Alice Claudia Oehninger

Being Human, a Biography of overcoming Limitations

AF212054

Alice Claudia Oehninger

Being Human

A Biography of overcoming Limitations

Impressum:

Bibliografische Information der Deutschen Nationalbibliothek: Die Deutsche Nationalbibliothek verzeichnet diese Publikation in der Deutschen Nationalbibliografie; detaillierte bibliografische Daten sind im Internet über dnb.dnb.de abrufbar.

Bibliographic information of the German national Library: the German National Library has registered this publication in the German National Bibliography. Detailed bibliographic information are available on the internet via https://www.dnb.de/.

© 2024 Alice Claudia Oehninger, zweite, überarbeitete Version

Verlag / Publisher:

BoD · Books on Demand GmbH, In de Tarpen 42, 22848 Norderstedt

Druck / Print:

Libri Plureos GmbH, Friedensallee 273, 22763 Hamburg

ISBN: 978-3-7568-9479-6

Prologue

I love to dance.

Lose myself to the melody.

Become one with the rhythm.

It reminds me like little else,

how good it is to be alive.

There was a point in my life, where I was ready to end the music. Instead, I promised myself I would dance until my heart gives out. The secret is to *want* to dance. Despite. Even when dancing seems impossible.

Because to dance is to feel life within yourself to the fullest. To be filled with fire and sparks, to set the ground beneath your toes alight and to feel vapour trails streaming off your fingertips.

To become your own storm.

There is a popular poem, concerning Life, and the enduring of its storms (*Vivian Greene, American writer and entrepreneur, 1979*). It has come to be one of my favourites, reminding me that fear is ever-present. An irremovable part of life. A necessity even, for our survival. Her poem reminds me, that I am constantly faced with nuisances and cataclysm, with irritations and terror, perturbations and heartbreak. And having worked through one challenge, it will be replaced by something else, equally dramatic, equally draining. So, the secret to dancing, is not to wait for the sometimes loud and seemingly atonal symphony of the life to end, but to hear the music within.

The quote also reminds me that dancing is a learning process. And that it is okay to falter. Or even, to trip and fall. To fail. But always keep trying. So, despite how badass aging yogis sound, when they teach their students to "Do. Or do not." And that *trying* implies failure by default, I disagree. Vehemently so.

Sometimes, even giving *everything* you have simply *fails* to turn the tide in your favour. Instead, you are swept off your feet and hurled against the rocks. The music is drowned out and you find yourself broken, seemingly beyond repair, without the means to help yourself, and without any idea or hope of how to carry on. Sometimes "doing" means simply pulling the blanket over your head, shutting out the world, trying to get through the pain. And telling yourself that tomorrow, you will try again. Because sometimes, trying is all we can do.

Often enough, people do not acknowledge others' humanity. We fear what we do not understand. We oppose change and we loathe what is "strange". We fight what we do not recognise as part of "our" group. This lies in our nature. In our past as a species, it was necessary to set cultural and traditional boundaries to survive.

Nevertheless, it is my conviction, that there is more to humankind than one-upping each other in the Darwinian arena. It remains my profound hope, that we as a species grow beyond these boundaries, into a society that thrives on inclusion, compassion, and dignity. And I believe that I, and people like me, have something unique to contribute.

I was raised as a white boy in Tanzania and Zimbabwe. Among a multitude of different cultures, far away from my birthplace, always on the move. And often singled out, on account of my appearance, on account of my identity, or both. It is only in recent years, that I have found something akin to roots, and they are not geographic.

I am trans* gender. I describe myself as a woman, who was born into this world without functioning ovaries or a womb. Which already says quite a lot of my views and my hopes for this life.

This book is a very personal account, and I would like to emphasise, it describes and expresses *my* experiences. My conclusions and my perspective of my life as a gender dysphoric, and my views on the lives that have touched mine.

I have written this with the best of intentions and the hope that it contributes to a deeper understanding of what it is to be human. That it enables people to be their best possible selves. And in doing so, contribute their best, our best, for society and for our future. I have tried to explore and illuminate some of the challenges I faced. Predicaments, emotional double-binds, and insecurities, causes for ambivalences or heartbreak. Many of which I saw, or see, reflected in those lives that touch mine. People I teach, people I counsel, people I love.

We humans are economic creatures. We like simple answers. But the world is complex. Being human can express itself in forms and variations so far from "normal," that we sometimes barely recognise this humanity in each-other. At the same time, my own empowerment was only possible, because total strangers were able to look beyond the immediate, and make choices based on imagination and compassion.

It is important to me, that this book is more than just my Story. I very much want to pass on some of the hope, the insight, and the sheer exuberance of having taken the leap and determined my own path. And that it is in fact absolutely worthwhile carrying on, in the face of a storm.

I have tried to be as authentic and true to myself as I can. Which is not always the socially accepted. Or the politically correct. So please forgive if I offend. I do not mean to. My life is a learning process, and far from over.

And finally, this book is… …how do I put it? You cannot have a breakthrough without something breaking. And sometimes, that which breaks is you. I have tried to be open, tried to be clear, without being graphic. There will be violence. There will be despair. There will be things that trigger people who are susceptible to flashbacks. There will be morally grey areas and reasons for ambivalence. There will be sex. There will be politics and science. There will be opinions and decisions, that will challenge a great many peoples' core beliefs thoroughly. Read with caution.

But happiness *is* a choice.

Well, no, it is not. Actually, left by itself, that is a very condescending and disempowering thing to say. But there *is* a choice to be made: whether or not to take that next step. Whether or not to look at causalities. And be mindful of what we learn from our experiences. It is human to be afraid. Afraid of change. Even if sometimes, something does in fact need to change, possibly to break, before we can recognise either choice, or happiness.

And sometimes, we just need to trust our hearts. We need to remind ourselves to hear the music, take the next breath, and just follow the rhythm.

Alice Oehninger

Second revised edition September 2024

Contents

(1) Being Different

Roots…

…I feel, I was born without them.

A part of me always felt lost.

Alone.

Which is untrue, of course.

Geography or family. Tribe or culture. I had plenty labels.

But the tags and the stamps I grew up with,

were things that were stuck on me

by other people.

Not mine.

When a child is born. What is *the first* question that is asked? The biological pre-rogative is universal. Pick any continent at random. Pick any culture. Pick any period in recorded history. In the overwhelming majority of cases, it will be;

"Is it a boy or a girl?"

And all those present to assist or witnesses the birth will check to see: penis means boy, vulva means girl. And that is it. Even today, the answer to that single, solitary question will determine the upbringing and socialisation of that child. It will influence how the child is integrated into the family, and what "value" or "worth" is attributed to this creature. Going so far as to predetermine what is invested into the raising and education of this human being. It has a far-reaching influence on what kind of character traits this human will develop, which of these are encouraged, which are discouraged, or supressed. It influences what kind of behaviour is tolerated, appreciated, or disdained. And all of this leads to career choices and career opportunities…

"Fremdbestimmt" dict.leo.org says: German, adjective. Externally-determined, heteronomous, other- directed.

…actually, it is quite incredible. This child, this new human being has barely taken its first breath. And already its future has been planned and chiselled in stone. Is that not frightening? How totally non-autonomous, how completely patronised and utterly domineered this child is? So absolutely dependent and helpless.

Disempowered.

All of this is influenced by the parents, by the immediate surrounding family, by the "tribe". By the community into which this young human is born. We cannot deny how deep and how lasting the parental imprinting of our personality is. In fact, the basic biological learning mechanism is enabled by mirror neurons, as our brains develop during infancy. We cannot deny that we are biologically conditioned to imitate and learn from the world surrounding us.

We are socialised into our gender roles. We are *conditioned* to respond in the patterns corresponding to our gender roles. Roles that someone else determined for us. Furthermore, we are conditioned to *react* when someone else deviates from those patterns. Breaks the mould. Steps across the immoveable borders of cultural taboos. Or even if they are in any way different.

Those reactions, forged by primal conditioning.

Often, those reactions are not kind.

Switzerland, 1970

I was born into a biologically male body. It was in a hospital near Zürich, and from what my parents have related, I broke my first gender-pattern there and then. Or perhaps, they broke it for me? Apparently, my Dad had quite the row with the nurses, who disputed the name chosen for me by my parents, saying it was an inappropriate name for a boy (it is a unisex name in a lot of countries).

Gender patterns and friction

I was a girl in kindergarten.

Pretty much everyone, with whom I have ever spoken about this, has asked me "how do you know?" As a matter of fact, every one of my therapists asked me at some point, what gives me the assurance and the security, that I am trans* gender? That I am female?

My first, impulsive answer would be, "Um... ...how do you *not* know ?!?"

How can any person not know what gender they are? And, yes, I did (and do) in fact tell my therapists, that I do not know how to define what I feel. That I cannot pinpoint what it is that gives me the sure knowledge that this soul of mine was born into the wrong body. I had extensive discussions with all my therapists, obviously, since this is the therapists' jobs. Nevertheless, the bottom line is, I cannot pinpoint why I feel the way I do. It just is.

Okay, so that is not really helpful. How *can* I be so sure?

I suppose, ultimate proof is the fact that, the feeling that I was a girl in kindergarten turned out *not* to be a phase I would outgrow. It accompanied me well through my pubescent years into adulthood, regardless of whether I got to wear dresses or not. My behaviour was consistent over decades.

A feeling of wrongness, a feeling of this body not reflecting who I am, a feeling of this body being somehow ill-fitting and always one step removed. Like wearing a left glove on a right hand. You can make it fit, but it is far from comfortable. And it always hinders your senses and restricts your self-expression.

To the point of where it *hurts*.

From a very early age, I developed strategies and coping mechanisms to deal with this feeling I had no name for. Not looking at my own body. From the age of six, right through to the age of twenty. No looking down. No checking in the mirror. Nothing. For fourteen years. Instead, I regularly used the mirror to make myself up. In the absence of any eyeliners or lid-shades, I used water soluble colour pencils I had. I am aware, stereotype, and not exclusive proof of femininity. But, it was what I needed, to feel more myself.

Of course, my parents did not dress me in dresses, or offer me girl-gendered clothing, this was not something parents did in the 1970ies. But I remember, we had a huge trunk of dress-up clothes, cloths, shawls, and accessories in our Kindergarten. I was a regular and a great enthusiast for dressing up. Always as a girl. So, yes, I was a total cross-dresser as a child. Mind you, I would hesitate to diagnose a child with gender dysphoria, simply because they enjoy dressing up across gendered borders at the age of four.

I gave myself a female name and requested of my nursery schoolteachers and the other children in kindergarten address me by this name. Some of those said playmates got on easily with the fact that I was "the boy with a female name". They took in stride the fact that I liked dresses, and they never seemed to be perturbed by the fact that the adults called me by a different name. We painted lots, sometimes pictures on paper, and sometimes each other. We crafted dolls houses and cars from cardboard-boxes, we ran round screaming and climbed trees. We played "Cops and robbers", where I was invariably the "suave blonde". As much as you can be suave when you are four or five years old. And we played "family", where I was invariably the mother or the daughter. Yes, total stereotyping. But, these were the 1970ies, and broadening horizons was work still in its baby shoes.

So. Since I knew I was a girl with such surety, why I did not pursue this with more vehemence or tenacity?

My deviation from my assigned gender caused immense friction with some of the other kids. Looking back, I assume that there were only a few actual instigators. But this was kindergarten. And children *are* uninhibited and impulsive, thus highly susceptible to mob psychology. This culminated in my being pursued and harassed by the outright majority. They made it *very* clear that my behaviour was undesired. On multiple occasions.

We had a "snoozing room" which was strewed with a kind of semi-hard pillows, stuffed with unprocessed cotton. The smell still makes me want to curl up into a dark, tight ball of silence and pretend I am not there.

They have found me. Shouting and shoving. More than I can quickly count. Running is not an option. I know that from experience.

I pretend not to care. Pretend they are interested in something else, try to slip past them.

There is always one. One who pushes the first shove, throws the first punch. Aims the first kick.

There are faces shouting and screaming at me, hands clawing. They cling to me, holding my arms, holding my legs. Panic rises hot and tight in my throat. I drop any pretence of being unperturbed and try to make a break for it. I struggle as hard as I can, I try to run, but there are too many holding onto me.

I fall. They drag me down, piling on top. So heavy I can't breathe.

I try to crawl forward. Away. There are fingers in my face. Fingers my hair, pulling. I feel that they are tearing off my clothes. I scream. I have lost my pants. I feel the cold air. I scream harder. I feel hands on the back of my head, pushing my face into a pillow. I cannot breathe. My chest hurts. It burns. My head pounds. I kick my legs to try to break free, but the others are too heavy. I feel hands grabbing my *anatomy* and yanking hard. They scream into my ears, "You are not a girl, you are a boy," over and over.

So yes. I can confirm, that when you are being asphyxiated, your sense of hearing is the last thing to go.

And, yes. I spoke up about this. I spoke with the nursery schoolteachers. Once. Maybe twice. I do not remember clearly. I went to see Erika. She was the child- minder to whom I had the deepest rapport so far. I remember her, saying, "But you *are* a boy." And, "Oh don't be ridiculous, they would never do that."

I became a *very* quiet child after that.

I became extremely careful to whom I spoke about who I felt I was. I did not address this topic directly with my parents for another forty years. Decades later, when we were talking about my childhood in another context, my Dad confided in me, telling me that the supervising nursery-school teacher did in fact suggest to my him, that he take me to see a child-psychologist. I understand my Dad avoided this at quite some effort.

You might think that an interview with a specialist, experienced in interacting with children, might have actually been the right thing, and saved me from a lot of grief. I will gently remind you, that in the 1970ies, the degree of enlightenment in things concerning sexual diversity and identity awareness was still at a point, where it was considered a crime against nature and a psychological illness to be homosexual. As for trans* gender? Whether or not such a thing actually existed, was still being hotly debated. It was only four years later that one of the specialists, who later interviewed me for a psychiatric evaluation, would leave the Gender Identity Clinic in Baltimore. He would take up residence in the University Clinic of Hamburg-Eppendorf, and later become one of the most widely known specialists concerning gender dysphoria.

In the meantime, I have spent several years supervising and counselling youths, who are either questioning their gender, or are decidedly trans* gender. And the things they tell me, about some of their so-called specialists and therapists, make me *very* angry. Even taken with a pinch of salt, to account for youthful exaggeration, some of those statements require me to take a deep breath, and then go speak to my own therapist, Dr Chamberlain, for supervision. That fact that we are twenty-odd years into the new millennium has apparently done appallingly little to improve either the mindfulness, or empathy of said school-specialists. Nor has it done much to provide for increased breadth of training for child- and youth therapists, or raising awareness over what some of humans can go through.

I am overall so very grateful that my Dad protected me.

Make no mistake. Those children in my kindergarten cannot be blamed for their behaviour. They behaved and performed precisely as they were preconditioned to do. By society, by the people around them, by their families and tribes, by their peers.

From infancy on up, humans are raised according to the maxim, that you need to be strong, you need to be tough, you need to assert yourself, you need to be better than the rest. And. If there is someone who shows vulnerability, who is weaker, someone who is *different*, you exploit it. You make best use of this opportunity to weed out the competition. And. If someone else was faster than you, to single out someone vulnerable, then you make sure to ally yourself with the strong.

What remains in the forefront of my memory, is how few friends or playmates I had that were my own age, and how much of my interaction was orientated towards the adults that surrounded me. Even more curiously, the children with whom I got on best were usually "outsiders" or in some way different themselves. Either having moved in from someplace else and thus spoke an audibly different language or dialect. Like Florian and Michael, who had moved to Zürich from Bern, and all they needed to do was open their mouths for this to be obvious. Or they had some kind of outwardly visible difference that ostracised them, like Lisa, who had a case of psoriasis, so bad, there were days when she would rub herself bloody.

I think adults simply did not take seriously what I claimed about my gender, putting it off as a game or a phase, whereas for other children this was indeed very real and deeply conflicting with what they saw and what they had been conditioned to believe.

My Dad

My Dad's parents were the epitome of traditional. When my Grandad lost his job in the 1930ies economic crisis, they were forced to move from the countryside to the city. Upstanding and conform, straight and narrow. My Grandad became a copper, and was later promoted to district station master or superintendent or something like that. My Granny was a housemother for their four children. From what my Dad tells, they were poor by standards (yes, there were and are poor in Switzerland, and yes, despite my Granddad's station). My Dad tells of his mother not knowing what to feed her family in the last week of the month for lack of there being anything edible in the house.

And my grandparents must have been very strict as parents. Not unkind, but certainly rigorous. So when my Dad went to study mechanical engineering, and he joined the students' union, that caused immense tension for a time between my Grandad and my Dad. My Dad met my mother in the various activities of the students' union (Vietnam protests, women's rights marches, rocking the roots of the establishment) and I assume, sadly enough, my grandparents saw my Mum as a bad influence. My being born, the first grandchild in the family, probably contributed to a significant degree to my grandparents mellowing considerably.

My Dad was and is one of the very few people I trust.

Which, I suppose is not surprising, considering the stretches of time he was alone with me.

He rode me to kindergarten and back on his bicycle when it was dry, or we rode the bus together when it rained. He was also probably the only person to truly realise, that I was not really happy in kindergarten. In retrospect, I get the impression, he did his best to make up for that in the time he was able to spend with me.

He spent hours making up stories or reading to me. He drew (technical) pictures for me and taught me how to draw and write. Or we played with my building blocks or Lego. I remember walking through the pedestrian areas or through supermarkets, and he explained endlessly, how escalators worked, or how trees drew water out of the ground, how clouds formed and rained water back onto the earth. He taught me to cut hazel branches and carve intricate patterns into the bark. As a matter of fact, I got my first (Swiss Army) pocketknife from my paternal Granddad at the age of five. We spent a great deal of time in the woods nearby, my Dad and I, walking, looking for pretty snail shells, watching birds and squirrels. We built kites, we build bows-and-arrows. My Dad was there for me, when I skimmed my knees with my roller-skates. He taught me to ride a bicycle.

So, yes, my Dad was *the* foundation in my life. My rock of reliability and refuge. And my source of warmth and love.

And despite this, I never emphasised or pushed the topic of being a girl. I am sure he caught that I liked to dress up. I am sure that he knew, I said I was a girl. I *know* he knew that some of the other children gave me a hard time in kindergarten. But I think he was ready to just wait it out, and see how I would develop. Not to mention that I am fairly sure, he saw himself helpless and overwhelmed with having a child that consistently broke gender boundaries, and caught loads of heat for it. And I am sure he saw himself powerless and abandoned by a society, and probably his own parents, because these were *things you just didn't speak about.*

I think I intuitively did not force the topic. I must have intuitively realised, how this would expose me in an extreme unfavourable light, and how it would create a great deal of grief for my Dad. So, yes, I kept it very low key. And no, my mother did not know, I know she didn't.

In connection to that, among the few things my Dad did *not* teach me, was to stick up for myself. Even when someone overstepped my boundaries so completely.

My dad is a tall man, and he was always very athletic. My mother is easily two heads smaller and of a much slighter build. And yet, despite all the physical abuse she gifted him with, he never once raised his hand against her. I believe he is one of those men, who has enormous respect of his own physical capacity. One very vivid memory of my parents, involves my mother tearing a whole bushel of hair off my Dad's head. He stoically shielded himself the best he could, physically and emotion-ally, and waited for her fury to burn itself out.

In fact, I do not even remember him ever raising his voice much. Withdrawal and mute endurance were always his method of coping, waiting for a more calm moment. Then he would patiently, diplomatically state his point of view and try to explain his reasoning. And after a point, give up in resignation. Because he perceived the situa-tion lost and any argument futile, since my mother was simply not prepared to come to any kind of compromise or to meet on common ground.

There were times we dawdled in the woods on our way home, sitting on a bench under the trees, just talking. Both of us afraid to go home to my Mum. As horrid as this sounds, these are fond memories. Quality time with my Dad. And. Fact remains, things were so much more peaceful when she was not there.

Looking back, the behaviour pattern of mute withdrawal and detached (dissociated) rationalisation reflects so plainly in my own behaviour through the years. I suppose withdrawing myself was exactly what I did myself for most of my life. So what I never truly learned, not from my Dad or from anyone else, was how to fight an honest, healthy, fair, and cleansing fight. And therefore, I never learnt that it was okay to fight. Obviously, I am not talking about physical violence. I mean a direct confrontation of wills and world-views. I never learnt as a child, that it was okay to get angry. And that it was possible to make up, and be okay again afterwards. Neither did I learn how to stand my ground when I saw my insight being ignored or depreciated, or my sphere of comfort or my person being violated.

But this is an insight that required many years to grow.

What my Dad *did* pass on to me, is perseverance and endurance to the point of being stubborn, along with endless patience, be it with machines or with people. He is my role model for accuracy and painstaking precision bordering on the obsessive. But all that springs from an ethic and a pride that we take in a job well done. In the same way, his unfailing loyalty to me, to Amahle (my stepmother) and my siblings certainly inspired me in how I modelled my later partnerships and how I picture a family to function. Not perfect, but real. And despite, or because of, my Dad not taking an active part in any conflict, he did instil me with a sense of fairness and justice. And he made it transparent, that he was and remains dedicated to furthering communication between peoples and the improvement of living conditions of the people he chose to share his life with.

As is evident in his biography.

I spent my most formative years with my Dad in Tanzania, where he taught at the faculty of engineering as part of the Swiss development aid programme. This was 1976 to 1983. In this time, my Dad climbed Kilimanjaro twice. Despite altitude sickness. He divorced my Mum in 1980. In 1982, he met Amahle, and they were married the same year. From Tanzania, we moved to Zimbabwe, where he maintained a chemical plant and trained new staff. When I left Africa at the end of 1989, my Dad moved on to Malawi, because at the time, moving to apartheid South Africa was out of the question. He worked as a technical manager for a textile firm, maintaining the plant and training new artisans and engineers. I visited him there once, and I have very fond memories of hiking in the majestic Mulanje Mountains and strolling along the beach of Lake Malawi at sunrise.

When South Africa passed the referendum to end the racist regime in 1994, he and Amahle moved to Johannesburg, Amahle's hometown. As exuberant the mood was in SA, so did it have its down-sides. He caught the full brunt of the wave of affirmative action and for a few short years, he did technical support for industries in the greater Jo-burg area. He was never really happy with that though, prevailing (lack of) work ethics and residual racism made it hard for him to fit in. Particularly with his boss, who treated company funds like his private purse. Today, I am particularly grateful, my Dad finally found a position with a medical aid organisation. Just in time, before his former boss absconded to the USA with all the remaining company funds.

The medical aid organisation placed him in beautiful, enchanting Lesotho, where he spent the better part of a decade maintaining six clinics, ensuring they had running water, ensuring the self-same water was safe, ensuring they had as few power outages as possible, making sure the medical wastes were treated before being disposed of, making sure that there was in fact, a reliable road leading to these clinics, some of which could only be reached with a four-wheel-drive. And ensuring that there was an artisan present in his absence. In all his placements, my Dad found fulfilment and connection, making many long-term friends along the way. Nevertheless, I have the impression, this job in Lesotho was my Dad's most memorable and rewarding, and of the many students, doctors and their families sent by the medical aid organisation, many of them were sad to see him retire. And I certainly take heartfelt pride in saying, that my Dad belongs to those people who moved mountains to empower the African peoples and contribute to improving their lives.

Following his retirement, my Dad and Amahle spent many rewarding and peaceful years in Johannesburg. He was attentive, when she suffered her first stroke in 2016, and I like to believe it was through his care, that she recovered all her faculties as quickly and completely as she did. When she finally left his side in early 2018, he gave up their house and moved into a home for the retired, with facilities for assisted living. That is my Dad, always prudently looking ahead.

What he did not yet know then, is, that a year after he would move into his new home, he would meet Khani (Khanyisile), a widowed nurse, also retired, who took a sweet and endearing fancy to him. I believe she is a source of inspiration and a focus for his care and attention, providing him with warmth and purpose in his late life. She certainly is someone whom I can call Mom with all my heart. I hope they still get to share many fulfilling years together.

My Mother

When I was approximately 16 months old, my mother spent some five or six months in a kibbutz, somewhere on the Palestinian-Israeli border. Around 24 months after my birth, my mother spent some time in the south of Switzerland in a community, that explored the possibilities of self-subsistence and independence from the "establishment".

One of my earliest actual memories of my mother, is, when she came back from Mexico. I must have been close to four years old. She had been living in a commune for about half a year, and she was seriously ill with something tropical.

To explain this, I need to digress a little: There are a lot of good things to say about the Swiss. They are industrious and dedicated, they are very keen on developing and improving processes. In fact, you can tell that this is a hardy mountain folk, who have had to fight for their survival in a potentially hostile environment, where ingenuity is a key trait to prosperity. They are overall kind, a joyous and sweet natured people. Once they have let you into their generous hearts, their loyalty is highly tenacious. Incidentally, much like the British, to whom I also feel quite a close connection.

Unfortunately, one thing that the Swiss are *not*, is particularly adaptable. Despite what I previously said about ingenuity. They are loath to change, and cautious to trust new things, new people. They are slow to accept, never-mind integrate, new ideas.

So many young women today are unaware, that the right to vote, is something that came to be only relatively recently. Finland pioneered in Europe in 1906. The Swiss, I am not proud to say, were among the last of the European countries, to acknowledge that women are eligible for this very basic human right too, followed only by Portugal and Lichtenstein.

The Swiss finally decided to grant women voting rights in 1971. The victory was hard fought for, and only partial. The voting rights were granted on a federal scale, but the regional (Cantonal) administrations still had the sovereignty over their local affairs. And it was in fact November 1990, that the federal government finally pointed out, that the regional (Cantonal) constitution actually contradicted the federal constitution, and passed a law that to the effect, that the boys were to finally put away their peckers, and let the girls play along.

My mother was one of those women who fought for voting rights in Switzerland in the 1960ies. She marched, chanted, and screamed for basic human rights along with all those other brave ladies. They chained themselves to the houses of government, they created roadblocks, they stood endless hours in public squares and supermarkets to collect signatures. They burnt bras, they threw paint-eggs (and bricks), and they danced in the streets.

My mother spent her entire adult life, working for the betterment of how women are recognised and treated in Swiss and European society, and sometimes beyond European borders. She and her friends /comrades formed communal centres, engaged in social and political reformation programs, ensured that women and children had safe-houses to go to. They argued and fought, rationalised and debated, begged and wheedled, coerced and blackmailed the patriarchal powers that were (and are), to not only tolerate women in positions of power, but cooperate inclusively. My mother fought her entire life so that younger generations would be able to lead independent and self-determined lives. Even today, she still remains an active thorn in "the establishment's" side, as well as spending hours a week being there for other people, by way of an emergency support hotline.

Mum, *I am SO DAMN PROUD of you*. What a gift! What a legacy to bestow your daughters with.

Nevertheless, my relationship with my birth mother was never an easy one. For as long as I remember, my mother always seemed angry. And being a child, I thought it was my fault.

Today, I get it. She had (has) loads of reasons to be angry. My Mum comes from a household, where verbal and physical abuse were liberally distributed. My maternal history is *RIFE* with violence and depreciation, the kind of archetypal abuse women globally face. My grandmother was first deported and abused as a young woman. By the Germans, for having the wrong faith. Then slurred a traitor and a collaborator by the French, and let me tell you, they were not kind. And finally, she was raped by the Americans. She fled to Switzerland, where she got pregnant by a man, who abandoned her. And the man who did marry her became an alcoholic, simply in order to survive the constant abrasion of her fury. As a result, my maternal grandmother was highly irascible, and did little to provide my Mum with a role-model of a loving maternal figure.

Fact is, I was afraid. I was afraid of my own mother.

Of both my mother and my grandmother.

My dad was, and still is, in so many ways, the traditional gentleman. The knight in, not so much shining-, but in definitely serviceable armour. My Dad most certainly questioned the system and the powers that were. Moreover, the fact that he was the son of a police superintendent, it was absolutely scandalous that he should be a spokesperson of the students' protests of 1969. And I assume this was a strong contributing factor to the attraction between my parents. Nevertheless, he was certainly so much more settled, steady, and rooted in tradition and "correctness". He is so much more a diplomat, rather than the anarchist rebel.

My mother was barely twenty when she became pregnant with me, and I speculate, she was in no way prepared. There were multiple instances when she implied, that she would have and should have "gotten rid of me". My Dad prevented this and did, what was at that time the "honourable thing" to do, and married her. I believe this created enormously conflicting emotions in my Mum. I assume there was enough in my Dad, that she loved and that she was attracted to. At the same time, it was the traditional role, which she so entirely abhorred, and she might have seen herself captured and enslaved into the same oppressive fate as so many other mothers.

So, yes. I get it. My mother was *not* a happy camper. Switzerland had finally come to its senses and granted voting rights to women. I would assume, she saw a central lifegoal realised, a door opened. And then along comes a baby. She was angry. She appeared ambivalent and unsteady in her loyalties and her affection. Both to me and my Dad. Above all, she was irascible and highly volatile. There were days, a lot of them, when she made it clear that I was unwelcome. I was in her way, hindered her from pursuing her own life, her dreams of liberty and her ambitions. And I bound her to this man, this gentleman. A man who was so "established."

On top of which, my mother carried, and still today carries, a searing, seething anger against anything patriarchal. It has coloured every one of her relationships to any man I ever witnessed. And then she bore a son. Perhaps that might have been like adding insult to injury? I do not know for sure if my gender truly played a role for my mother. When I think of *my* childhood, it certainly seems likely, and when viewed in the light of my mother's often openly displayed misandrogyny, even more so.

On the other hand, when I look at the childhood Eirian experienced, that at least raises some doubts, as to just how personal my mother's anger, impatience and rejection was. Eirian, my sister, was born seventeen years after me, and she grew up with a different Dad, Francesco. And yet, the tragedy is, when I look at my sister, when we speak with each other, she, too, carries psychological scars that are all too similar.

My impression is, like some Artists and other great People, my mother saw her Children as obstacles. As challenges to overcome. Things that hindered her in her work and her passions for creating a world in which women would thrive and decide unhindered. I am aware, this not how my (our) mother would describe the situation. Bottom line remains. I felt unloved by my mother. Not welcome. Not good enough.

And that was the first of a long line of "not-good-enough"s that would continue to prevent me from ever developing a healthy self-esteem.

Today, my Mum and I share an amiable bond of mutual affection and respect. But this took my becoming independent. Legally and psychologically, emotionally capable of stating my own case, naming my needs, drawing up and maintaining my own boundaries. Things are still not without effort. We both still hurt at the past. And sometimes she struggles with what I am and who I am today. But more than anything else, she respects the choices I made, and she acknowledges the battles I have fought to determine my own path. I dare say, that is something that she sees reflected in herself, and appreciates.

The mother I chose

There is a lovely parable, possibly Buddhist, of which I am extremely fond. Unfortunately, I have not managed to find its origins, despite extensive research. I barely remember where I heard it, I believe it was in Dar es Salaam. It states that a man (yes, a man, of course a man) can have three fathers. The one who gives him life (gets the mother pregnant), the one who clothes him and provides him with a roof over his head. And the one who teaches him a craft, and imparts wisdom and the ways of the world. It also states that, *these three fathers can, but need not, be one and the same person.*

I have four mothers.

The other person I learnt to trust, as a child, was my babysitter, Evangeline. And she was to some degree, the counterpoint to my father's very technical way of analysing and detailing the world. And, heartless or cruel as it sounds, she was everything my mother was not. She had time for me. And more than anything else, she showed me unlimited tenderness, patience, and affection.

Evangeline read to me endlessly, told me stories of brave girls who rescued their brothers from selfish ice-queens, of boys who befriended dragons, of flowers who wore clothes and played musical instruments, and of winds with names and families. She told me stories of fairies and elves that populated the woods and hid behind ferns. Tales of gnomes and dwarves that lived under rocks and gleaned precious treasures from books. Of unending tunnels of libraries filled floor to ceiling with the most wondrous of tomes and scrolls. We spent countless hours together building villages of fruit, painting pictures or puppets. And she usually had a shawl or a pretty scarf I could borrow.

Above all, Evangeline was gifted with the patience of an angel. She still is. She very much became my "ersatz" mother, and when my parents decided to have me baptised at the age of five, I was permitted to choose her as my godmother.

She must have shown me tough love as well, but she obviously managed to do so in a supportive and appreciative way, because I have no memory of feeling anything other than welcome and cherished.

I have no memory of any kind of competing tension between Evangeline and my mother. Considering that my godmother was still in her early to mid-teens, there was no danger of my birth mother being "replaced" (aside the fact that this would have been so far out of character for my Dad). Remarkable is, that decades later, my mother recalls that she was indeed very jealous of the rapport between Evangeline and me. To counter this, my godmother recalls very fondly, my parents as being so very much older than her. She told me, how being introduced to my parents' circle of friends, how being in on their discussions, had long and highly impressive effects on her way of thinking. How she felt treated as an adult for the first time. I also know that my mother met Evangeline, years later, when I married Wiebke. And that she thanked Evangeline profusely, for being there for me all those years.

Today, Evangeline has her own practice for art therapy, working with children traumatised by war and abuse. Alongside this, she has a part time job, working with families with a migrative background, facilitating their integration into Swiss society. This she does mainly by empowering the mothers through a large network of helpers and employees, and ensuring the placement of their infants and children in communal kindergartens and health care. The well-founded success being, that if the children are well integrated, then their parents will find it all the more easy to follow.

Above everything, she is guided by common sense and a deep love and respect for humans and their needs. She is empowered by the singular trust that *we all love our children* and want nothing but their best. If we had more women, more *mothers* like her, politicians would be out of a job, warlords would be out of soldiers, and fanatics would be out of zealot followers. Of course, individuals disappoint her every once in a while, but she remains committed and unshaken in her faith in the good in people.

She was, and remains today, my role model for everything that is gentle but steadfast, boundlessly creative but realistic, opinionated but fair.

We write as often as both our very busy lives allow for, and every once in a while, we visit one another. Her support and her counsel remain invaluable to me. And cautious as Evangeline was about some of my transitioning steps, she always managed to convey that she had my wellbeing and my happiness at heart.

Tanzania, 1976

I was six years old when my parents emigrated with me, to Dar es Salaam, on the East African coast.

Tanzania, most particularly Dar es Salaam, was an extremely interesting and remarkable place in the 1970ies. The country had been an independent member of the British Commonwealth since 1964. At that time, one of the poorest countries in Africa, and yet, the income gap was not that steep. Unlike today, there were few super-rich people (of any skin tone), the majority of the population existing more or less securely. The indigenous population was largely indifferent to friendly to the large number of expatriates living there. Despite no notable mineral riches, it was strategically well placed, and the Chinese generously offered to build a railroad, from the port city, around to Lake Tanganyika, past the East-African rift, and further into the heart of the continent, where the more exploitable mines lay. This was also the time when the Leakey family was discovering lots of hominid remains in Olduvai Gorge.

There was an open, ongoing armed conflict along the border to Uganda (check out Vita vya Kagera, and the Ousting of Idi Amin). The repercussions of this were of course an even further strain on resources and infrastructure. Any strategically important structure, like bridges, basic public service buildings, and of course water and power supplies, were guarded by heavily armed soldiers. There were checkpoints every fifty kilometres or so, and overall, there was a heightened military presence in the streets. Nevertheless, apart from the actual zone of conflict, Tanzania was by and large peaceful and even the soldiers were mostly good natured and easy going.

Dar es Salaam was at that time still the capital, and there was a large, sometimes thriving, sometimes grumbling community of expatriates situated there. The "old colonials" were dying out and being replaced with cheery idealists like my Dad. The Swiss have long roots, dating back to mission hospitals dotted across the country. There was a large German community, there were Dutch, Swedes, Norwegians, British, and of course a great many people of Indian origin. There were Yugoslavian refugees, even then. There was a very large Chinese community. And there was a strong community of Americans, most particularly of Americans of African descent, looking to find peace from racial conflicts, and rediscover their roots.

For any family that could afford it (pretty much all the expats), and even some that could not, it was a matter of course to have domestics. I realise that this is a topic of a somewhat delicate nature. And while this has its roots in the colonial hierarchy, it was simply natural to have somebody helping in the household and / or garden. And thereby provide opportunities for semi-skilled employment. But more on that later. Fact is, probably none of the expat wives had to work if they chose not to.

My Dad took on a lecturer's position at the faculty of engineering in Dar es Salaam, and for several years, he was the coordinator between the Swiss development aid community and the Swiss embassy. For my Dad, this was possibly the closest to perfection he could have, jobwise. It was a highly practical, highly makeshift environment which required ingenuity and adaptive thinking. And it gave him every opportunity to pass on his experience and expertise.

For my mother, it was a dead end. As far as I know, the decision had been a unanimous agreement between my parents. I believe, she had supported the move to Africa, driven by ambitions to further women's rights, women's emancipation, and the ideology of gender equity in Africa. I believe she had all the hopes and good intentions, to bring the "good fight" to Dar es Salaam, and improve living conditions for women, strengthen their rights within society and within marriage, and ensure their right to education. I would think she still felt the rush of victory from the changes that were coming to effect in Switzerland.

Tanzania has a very diverse background, culturally, with a very strong influence of the Arabic traders, that came south by way of the Indian Ocean. Independently of the Muslim culture, there was, and still is, a deeply rooted highly patriarchal system in place. And Tanzania was at that time a picture-book example of a country where the women did pretty much all the work of keeping society alive, i.e., tilling that land, fetching the water, and raising the children. Things have improved since then, for example, in 2000, an amendment to the constitution was passed to strengthen the rights of women to own land, just to give you an idea of what kind of challenges we are talking about here.

So, what my mother found, was that empowering the local women consisted mainly of teaching them to make better use of the land, getting the land to yield more and better crops, encouraging them to sew and craft items they could sell, and thereby securing independent existences and improving living conditions. Perhaps most importantly, making very cautious, very tentative headway in teaching sexual hygiene and family planning, both being enormous taboos in East-African cultures. In pretty much any African culture I ever met, for that matter. The hot-plate of plain basic disposability (deliberate choice of word) of women for sex, was more than a generation away. Maybe more than three.

So despite the fact that most of the wives of all the expats had profited from education and vocational training, the vast majority of the expat women maintained a low profile as homemakers and mothers. A lot of them took up creative hobbies or other pastimes. A fair number contributed a lot of time and effort as volunteer work in the afore mentioned projects to strengthen the rural communities. But the progress was painstakingly slow. The thought of women's lib and emancipation was, in Africa, more than a generation away. Women are still fighting for basic recognition of human dignity and self-determination today.

So instead of leading women to revolution, my mother found herself trying to teach *me* the basics of English and mathematics. She was not particularly patient. My being afraid of her temper did nothing to facilitate my learning. I still remember the seething frustration and agitation radiating off her, as scorching as the tropical sun.

The fact that there were beaches to explore, starfish to prod, sandcastles to be built, did not improve my interest. There were trees to climb, fruit to find, animals to marvel over… …so much to do, so little time. And all these fascinating dark-skinned people to follow around. The Tanzanians were (I presume still are) extremely fond of children, and any expat family with kids found themselves swamped by inquisitive and friendly people, who either wanted to touch the "Mzungu" (Swahili: white person) because touching straight blonde hair will bring good fortune. Or to sell then something. After all, everyone knows that all "Wazungu" (Swahili: white people plural) are richer than kings and more gullible than cows by standard.

Custody issues

My parents took me with them, when they went on a very long car journey, picking their way into the heartland of Tanzania, passing Mbeya, and approaching Lake Tanganyika that borders the East-African rift valley, going from mission station to mission station.

To be honest, in my memory, all of it blends together in a wild profusion of exuberant adventure, fun, and sheer sensory overload.

Exotic sounding names. Bagamoyo, Chalinze, Tabora, Iringa and Arusha. Settlements, ranging from innocently crumbling concrete, flaking bricks and corroded girders. With tarred roofs, sagging just slightly under the tropical sun. Windows, sometimes blind with age, or patched with plywood. Walls painted with advertisements in colours that must have at some point been vibrant. Villages of original wattle and daub, thatched with the typical "Elephant grass" (Pennisetum purpureum), complete with "bomas" (Swahili: livestock enclosures) and "shambas" (Swahili: tilled and cultivated fields).

Petrol was rationed, Diesel was in very short supply. Main roads were sunbleached tarmac, sometimes with vicious potholes, that could neatly swallow a tyre of a small car. Side roads, ranging from pebble-strewn tracks to sand-drifts, were a challenge to any ordinary vehicle, and even off-roaders had it hard.

Entire villages flocking around our car, so they could witness the Wazungu. With lovely colourful markets, and laughing dark-skinned faces of people who wanted to tousle my hair, women whose own hair was coiffed in coils, plaits, and even pyramids, so lovely that I, too, wanted to reach out and touch. Farmers, or their children, selling delicious crunchy corncobs straight off the embers. Baskets, woven of palm fronds, full of fragrant rice, fruit, and vegetables, deliciously colourful and enticing. Caravans of women and youths, artfully balancing burdens of wood or water on their heads. Goats bleating, cattle lowing, dogs barking and cats languorously sunning themselves, judging the world through slitted eyes.

Craft markets populated with artisans; the air filled with the tick-tick-tick of their tiny chisels. Fragrant ebony, dark as charcoal and heavy as iron. Rose coloured mahogany, responsive and warm to the touch. And, yes, ivory, pale like a moon in a midnight sky. Chagga and Makonde carvings, intricate worlds within worlds, one piece telling entire folk tales or recounting histories of tribes. Baskets, bowls, and mats of woven grass, sisal fibres, raffia, and other palm fronds, in pattern so intricate and beautiful that it took (takes) your breath away.

Tall Maasai, elegant as giraffes, proud as lions. I swear, Maasai can bend spacetime. The number of people they pile into one car defies physics.

Savannah so endless it melts into the sky, dotted with balloon-like Baobab trees and dainty umbrella-top acacias.

And the road trip was, in significant parts, sheer horror.

At this point, I understood nothing. No English beyond "hello, my name is," and certainly not Swahili. My parents were inexperienced with the dust roads, and our car overturned. This stranded us one week's drive in the middle of absolutely *nowhere* with a damaged front axle. With no food or water. When finally a lorry came by, my parents decided that my mother and I should head on to the mission house we had been heading for, and my Dad would stay with the car, in the hopes of getting help and repairs. I remember realising, that kicking up a fuss would only worsen an already bad situation, so I kept my mouth shut. Riding in a lorry that shook and groaned with every bump, and needed a stop every half hour (there were many) or the engine would overheat (the radiator was broken and continuously lost water).

The six-year-old that I was, was incapable of seeing the positive. I remember sleepless nights, thinking I would not ever see my Dad again. Much to my shame today, I was incapable of seeing all these helpful and kind people for what they were. You may think, "your Mum was there." Keep in mind that in my world, my mother spent more time avoiding me or shouting at me, than spending quality time with me.

Fact remains, the lorry drivers took us to the mission, where we spent about half a week. Lucky for us, out of sheer intuition, the people there pointed us in the right direction. They packed us on another lorry, headed for tiny district town at a road junction, with the only workshop in a radius of several days journey. And that is where we found my Dad again.

The fire might have been the straw that broke the camel's back, because my mother opted to move back to Zürich. This being the 1970ies, where children belonged with their mothers, I was never asked whether I wanted to stay with my Mum or my Dad.

Shortly after we moved into our first home in Dar es Salaam, this was broken into. And by sheer freak accident, the burglary caused a fire and the building burnt out completely. I remember being devastated with finding the charred remains of my cuddly toys. And yet, the smell of picking through the rubble for salvageable items, this was still not as bad as spending the first few nights back in Zürich on the living room floor of one of my mother's friends, where the carpet smelled of cigarette ash (this was the 1970ies, where people smoked like industrial stacks any-time, any-place).

My mother and I settled into a routine of where I went to school during the week and I spent most weekends with my paternal grandparents. Spending the weekend with my them was of course a sweet deal. They doted on me, providing me with a bicycle to ride to school with. And my Granddad had a huge den full of wonderful tools, including a pillar-drill, a lathe, and a great big workbench. It was with my Granddad that I crafted my first weather vane from plywood. It had the shape of a running fox, and of course I painted it bright red.

Evangeline, my godmother, was at this time in Greece as an intern, so we did not get to meet. I missed her terribly. Just as I missed my Dad.

I have no idea what the other children saw or perceived. But it was clear I was not one of them. I did not make a single friend then. There were a lot of whispered remarks and ill hidden smirks. Well, no, actually the smirks were not hidden. There were scuffles and there were shoves. I think even our class teacher, Ms Graf had a dislike for me; her jaw always went tight when she saw me.

I spent the weekday in school, from seven-thirty, and I think that ended around four in the afternoon. I have no memory of what I did around lunch, but I do remember hanging around the schoolyard on my own, playing ball or riding my bicycle until after dark. My mother was off at work or in some lectures. I admit, I was not really bothered, being alone. Quite to the contrary. The other children picked on me regularly, so their absence was a relief. And my mother was usually tired, or irritated and impatient. Or all three. In my memory, there was always a tension in my mother, like a coiled spring. An ill-chosen word, or just doing something that displeased her, might trigger a violent reaction.

I recall one of the teachers happened past one evening, not Ms Graf, one of the other teachers. And she asked me, what I was doing in the school yard all on my own and after sundown? She must have called somebody after that brief conversation. I have no idea what went on behind the scenes, but not long after we had arrived in Switzerland, only about twelve to fourteen weeks, I was on a plane back to my Dad. I was very sad to lose my grandparents, but all considered, might even have been a good thing. They would have spoilt me entirely.

My parents finally got divorced three years later in 1980. My mother made one more very valiant attempt to try and reintroduce herself into our lives, but that did not go as she had planned. I think for my Dad, too much time had passed, and he had emancipated himself to the point of where he was gentle but quite rigorous about where he belonged, where I belonged, and where he though my mother belonged. And despite her honest desire to be with us, I do not think anything had changed about who she was at heart.

Today, I grieve for her broken heart, but I maintain that it was the best for my Dad, and the best for me. And the best for her too.

Looking back, it was the car accident that gave me the first true realisation, that life and death were but a heartbeat apart. And with it, the idea that I could lose my Dad, the only adult apart from Evangeline whom I felt dependable. This instilled in me a deep insecurity. A permanent fear that I would lose people I loved, people on whom I was dependent. I suppose the move to Tanzania was the first realisation I got, that in a blink of an eye, my life could change drastically. That I could be thrown into a world where I had no means of communicating and therefore existing without being dependent. But being confronted with the very real possibility of losing my Dad, intensified my anxiety immeasurably. On the contrary, the extreme vulnerability of being dependent on my mother in an environment where I was completely unable to communicate, only served to heighten my distress. Much of my life has been ruled by this fear of impermanence, of things being totally beyond my control. Or of being wilfully abandoned, for not being good enough.

But of course, these are adult reflections. Made decades later, from the comfort and safety of a therapy room, trying to come to terms with my own patterns of developing dependencies.

Home, sort of

Still in 1977, while I had spent those three months in Switzerland with my mother, My Dad had moved into another house that had been allocated to him by the university. This was part of a small collection of maybe thirty or thirty-five identical houses. Ours was a cute two-storey, three bedroom structure, that was to be our home for the next seven years. There was a carport of woven palm fronds out front. It sported a colony of silk-orb-weavers, with leg-spans the size of an adult's palm, vividly coloured and mandibles visibly glistening from ten metres away. My Dad planted two large frangipanis, with sweet smelling yellow-and-white blossoms. Also, several banana plants, which thrived wildly, presumably because some of the roots had found access to the sewage drains. Out the back, we had a huge bamboo, taller than the house and pillars thicker than my leg, as well as several Flamboyant trees. I loved those in particular, for their flaming red blooms, and because they were so very climbable.

The homes were lined along a central drive, next to which stood a huge and proud mango tree. Not my favourite, because its sap was very sticky, making climbing a messy affair, but still, it grew mangos, right? These houses were perhaps not as generous or spacious as other staff quarters on the university campus. But the Darajani (Swahili; "by the bridge" or "by the causeway") did have the highly fortunate advantage of being situated slightly lower than all the surrounding neighbourhoods or the student flats. It was among the last collection of houses to lose access to running water when pressure dropped.

Which it did frequently. Every once in a while, water would simply stop running. Sometimes for hours, sometimes for weeks. If the latter was the case, my Dad and I would fetch water from a cartesian well, some kilometres away, filling it into large orange plastic buckets in the back of our jeep. The water that came from the well was not really different from the water that came from the taps. Sometimes clear, sometimes cloudy with silt residue and mud. *Always* with the possibility of Cholera. We boiled and filtered our water on principle. Caution of infections and tropical diseases or parasites was ever present. Malaria, Typhoid, Hepatitis, and a long list of others were facts of life. Even as a child, you learnt this quickly. Crippling injuries and debilitating Infections were a matter of course, as were accidents due to road conditions or the (un-) states of vehicles.

I was not yet seven years old when I met my first victim of leprosy. An elderly man, sitting on a very tattered and grimy mat of woven grass. He was begging for coins outside a hardware shop. Today's zombie movies had nothing on this pitiful husk of a human being, who seemed more dead than alive. One of his legs ended at the ankle, the second leg ended at the knee. The man had two digits (digits, not fingers!) left on one hand, and no fingers on the other. One of his eyes was opaque, and the teeth in his mouth barely outnumbered his remaining limbs. I remember being completely overwhelmed with a mixture of horror and pity at this wreck of a human being, forced to survive under such circumstances.

Another thing that shocked me deeply, and left me floundering in a turmoil of emotions, was how these easy going, gentle people dealt with crime. Poverty was a part of life, so it was natural, if unfortunate, that some of the more desperate individuals would resort to taking what was not theirs. I remember witnessing how a mob, and there is no other way to describe it, a mob of people force-marched a young man to the police station. One of my older friends, Ambokile, was among the mob, and he told me, the young man had been caught stealing a loaf of bread.

I was struck speechless by the complete lack of inhibition, with which the young man was beaten with sticks. People flung fist-sized stones. The young man was kicked and shoved around. And I was absolutely horrified and deeply disturbed by the blatant *glee* with which these people unleashed their rage on this unfortunate individual. It was ugly. I have no idea if the young man even made it, but he would have been lucky to reach the police station alive. Or not so lucky? I ran home in tears, and even my Dad could not console me.

I am not even going to start on what they did (do) to people accused of witchcraft. Or how albinos are treated. And, no. Female genital mutilation was not a public topic in the 1970ies.

Despite all these things, Dar es Salaam was as close to paradise in so many ways. Despite being one of the most impoverished countries in sub-Saharan Africa, Tanzania had an abundance of fruit and vegetables. A biannual rainy season, giving rise to a variety that put any modern, globally supplied supermarket to shame. So while basics like salt and sugar, cooking-oil and toilet-roll were almost constantly in low supply, and to obtain exotic goods like noodles or toothpaste, you needed to be extraordinarily well connected (and illegally fluid in hard currency), my Dad and I were always comfortably stocked. There was pretty much always rice, maize, sweet-potato and cassava available. There was wheat flour available, but it was invariably "inhabited".

We discovered cassava, sweet potatoes, and yams. So many varieties of rice and potatoes. There was spinach, okra. Although I only ever got the hang of preparing okra in a palatable way in recent years. A wide variety of cauliflowers and cabbages, a diversity of beans, lentils and other Leguminosae. There were tomatoes and onions, zucchini in abundance, squash, and pumpkins. A variety of carrots, leeks, and eggplants. I remember discovering bok-choi, cooking bananas and green papayas. An abundancy of peanuts and cashew nuts. There was a seasonal variety of apples, pears, and plums, while citrus fruits, mangoes, passion fruit, physalis, pineapples and papayas were available all the year around. I learnt about guavas, whose sweet buttery taste I still miss today. And there was a variety of bananas, the likes of which few Europeans ever even learn about, regardless of how globalised the produce section in supermarkets are these days.

Fresh milk was scarce, and aside from butter (salted only), any other dairy products were entirely unavailable. For My Dad and me, typically Swiss in this particular respect, the absence of some savoury cheese was hard, but it was something we dealt with. At some point, my Dad and some other parents organised a connection to a dairy farm and we had a weekly supply of fresh milk.

There was meat available, but you needed to be wary. Or you needed to be hardy. Or both. Either way, meat needed to be cooked well, but I was never really enthusiastic, and my Dad was chronically worried that I would be malnourished. Fish was an interesting topic, because despite Dar es Salaam being a port city and despite fishermen bringing their catch straight off the boats, our experience with fish was such that eating fish bore an enormous risk of food poisoning. So fish was not on the menu.

Today, I fully appreciate that at the time, budget and prices for food were of no concern to me. Despite this, I was entirely aware of my privilege to be born rather better off than most of the children that surrounded me. And while there was little starvation as such, children that suffered from severe protein deficiency oedema (Kwashiorkor) were a common sight. My Dad still hates any kind of beans today, but we certainly never went hungry, nor did we suffer any deficiencies.

Another thing I only began to appreciate many years later, was that all the homes and houses on the campus came without any kind of fence or enclosure. I mean, yes, every home had a sort of a yard, that was planted and tended in a way as to show that this was where the "home zone" began. But other than that? No fences, not even low fences. No chain-link, no walls, no barbed wire, no broken glass set in concrete. No high-tension electric security fences. No signs that threatened with mauling dogs or armed response.

If you wanted to visit someone, you walked right up to their door and called a cheerful "hodi, hodi?" (Swahili: "Hello, hello," or by context, "may I come in?"). If someone was home, you got the equally cheerful "karibu, baribu!" ("Welcome, welcome"). You didn't call ahead, you did not make an appointment. And you did not cancel five minutes ahead of set time because you got distracted.

Come to think of it, none of the homes had a phone. And by phone, I mean the telephone device with a dialling disc and the funny thing that looks like a plastic banana with bobbles on either end. Mobile phones were huge, heavy, battery-operated devices that ran via satellite uplink. You needed a car to lug them around. Television was something that happened in other countries. Smart phones were more than three generations away. If my Dad wanted to talk to his parents, to tell them of our imminent arrival for a holiday in Switzerland, he would schedule a timeslot at the central post office in Dar es Salaam. On the phone, I imagined you could hear the echoing emptiness of the vacuum between worlds, and there was always some seconds of delay, before a reply would be heard. We spoke for two or three minutes, because anything else would have been ruinously expensive.

Amongst us kids, communication was very direct. Very basic. When we wanted to meet, we simply went out and *did*. We walked, or rode our bikes, to our friends' houses and we checked to see whether they were there and whether they had the time to play. It happened independently and without supervision of our parents. Any feedback, from either your friends or your not-so-good-acquaintances, was immediate and unmitigated. We did not have anyone drive us anyplace, we did not have a week crammed with activities and extra schooling. And apart from homework, we made our own schedules. And it worked.

In retrospect, I am aware that the picture I paint is rather rose-tinted. But then, Life is so much simpler when you are a child. I was simply unaware of so of the complexity much that went on in the remainder of Tanzania.

So yes, this was home. Even if a part of me was always apart, watching from the outside.

Friendships

I went to the international school of Tanzania in Dar es Salaam. I started school, speaking hardly sufficient English to tell people my name. But that was okay, because I was far from the only one, and the school was in fact equipped really well to support those children who were learning English as a second, or even as a third language. There was a huge variety of nationalities in school, with about a quarter of the pupils being from the more well-off Tanzanian families. All of the teaching staff were expatriates, and obviously very well qualified. They were overall friendly and good natured towards all their students.

I came to abhor school uniforms, though. I was forced to go to school as a boy. I was not even able to retreat into something gender neutral. I had to wear my hair short. It felt horrible. I felt horrible. This was not so much a sharp kind of pain, but it was a constant, continuous weight which chafed at my soul and grated on my nerves.

I am well aware of the abundant arguments pro school uniforms, all of which go along the lines of that they create an environment of equality and reduce social tensions by minimising the obvious income gaps between the families. I will say, as politely as I am able, that this is just so much bull dung. For starters, there is a blatantly obvious difference between the uniform that is fresh and crisp every morning because it has been laundered and pressed by a domestic, and the uniform that is worn for a week and smells of wood smoke and sweat, because there is only one set, and it gets laundered on the weekend. Secondly, there is the difference between the uniform that has been bought fresh off the rack every season, and the uniform that has been worn by the five previous siblings, and will continue to be worn until the shirt is held together by the seams, where the fabric is double. And finally, there is the difference between the uniform that is mass produced, preferably in polyester because that will endure more than one generation, and the uniform that is custom tailored. You think school uniforms are uniform? Wake up!

What remains today is a deeply rooted dislike for knee-high stockings combined with shorts. I mean seriously? Shorts, yes, of course. This is Tanzania coast-side, it is thirty-eight Celsius in the shade and humidity is approaching one-hundred percent, of course you wear shorts! But who in their right mind wears knee-high polyester stockings? And of all possible aberrations in fashion or absences of good taste, to shorts. Must be the heat…

I like to think I am like my Dad. To a high degree: colour blind. This was *not* something I was born with. On the contrary. Looking back, being exposed to my grandparents, and their concerns and conversations prior to our emigration for Dar es Salaam, did imbue me with prejudice. And the views on "Africa" of the main Swiss populace in the 1970ies were not that far removed from what they were at the height of colonial times. But my experiences in school and our neighbourhood, my playing and *living* with the people in Dar es Salaam realigned that. And of course, my Dad's mind-set modelled mine. As I said, there was an abundance of nationalities and skin tones at our school, and I had friends and acquaintances all across the board of ethnicities. At this period in time, language was the greatest barrier, and culture the second. Meaning to say, I was aware that the majority of the children in our school and neighbourhood had a different skin tone. But what really had an effect on my choice of friends was whether or not we managed to communicate along common ground.

I believe soccer is the most successful universal language spoken on this globe, and soccer is played with a passion all over Africa. It was not my strong point. I played along every once in a while, but overall, Ambokile and his pals always played a little too rough for my liking, and the other girls did not seem all that keen on shooting goals either. To be honest, I too found, and still find, soccer overall rather pointless and boring. I did rather enjoy playing softball, but that we played only that at school. In our neighbourhood, bats or balls seemed unavailable.

Ambokile and Sharon were siblings, originally from Uganda, and I dimly remember that their Dad had needed to go into exile, for having fallen into disfavour with the Ugandan government. Sharon was about my age and Ambokile was some few years older. They had a youngest brother, Dennis, cute as a button, whom I doted on, even if he we hardly understood each other. Sandra was Swiss like me and lived two houses over. We got on really well most of the time, and at other times, we fought like siblings over the most stupid of things. Adrian was another Swiss boy, who lived a ten-minute bicycle ride away, with whom I spent endless hours. Scavenging for usable raw materials, constructing model cars, finding fruit in the wild, trailing through the bush were unifying activities. Playing Lego and listening to music (Abba, Simon & Garfunkel, Beach-Boys, ZZ-Top to name a few). Cheong was a sweet if shy Korean boy who had been adopted by a family from Sweden. The stunts he pulled on his bicycle were breath-taking, and he could outrace us all, on two wheels or one. His giggle was entirely addictive.

One of my closest friends was Jeremy. His family moved in a couple of houses down the road in the Darajani about half a year after we did. They were a family of emigrants that left the USA to get away from poverty, racial tensions, and the increasingly violent crime of Boston. Jeremy and I got on well, sharing our love for stories and wild adventures, comics, and books. Jeremy too was a great fan of Batman. He was not such an avid player of Lego, and yet we were very good friends and play-mates for about three years. One of my fondest memories is his mother, baby Joy on her hip, showing us how to make peanut butter, and the two of us playing Lego with his younger brother Raymond, with plates of some kind of corn-crackers with peanut butter on the side. And ironically for being an American, Jeremy introduced me to the Beatles.

Lego was one of my greatest enthusiasms, which could absorb my attention like little else. I could spend entire rainy weekends (and quite a few sunny ones) searching for the right bricks, patiently developing the most elaborate space-ships, cars, pirate-ships, evolving whole worlds and universes in my mind. Cheong and Adrian were usually with me, and together we would derive the kind of intricate plots, that might give Big-Bang-Theory, Deep-Space-9 and all the Trekkies-fan-fic some serious com-petition.

Books, comics, and novels were my food for soul. Jeremy and I would soak up all the stories, adventures, and reports of exploits we could lay our eyes on. We loved drawing and colouring, depicting scenes from books as we imagined them or drafting our own comics and stories. We used any available paper. Luckily my Dad brought stacks of redundant printouts from university, so in a world where stationary was practically non-existent, my friends and I had an unlimited supply. If you were pre-pared to disregard that the paper already had print on it.

There was an abundant supply of wood to carve, grasses to weave, and animals to discover. I had free access to all my Dad's tools, and his trust that I would put them to good use. We build tree-forts, connected my rope bridges and rope ladders. We had the bamboo in our own back garden. Wire and cut-up bicycle tubes were always to be scavenged (Tanzania in the 1970ies was held together by wire and rubber bands). I quickly picked up the art of fabricating cars and trucks from small boards, wire and cut tin cans, with wheels cut out of flip-flops. The ingenuity of providing them with steerable front wheels and creating a steering rod, long enough to guide standing up. Or running. My friends and I would race these vehicles through the dust, screaming like banshees (Yes, we actually played with these models, instead of put-ting them on display). All of us dreaming of owning fast cars and invincible trucks.

There was an abandoned nursery not far away, where we children would scav-enge for mangoes, cashew fruit, physalis, guavas and passion fruit, in the trees that had grown wild. There were fields and woods in which we could roam free, the only real hazards being broken glass. Or puff-adders, which would rely on camouflage rather than flight. Any other snake or predator would surely have cleared out from the amount of noise we were making. There were ravines to explore, there were riverbeds that carried water only after rains, an endless source of polished quartz and agate stones. If you wanted to find water, you needed to dig into the sand, like the elephants did in the game reserves, and about half a meter down, the hole would slowly fill.

As close as Dar es Salaam is to the equator, the sun rose at six in the morning, and set at six sharp in the evening, all the year round. Dawn and dusk were short affairs, but hugely colourful. And since there were no streetlights, the stars cast a brilliant canopy across the heavens. Temperatures would fall quite sharply, and my friends and I would sit, or even lie on the warm asphalt of the single lane running through the Darajani. The danger of being run over was smaller than chancing upon a snake, enjoying the very same warmth. Very often, several families would gather in one of the gardens or backyards, a fire would be lit, and the adults would have a barbeque, and we children would play hide and seek or chase each other around the adults, until our parents packed us off to bed.

On weekends, four to six families would very often go to the one of the beach hotels and spend the entire day there. Swimming, exploring tide pools, re-routing rivulets running back to the sea. We spent hours playing hide and seek in the seaside resorts. My Dad would play volleyball with the other parents from the campus, and we children would watch and build sandcastles.

So, yes, I had it good. I was privileged.

When I tell people of my youth, I very often get a wide eyed "Oooh" and they ask me about safaris and if there were a lot of lions and elephants in our back yard?

Um. Seriously? But unfortunately, No.

After all, we lived on a university campus on the outskirts of a sprawling port city. We did not live in a game reserve and my Dad was not a trophy hunter or a game warden. I went to school. My Dad taught engineering and design six days a week.

Nevertheless, of course my Dad did take me on safaris. Once a year perhaps. The Mikumi Game Reserve was the most easily accessible for us. To be perfectly honest, I viewed our journeys with a mixture of deeply rooted anxiety, dating back to our car accident. And exuberant enthusiasm at seeing such a rich abundance of wildlife. One trip stands out in particular, because Evangeline and René, her significant-other, came to visit us in Tanzania. Some of my favourite memories are from those days.

Another highlight shared by my Dad and me, was that spent several easter holidays at a quinine plantation, set deep within the Usambara Mountains (home of the

Usambara Violet). It was run by a Swiss family, somehow connected with my Dad, and they took us hiking, bird watching. And I spent afternoons painting eggs and baking cookies with Heidi, the "Mom" of the plantation. It was a deeply enriching experience, because the lush rain forests of the Usambara mountains were such a stark difference to the scrub and grass savannah that was so abundant. This was jungle in its absolute primal state, with creepers as thick as a grown human, with trees with channelled roots, beset with their very own ecosystems of orchids and lichens. There were birds the likes of which you never found in the plains, and there might have been gorillas and other primates.

I am deeply grateful for all these experiences and all the memories that I took with me.

Hardships

And yet, next to all this beautiful and varied abundance of passing time together, of exploring and learning, I found it very difficult to keep friends.

The expats in our community and some of the more well-off local families on the university campus, all sent their children to the international school. This was situated in the outskirts of Dar es Salaam, about forty to fifty minutes cars' drive away. Since there were no school busses, the parents organised themselves in carpools and took alternate turns in making a tour of the campus and picking up all the children. In the afternoon, the same again to pick up the children from school and drop them off at their respective homes. I still remember the smell of as many as twelve kids packed into a station wagon, whose PVC-leather seats had sat in the sun long enough to scald the bare skin. Air conditioners for cars were two generations away.

I have come to find the taste of sweat is almost indistinguishable from the taste of tears. Getting to school was a gauntlet. Getting home again just as much. I was obviously the odd one out. Even among the Swiss kids, which were a minority anyways, I must have somehow stood out, seemed to somehow be different. And therefore, a predetermined target. The teasing was something was something that I was already familiar with from kindergarten. And yet, the viciousness and the malignancy of this steady stream of verbal abuse was something new. Coupled with pinches, cuffs, and shoves, pulling hair, or spitting on me. In some instances, using compass needles or freshly sharpened pencils if they could not provoke a reaction with the usual methods. My spine still goes rigid today, and my breathing goes flat, when I remember how I swore I would not give them the satisfaction of seeing me cry.

Despite all this, possibly because of all this, I tried my best to "be good". I paid close attention in school, I was diligent and studious, I got good grades. I tried my best to pretend nothing bad happened and to put a brave face on my dread of being picked up for school the next morning. I was deeply afraid, that if I did not make this work, then I would be sent back to live with my mother. I had never been asked whether I wanted to stay with my Mum or my Dad. It had been decided for me that I should remain with my mother and return to Switzerland. And then faceless people had decided that I should stay with my Dad instead. So obviously, the same faceless people could revoke their decision.

Like in Zürich, I know my Dad was fully aware of the grief other kids gave me, and I know he spoke to other parents on my behalf. At some point, I think he simply stopped trying because he realised that, while this would grant me a short reprieve, the backlash was so much worse. Instead, he gave me the most valuable gift he was capable of, he spent so much of his time with me, and he made it count.

On pretty much every working day, my Dad would spend about an hour reading to me after lunch from my favourite books. Books that were chosen and sent to me by my godmother, Evangeline, and thus always something special. On the weekends, we would spend time with other families, in their gardens, or go to the beach together. Or my Dad would spend time with me, building or crafting all kinds of things. He showed infinite patience in teaching me more on how to use tools. We worked together for more than a year on a glider plane with a wingspan larger than I was tall. By and by, I learned to do these things all by myself. And I became a voracious reader.

In all the books and stories that I devoured, I always identified more easily with the female characters. In all the adventures that I fantasised with my Lego, my character was a girl, a woman. The tendency to dissociate and to distance myself from the "real" world is clear, even at this early age. I suppose there is even some irony, that one of my favourite characters was Susan Storm, the original invisible woman (*"Fantastic Four" by Stan Lee & Jack Kirby, Marvel comics*). Aside from Batman of course, on whom I still have a crush (*"Batman" by Bob Kane & Bill Finger, DC Comics*).

There were no shawls or dresses available, there was no magical box of clothes or dress-up gear. And yet I still found a way to fabricate clothes that were almost dresses from worn-out t-shirts. I had an expansive set of water soluble colour pencils or crayons, that were quite soft, and I got quite proficient at applying eyeliner and lid-shade. Come to think of it, I even managed to organise some blue leggings along with a matching blue polar-neck (in the tropics, goes to show what children are capable of) and in that get-up, I felt pretty much like Susan Storm. I even made myself a utility belt and a set of chest prosthesis from a tennis ball I cut in half. Um, yes! Chest prosthesis at the age of seven. Hey, I was being Sue Storm.

Our domestic's name was Mister Williams. That was not his family name, but to my shame, I only remember how I addressed him as a child. He was a very fine Muslim gentleman, with simple education but with distinguishing and impeccable manners. He had a thin and exquisitely manicured moustache, which he liked to stroke, and his cheeks were splashed with tribal scarring patterns. He always wore freshly pressed shirts that smelled faintly of polished ebony and strong tea. He lived about half an hour's walk away in a cabin that was his own.

During the week, he would cook excellent lunches for my Dad and me, and he took care of our laundry. I believe he was quite fond of me, and he showed me lots of patience and care. Once, sometimes twice a year, my Dad would be away on a congress, a convention for development aid, or some other form of business trip. During these absences, he asked Mr. Williams stay at our place in our guest room, and take care of me full time.

It was during one of my Dad's absences that Mr. Williams happened on me in full Susan Storm mode. I think it is fair to say, he was at least as shocked as I was. I certainly wished I were invisible. I was deeply worried that he would tell my Dad and that my Dad would send me back to Switzerland. Nevertheless, I realised pretty quick, that Mr. Williams was, more than anything else, frightened. I am not sure exactly what he was afraid of. Being blamed for my aberrance, and therefore being let go with a bad reference?

Or possibly, he was afraid that someone else would discover my tendency for female clothing? It is entirely possible, that he was very much afraid for my safety. Today I know, there are a lot of African cultures, where people, whose gender expression or whose sexual preference deviates from the norm, are mutilated, beaten to death, stoned, chopped apart with machetes, doused in kerosene and burnt alive… …no, that is not an exclusively African problem, there are a lot of cultures like that world-wide.

Fact remains, his genuine fear left a deeper impression than any anger, chastisement or depreciation could have done. That was the last time I played Susan Storm.

Of course I made friends, but somehow, that never really lasted. The most natural cause was that families would stay in Dar es Salaam for a year, maybe two, and then return to wherever their home country was. At some point, Ambokile and his family left, when their Dad was given tenure at another university. And from that point on out, Raymond, Jeremy's younger brother would tag along regularly. Sandra stayed a good friend for two years, before she returned to Zürich with her parents.

Getting to know new people was not usually a problem, since new families were always introduced to everyone, very often in the form of a garden party at someone's home, or all the families meeting at the beach.

In Dar es Salaam as in Zürich, I kept my feelings of who I was, what I was, as well hidden as I could. But looking back, I realise how miserably I must have failed at that. I suppose the girl that I was at heart would simply not be subdued. She always made herself known in one way or another. I was inconsistent in my own name, as much as I tried. Susan Storm was something I kept to myself entirely, and yet I kept being caught in clothes that were almost-dresses. And I am convinced my body language was at least as ambiguous. I am also convinced that this is what provoked the rumours and the whispered comments among the other children.

The slurs and the names.

Children that befriended me did not have it all that easy either. At best, they needed to disregard all the rumours about my being a freak, mentally sick, a perv, a faggot or a queer, just to name a few. I wonder if those kids even knew what it was that they were saying? If the worst came to the worst, then my friends, Sharon, Sandra, later Adrian would catch the collateral, simply by being in my presence. Or they were attacked as accessories. Mostly this was just verbal abuse, but scuffs and shoves were regular, along with punches and kicks. Stones would get thrown, mud would be flung, sticks would be picked up. Perhaps I should be grateful. Those were the days before baseball bats became universally available. There were days, where spending time together with Adrian and Sandra meant sitting in a group in one of our backyards and repairing our bikes, because our tyres had been slashed.

And every so often, I lost friends, simply because they tired of the constant friction I seemed to attract. At some point, both Adrian and Cheong simply turned mute and kept their distance. There were times when this was really bad, where I felt utterly alone in the world, where I *was* alone. Despite having my Dad. There were times, even before I turned ten, that I reflected about what I wanted from life, who I wanted to be. And it was clear, I did not want to be the weird kid, the freak who was utterly friendless, ridiculed, and kicked around by the neighbourhood.

You can feel cold, even if it is thirty-eight Celsius in the shade.

Things grew slightly more tense when one particular family moved into our neighbourhood. Joey, his two sisters Olivia and Prudence, and their considerably older brother Martin. Also Americans of African origin, they had emigrated from New York and first moved to Zambia, before settling in Dar es Salaam. I understood they had a lot in common with Jeremy, and I believe, they had a strong influence on how his life later developed.

It was clear; Joey's family was of a different mind-set. Joey was aggressive to downright abrasive in establishing his place in any given group. And he was extremely quick to cry "racist". Still, he was an overall curious and adventurous boy, and he loved playing hide-and-seek, raiding kitchens for food, or climbing trees. In my memory, I think he rather enjoyed exploring the bush together with Jeremy, Raymond and me.

Olivia and Prudence made it clear that I was beneath their grace. In fact, they rather treated me as something half-digested a cat might have thrown up. And if their vitriol failed to convince me to vacate the premises fast enough, they impressed their disdain with more pointed arguments. Freshly sharpened pencils, for example. I learnt to stay clear. As for Martin, he must have been between sixteen and eighteen, he was a very angry young man. I dare say, he certainly did not live up to his namesake, Martin Luther King. Some of the movies Martin and his siblings had seen, must have been excessively violent. And racist. Of the kind that seeks retaliation and vengeance.

While Jeremy did not condone the violence, he did not exactly condemn it either. And from his overall attitude, it was clear that he was beginning to question if I was "appropriate company" for a budding Black-rights activist, exploring his African heritage.

Jeremy would later acquire quite some fame as an editor and a writer, exploring the evolution and influences of African and Afro-American culture. I am sad to say, our friendship ended rather dramatically during a sleepover.

I am at Jeremy's place for the night.

His mother has sat us round her table in the Kitchen, together with Raymond and Joy, the youngest. She is feeding Joy, while she supervises us making peanut butter. I enjoy this immensely. Peanut butter itself is a novelty to me, and making it myself doubly so. I am fascinated and delighted by this taste and texture. And making food myself from scratch is just so empowering.

Later, she sends us upstairs to get ready for bed.

We are in Jeremy's bedroom and we are talking, like we always do, about books' characters and comics' heroes. Who our favourites are, and why we think these in particular are so great.

And as usual, I enthuse about Sue "invisible woman" Storm and Kate Kane aka Bat Woman. It is a great way to spend time, it's fun. I am at peace.

We have been talking for a while. Jeremy asks why I always talk about the girl characters. I am careless enough, or honest enough, to outright tell him, how it is an obvious choice for me. I am a girl. This puzzles him. I can see thoughts flash across his face while he processes.

Without warning, he strikes me straight across the face with his fist. He shoves me roughly away from him. My head hits the wall. He is literally panting with... ...emotion. Fury, disgust, hate.

"If you ever *come near me or my family again, I'll kill you!"*

So that's how I ended up, standing on my Dad's doorstep shortly before midnight on a Friday, clutching a bedsheet and bleeding on my PJs. And yet, looking back, what hurt (hurts) more than my cut lip or my nose was the look of revulsion on Jeremy's face.

Of course, my Dad asked what had happened. And if my memory does not deceive me, this was probably the only time ever, in the years we spent together, that I told him. That I was a girl. In retrospect, it probably got lost in all the tears and wiping away blood and trying to disinfect the cut lip of a child wriggling in pain.

Innocence lost

I know for a fact that I was not all innocent. Far from it. In retrospect I know my insecurities made me rather clingy. And that is most likely an understatement. Half the time, I was probably far too eager to please. I rather think I was possessive, possibly even emotionally manipulative in trying to ensure my friends' loyalties. And the other half, I was slow to trust and quick to retreat. I was silent. A lot. When asked for my opinion, I stated my direct and unmitigated state of mind, something that few people were prepared to deal with, even more so, since I rarely spoke much.

For a time, I wanted to appear hard. I wanted to appear tough. And the constant exposure to all the verbal flack did nothing to improve my communication skills. I am not proud to say, for about two years, I was quite the foul-mouthed little punk. I dare say I possessed all the diplomatic skill of an eight-year-old, and I certainly did not think everything through.

Come to think of it, *I* probably appeared as if I was angry most of the time.

And yet, at some point I realised, being hard, being tough meant being alone. And that was something I simply did not want to be.

I am quite grateful for a number of people's intervention and feedback. Adrian, Mr. Williams, Jeremy's mom. A number of my teachers in school, in particular Mr Evans, who loved reading to us. I rather like to think my social skills improved considerably from there on out.

Ironically, Joey's uneasy friendship registers prominently in this respect. His hair-trigger chip-on-the-shoulder behaviour contributed immensely to my ability to reflect what I was actually saying, what words and expressions I used, how that was perceived by other people. What kind of an impression it created about what kind of a person I was. And I got so very sick and tired of attempting to convince Joey that I had slurred him, not because of his tone of skin, but because of his tone of voice. I was irritated by his steady stream of challenging remarks and casual insults, unable at the time to call him out on his hypocrisy.

There were enough stretches in my time in Dar es Salaam, where I was apparently without anyone to play with for days to weeks on stretch. Moreover, spending time with other children seemed to always entail being made fun of. Being teased, being picked on, up to the point of being beat up. Regularly. Regardless of whether I adapted and accommodated the needs and whims of the others, or whether I did my best to keep my own straight line, I always seemed to lose the loyalty of my playmates, or their commitment to any lasting friendship.

Nothing was good enough. I was not good enough.

And yet, from all the years of abuse and antagonism from the children around me, one of the most important conclusions I reached, was that violence only ever engenders counter-violence. To this day, I believe and I maintain, that nothing is to be gained from anger or retribution.

And what I can say with certainty, is that that race, geographic origin, or tone of skin was never a decisive factor in my loyalties or affections.

Confirmation

My Dad had subscriptions to several Swiss newspapers. They chronically arrived slightly late, but that did not really matter, since the world turned at a completely different pace in Dar es Salaam anyhow.

I was eleven years old. I was an addicted book worm, and I went through books like the proverbial monkey though a banana plantation, often rereading books I was particularly fond of. Michael Ende, Kurt Held, Heiner Gross, Lewis Carroll, C.S. Lewis, Alexandre Dumas, Robert Louis Stevenson, Victor Hugo, Charles Dickens...

Completely off topic, but significant to the timeline, and significant to my development. My Dad had a girlfriend for some time, Ms Muchumba. She had one of those beautifully crafted hair styles, with pyramids and coiling plaits, that I saw only in East Africa, and she loved wearing those rich, vivid prints that are so typical. She dined with us regularly for a time, but truth be told, I remember little of the conversation with her. At some point, I found a condom packet, and I asked my Dad what that was. So that was when my Dad saw himself faced with telling me about anatomy, sex, and pregnancy, and why this was so important to adults.

During week days, my Dad still read to me after lunch, more out of habit and kinship than anything else. Or we would both share a book in companionable silence. And sometimes we would share the paper. He would take the politics and front pages, along with technical and research, while I would focus more on the culture and arts. Every once in a while, we recommended each other articles of particular interest. And of course, my Dad would explain to me, how the world worked.

My lips still go numb, when I remember sitting opposite my Dad, the sun shining through the window in my back, bringing out the cheerful orange of the armchair I was sitting on. My mouth went dry and my breathing became so shallow, I barely dared turn the pages, so as to disappear entirely. So as to not have my secret revealed. I was so afraid...

...I cannot even truly say of what I was afraid of. Of my Dad finding out and not love me anymore? Of being sent back to live with my mother (Yes, this was a very real fear). Of me *being* the crazy queer everyone said I was? Of it being Real? Of me having to face this? Alone?

But that was precisely the point. I was *not* alone.

By pure utter coincidence, the article in the newspaper described the life of a person, born into a male body. How this person had always known that this was wrong. How she had always known she was a girl. A woman. How she had fought, literally, for years (this was 1981) for legal and medical recognition of her state of being, of her state of mind. How she had to spend years and a fortune in hard currency to pay lawyers to fight for her right to a name. And more years and more currency to pay surgeons to enable her to finally feel more or less comfortable in her body. How she had to undergo surgery that at the time was radically new, how the surgeons had no experience, how everything might have cost her life. All this, to live a self-determined life.

I registered all the hardship this woman endured to be granted to live the life she sought. The life she deserved. But only barely. What I *did* register, was that I was *not* alone. That what I felt was *real*. And that something could be *done* to help me.

I learnt I was trans* sexual.

And despite my eleven years, I recognised the scandalised undertone of the newspaper article. How the journalist sceptically analysed the lack of "proper" experts to examine this poor soul and give *him* the "right treatment." To set him back in the right path. I remember the insinuated suggestion that how it could be possible that any sane creature could feel that way, never-mind letting someone cut off your penis! Oooh, yes! That really tickles people's imagination, does it not? Let that sentence dissolve on your tongue…

…forty-odd years later, and you still cannot tell a cis* man you are trans* gender without him flinching and instinctively reach protectively for his genitals.

And yet again. I said not a word to my father. I quietly let the newspaper disappear.

Today, I would urgently hope that any child feeling like I did, should have the trust in their parents to do the right things and to support and empower their children in their identity. And I would fervently hope that any parents would in fact be educated enough, open enough and confident enough in their own identity and in their trust in their child. To empower their child.

Today, I weep over the years lost to me. The years I could not live as a girl. The years I could not grow into this better version of *me*.

And yet, today, rational analysis tells me, that this was probably for the better. The world in 1981 was not ready for the likes of me. And I not ready for the world.

Nancy

In the same year, I came back from a holiday in Switzerland, to find our neighbourhood had been enriched by a new family from the UK. Marc was about my age, give or take a few months, and Peggy was about two years younger. They had two even younger siblings, Lizzie, and Tommy, but they were rather too young to really play with us. We got to know each other through soccer, ironically, since that was the "done thing". But it was soon apparent, that Peggy and Marc were rather more keen on other things.

Marc and Peggy introduced me to the fabulous worlds of Enid Blyton, Arthur Ransom, Ruyard Kipling, Roald Dahl…

Marc was really good at knots, and he taught me loads of things I still use today. I introduced them to art of building cars from scrap metal and other detritus. They were enthusiastic about climbing trees, particularly if there was fruit to be found. We built rope-ladders and tree forts. We found that Lego was a passion that we shared, dreaming up universes of our own, much like I used to do with Adrian and Cheong.

I kept my distance during our daytrips to school and back. I was ever so grateful that Marc and Peggy were driven in another car by different parents, and that they were not in the same class as me. That way, they avoided at least some of the collateral that spilt over from the routine daily abuse I still faced.

We became rather close-knit, creating our own world of Amazons-Pirates, based very loosely on ideas and characters gathered from the books by Arthur Ransom. Even Marc took on the female name Ruth, as in, being a ruthless raider. I took to calling myself Nancy.

That name and our friendship would stay with me for years to come. In fact, I came to love them much like siblings.

Although it was very clear to me, that for Marc and Peggy, all of this was a make-believe fantasy. When they returned home to their parents after a day of corsair activity and defending our island against hordes of imaginary invaders (anything from alien space invaders to competing crews of cutthroat pirates), then they would be tucked into bed as Marc and Peggy. And go to school as Marc and Peggy.

For me, the name Nancy grew to be more like what I called that part of me, which was always there, but never truly present.

And in my mind, I began to envision what Nancy looked like. How she moved, danced, climbed trees. Laughed, cried, hoped, and brushed her teeth. I imagined how she would go to school instead of me, and how she would be so much tougher in facing all these bullies. How she would be strong and wise at the same time. Invincible in the secure knowledge that she could have wiped the floor with all of the ruffians if she so pleased. This was the solidification of a complete second life I lead, entirely in my own mind.

I think Peggy and Marc's parents were well aware of our making costumes and female apparel, just as they good-naturedly went along with all our diverting water courses and building forts in their backyard. There were simply better suited trees and more space in their garden than behind the house where I lived with my Dad.

Plus, their mother was either a witch, working miracles, or maybe she had just the right amount of vitamin B, to always be stocked with wheat flour and yeast, with jam and some form of cheese. So, their family actually had bread and cheese (not Swiss though), and she did not seem to mind feeding me on so many occasions.

First base

Another rather noteworthy line of events happened during my school hours.

Dharinee, one of the girls in my class, asked me if I liked her. Considering that she belonged to the few, who did not call me names, or prod me with freshly sharpened pencils, yes, I liked her rather more than others. Dharinee had charcoal dark hair, flowing like a river, and I was so very impressed by that. Plus, she had a peach-scented eraser in the shape of hello-kitty. She was bright, outgoing, and above all, friendly. We lent each other colours, to copy the diagrams from the board, during lessons.

One day, she asked me to stay behind in the classroom during breaktime, and I found out in short order, that she liked me so much, that she was prepared to kiss me. And not just a kosher peck on the cheek either. Full-out French.

That was quite an enlightening experience.

Entirely surprising and astonishing. Very much so. Slightly confusing, moist to wet, but overall, highly enjoyable. Certainly something to keep on a bucket list.

So, during breaktimes, Dharinee and I would sit by ourselves, holding hands, and when we felt we were not observed, we would make out. Yeah, twelve. I know. Slightly soon. But it was an innocent exploration, and it never escalated to anything else. At this point, I did not even associate it with anything sexual. Today, I rather think she might have been inspired by older students. Or possibly from observing her parents.

It did lead to two things.

Guang was another in my class. A delicate boy, smart as an encyclopaedia, timid as a hedgehog. Sitting next to him was almost as good as sitting next to the teacher. He had a buzzcut that simply screamed my name. I loved to let my fingers run across it, in an appreciative caress.

We were sharing a break together. At some point, I asked Guang, whether he would mind, if I kissed him. He was so surprised, he forgot the sandwich in his mouth. He chewed thoughtfully, and then asked, why I would want to kiss him. I told him that I liked him, that a kiss was a way of showing affection. And, after all, when girls like boys, they kiss them, right? Guang looked at me, slightly sideways, apparently giving this a lot of thought. He finished his sandwich, and then said, "Yes, okay".

My guess is, that either, he told his parents of the girl who looked like a boy. Or, that the teachers had, at some point, seen us, and intervened.

With the change of the school year, both Dharinee and Guang were placed in separate classes, with different schedules, and that was the end of our explorations.

I have no idea, if there truly is a connection between our kissing, and our being separated. I have no idea if the school ever contacted my Dad over this. Neither do I have any idea, whether Marc's and Peggy's parents ever spoke with my Dad over my gender ambivalent behaviour, when hanging out with their children. I am sure my Dad spoke with their parents on many occasions, so he must have known at least some of the things going on. But whether he was aware of any of the specifics?

I remember a very noteworthy conversation with my Dad, when I was twelve, soon to turn thirteen. We were sitting in our favourite armchairs after Lunch. As per usual, we were enjoying our mostly silent companionship and connectivity, reading. I do not remember how the discussion started, but my Dad got to talking about the time he spent working at the faculty of engineering in New York City as a very young man.

Apparently, my Dad found friends easily, and he told me of exploring the city together with them. One in particular must have been deeply impressed by my Dad, to the point of being smitten. And he went on, to make my Dad an offer, that was decidedly more than friendship, an offer that was very clearly intimate.

My Dad told me, how he declined, as politely and mindfully as he was able. And he recalled, how this friend had been really upset to be turned down.

And my Dad asked me, how I felt about that. And if that had ever happened to me?

My thoughts immediately went to the newspaper article more than a year ago. And I told my Dad, truthfully (to my perception), that no, this had never occurred between any of my friends. That I had liked Guang, that we had been good friends, but that we no longer saw each other. And that, while Marc was a very close friends, of whom I was very fond, then I did not feel myself drawn to him in that particular in that kind of way. Or to anyone else.

Looking back, I believe I was so preoccupied with playing at being a boy for part of my life, and being tom-boy Nancy for the remaining time, I had never thought about attraction to anyone. Neither did I remind my Dad, that my experiences with letting people too close, lead to punched noses and split lips.

I remember my Dad pausing, as he tried to find the right words to say. And then he stated that, should I decide that boys were cool and attractive, it would be okay for him.

Looking back today, that was probably *the* most awesome thing a father could have said to his child. Any child. In 1983.

I am quite sad that he no longer remembers that conversation today. When I told him thirty years later, that he never really had a son, that he had had a daughter instead all along, he was entirely surprised. He is still as awesome, as open minded and kind-hearted as he was then, and he still remembers how worried he was about my being picked on in school. But he seems to have forgotten the dresses and the ambiguous behaviour altogether.

I think I blushed redder than a beetroot and I probably said something noncommittal along the lines of, "okay, thanks." And then asked some distracting question to get the topic away from the hot-plate that was my awareness that I was trans* gender. And again, while I am extremely sad, that I did not have the trust and the confidence to tell him then, I maintain today that 1983 was not a good time to be "different". And certainly not a good time to be trans* sexual. Never mind the fact that this was East Africa, where gender roles are so deeply ingrained in the culture, they might as well be part of the bedrock.

Nevertheless, the years where I was between eleven and thirteen were probably my happiest and freest in all my childhood. All my fondest, most unencumbered memories are of that time.

I have often been asked, where my roots lie. It would be wrong to say, I do not have any. But they are…

…intangible. And they are not anchored to culture or to patriotism. The roots I was gifted with over the years are spread so far in both geography and in the people whose souls have touched mine. Home is where the people are that mean something to me. And I think I am blessed that this means, home can be so many places on this globe.

Most of all, I am blessed today, to have found a home within myself. But that was a long, long time in the growing.

(2) Being Normal

Normal…

…there is no such thing.

It is an entirely human invention.

To protect us from the incredible profusion that exists…

…outside the horizon of our perception.

A newborn child has

no gender

no culture

no skin colour

no sexual orientation

all these things are yet to grow

some are pre-specified, some are conditioned

"Why can't you just be normal?"

I have been asked this often enough as far back as I remember. And often enough, I have asked the same myself that. I have been called a freak, an accident, a perversion of nature.

But what exactly does that even mean, being normal?

This is not part of the chronology. This is a detour into explanations, statistics, and attempts at definitions. Every once in a while, the scientist in me slips her leash…

Defining what is normal

Without going into the actual statistical mathematics, I still find the "Gaussian mean" to present one of the clearest and most irrefutable definitions of "normality". Take a large enough population of anything, and consider a single parameter or measurement. Cassava roots and their weight, tulips and their tallness, bumblebees and their top velocity, the volume of raindrops, the fluffiness of sheep, correct answers in a maths exam…

…and yes: the values, beliefs, and core-ideals of humans. Or how easily you accept and live with your body's biological specification.

Set up a graphical distribution of your single parameter or measurement against the number of times it occurs, and you get what is called a Gaussian or a Laplace–Gauss distribution curve. This expresses itself as a kind of symmetrical bell-shaped graph. The hump in the centre essentially symbolises that the most common value, hence the average or standard mean, while the skirts that taper off on both sides show how the further away you get from the standard mean, the less frequent those measurements will occur. This bell shape can be kind of flat-ish or more steep, depending on how widely the variation is within a population.

There is such a thing as the standard deviation, which is a mathematical term for how much any single given value will deviate on average from the standard mean. 68% of all values of a population will be within one standard deviation, plus or minus. 95% will be within two and 99,7% are within three standard deviations of the standard mean.

If you want to know more about it, please go ahead and read all about "normality nest" in Wikipedia, or look at a textbook on statistics and distribution. It is actually quite cool logical stuff and it might contribute quite some insight to how you look at the world around you.

What I really find so intuitively and convincing about this mathematical model, is that *all* the values belong to the curve, and *all* the single values contribute to make the whole. The standard mean is per definition and per calculation dependant on *all* the values, even the ones belonging to the 0,3% that deviate from the standard mean by more than three standard deviations.

Or, to put it another way: *that which we define as "normal", is always relative*. It is always dependant on *all* members of the population. How we define what is "normal" is always from a perspective that is based on an average of a large portion of the population or collective. A standard mean. And yet, the outlying, more deviating values also belong to the whole of the population. Even if they differ strongly from the standard mean, they still contribute to our view and our definition of what it is to be normal.

They have a value and a purpose.

And it is normal for there to be deviations.

Furthermore, the standard mean is itself is subject to variation. The moment you change any of the values, you change the average. And perhaps more importantly: the moment you *choose to exclude* particular values for whatever reasons, the moment you begin to *arbitrarily select* your data, you are changing the whole fundamental structure and you are changing the centre of your distribution curve. And that would be a false basis on which to ground any choices or build any rules.

You would be cheating. Yourself.

It is normal for there to be diversity.

It is this exact variation, this *diversity* of people with different gifts, different strengths and talents, different points of view and core-values, that has in fact ensured not only our survival on this beautiful little planet, but brought us prosperity, and founded our immense creativity.

Perhaps though, a word of clarification.

Please bear with me when I speak of "deviation". When I use the word, all I mean is that the observed parameter does not correlate with the standard "normal" as defined by being close to the standard of the mean. I place no moral weight or ethical *value* on any of this. It simply *is*. Just as beliefs, dispositions and core tenets of people will differ, depending on their up-bringing, on their cultural and hereditary background.

Fact is, there are a number of biographical parameters in my life, whether I think of my being trans* gender or whether I look at the variation in my geographical time-line and the diversity of cultures I have learnt from. Some of these parameters certainly lie outside of the norm, and the multitude of variations in my biography are extreme. Maybe even beyond the 0.3% standard deviations.

Being Queer* (LGBTIQ*)

What I do find highly important to clarify, is how biology, identity, expression, and sexuality are very different things.

Biology is what your doctor or your specialist sees. To some degree, this is what is determined when you are born. Simply put, we define that it is normal for am human with testes and a penis to be a man. The biological sex is male. And a human with a uterus, ovaries, and breasts to be a woman, the biological sex is female. We base this definition of "normality" on the fact that this is true for a very large part of the population. And that it fulfils the biological basis for procreation.

But already, the dichotomy of male and female is shown to be untrue. There are people whose bodies are in fact a transient between the male and female, either in the development of the sexual organs, or in their hormonal balances. There is an entire spectrum of different states, all of them being *a purely biological condition*, where both expressions are latent, but developed in different degrees, to the point of where there may or may not be visible differences. Some intersex people do not even register this, if the development is minimal. Sometimes, the condition is recognised with the onset of puberty, and sometimes only recognised as late as when the person is diagnosed with infertility.

Oh, and guess what: this is normal.

Permit me to clarify. The huge advantage of sexual reproduction is that it is *prone* to produce deviations. It is precisely this variety that has produced this enormous abundance of species on this planet. It is the deviations that have ensured the *adaptability* of the different species under so many different environmental conditions, and *secured the survivals of biological life*. It is normal for there to be deviations.

Gender identity

Or, how you feel about yourself. Your deep-seated psychological sense of self. Your identity.

The vast majority (approaching 95%) of the human population of this planet is what we have come to call cis* gendered and heteronorm. That is to say, you are born into an ordinary binary biological body, and you are comfortable with the biological sex into you were born. You live and fulfil the role, which for most people is "normal" and "natural" to be associated with this biological sex. You are born to develop ovaries and breasts, you are a woman and you live the social expression, take on the social role of a woman. And you are at peace with this. You have testes and a penis, and you identify as male and you are comfortable being a man. And that is cool with you.

Nobody asks a cis* person, "how do you know?" Even more to the point, as a cis* person, you yourself will not ever question your own gender identity.

Per definition, trans* gender do not identify with their biological sex. Most people I know, suffering from gender dysphoria, are binary, or near-binary. Meaning, they are born into a biologically male body, but they identify as female. Hence they are male to female (mtf) trans* gender. Or they are born into a biologically female body, but they identify as male. Thus female to male (ftm) trans* gender.

Trans* sexuality is more of a medical term, and is used widely in professional and health-care circles. The concept of trans* sexuality has come to be recognised by medical and legal authorities in more and more countries including by the WHO. I understand it was originally coined by Dres. Harry Benjamin, Magnus Hirschfeld and Arthur Kronfeld who worked with a great many gender dysphoric people. Their publications and guidelines still bear a great deal of influence. For their times, their research ushered in a renaissance, breaking many taboos, and casting an entirely new light on how we view sex, gender, and gender-roles in societies across the globe. They contributed the basis to today's standards of medical care.

The World Health Organisation WHO today defines trans* gender as having a gender-identity and gender-expression that differs from the biological sex assigned at birth. The term gender dysphoria is a more modern wording, used more specifically by psychotherapists and their circles.

Most trans* gender will pursue hormone-replacement-therapy (HRT) and gender-realignment-surgery (GRS), since living in a body whose biological sex does not correspond with their gender identity causes them excruciating grief and anxiety. This *transition* is a one-way street, with the trans* person establishing and evolving their true gender-identity and being able to live a life according to that. This involves being socially recognised, integrated, and included, since this is a basic human requirement for being at peace with yourself and living a fulfilling life.

It is important to be aware, the self-perception of a trans* gender is not necessarily dependant on what is biologically there. Not all people who identify as trans* gender need or desire gender-realignment-surgery. Meaning to say, there are people identifying as male and they are men with a womb and ovaries. In exactly the same way that there are people who identify as female and they are women with testes and a penis. Curious perhaps, and maybe difficult to comprehend for other people. Nevertheless, it remains irrefutable that this is how these people feel about themselves.

64

Which just goes to prove, that gender is what is inside your head, inside your heart, and not what is between your legs.

I would think the most important thing to take from this is that the gender identity of a person is not necessarily dependent on the biological sex. Fact remains that trans* gender people go to extremes to *become* the person they feel they are inside. That which the world around these people experiences as a change, is in fact just the actual person coming to the surface and establishing their own roots in society.

I would like to re-emphasise, that we are talking about identity. We are talking about how you feel about yourself. About *whom you are*. All of this of course may have an influence in what you wear and how you present yourself in society. But not necessarily so. Just because a person wears trousers, a shirt-and-tie does not make them a man. And there are such things as men-skirts.

The self-perception of being genderfluid is possibly the easiest to try to explain to a person whose mind is heteronorm and binary. In today's modern world, the question of gender identity has at least evolved into something approaching a matter of course, that all people have typical male and typical female attributes. It has become accepted that nobody is just male or just female, but that all people are to some degree guided by attributes that are designated as male, or described as predominantly female. People who identify as genderfluid might be described as being able to feel one way or another, depending on situation or time. If you are genderfluid, you might describe yourself as male or as female, or possibly somewhere in between. And the important thing is, *that this is dynamic.*

And some people are neither. Not male, not female, but they certainly have a gender and they are completely cool with that. They defy definition, they baffle the binary, they negate the norm, they elude any labels. They know what they are. But it is not male, and it is not female. Any non binary reading this, please do not think I make light of the process of finding out what and who you are. I cannot imagine discovering that you are apart from binary genders to be any more easy than coming to the conclusion that you are in the wrong body. Never mind expressing and upholding these findings in the face of a sceptical and possibly depreciative society.

Of course all of this can be extremely vexing. For all sides concerned. For the person coming to terms with their being genderfluid. After all, constantly recalibrating your own perception is work. Constantly making the effort to be in touch with your own deepest needs and values, while stemming the flood of sensory input from the surrounding world.

For some heteronorm binary people, this might be completely impossible to comprehend. They might misinterpret this as if the genderfluid person is putting off making a choice, playing games or being intentionally manipulative. Which, I dare say, is a projection of their own insecurities onto the genderfluid people, the inability of many heteronorm binary people of coming to terms with ambivalence.

There are people whose perception of self is, that they are devoid of gender. Not even that they feel not-male or not-female. They feel themselves to be apart from any kind of binary or non-binary identity and seem to disregard the actual concept of gender. Perhaps agender people themselves are even nonplussed or confused by how the world around them is so obsessed with this binary dogma.

Gender expression

Gender expression is a way of describing how you present yourself to other people. To your family, to your friends and your social circles. And to society as a whole. How you show, how much you show and what you choose not to show is all part of a language with which you interact with the world in which you live. In reference to Mr. Paul Watzlawick, Austrian philosopher, and expert on the science of social interaction, *there is no such thing as non-communication*. Clothing, style, and fashion has volumes to say. In the same way that the language you speak, your vocabulary and your slang illustrate your background.

Body language is the most powerful tool of social integration. Or ostracism. Each of us has our own very personal dialect, honed and perfected by a lifelong exposure to family roles, or tribal expectations, society rules, hierarchies, and stereotyping. So in all of these ways, we are constantly broadcasting who we are. And how we wish to be seen by our families, work colleagues, your friends and by society.

The profound impact of body language lies therein, that we are constantly communicating without even being aware of it. Body language is subconscious, *and we cannot control it*. Not truly. It is precisely our body language that contributes to the greatest diversion between our self-image and how others perceive us. It is also our body language, that betrays us if we are attempting to generate an image to which we are not congruent.

I would assume that for most people, how they present themselves is a reflection of whom they are in their identity. If you identify as an easy going alpha male, chances are, you are going to behave and dress in a ways that presents your male attributes to their greatest potential. After all, you want attention. Why else would there be workshops offered by life-coaches to polish up your image and work on how to present yourself. Dating, job interviews, getting that promotion…

I am stereotyping?

Let us be realistic. Stereotypes exist because there are so many examples that support and confirm their defining characteristics. As Chimamanda Ngozi Adichie, Nigerian author and activist, said, "The problem with stereotypes, is not that they are untrue, but that the stories they tell are incomplete". Or to put it another way, there are enough people whose identity, and whose behaviour and outward expression correlate in such a way, that if you consider all the things they have in common, you will find they share a measurable standard of the mean. Stereotypes are nothing other than a standard mean of a particular subgroup. The important thing is, not to ignore everything else that is there, to remember not to *reduce* a person to a stereotype.

So, yes; it is normal for there to be stereotypes. Quod erat demonstrandum.

There is an immediate correlation between how closely your outward expression fits your inner identity, and how confident you are about your inner identity. You might think, well duh. Obviously. Nevertheless, the point is: Communicating who you truly feel to be, on such an intimate level, has everything to do with self-confidence. And this confidence has everything to do, with feeling secure of acceptance and inclusion in society. We only feel free to express ourselves, to evolve and *be* the person we truly *are*, in a society that encourages and appreciates freedom of mind and soul, a society that welcomes and respects a commitment, to exploring your own inner world and bringing this to the surface.

I have met a fair number of cross-dressers and trans* vestite artists. As a trans* gender, you invariably do. Every trans* gender is at some point of their existence a trans* vestite. But *not* every cross-dresser is trans* sexual. Or homosexual either.

Trans* vestites and cross-dressing people present a type of trans* identity or trans* gender that is, more often than not, a form of art. Meaning, *it is a show*. A portrayal of a fictional character. You might even say, this not unlike cosplay. For a great many cis*-gendered people, including even some gay or lesbian people, this causes a great deal of confusion. What they see, is a person who wears clothes whose stereotype do not match the biological sex of the wearer.

There is a clear and important distinction between trans* vestite artists, and the trans* sexual trans* gender. A trans* vestite performs a role as convincingly as to be nearly real. And then after the performance, they will proceed to "take off" that persona and all the accompanying accessories. At the end of the day, they remove the make-up, disrobe the dress, and hang the set of silicone boobs in the wardrobe. Or unwrap their natural breasts and put away the packer. And they return to being the person whose existence is anchored in this "real" world.

On a personal note, a thing I continue to find decidedly remarkable, is how many trans* vestites present themselves in roles so conspicuously stereotype. I would assume, this is another reason why a great many cis* people have such difficulty being able to differentiate. The majority of those trans* vestites I have spoken to, mainly men presenting themselves as women, present themselves in roles of *stereotypically cis-het* male-fantasy ideals*, to the point of portraying females of downright playboy or centrefold qualities.

Over-sexualised and *very much *reduced* to just that.*

Which might possibly imply, by inverse psychology, how very cis-het* male their mind and spirit remains? Which would be decidedly odd, if they happen to be homosexual. But to be honest, I have no answer to that. My guess is, that many of these behaviour patterns root back to the nineteenth and early twentieth century, when the only way for homosexual men to meet publicly, was in burlesque clubs. But I emphasise, that is a guess.

A trans* sexual trans* gender, on the other hand, *is* the person. If observed from the outside, it may appear that they are crossdressing. Wearing clothes that do not match their biological sex. But. They are wearing clothes that match their gender identity. That which is their soul. They *are* this person, whether they go to parties, dine out with friends, or brush their teeth afterwards. They remain this person when the sleep and when they get up the next morning. A trans* gender person is playing a role, when they pretend to be a cis* person, living a life that matches their biological sex.

In contrast to most trans* vestite artists, trans* gender most often try to remain entirely inconspicuous. For most trans* gender, blending in is their ultimate goal. Being "normal". It is exactly this contradiction of intentions and expression which contributes to a certain amount of friction between trans* gender and trans* vestites.

But it does prove: do not jump to conclusions, make no assumptions, take nothing for granted. If you continue to be open for surprises, then life will continue to bestow you with all kinds of wonderful meetings, friendships, and experiences.

Give me the proper occasion, and I will so absolutely wear a one of my old formal suits, and confuse the hell out of everyone. Just for the fun of it.

Sexual orientation

We all have our preferences. We have a type. We simply do. There is a pattern of biological sex and gender expression to which we are naturally drawn and which we find attractive. Desirable. Sexy. Or just plain beautiful. And along the same lines, there are characteristics, personality traits and social expressions that we find endearing, impressive, comforting or just plain fascinating. Just as we have a preference for plain buff, black-leather-and-lace, or pink-and-white fluffy tutus. Missionary, doggy, cow-girl/-boy/-person, jumping through hoops, etc. We have a preference. Full stop.

For the majority of people, this is straightforward (pun intended) boy meets girl, romance happens. You identify with your biological sex, you are attracted to the opposite biological sex. End of story. It is what we term "**heteronorm**".

I think for the vast majority of people, the term homosexual, too, is self-explanatory. Or at least so widely present in the media, that heteronorm people are at least aware that there is such a thing as being gay or being a lesbian. After all, heteronorm society does seem to find the concept piquing to the curiosity and certainly entertaining to some degree. I would venture to speculate, that this is due to a latent homo-erotic tendency in each and every-one of us (Yes there is. Unless you find being sexually aroused a nuisance). And I will dare state, it is precisely this latent homo-erotic tendency that a lot of people seek to supress and deny, that sparks such enormous capacity for violence and hate.

Most, most unfortunately, that, too, is normal.

As in, it is an expected and natural reaction. Just as it is my expectation that in an inclusive and educated society, people should be in a position to recognise their own prejudices and insecurities. And be able to control their urges to lash out.

Less widely spread, is the awareness of all the myriad shades of differentiation of preferences. In my experience, things are rarely in a binary one-bit state of being, male or female, this or that, heterosexual or homosexual. As a matter of fact, just like most of us are male or female by different degrees, how we evolve particular characteristics in a whole spectrum of sliders, there are people who experience their emotional and sexual attraction by degrees. I dare say, for most of us, this is a matter of personal evolution, and likely to change over the years. For some, it even changes overnight.

Moreover, some few people find an emotional bond to another human to be entirely sufficient and fulfilling, and have no own innate desire to become sexual. A close friend of mine is married to a wonderful man (her words). She describes that she herself feels no sexual desire or longing for her husband (or anyone else), but simply acknowledges that this is something that is important to him and to the functioning of their relationship. I suppose that would make her demi-sexual?

Be aware

Incidentally, I believe it is an entirely heteronorm concept, that of any homosexual couple, one should be "the man" and one should be "the woman". If you really think about it, the need to stereotype into binary is so altogether heteronorm, it is just funny. I suppose there *are* lesbian couples where one of the partners is butch and her partner is femme, just as there are gay couples where one of the partners is more effeminate. Maybe even a drag queen. However, please remember that this is a cliché generated and propagated by the same heteronorm binary dominated media industry that introduced the quota-person-of-ethnic-origin.

The roots of some of these homosexual stereotypes, as presented by the media, go way back into the post-world-war-II era, when *global* society was picking itself up out of the rubble, and the different subgroups (Including women. Remember Wendy the welder? Rosie the riveter?) had been given a taste of being integrated into a functioning society at eye-level, and with something approaching equal rights. A society under duress and driven by pure necessity, surely. But nevertheless, the strains of war did force a great many people to look beyond their own horizons.

It remains proof of just how adaptable and versatile humans can be.

Another thing I would like to emphasise very, very clearly. This is essential to understanding and interacting with other people around you. Everything I have so far described, everything about the non-dependence of gender identity of a person on their biological sex. Everything concerning the variety of gender expression. *None* of these things is in any way secure evidence of emotional preference of attraction. Nor does it permit any concrete conclusions to be drawn about the sexual orientation of a person. Any conclusions you come to is based on your assumptions. Based on your observation of, or interaction with this person. Which in turn is based on your life's experience. On your unconscious bias. Or even on your conscious bias. Whom I love, to whom I am attracted, of course I describe this as part of the person I am. And yet, it is not the same as the identity that of how I describe myself to be.

Concerning trans* gender people, most trans* women I know describe themselves as lesbian, and most trans* men I know, as homosexual, gay. Which I personally find in itself to be just way, way curious and remarkable. As if part of original biological hard-wiring in the body was maintained. Like a biological male should be attracted to a biological female, and vice versa. But I have absolutely no idea how this correlates with the emotional and sexual preferences of trans* gender people globally.

It would be entirely curious to find out.

I personally do find myself attracted to both men and women. But then, if I am honest, I don't think the biological sex of my partner really matters that much to me. I suppose if you *must* use a label, then it would be bisexual or even pan-sexual. But then I really don't believe the label to be of any import. I know who I am. I know whom I love. I know whom I desire and long for. And so does my significant other. Case closed.

The VUCA / BANI world

A gentle word of warning.

There exists a *wild* profusion of labels and designations and symbols. With each subgroup, and subgroup of a subgroup, developing their own brand of identity and their own self-designation which they feel is just right for them. And unfortunately, some few are quite militant about impressing their label on their fellow humans. A label implies surety. Security. Order. Normality even. To some people, it is an anchor that is vitally necessary to provide them the necessary place and stability in their world.

I am not going to go into the myriad of other labels. I frankly do not feel qualified, despite the fact that I self-designate as Queer*. But if you are curious, go ahead, read up. You will find a freight load of information about this on the web. And a lot of sites make a supreme effort to try and engender clarity and structure. Pun absolutely intended. I do find it important though, to emphasise, that all of these designations, all of these symbols and signs are labels to drawers.

We humans require drawers into which to sort information. And yes, this is normal. It roots back into our very reptilian instincts, to be able to make split-second decisions between "dangerous" versus "food", between "sex" versus "boring". And we still use those drawers today, although our cabinet has possible grown slightly larger and more complex.

So, the drawers are still there, and we still categorise information as a matter of course. All of this has been imprinted into our brain by our upbringing in our families, by society, and by our very own personal experiences. Our perfectly normal unconscious bias.

But it does remain an excellent idea to be *aware* that we are using these drawers. Be aware that we are selecting and prioritising our input, according to our own personal preferences.

And concerning the wild profusion of self-designations and symbols, all of this only goes to prove that we are trying to pack into drawers what in actual fact is a conglomeration of countless sliders, each variation being a parameter of character expression and individual preference. We need to remain aware that each of us is a single individual. A tiny cloud of points (sparkles) in a multi-dimensional spectrum of personal evolution and the summary of our life's experiences.

Not only that. The whole system is in fact alive, shifting and dynamic. All the time. That is VUCA for you.

Disclaimer

In my examples and descriptions, I stereotype a lot.

For the sake of simplicity and understandability, I summarise and generalise. I do so consciously. In the full awareness, that a small minority of people are going to kick up all kinds of fuss, because they feel left out, or misrepresented. And the plain basic fact that this disclaimer is even necessary, is also a result, that a few people are going to be so upset because they feel threatened in their comfort zone.

But guess what? That too, is normal.

Numbers

The numbers and statistics provided on the various subgroups of the Queer* peoples are extremely unreliable. The estimated number of unreported or supressed cases is probably high. In some countries, higher even than the actual statistical number given. It depends very much on whom you ask, and where you are geographically, politically. There are still enough countries where any deviation from the heteronorm binary is illegal, and where transgressions against Queer* people is considered a bagatelle or a negligible offence. If, at all, it is considered and offence.

The studies of the WHO show, that 5.0% - 7.5% of the world's population is homosexual. That is, these are the people who *know* they are homosexual. These are the people who openly live by this and choose a partner by this. Not the people who have supressed ambivalent feelings about the same sex. Numbers vary according to which study you draw on. Along the same lines, 0.5% of the world's population are trans* gender, and 0.2% are intersex.

And perhaps this is a good opportunity to take another look at statistical mathematics. After all, it is not our ability to count that makes us human. Although, our being able to count well, will have contributed to our successfully surviving on this planet.

What makes us human, is the ability to look beyond the pattern that is immediately visible. And to engage our imagination. And to empathise with our fellow humans. What makes us human, is to sometimes accept, and include, what is not immediately normal. And in doing so, step out of our own limited borders of perception. Out of our own comfort zone. We are capable of welcoming and embracing someone simply because we recognise a fellow human struggling in, or with, the same harsh environment.

It is normal to struggle.

We all do at times.

I know I do. I still do.

I guess I am normal after all.

(3) Being a Girl

Masks…

…we all wear them.

Possibly even multiple layers, shifting and changing.

Depending on with whom we interact.

We are taught this by the society we grow up in.

We are taught to hide our true selves.

To hide our vulnerability.

To hide our humanity.

At some point, we learn to hide from ourselves.

A great many things in 1983 announced changes.

As fulfilling as my Dad found his work in the faculty of engineering and how it was a high-value-adding input, he was contributing, he was sorely sick of marking papers and exams. Consequently, he started looking for other meaningful things that would earn our existence.

Decades later, I was to discover that he had been offered an *extremely* lucrative placement as an engineer in Saudi Arabia. Apparently, he turned it down because he was worried that this would not be a good environment for me. Not for any concrete reasons, just an intuition. My Dad never told me of this offer. Yet despite this, as I transitioned, decades later, I had reoccurring nightmares. I dreamt the same dream so often, I have it memorised. This is one of the most peculiar and remarkable coincidences of my life, that cannot be explained in any way.

I find myself wearing something of white chiffon, airy and free flowing. I am walking through a most lavish garden. There is a soft breeze, warm as a breath. The garden is huge, almost park-like in its beauty, perfectly manicured lawn, with soft grass of juicy green between my toes and huge trees offer refreshing shade. There is a sparkling fountain surrounded by flowering bushes, with bees and butterflies. On one side, there is an infinity pool, tiled in deepest azure, the water reflecting the immaculate sky. There are fruit trees to one side that bloom and are laden with ripe and inviting grapefruit. I inhale their fragrance longingly (I am not allowed to eat grapefruit). *In the background rises a modern and elegant house, with ceiling to floor windows, minimalist geometric architecture, the kind of home I would find extremely desirable. The garden is surrounded by a concrete wall, three metres high with spikes glinting in the bright sunlight. At regular intervals, there are "windows" to the avenue outside, barred with stainless steel, permitting a view of a road with an equally well-tended lawn and the palm trees beyond.*

Outside, on the road, there is an elderly man with a grizzled white beard, wearing a white kofia and a sand-coloured caftan. He is watching me, with unmitigated hunger in his face.

And it comes to me, like being plunged into icy water:

This garden is my prison. *I will never leave it without a male escort.*

Like in a movie, there is a cut, and I am in my bedroom in Dar es Salaam. My first bedroom, the one that burnt out. I am going through all my possessions, one by one. I am tossing all my pants, all my shorter skirts, all my t-shirts, anything remotely revealing (clothes I have never possessed). *I am packing up all my study-books and novels, anything that implies that I am educated. I pack my laptop* (a complete anachronism for the 1970-80ies) *to be given to charity. I remove any trace that my Dad has raised me to be a self-reliant, self-assured young woman who speaks her mind. There is a clothes rack from which I pick veils for myself, hijabs. I hear his voice calling me, we should be leaving, if I am ready?*

The scene changes again, and I am back in the beautiful garden. James, the older of my two (step-) brothers stands behind me. This is the only change in the dream, and there are two versions that alternately repeat themselves.

The first is, he looks around and enthuses, "Is this great or what?!?" Inwardly, I feel a nauseating sensation of vertigo as I think, "Dude, are you not aware that you are as much a slave in this place as I am?"

In the second version, he looks around, his face clouded and thoughtful. He places his hand on my shoulder and squeezes gently as he says, "We will get through this. This too, shall pass."

Looking at this dream today, it is just incredible how the past and present have melted. Integrated. And I am still speechless at the things my subconscious has picked out.

My third mother

In 1982, there was a global congress for peoples that worked in, or contributed to, the commercial development and technical evolution of African countries. The congress took place in Lisbon, and people from all over Africa, the US and Europe took part. When my Dad tells this story, his eyes still mist over with sentiment and emotion.

He was on a flight from Dar es Salaam via Nairobi to Lisbon, and the aircraft was booked to the absolute very last seat. Being his usual well-organised self, he had booked his seat well in advance, and he was fortunate to have a window seat. The departure was slightly late, because they were waiting for the last passenger, who had been delayed. Finally, the captain announced that all passengers were now on board, and that they would be taking off shortly. A flight attendant escorted the last passenger to the very last empty seat on the entire aircraft, the seat next to my Dad.

My Dad recalls how his breath was taken away by the most beautiful woman he had ever laid eyes on. And he also recalls, how this woman bluntly and adamantly refused to sit next to a White man.

Since they were already late, the crew was not inclined to accommodate her wishes to sit anywhere else, as this would have involved shuffling around passengers. So, with a demeanour that would have frozen an ocean, the lady sat herself next to my Dad.

Up in the air on a cloudless and bright day, and some couple of hundred kilometres from Dar es Salaam, my Dad plucked up all his courage and addressed the beautiful lady next to him. He said, they were passing Kilimanjaro, one of *the* most spectacularly magnificent sights in Africa. And while he understood that she was not comfortable with his presence, then she should not let such a unique opportunity be ruined on his account.

And would she like to trade seats, and sit by the window?

Apparently, that was sufficient to break the ice. And apparently, they had a very long and fruitful conversation on their flight to Lisbon. My Dad and Amahle were married later in the same year in the circle of my Dad's friends in Dar es Salaam.

And in order to give us all a fresh start, we moved to Kwekwe, Zimbabwe.

Zimbabwe, 1983

The elections, that finally achieved the end to Zimbabwe's oppressive white Rhodesian regime in 1980, spelled an end to fifteen years of ongoing guerrilla bush-war of the bloodiest kind. There were mercenaries involved, there were pro-western and pro-communist imperial states shuffling for power and influence in the background (there was such a thing as the cold war), arms were supplied, black-ops and assassins sent, humans demonstratively executed. All sides were deeply guilty of the most unspeakable of war crimes, with countless civilians fallen victim to the waging of psychological warfare or misused as substitute targets in absence of the actual militias.

When viewed in the light of South-Africa's bloodless miracle in 1994, this was a pitiable failure of humanity. It was ugly. And when the dust finally settled, when the blood dried, everybody was apparently so relieved over the cease-fire, that nothing was done at all, to address all the injustices. It seemed the civilian population was so entirely loath to speak up about violence. So intimidated were they by the recent past, it permitted the ruling party of the Shona tribes, and their leader Robert Mugabe, to secure their power by means of massacring an (conservative) estimated 20'000 of the rivalling Ndebele peoples, retribution for rivalry and defiance during the struggle against white oppression. This in turn was rooted in tribal competition and feuds, going back to before the Europeans showed up (I am referring to the Gukurahundi. Overall, the history of Zimbabwe is well worth reading up on, touching on many kinds of human struggles). Incidentally, in 2005, Nicole Kidman and Sean Penn starred in a movie called "The Interpreter". While never actually naming any names, the movie laid (lays) its finger grimly and implacably into the festering wound of Zimbabwe's botched caesarean birth.

However, in 1983 Zimbabwe was a "free" country. With South Africa still under Apartheid rule at the time, moving there was out of the question.

Radically different

The part of Zimbabwe that we moved to was arid scrub savannah.

If you look at the continent, then Zimbabwe lies on the tapering-out southern end of the African rift. As a result, the bedrock is rich in minerals, the topsoil is thin, and the landscape is dotted with typical protrusions of basalt and granite, majestic "kopijes" (Afrikaans: "small heads"), spectacular piles of boulders, from soccer-ball sized to towering multi-storey spheroids, exfoliated through millennia of extreme weather conditions, baking under the bleaching sun and venting their stored heat into the endless midnight sky.

And home to a profusion of life. The kind of life that required little water, little soil, little of anything in fact. The vegetation was spare, trees were stunted, scrub like, and there was a profusion of succulents, aloes, and cacti. Flowing water was even rarer than in Tanzania. What delighted me in particular, was the abundance of non-threatening reptiles, skinks, iguanas and "dragons", which I had hitherto not encountered. However, I was less fond of the wide variety of arachnoids to be found, ranging from camel spiders the size of a saucer, and evil-looking little scorpions. And for some reason, geckos were scarce. The birds were different, smaller, less colourful. But no less beautiful.

Kwekwe was / is a town that grew around a crossroads near the fork of the Sebakwe River. The point where the rail lines that shipped coal meet with deposits of chromium and iron ores. In addition, Kwekwe lies along the so called "greenstone-belt" which was high in exploitable gold deposits. Later, a chemical plant was added, that drew water from the Sebakwe River and manufactured ammonium nitrate.

As sprawling and huge as Dar es Salaam was, so was Kwekwe tiny. And radically different.

What I registered immediately were basic things. Roads were well maintained, easy to travel. Power-cuts and black-outs were seldom, in fact there were hardly any. Despite Zimbabwe being quite an arid country, there was (in the 1980ies) no shortage of drinking water. Water could be drunk *straight off the tap*! OMG! Even if it tasted so strongly of chlorine, you might have possibly bleached hair with it. And, as I found out many years later, the drinking water was conducted via asbestos pipes. Fuel was always available. There were supermarkets! With filled shelves! There were frozen goods! There was milk in variety and there were dairy products! There was cheese! Only two types, Gouda and Cheddar, but hey, there was cheese.

There were ice-cream vendors, and you did not need to worry about cholera or typhoid. There were Hardware stores that were *always* stocked. With variety to choose from. There were bookstores, oh joy! With well stocked fantasy and science-fiction sections. There were Stores filled with clothes and shoes to buy. OMG! There was television. And VHS video libraries.

People were well dressed. In clean (cleaner) clothes. Okay, let me rephrase; there were significantly fewer people living under conditions as to be at the bare margin of existence. There were virtually no visible victims of hunger, malnutrition or even disease (again, not in the 1980ies). Due to the arid climate and well-maintained infrastructure, malaria, typhoid, and cholera were distant rumours.

The supply and availability of basic goods, rice, wheat flour, salt sugar, cooking oil, and toilet paper was secure and readily available. Guaranteed. There was an abundancy of good quality meat, and as I learnt quickly, a braai (Afrikaans: barbeque) was the foundation of the local way of life. This was one of the things, all peoples, independent of skin tone and cultural background, were unanimous on.

To my great joy, apples were available all the year around. As were oranges. Ironically, and to my extreme disappointment, what was completely lacking were all the fruit that I had come to associate with Africa: papaya, mangoes, guavas, passion-fruit. Even tangerines were scarce. Along with this, the variety of vegetables in the supermarket was devastatingly limited by comparison. Cabbages, cauliflower, onions, carrots, spinach, and tomatoes. Peas and beans. And that was pretty much it. Even peanuts were hard to come by. Cashew nuts were entirely absent. New were watermelons, but to be honest, I never really got enthusiastic about those.

A significant number of the private homes had a swimming pool in their garden, something I was entirely unfamiliar with. Of course, this was dependent on the neighbourhood. In our quarter, I would estimate about half of the gardens sported a pool. Considering the climate in Zimbabwe, this is as close to decadence as you can get. So dry as to require prohibitive amounts of drinking water, and entirely unusable for six to seven months of the year if you did not want to risk pneumonia. In the months Mai through August, temperatures sank to where there might be frost in the morning.

Today (early 2020ies), Zimbabwe is radically different yet again. Rampant corruption, tribal and political rivalries, racism, failure of infrastructure, collapse of the economy, raging HIV, the return of typhoid and cholera, all these have persuaded those with any means to make a living elsewhere, to up and leave the country. In other words, all those with any kind of education, training of craft and vocational expertise. Regardless of their tone of skin. Apart from the high-gloss tourist industry, pretty much all thriving commercial enterprises, and all the farms that had permitted Zimbabwe to *export* wheat and maize in the past, were "nationalized". In other words, given to high-ranking party officials. Who in turn had little to no interest, never mind the know-how, to keep them thriving. The country is destitute, with severe shortages of basic existential prerequisites for the general populace. Today, Zimbabwe is a portrait of some of the most self-destructive behaviour patterns humanity is capable of.

Adapting

A lot of things dawned on me when we moved to Kwekwe.

I suddenly came to appreciate, how on the university campus in Dar es Salaam, all the homes and houses on the campus were without any kind of fence or barrier.

In Zimbabwe, each and every house, tenement, block of flats was enclosed. Each home, was indeed, a fortress. With a locked gate. The simpler fences were chain-link. Two metres were standard. Barbed wire was liberally employed. The more established homes had a hedge behind the chain-link, obscuring any view. From there, the enclosures progressed to slatted wood walls, concrete pre-fab walls or brick-and-mortar. Spiked with broken glass, barbed- or razor wire. Signs warning of dogs (Rhodesian Ridgebacks are a sight to behold, bred for all the wrong reasons) or announcing armed responses. In some areas, you found the wall topped by fine cables, carrying some fifteen to twenty-five thousand volts.

The irony of this is, in Dar es Salaam, our home was broken into seven times. Clothes, shoes, and food went missing, but that was it. In Kwekwe, break-ins were unheard of. If there were transgressions, and they were rare, they happened on isolated farmsteads. And they happened regardless of any fences, dogs, walls, or security systems. And *if* something *did* happen, very often, *severe* arbitrary and unbridled violence was involved.

In Kwekwe, I met no one. There were no other children about. People simply did not go out and meet people. It was not the done thing. Due to the move to Zimbabwe, my re-entry to school had been shifted by six months, so I had no contact there either. And either most of the other children were away in boarding schools, or they did not seem to be interested in anyone outside their own fence.

For the first six months, I was utterly and completely alone.

Another thing that truly shocked me, was how openly present racial tensions were. I realised all of a sudden just how uncomplicated and chill so many things had been in Tanzania. How easy going and mellow people had been. How self-assured and confident *all* people carried themselves in Tanzania. Yes, life was hard, within reason. But Life was hard for pretty much most people. The regular shortages of all kinds of essentials affected everybody. But people got by, and people more or less got on with each other. In Zimbabwe, most people of African origin were timid and reserved, some were openly distrustful or, in some cases, even hostile and aggressive. Which in turn made me question, what kind of treatment they had been accustomed to in the past.

In retrospect, it was a good thing to get to know Joey. He was far more direct and upfront than Jeremy, about his anger over being stigmatised and discriminated as a person of colour in his life in the US. As annoying and downright disrespectful as I found Joey's constant accusation of racism, it worked a long way to my being sensitised to the living conditions, and the matter-of-course abuse and discrimination that people of colour faced.

Face.

Amahle

I am extremely sorry to say, Amahle, my stepmother, and me did not hit it off well. Not at first anyway. She was, for many years, another maternal figure whose tempers and moods I came to fear.

Amahle was born and raised in Alexandra, one of Johannesburg's largest and sometimes roughest suburbs. It also turned out, she had been at that congress in Lisbon as an envoy and representative for the ANC, for which she sometimes ran errands or organised "things." Fact was, she had a long list of excellent cause to react to my Dad the way she did, when she first saw him on that airplane. *Up to and including the why and how she was widowed*.

I was a shy child. For any number of reasons. Being out of sorts with my own body, to a degree that most people never even begin to understand, did not make approaching new people easier. Amplified by the slow but sure onset of puberty.

Very early on, still in Tanzania, one of the things that left a lasting impression, was, when Amahle had some friends over. I saw from the doorway to our living room, there were guests, having tea and biscuits, talking. I thought I would be as little intrusive as possible. I said hello from the doorway, one of the people even looked my way, and I disappeared again. Later, I passed the doorway again, and Amahle called me back and asked me to greet her friends. I said, to my perception truthfully, that I had already greeted her guests. Considering that she had missed my doing so, I understand how irritated she was. As sorry I was for the misunderstanding, I was deeply wounded at being called a liar in front of her friends.

At the same time, I obviously wanted to make a good impression, so there were a number of things I tried, to impress Amahle, trying to engage her in conversation. But at this point, she had already formed an opinion. Sad and unfortunate as it was, at precisely this point, our cultures collided heavily. Amahle herself had been raised in the understanding, that adults are always right, and that children should wait until spoken to before opening their mouths. She raised her own children according to this maxim. Needless to say, this was in direct contradiction to just so many things my Dad expected of me.

Another example was, where we were sitting around our dining table. My Dad was cleaning a piece of equipment with methylated spirits, and I opened a window, to let the fumes dissipate. It happened to be the window next to Amahle, quite simply because it was closest. She interpreted my behaviour to the effect, that I was implying she smelt bad. And, yes, there were (are) people who will stoop to this kind of behaviour, so I do empathise very well how wounded Amahle was. But I was equally hurt that she should be unable and unwilling to differentiate.

There were many of these incidents over the years, greater and smaller. These two in particular stayed impressed on my memory. The first, because being called a liar in front of her friends hurt deeply. The second episode I described occurred some four years later. I recall it this clearly, because it was one of those times, where I tried, with all the rational reasoning and diplomacy I was capable of, to talk it through with Amahle, and make it clear that my opening the window had nothing at all to do with her, never mind her skin colour. She flat out refused to believe me. In fact, she went on to give me a solid talking to, about the abuse she had to put up with in her life, and how she would not take any sh!t from a lying racist.

She ended with the statement, how she would never forgive and never forget.

Those words, more than anything else, shocked me deeply. I was always acutely aware, that, while I was certainly saddened and irritated by the friction between us, I did not have to spend time with Amahle if I did not wish to. But it was my Dad, who really came away with the deepest injuries. I was sixteen at the time, and I like to think I was capable of rather more than just connecting the dots. More than her dislike of me, what deeply disturbed and made me thoughtful, was how she obviously bore this constant burden of anger, loathing, and grief, over the injustices she had suffered. And how this coloured her entire life (pun intended) and impaired her own judgement, to the point of where she was so angry, that she was no longer capable of recognising good will and amical intentions in another person.

And what did this imply about her affection for my Dad? What was my Dad to her? The solitary exception that proved the rule? A dupe? Or a trophy? And yet, there *were* times when it *was* clear that they shared a deep and meaningful connection. That the time they shared was enriching and fulfilling for them both. Amahle and my Dad remained married until she passed in 2018. She suffered a mild stroke in 2016, from which she recovered to some degree, but she thrived explicitly due to my Dad's diligent care. Theirs was not a marriage how I would have wanted mine to be. But even as I write that, I am thinking, "glass houses, Alice, glass houses." I like to think, in their years together, they were happy. Or at least content and at peace.

For my part, I am deeply sorry we did not get on better sooner. After all, we shared the same roof and table for so many years. Amahle was extremely talented with a sewing machine, and she had a great eye for colour and fabrics. Never mind that I am sure she could have told endless anecdotes of her growing up in Alexandra, or her years spent in exile.

I could have learnt so much from her…

And my Dad really misses her.

Menials and domestics

We started out in a bungalow, rather nondescript, with a "garden" that was mainly sand or packed earth. It was odd. Despite best concerted efforts of Oubert, our gardener, and my Dad, nothing grew. I welcomed the decision to move to another house, just a few blocks down the road. This was a pretty two-storey structure, surrounded by lovely trees that afforded beautifully cooling shade in the scorching Zimbabwean summers.

The garden of our new home was lovely, and plants and flowers grew well. I spent hours watching birds, geckos, and lizards of which there were plenty and a beautiful variety. Weaverbirds are still among my favourite, as are blue-throated agamas.

We had a swimming pool in the garden, which was a novelty, but to be honest, it lost its significance to me rather quickly. All these garden pools look really sweet and flashy, but the fact is, all they are good for is getting wet. You swim more than three strokes, and you hit the other side. As I mentioned previously, Kwekwe, in fact Zimbabwe as a whole, was way too chilly for at least six months of the year to go for a dip. And finally, there was the fact that showing my body in a swimsuit really boosted my dysphoria.

In Tanzania, I had been to Mister William's small but tidy little hut several times as a child. It was a very simple structure, with basic amenities, it was functional, it afforded some comfort, and he had decorated it sparsely but tastefully. I remember his pristine caftan for special occasions hanging off the wall in his bedroom. I still recall the feel of the embroidery under my fingers. I remember the creaking of the springs when I sat on his bed. The familiar smoky scent of ebony and black tea. He always took three heaped spoons of sugar in his tea. If sugar was available.

In Zimbabwe, most single-house homes had a servants'-quarters built into the backyard. I came to learn, that this was perfectly normal in the entire southern African continent. The sole fact that an employee should reside on premises, and therefore by implication, be available and accountable twenty-four / seven spoke volumes of the conditions under which people had served their "masters" in the past. Pretty much all the servants'-quarters I came across, were built along the same line. Blocks of bare, square concrete, cold even in summer and cold enough to drain your soul in winter. Minimal, and as homely as a maximum security prison cell. With the difference, that in a prison, there are laws dictation the minimal allocated space to one person, and prisoners could decorate and personalise their four walls. I do not believe any of these servants' structures would have passed an audit.

We had Mariah, a young woman, who did our cleaning, cooking, and laundry. And we had Oubert, a young man, who took care of the garden and the swimming pool. Considering the risks young women ran in Zimbabwe, I understand entirely well that Mariah kept her distance and her head down around any males. She had a home she could return to in the late afternoon, so that was okay. Oubert was a cheerful and creative young man. He had a family some distance away, which he would be with on weekends. During the week he lived in that concrete excuse for a stable. My ears burn when I think of it. My Dad did his level best to keep the place dry, keep in the warmth and to improve sanitary conditions. At some point, he gave up in disgust, turned it into a garden shed, and arranged for Oubert to afford more comfortable accommodations.

But not one of us, not my Dad nor me, and not Amahle, ever built that kind of level of trust or bond to any of the employees we had in Kwekwe. It was just that. They were here to do a job, and they did it more or less satisfactorily, but there was no commitment or interest beyond that. On neither side. Strange. Or perhaps not strange? Perhaps just new and different, but certainly less personal, and less humanly in-touch.

Just the way it is…

On the surface, people of all colours and ethnic backgrounds walked the same sidewalks, sat at the same sports fields, shopped at the same stores, and went to the same movies. Drive-in cinemas were popular throughout, and as I said, so were braais (Afrikaans: barbeques). Children went to the same schools, played soccer. No, let me correct that: Children played rugby and cricket together, or hockey. Children spent their school break-times…

...it was a surreptitious thing. You did not notice immediately. If you looked a little more closely, it was clear: here in Zimbabwe, it did indeed still matter what colour your skin was. Despite the newly gained freedom of movement, and freedom of education, people were still very much slaves to their ethnic heritage. Evolving out of that mind-set was something that had only just begun. People with European background kept their own circles. They were almost exclusively British, with barely any exceptions coming from other European countries. And yes, there was a "country club". As with all British colonies, there was a large Indian community, which kept its own counsel. Along with their rigid caste system. There were virtually no people from East Asia (not yet, the Chinese would come later). I found it altogether remarkable how the better situated, better educated native Africans took themselves apart from the majority of people of less erudite means. It was very clear indeed, people getting their hands dirty on the job were considered inferior. I remember the mother of a school mate of mine, refusing to give her housemaid a mop with a handle, stating that a servant belonged on her knees. Both women were indigenous Zimbabweans. The Shona eschewed the Ndebele, and vice versa. And heaven forbid you were a Shangaan, a Khoi or a San. And the peoples of coloured or mixed background were shunned by *all* the groups, belonging nowhere.

Now that the Indigenous Africans had regained their basic rights, they set about righting the wrongs and settling scores. All of a sudden, white people found themselves not just at a statistical disadvantage when applying for jobs or negotiating for contracts. Even things like getting a bank account or getting their car registered got to be more complicated. Even at the age of thirteen, I realised these people were traumatised by the recent years and everyone was on edge, everyone was looking out to gain the greatest possible advantage over others, because you never knew when the tables could turn against you.

So it was into this somewhat uneasy and distrustful climate that we settled. My Dad was *the* oddball of the neighbourhood. Probably of all of Kwekwe. A White married to a Black. In Dar es Salaam, this had been uncommon, but uncommented, certainly more frequent than in Zimbabwe. In Zimbabwe, I know for a fact there were a lot of comments along the lines of "married his house-girl, did he?" Amahle was a Zulu, and the Zulus being a tribe with quite some history of violence and invasion, she too was viewed with some distrust, even hatred. Not to mention her marrying my Dad, of course. That put her in the firing line as like nothing else. After all, she was "the housemaid that had seduced her master, what a slut!" I sometimes ask myself what her erstwhile ANC friends said about her. I imagine the accusation of "diluting the blood" came from both sides. Which, incidentally, contributed reasons to why my

Dad and Amahle decided to not have any children together, despite the fact that they both would have wanted to.

Some few families did in fact see this marriage across ethnical boundaries as a step out of the dark ages, and forward into a better and more inclusive future. Thankfully, one of my Dad's closest working colleagues was amongst these. They were guests in our house relatively often, and we visited their farm on occasion. It was thanks to his influence (his cousin's influence) that disaster was later averted. Still, I think my Dad had few true friends in Zimbabwe.

It was ultimately my Dad's frankness, his integrity, and the core fact that he appraised (appraises) people by what they were (are) able and willing to contribute, instead of their tone of skin or their political connections, which cost him his residence permit and his job in Zimbabwe.

However, I am getting ahead of myself. That came much, much later.

School

Despite being rather modest, Kwekwe High School was one of the better schools in the country. Certainly not as renowned or glamorous as say Plum-Tree private college, or Harare International School, both of which were boarding schools. But it was by standards, a well-equipped academy. Staffed by a colourful mixture of teachers, both in heritage and in character. Some Zimbabweans, some British, one or two of Indian background, and one solitary Teacher from Mauritius, with different teachers for the different schoolyears and syllabus contents.

One of my favourite biology teachers was Ms Chisawa. Far too seldom, she told fabulous stories, of how she had studied in India and Nepal, how she had lived in a cloister together with the monks. How intricate and mindful the lives were there, and how she was deeply impressed that even the poorest of the poor were assured their bowl of rice. She had integrated a great deal of that mindfully gentle, yet adamant way of regarding the world, something her home country desperately needed. We had a French teacher, Mr O'Connor, from Ireland. I think he and I got off on the wrong foot. But we both managed to recover from that, and he was always delighted by my pronunciation in his classes. One of our Maths Profs, Mr Moyo, was chronically late for class. He would rush in, loudly and agitatedly, solve an example on the chalkboard (yes, real chalkboards) at speeds impossible to follow, and then rush out again. He was undoubtedly a genius at maths, but a pedagogue he was not. Another of my favourites was Mr Rooney, an elderly gentleman, always impeccably dressed in a three-piece, complete with silk-handkerchief, even if it was barely below forty Celsius in the shade. He was a passionate advocate of Shakespeare, a compassionate advocate of human rights, and a secret blues and jazz pianist. When he thought he was alone, he would sit at the grand piano in our assembly hall. I could have sat and listened for hours.

The school had enough books for almost half the students, so most of the more well-off families bought books for their children. And paid an extra levy for books, desks, equipment for the laboratories and general maintenance. With all this, the school was able to provide us with practical experimental education in biology, physics, and chemistry. I really enjoyed these lessons in particular, and this went a long way to setting the prerequisites for my choice in vocational career.

Above board

I consider myself so very extremely fortunate that my Dad permitted me to be a day-scholar. As opposed to sending me off to boarding school. Which was what most parents, with the means to do so, did in Zimbabwe. I think the pure lack of privacy in a boarding school would likely have driven me to do something drastic and stupid. Either kill myself slowly though drugs, always a *very* attractive option to troubled youth, and entirely popular at boarding schools. Say it is not so. Or I would have stepped in front of a bus. There were plenty of those too.

For all those avid fans of "insert your favourite book-title on boarding-school-heroes, magical or otherwise, here": Really?

Honestly? You would want to be sent away from your home and your parents? Or you would want to send your child away? To be raised by strangers, impersonal and distant? To be stamped into a rigid mould dating back to the previous millennium?

Yes, I am aware, that there was a time, where schools were so rare, that for most people, they were far away. And you would rather entrust your children into the care of strangers, than not have them educated at all. But that was then. This is now. Today, we have the means and the availability resources, to have a school right in the neighbourhood.

Yes, we do. Do not tell me, we do not. If you tell me, there are no resources, I will tell you that humanity is currently burning significant amounts of currency. But more of that later.

Boarding schools. I mean, look at the system for what it *is*. Any emotional role models are absent. There is only a cold system of rules. Enforced by teachers who cannot favour any single child, nor *have the time or the resources to mentor and guide several hundred of them*. Never mind build a nurturing personal relationship. This is not some high-end elite college for the puissant progeny of those who have several accounts on the Cayman Islands. We are talking about classes between thirty-five and forty-five pupils to a class. I grew up in countries, where eighty students per class in state schools is a matter of fact.

I am aware that schools exist, be it boarding schools or otherwise, that offer one-teacher-to-five-student ratios. Where each and every pupil is lavished with just the perfect individual guidance and counselling. Where all of the school staff, up to and including the plumber, are entirely benign, at complete peace with themselves, and come equipped with a degree in child-psychology. But none of this is for ordinary people. Such schools serve a minute fraction of the worlds' population, and despite of how being-a-minority is not a valid reason to be disregarded, then it remains this exact minority, that reaps all the privileges. It cannot serve as a standard.

Besides, seriously, picture that. Picture what would happen if a teacher were to truly adopt the role of an attentive and devoted parent. That teacher would be out of a job, and out of a life, so fast, they would not have time to tie their laces.

So? Who actually raises those children?

They raise each other. As a result, you have a next-generation conditioned almost entirely by bullies and would-be tyrants, guided seemingly entirely by their baser impulses. Emotional eight-year-olds, those ruthless enough or ambitious enough to become influencers. And, yes, of course this leads to lasting bonds of loyalty and friendship. Which is just fine, because the protagonists of such high-gloss fantasies are always in the focus. They always win. And while they might not always be the best of role-models, these heroes remain basically noble and kind-hearted. They grow into mature adults of loyalty and integrity. They care about more than just their own immediate safety and gratification.

We know what happens with the hero. Boy gets girl, vice versa, happily ever after. What if we follow the story of the opponent instead? No! Not a book with a lovable, down-on-their-luck, inhumanly sexy bad guy/girl. I mean the antagonist from the first "happy-end" novel you thought about. What do they get in the end? Or better yet, what would the villains' faithful sidekicks have to say about all that? What would they say about all the secret and not-so-secret societies, the fraternities and sororities that exist worldwide? Interesting, is it not? Now imagine this person walking around a school, being cruel simply to cope with the overwhelming insecurity and the completely excessive demands with which life floods this child. Or even worse: for the sake of being cruel, because cruelty has become a means to an end. The only way they feel empowered to experience any kind of self-actualisation and control. Yup, great parenting material, right there. Wonderful future generations of leaders will be imprinted by these exemplary specimens of arbitrary despotism. Leaders full of inspiration and zest, role models of empathy and mindfulness.

Sorry, I got carried away there. As Vanessa, a close friend of mine, says, "Alice speaks fluent sarcasm." But the sarcasm does not invalidate my points.

Prefect students? Oh joy! More school uniform. I made my first experience with prefects on my first day in Kwekwe High School. He made me do twenty push-ups because I did not have the right colour shoes, and threatened to have me dig a hole in the ground if I did not have appropriate shoes by Friday. I did not have the right shoes because in Dar es Salaam, you were lucky to have *any* kind of shoes, and it was okay as long as you had the proper shirt and shorts. It eludes me to this day, how doing push-ups would change anything about the colour of my shoes.

We had School houses. Montgomery, Tedder, Eisenhower, and Mallory. There is a tale right there. And, yes, the houses competed with one another in sports, winning all kinds of trophies and things. And if they won, they would get to compete with other schools. In Dar es Salaam, I rather used to enjoy softball, but unfortunately that was not known in Kwekwe. So instead, I opted for another sport with a ball and a stick and as little body contact as possible, I tried hockey. It became very clear that I was nowhere nearly competitive enough to get anywhere, and the constant pressure and demands took any kind of fun out of the equation. Cricket was just as bad. As for rugby? Piling up with ten to twenty sweaty, grimy bodies? Boys? Touching me? Um, *NOPE*, not happening! I opted instead for some twenty months of detention, by flat out refusing to take part in any kind of school sports. After that, I think the school simply gave me up as a lost cause.

To make matters more interesting, and for all those fans of so many shades of ignorance; yes! Yes, most my teachers *did* in fact sport bamboo canes. Or rubber gas-hoses, diverted from their intended use for Bunsen burners. And some of them were quite liberal in using them, to enforce something labelled discipline. What it taught me almost immediately, was a clear distinction between fear and respect.

Incidentally, my Dad was on the chairing committee of the PTA, and he spent futile *years* trying to argue with teachers and parents alike, that "sparing the rod and spoiling the child" was not the optimal way to achieve intrinsic motivation in youths.

Yes, that was pretty cynical and depreciative of me. And yes, my opinion of boarding schools, perhaps my opinion of all schools, is biased. *Based*, I might add, *on actual experience and observation*. Maybe I should add, that I am aware, that in a lot of countries, corporal punishment has been declared illegal. None of which changes the fact, that in so many societies worldwide, a swift slap to the face, or deliberate public humiliation, even a whipping with belts or sticks, *are accepted standard methods of raising children*. An integral and taken-for-granted part of growing up. The legal situation changes nothing, if the basic cultural mindset is still stuck in the Middle Ages.

Of course I would like to say that this experience taught me to be *aware* of how daily exposure to physical and psychological violence leads to us accepting it as normal. And how this in turn contributes to the further propagation of abuse. And to be aware of how misuse of power is embedded in our societies. I would like to say that this empowered me to call out any injustice and engendered in me the ability to resist any attempt of force or coercion. But as a teenager faced with an environment that is exclusively accepting of violence as a means of upbringing, rebellion is not really an option.

Closer to the truth is, that this system has left me highly adaptable and diplomatic, to allow me to remain unnoticed und unremarkable. And it gifted me with a high tolerance for pain. Even in later years, faced with plenty of opportunity to test my ability to constructively defuse tensions into win-win situations, I think I rather failed at this. I learned that way, way later, and I like to believe, that I am putting it to best positive use in my function as an educator today. I comfort myself, with secure knowledge of having at least spoken up against racial discrimination, although I most certainly could have done more.

Overall, my experiences in schools taught me the value of perseverance and persistence. My sheer ability to endure pretty much anything without showing a reaction, was my way of dealing with bullies and adverse conditions. I was, and still am today, easily more patient than most people, certainly more patient than any menacing rough-neck, anyone needing to down-play their insecurities, or anyone naturally predisposed to enforce their will by way of intimidation. I have always ultimately found a way to get through rough situations and achieve what I set out to do. Sometimes by waiting long enough and doing what I needed by myself.

And in time, I learnt to do so by talking it through with the person or people involved, and finding common ground. You learn to compromise. And you learn to adapt. You learn to look for solutions that engender a win-win. As a trans* gender, you have to. Moreover, you need to do so in a way that does not rely on physical exchanges, whether in the real or in the metaphorical sense. You are the weaker. And you are the petitioner. The rules of societies are set out by others, by the gatekeepers. And if you want to transition, then you follow those rules.

So, yes, of course I learnt a great many lessons that proved invaluable in later life. But frankly, I am sick and tired of hearing, "But it was good for you. It made you hard. It made you endure." Peoples! Why on this lovely great green frikkin' earth would I need or *want* to endure?!?

I do not want to be hard. I want to be loved.

I imagine, I am not the only one.

Being a teenager

The most severe infringement into my sense of wellbeing was the onset of puberty.

Gradually, gradually, I noticed my body start to change. Hair sprouting in all kinds of places. And to make matter so, so much worse, my anatomy reacting dependently and sometimes independently, of all kinds of things that happened either around me or in me. And, yes, I noticed all this without ever looking down at myself or without ever looking in the mirror below the neckline.

Of course, puberty happens to everyone, and we all think it sucks. Probably our parents more than ourselves. And yet, I will maintain that for youths suffering from gender dysphoria, puberty is hell. Plain. Explicit. Hell. And for many trans* gender, this is the beginning of a cruel and excruciating descent into self-harm, dissociative- and borderline behaviour.

For me, Puberty was very much a loss of innocence. I lost touch with myself. With my body. I felt betrayed. I felt violated. My body suddenly behaved like a stranger. Like no longer a part of me. Up until now, I had been able to ignore that I was born with a penis. I simply blended out that part of reality. Not looking at myself was easy. I had done this for the past eight years, I was used to it. But nothing pulls you into the here-and-now of having a male body like an erection.

Which, if you happen to be a cis* gendered male, may be the sprinkle topping to your ice-cream bone, sorry, I mean -cone. But if you are a girl, having an erection is…

…there comes a point where you find yourself in the bathroom, holding a kitchen knife. I believe with all my heart, each and every trans* woman at some point ends up exactly there.

Bathroom. Knife. Decision.

Incision?

And then of course, there was the horror of body hair, suddenly sprouting everywhere. I was able to blend out the awareness of hair on my body, but facial hair was something I failed to deal with. I organised myself an electric razor, and I started shaving from the moment I saw the first development of colourless down on my upper lip. Looking back, I realise my stubble stayed colourless for my entire teen years. Which I am sure contributed to my being looked upon with belittlement and ridicule by some, even in my late teens. I remember Dalvinder, one of my class mates commenting, on how I was still a baby, and she did not mean that in a kind way.

Half-life

I became *excellent* at compartmentalising my life.

I compensated my isolation and my revulsion for this body by removing myself from it as completely as possible. What had developed itself in Dar es Salaam in my imagining how life would be as Nancy, proved to be just a foreshadowing. I began a nightly routine of reliving my entire day as Nancy. I played through conversations, made decisions, and visualised myself in interaction with all the people I had met that day. I went through my day at school, I relived the lessons. I even redesigned the time I spent all on my own, to the point of where I imagined friends for myself which I failed to find in the "real" world.

And in so many ways, I completely isolated Nancy as well. She no longer surfaced outside of my own perception. On rare occasions, I would bring out my soft colour pencils and apply eyeliner, and lid shade, perhaps even a little red to the lips. But I only ever did that in a locked bathroom. I no longer wore skirts or anything that looked remotely female. This was simply not the place for it. I made no mention of my alter ego in Zimbabwe. To absolutely no one. Although I know for a fact, that she had a great deal of influence on my vocabulary and my body language.

I suppose in many ways, I became the perfect teenager. From a grownup point of view. I did what I was told (true, Amahle would have debated that), I hardly argued, I was soft-spoken, attentive, and cooperative. I got excellent grades in school. I was creative in a quiet, clever way. I absolutely never picked fights. I tried as much as possible to remain invisible.

Amahle had three children. Her eldest, Sindisiwe, was away in Cuba, studying electronics. The older of the two boys, James was apparently living with his family in Johannesburg, for reasons nobody *ever* managed to explain to my satisfaction. It would be several years before I was to meet him. The younger of my two brothers came to stay with us about six months after we had moved to Zimbabwe.

His name was Quiniso and I was enthralled by the endearing click-sound that was a part of his name. Quiniso was four years younger than me, and he was adorable. He had a most luxurious afro, which he pampered for the better part of fifteen minutes every morning. Wildly enthusiastic about "Knight-Rider" and "The-A-Team", he told me all about what I had been missing by not having access to television. He was also an avid BMX rider and he practised stunts and tricks for days. One of Quiniso's favourite foods was strawberry marmalade spread thick on slabs of cheddar cheese, and if I annoyed him, he would dare me to try.

I was happy to see, that Quiniso was easily more fortunate than me in finding friends. The kids his age were all day-scholars, and the primary school of Gold Ridge was not far, so he could actually meet his friends from school.

My making friends in our neighbourhood turned out to be nigh impossible. Most of the kids my age either really were away as boarders at school, or not interested. At school, finding friends turned out to be just as difficult. A great many of the pupils had been in primary school together, and the close-knit groups from there still persisted. I was "the new kid", despite the fact that with the switch to high school, the environment was new for everyone. But perhaps that was the precise reason, why all the little peer groups that were already familiar snuck together a little closer still, and presented a united front to all the other little peer groups? Whatever the reason, I must have stood out like a sore thumb.

This was the time where Margaret "Maggie" Thatcher closed the majority of the UK mines, and great many families were suddenly without a means to support their existence. Those in a position to do something about it, emigrated to where there were mining operations. For example, to Kwekwe's neighbouring town of Red-Cliff, where there was a mine for iron ore and a smelting operation.

So after a first few weeks of familiarisation, it turned out that I was not the only "wierdo", and I got "adopted" by Henry and Josh, with whom I shared at least some common ground. They were two of boys whose families lived and worked in Red-Cliff, and I think Josh had a younger brother.

It was an odd kind of companionship. In the entire three years that Henry and Josh went to Kwekwe high school, the only time we shared, was at school. If we had study periods together, we would always intuitively find each other and learn together, quizzing each other, comparing notes, helping each other with queries and diagrams (I was good at those). Or we goofed off, playing hide-and-seek in the first year, followed in the successive years by fencing with sticks and epic chess matches. It was Henry that brought Stephen King, Frederik Forsyth and most importantly, John Ronald Reuel Tolkien into my life, for which I will be eternally grateful. But we would never, not once meet outside of school hours. And despite similar reading interests, we were never very close friends. I would not describe our friendship as deep or even very emotional.

Outside of school, I still had no friends at all. I spent my solitary time reading, playing with my Lego, or building model boats in our garage, where my Dad had all his tools. Sometimes I would just ride my bike or wander through the bush, watching birds, tortoises, and lizards. And I still spent nights fleshing out my daily adventures with imaginary friends.

All girls love horses

Joining up with the equestrian society pretty much saved my life. Or at least it saved me from complete isolation and a deterioration of my social skills.

By pure chance, I found a flyer pinned to the school notice board, offering riding lessons for a very affordable price. My Dad's income allowed us a very comfortable life, but certainly not an extravagant one. And to make matters even better, it was within bicycle distance, so my Dad would not have to take me.

To begin with, riding horse was something I did once a week. The days Monday through Thursday were blocked by hockey practice. Or detention. For not being at hockey practice. Every Friday, after school, I ate a hurried late lunch and rode my bike, at speeds beyond anything sensible, out of our neighbourhood, and down a dust track to a farm on the outskirts of Kwekwe. If you are riding a racing bike with thin tubes, it is better to take sandy stretches at high velocities, or your tyres will sink into the sand, and you will be catapulted straight over the handlebars. Hey! It made perfect sense at the time. Besides, I was wearing my riding helmet, right?

The horse stables were part of a farm which focused on cattle, and most of the horses were "bush ponies." In other words, small, agile, and very robust, capable of dealing with the rather unforgiving climate of Zimbabwe. Five of these belonged to Gillian, along with a thoroughbred named Sunsetter (as in sunset red). He certainly had a temperament to suit his fox coloured coat. The other horses belonged to a variety of other owners.

Gillian, my riding instructor was a cheerful young woman, barely out of school. She worked some office job someplace, and her only interest in life seemed to be horses. And her boyfriend, Zach. In that order. Concerning safety and wellbeing of the horses, she had zero tolerance for nonsense, but other than that, she was good humoured and not above wrestling each other into the horse-trough after a dusty outride into the bush under the scorching sun. If ever she found it strange that a "boy" should spend so much of his spare time rubbing down horses, or show so little interest in pursuing girls, she never mentioned it.

She took care of all the horses, together with Earnest and Chisembo. I never saw Earnest on horseback, but he was a talented farrier, and he took care of all the injuries any of the ponies would return home with. Chisembo was a prankster, and he had a laugh that was contagious. He was a skilled horseman and he repeatedly proved himself to be just as good at first aid. With humans. Chisembo picked me up off the ground quite a number of times, when I was thrown off a horse, checking my limbs and on several occasions, massaging the air back into my lungs because I was winded so badly. He always came along when we went out into the bush with our horses. I think I rarely saw him as cheerful and free-spirited as when he was swimming next to his horse in the water reservoir.

To begin with, Quiniso joined me. I rather think he did so to please me, rather than that he truly wanted to spend time with horses. I on the other hand really blossomed in this environment. I loved the smell of the fresh hay, even if mucking out stables was not really my most favourite of pastimes. The velvety feel of a horse's snout is something I remember so very fondly. The soft sounds, the snuffles and shuffles of horses shifting around me as I combed their manes and tails. Or leaning into my currycomb with half closed eyes, lost in bliss.

I like to think I was a quick learner. To begin with, Gillian offered to teach me polocrosse, lacrosse on horseback, but I found the concentration and the precision of dressage and show jumping more appealing. And if she had thoughtful moment, even Gillian admitted, polocrosse was ludicrously dangerous. Time passed and at some point, I got less detention, as our sports teachers and prefects lost interest in me. Or gave up in frustration. I spent pretty much all my free afternoons at the stables, and after about two years, Gillian approached me. She told me, I knew where kit and gear was, that she trusted me with the horses that were hers, and that she was grateful if I would just exercise them whenever I could make the time.

Ha! Paradise! I still paid for lessons and training, but that was more of a symbolic thing. It was more like I was contributing to the upkeep of the horses.

Having a social life

It was through horse riding that I was introduced to a great many families who were into riding. Most had children, youths my age, and in a lot of cases, the parents themselves were enthusiasts. In this environment, it was not only okay to be rather quiet, it was considered a perk, to be considerate and patient. The fact that I guided the horses gently and with persuasion, rather than force, was appreciated as proof of skill and empathy.

Aileen grew to be one of my closest friends. She was at the stables at least as regularly as I was. A lanky beanpole of a girl, easy going and always ready to share a joke. Or an apple. Unafraid to get her hands dirty, and extremely generous with her mother's most expensive shampoo, when we washed our horses. She had her own horse, Arthur, but most frequently she referred to him as Loskop (Afrikaans: "loose head" dummy, silly person). Arthur was a mixture of Arab and bush pony, magnificently teak coloured, with a glossy shine, and quite the independent thinker. She doted on him, and he used that to his full advantage.

Gillian supported and encouraged me to train two of her ponies. Thor was a handsome grey, and for a pony quite tall. He was good natured and patient, excellent for dressage. He had a snow-white coat and an adorable forelock that hung cutely over his forehead. Anthony was the opposite, a piebald of chestnut and grey, playful and mischievous, always with food on his mind. But he could, if the whim took him, jump clear out of a stand-still over the gate of his stable. And make his way to the feed-locker.

Twice a year, there would be nationwide dressage and show jumping events. I remember being almost speechless with gratitude, how the other families would pack my gear and me *and* both my horses into their trucks and trailers and take me along to wherever the events were taking place, Bulawayo, or Harare. My Dad would have driven me, had I asked him, but there was no way we would have gotten the horses transported. As I said, we were comfortable, but there was no way My Dad could have afforded to come up with the funds, had I needed to pay for a horse box, or accommodation. As it was, there was simply no necessity, there were always generous offers of, "Hey, you wanna ride with us?" and people seemed just as happy to offer me a pad to stow my sleeping bag. The best I could do was show my appreciation for such generosity by offering my help all around.

Or, we would host the events ourselves. We spent days, prepping makeshift stables, raising tarpaulin roofs, and constructing fences, readying extra sleeping accommodations, looking after catering. It was a huge lot of work, but loads of fun, and just so rewarding. There was so much connectivity and shared joy and pride in having hosted a successful event.

It was my third year in high school, I was fifteen, and the farm where Gillian offered board for horses had to close shop. She and all her horses had to move to another farm quite a distance further out. I was dismayed at this, because this would not have been feasible by bicycle. Instead, three times a week, Gillian would pick me up in her fire-engine-red mini cooper and drive as if the stables were on fire and we were the only fire-engine on the planet. Usually Aileen would be there too, being dropped off by her Mom.

We would then spend a companionable afternoon mucking out, cleaning horses, training or enjoying a leisurely outride into the bush. We would discuss school and teachers Aileen and I shared, discuss social patterns of Zimbabwe and South Africa, discuss Gillian's boyfriend Zach and why he hated her thoroughbred Sunsetter, "One day that bloody nag (Slang: ill-tempered horse) is going to kill you!" "You spend more time at those f*cking stables then you do with me!"

I think what I appreciated so much, was, that Gillian treated Aileen and me like adults. And working or training with Aileen was simply smooth, without any kind of friction, we complemented each other wordlessly.

At some point, Gillian married Zach, and this cut deeply into her horse-time. This also meant, she would not be able to drive with me to the stables. Without much ceremony, the Mackay family more or less adopted me. And as long as my Dad knew where I was, whom I was with, and that I was safe, he seemed comfortable with my choices. Michael Junior and Andrew were avid horsemen. Of course Michael Junior went as Michael. He was, I think, five years younger than me. A very eager to please, a very polite, and helpful boy. He had yet to grow into his tallness, but he was undeterred to prove he was capable of pulling more than his own weight. Andrew was two years younger than Michael, and a very bright spirited and cheerful boy. Most of the time. I sometimes got the impression, that being the youngest also granted him liberties that his two older brothers had had to fight for, and that he was not always appreciative of this.

Michael and Andrew were weekly boarders at a School run by the Adventist church. Their parents picked them up from school Friday afternoon, and together, they would pick me from my home, and we would spend the afternoon with the horses.

Michael did not own his own horse, so he often rode Thor when I was not training him, or he would ride one of the other ponies. He was a patient and dedicated rider, just as he tackled everything in life. Andrew had his own pony, and she seriously challenged his patience. Sue was a short little barrel of a pony, and she could have been taken straight out of a Norman Thelwell cartoon. Moody and devious, she was a b!tch. Quick to nip you in the rear if you were not careful and always ready to give you the slip of you were not on your toes. We spent hours trying to catch her.

Dave Mackay, the oldest of the three Mackay brothers, was in my year, but not in my class, as he took the accounting branch of education. He did not get along well with horses, quote, "one end bites and the other end kicks." But Dave turned into being one of my most loyal friends.

He could be very a thoughtful and serious young man. I dare say this was engendered by the responsibility he was burdened with in his role as firstborn. I also caught some underlying friction between Dave and Mike, the father of the family, making me wonder if Dave was born out of wedlock (Yes, Zimbabwe in the 1980ies this was an issue). Or maybe just the fact that he was born into a difficult time of political upheaval and war, and that his parents had had to deal with a great many challenges and insecurities during his infancy.

Dave sported his Dad's reddish curls and his square jaw. And shoulders like a stallion. Quite the looker, actually, if a bit short. When he laughed, his whole face lit up, showing his white and slightly rugby-traumatised teeth. He had a quick wit and a wonderful sense of humour. He was so generous with that. And he was easily capable of laughing at himself, which made him so endearing.

His primary interest was herpetology, and if people found a snake in their home or garden, they could call him, and he would catch the creature. He would keep it for a few days, make sure it was healthy and uninjured, and the take it far into the bush and turn it free. I think it was Dave that realised how little connected I was, and more or less took me under his wing. We came to spend a lot of afternoons studying together. And we spent entire weekends scouring the bush for animals to watch.

Fiona was the mother of the three boys, and entirely devoted to her family. Fiercely proud of her boys, all four of them, and despite her rather petite size, she was a force to be reckoned with. At the time, I think Fiona, rather thought I needed a mother, and from between the lines, I think she thought rather poorly of Amahle. For reasons other than skin colour. I often felt a little guilty and extremely nonplussed by the attention and warmth she bestowed me with.

My Dad seemed to accept this as part of my natural growing into independency. I still spent Saturday morning with him, doing our weekly shopping. It was *our* time, where we talked. What had my week been like, what had his week been like. What were the latest rumours and political developments. Sometimes of the tensions between me and Amahle. And usually Sunday night was spent with our family together, Amahle watching Denver Clan or something, and Quiniso and I reading books, my Dad usually reading the paper.

Friday afternoons riding horses, turned into Friday afternoons riding, followed by Friday evenings having a garden supper, and playing volleyball with the Mackay family. Which then turned into Friday afternoons on horseback, supper and volleyball in the Mackay's garden, followed by either drive-in cinema and / or playing squash at the sports club. Almost regularly, Oscar joined along as well. He was very much another "stray" the Mackays had "adopted," and he was a former rugby buddy of Dave's.

Almost every Friday, the four boys and I would leave the Mackay's home, either after returning from the drive-in, or from an excursion into the bush. We would head for the squash-courts and drive each other to the brink of exhaustion until three in the morning, with the boom box playing at full throttle (portable cassette player, not a blue-tooth box). Sometimes rum-and-cola was involved, although I stayed away from those. I relied on the sugar kick from tonic water.

Riding home on my bike under the stars always had something so refreshing and invigorating. Cleansing even. I had my own key and let myself into our home without ever turning on any lights, standing under a cool shower in the dark until my pulse slowed. Fall asleep looking forward to spending Saturday morning with my Dad.

Life was good.

Casually racist

Welcome as I was, as much at ease as I was in the equestrian community, there was a discordant note that bothered me. I did notice how people were racist in a completely subconscious and off-hand way. I do not think that the Mackay family were more so than any of the others, but spending so much time with them, of course made it more obvious. They were not so much openly hostile or antagonistic. It was casually depreciative remarks like, "Oh, that's pretty good for a hout-kop" (Afrikaans: wooden head). What irritated me even more is that to some degree, they *were* aware of this, and would make jokes about it. When I called them out on this and stated, that this was really hurtful thing to say, they excused themselves with that it was meant in humour, not in harm. And that they did not really mean it. That irritated me even more.

I was aware that Mike Mackay had been a trooper and a police officer in the days *before* independence in 1980. On very rare occasions, when conversations took unexpected turns, he spoke of things that implied he had been there to "clean up" the aftermath of unspeakable violence, be it intertribal genocide, mercenaries massacring "sympathising" villages, or retaliating "freedom fighters" wiping out isolated white settlements. I also knew he had friends of all ethnicities where he worked as an artisan, and I dare say, they were used to his way, and they took it in stride. I also dare say none of these people knew anything else, having grown up with this ever-present, all-pervading mind-set.

I am also aware that, while I openly challenged racist remarks, I never would have considered leaving the equestrian community or withdrawing myself from the Mackay family. But I do believe, my statements and opinions left an impression and hopefully even effected some changes in people.

Dave was the only one to be at my home with any regularity, and even then, we did not usually spend much time there. It was never openly spoken of, but I do think the Mackay family thought it odd that "my Dad had married a Black", and Dave was a little awkward around Amahle. But then, so was I. I was always checking everything thrice in her presence. Watching my words or my actions.

I never caught anyone making depreciative quips or even thoughtless remarks around Quiniso. I would have given them hell (or I like to believe that). And he never said anything to me in this regard. Despite this, and as much as I hated admitting this to myself, all these circumstances may have contributed to his giving up on horse riding. Perhaps he felt awkward and maybe unwelcome in this crowd? That it was not just the clinging fragrance of horse sweat? At the same time, he *did* in fact have his BMX crowd, which he seemed to enjoy rather more and which absorbed a great deal of his spare time. At some point, he took up tennis, either of which had about the same ethnic distribution. And yet, despite our both being fulfilled by our own circle of friends, we still shared our interests of movies and television series and I like to believe, he was fond of me. Quiniso was certainly a brother to me, and I loved him dearly.

Another topic over which the Mackay family and I frequently collided was the matter of wild-life conservation. The Mackays were (are) vegetarians and they were passionate protectors of animals. We spent a great deal of time together, raising awareness and collecting funds for maintaining and upgrading parks' fences and water supplies. And I was proud of my contribution to this. I like to think we achieved a great deal (highly relative of course) in making lives of rhinos safer in Zimbabwe (This was before the economy collapsed).

But the Mackays were not just passionate, they were downright militant. Driving through game-parks at night with flood lights, is something I enjoy immensely, if it is for game-viewing. But when game-viewing turned into poacher-hunting, I no longer found this to be at all okay, never mind entertaining. To be clear: I find it despicable and wretched, when professional soldiers turn poachers and target high-profit game, like rhinos or elephants, with fully automatic weapons, for horn or ivory. But when starving people feed their kin and communities, by trapping and killing impala or warthogs, I find myself torn between empathy for the animal and empathy for the people.

Ultimately in such things, my heart went (goes) with the people. And while it is illegal to poach wildlife, it is also illegal and ethically highly questionable to restrain and beat up people who are simply desperate to survive and feed their families. And I simply *failed* to understand how the Mackays could be so empathic where cruelty to animals was concerned, but so callous and dismissive concerning transgressions against human dignity and welfare?

It was one of the things where we agreed to disagree. That in itself was a novel experience for me: having someone disagree with me, but still appreciate me.

The fact remained that I felt very welcome and at ease in this social circle. In a very long time, I no longer needed to put up a front of being tough or being hard. To people, I appeared as a quiet and perhaps timid boy / youth, who was good with horses. Nobody addressed me as Nancy. But then nobody called me a freak or a mistake of nature either.

People did not just tolerate me. People brightened up when they saw me. People appreciated the way I handled horses, people appreciated the work I put into projects. And above all, I believe, they appreciated how I treated *everyone* with kindness and respect. People welcomed me into their homes and into their hearts. This was an entirely affirming experience.

Sweet seventeen

When the court ruled that custody over me was to go to my Dad, they also dictated, that I was to spend a certain amount of time together with my birth mother, so as not to have me grow up completely estranged. At the time, I would have flat out refused to spend five weeks with my mother. I simply did not trust her, and being dependent on her moods was extremely distressing.

Instead, I did get to spend the winter holidays (European winter) in Switzerland. So every year, I got to stay with my grandparents and visit the rest of the family. Among these were my cousins, Urs and Remo, the sons of my aunt Lisbeth and her husband Walt.

And of course, I would spend some days with my mother. She too had re-partnered, although it was going to be some years before they would marry. Francesco was (is) an extraordinary man. Patient and observant. Deeply empathic and thoughtful, very kind and mindful, to the point of being downright submissive. At the time, he was making a living by harvesting pieces and components of trashed bicycles to recycle (pun intended). He then sold his rebuilt bicycles. I have never again encountered the creative and the self-destructive so close together in one person. But thirty-four years later, and he still has her back. So somewhere in all malleability of his, there is obviously a great endurance, capable of coping with my mother's volatile mixture, absorbing the impact and turning it into something good.

But even my mother was ambivalent about my presence in her home and her life. One episode stayed with me particularly clearly. I was fourteen, when she demanded Francesco and I spend the night in the forest, away from the isolated farmhouse she was living in at the time (on the forest floor, with nothing but a blanket and a damp sleeping bag). The reason for this being, that there was an astral conjunction, and she wanted to perform a ritual with her coven (Yes, coven. As in wiccan and paganism), which demanded no males present, or even in close proximity. Nevertheless, I think she had her days when she clearly felt family ties and did her best to cultivate an amicable relationship to me. And I do believe I she was pleased to see I had inherited some of her creative talents.

Being in Switzerland also gave me the opportunity to spend some days with Evangeline, my godmother, who had moved to Bern in the meantime. She shared an apartment with her significant other, René. To be honest, that was something I lived for. Her mindful and delicate way (no other way to say it) of sharing her time with me was immeasurably soothing and calming for what I felt was my soul chafing inside the ill-fitting shell that was my body.

In January 1987, my mother gave birth to Eirian, and Evangeline gave birth Seraphina, both born within two days of each other. I was blessed with two of the most wonderful sisters possible. I tried to see them as often as possible. Which was not often, obviously.

Every other year, I was able to visit Peggy and Marc, whose family had moved from Dar es Salaam back to Manchester. Marc introduced me to Terry Pratchett, whose colourful complexity and satirical mirroring of our world as the disc-world, enriched my life immeasurably, and who permitted me to really appreciate a well-worded and reflected argument. Marc also introduced me to more music. It was Dire Straits that really got me into actually *listening* to music, appreciating the complexity of melodies and rhythms and the skill behind the interaction of the instruments, and not just singing along to the words. Marc, I am forever grateful.

Christmas of 1987, I was seventeen, was also one of these holidays. Plus, I had just completed my O-Levels (intermediate exams), and my holidays were slightly longer than usual. I began my holidays in Switzerland with my paternal grandparents. Following which I got to stay some days with Evangeline, René and one-year old Seraphina. It was a truly fulfilling time, and it renewed the deep trust and affection that I had for Evangeline. I spent Christmas and New-Year in England. Strangely, we fell back into our old ways of being Peggy, Ruth and Nancy, the fearsome Amazon Pirates. Marc's dad took us to the Lake-District to go hiking for New-Years-Eve, and all of this just perfected the backdrop for stories of lost islands and sunken treasure. Marc and Peggy's stories. For me, it was a brief breather. A break from reality, permitting me to being myself. Being free and unfettered. I could almost forget my body.

Curious how none of us hesitated to immerse ourselves in our "game". Not even Marc. I think he too enjoyed the illusion of being pre-teen again and just letting the years slip away. So it was in this frame of mind, being Nancy, that I returned from the UK back to Switzerland. And it was with a lighter heart than usual, that I went to stay with my Mum for a couple of days.

Community

True to her ways, my mother was still testing the limits of societies' constraints and exploring new paths to empowering women. She was no longer living in the commune she had previously founded. Instead, she had taken a small apartment, in order to provide a safer environment for Eirian, my sister, who was one year old at the time, and two days older than Seraphina. Francesco, Eirian's father was still living in the commune. Probably better so, I believe my mother might have done something drastic, had she and Francesco shared the tiny apartment.

The commune was a loose congregation of people, a whole spectrum of characters, ranging from tight-strung far left, through loose-hanging shaggy hippies, all the way to hard-core-eco-environment friendly. Although in some cases, "friendly" was not the word I would have used. Some of these people apparently had no sense of humour. Regardless, and truth be told, talking with these people was way, way interesting. And some of them really made time to explain their ideas and muse with me. Come to think of it, it must have been similar to what Evangeline felt like, when she met my parents as a teenager, and she was introduced to their friends. Bouncing ideas off these people had unexpected and sometimes alarmingly fun consequences. Even if the standards of hygiene tested other limits, namely those of my comfort zone. And that is coming from someone who spent fourteen years sharing a bedroom with colonies of ants and nesting geckos, or hunting for silk spiders (Nephila) in the bedroom corners and camel spiders (Solifugae) under the toilet seat. You think I am joking? Google them, I dare you.

Francesco, and his projects for constructing useful and fun objects from bicycles remains, felt right at home in this environment. I really enjoyed spending time with him. I was already fully capable of stripping and reassembling my bicycle, but still he was able to teach me loads of stuff where there were either easier ways, or he had the tools and expertise that I had previously lacked. For example, I had never before disassembled, cleaned and greased a pedal-shaft, right down to the ball-bearings. Even better, we found we actually shared quite a lot of know-how on crafting model vehicles form tin cans, and I like to think I quite impressed him with that.

Time spent with my mother was… …uneasy but very educational. Little, if anything, had changed about my mother's shifting moods and her simmering temper. And nothing had changed about my being outright afraid of her. She *did* however show me how to operate her sewing machine, something for which I am extremely grateful today, and she gave me a basket of rags I could make use of. I did exactly that. From embroidered pirate flag to skirts, I made as good a use as I could in the short time.

So you wanna be a girl?!

Had this been Zimbabwe, I might have, I would have, probably been more on my guard. As it was, I was more at ease than in the past. And having Eirian to pamper, when she was awake, drew me out of my shell.

I do not know what kind of connection Andrin had to Francesco's circle of friends, or how he came to be in that commune. I thought he might be someone's son. My Mother had specifically arranged for his presence, so I would have someone of my age group to relate to.

Andrin was an easy-going, tough acting nineteen-year-old. About a head taller than me, sandy brown hair, and pale blue eyes. We goofed off together in Francesco's workshop, we helped ourselves to the fridge, and we raced bicycles (you're never too old or too cool to race bicycles). We made a cardboard silhouette of a cat and giggled ourselves silly as motorists went full on their brakes, because we made them think there was an animal on the road (you're never too old to realise how stupid you once were).

And we talked about sex.

Let me rephrase that. Andrin talked about sex. I had very little to talk about, but I was certainly curious, because he was the first person *ever* to actually mention things, that drove the blood into my cheeks. And he did so much more than just mention. In my memory, the moment there were no adults present, Andrin would happily, and with complete lack of inhibition, monologue in great detail, how he would like to "do it" with girls.

He was imaginative in creating a metaphor of just about all and any daily topic. He was highly creative in demonstrating his ideas with the use of commonplace objects as visual aids. He was proficient and versatile in supplementing the appropriate sound effects. Or those he imagined appropriate. He was, in fact, capable of maintaining this, to the point where I began to lose interest.

After two days of this, I did find it disconcerting, that all the terms he used were… …derogatory. Language that would not have made it past my tongue. The days of my being a foul-mouthed little punk were far behind.

But still. I was intrigued. I would be lying if I said otherwise.

Trigger warning.

There was a room, I assumed it was his bedroom, just below the attic, where the two of us withdrew to, to be out of the way of all the adults. Oblong, with walls that were once whitewashed, now speaking of age. A glossy grey door frame, that shed flaky paint, smelling of time passing. The floor was bare wooden boards, hollowed out by generations of feet walking across them. There was a single lightbulb, cradled by a yellowish lampshade hanging from the centre, casting the high ceiling into shadow. There were two bare windows on the left. The old kind of windows which are actually two separate windows, one behind the other, doubled against the cold, with a deep window ledge. The single bed placed up against the right corner was the only piece of furniture. It was covered with a heavy blue-and-grey duvet and pillow, both smelling slightly of damp goose down. Andrin's backpack, khaki and olive, was an anachronism in this room. Leaned up against the bed, it was the only splash of semi-colour.

Andrin and I are standing by the window. The streetlight picks out three motor scooters. On the corner below are some youths, eight, maybe ten boys and three girls. They are talking, joking, laughing. The catcalls and laughter echo between the houses. I catch nothing of what they are actually saying, but that is unnecessary. Hanging out as youths do.

They are unaware of Andrin and me in window overlooking the street.

Two of the youths are slightly apart. Her back is against the wall. He is standing between her legs. They are making out, obviously immersed in this. They take no notice, or pretend to take no notice, of the others who are hooting and jeering at them.

My mind goes to Dharinee and Guang. Tasting their lips. I admit. I would not mind experiencing that again myself, just to see what it's like today. Self-consciously, I glance at Andrin, to see if I have been caught blushing. But I need not worry. He is completely engrossed.

The boy's hands drop to the girl's waist. Literally, I do not believe I am seeing this. He has opened her belt and is obviously working on her zipper. I catch the precise moment her mood tips. *It's no longer a game. She no longer wants this. And neither do I. Below, the girl roughly shoves the boy away and shouts at him. She turns away and closes her pants, visibly angry. And scared. The boy and the other youths are laughing. Beside me, Andrin sniggers,* "I'd give her something to scream about, that's for sure."

Like the girl, I turn away. I no longer want to see.

Andrin catches the change. He repeats what he just said, gauging my reaction, "I'd give her something to scream about, that's for sure. What about you?" *I make a non-committal noise and go over to sit on the bed. He is now visibly irritated.* "What, you don't wanna f*ck her? You don't want to make her scream on you dick?"

This thought, more than anything so far, the mention that I have a "dick", drenches me like a tub of filthy ice-water. I am irritated. Confused. Nauseated. I shake my head, as much to shake off the confusion as to emphasise, "No! No, I wouldn't."

This really catches him off guard. Perplexed, he asks, "What do you mean? Why not? I mean look at that ass. C'mon, you don't wanna shoot her full of your spunk?" Now I am upset. Even more confused. And I am worried about that glint in his eye. I do not know what to do.

Out of the sheer lack of anything to say, I tell him, "Because I'm a girl!"

That has him completely stumped. "What ?!?"

I should not have said that. But now it's out and I cannot make it go away. My face is hot, I cannot feel my fingers and my ears are ringing. I try to explain that I am a girl. In the body of a boy.

He is silent. And then, "We could pretend?"

What? Where did that come from? I don't understand, shake my head. So he says, "We can pretend to f*ck." No longer a question. He is growing visibly more agitated by the second. In two steps, he is in front of me. He shoves me onto my back. Rough. I feel his hands fumble for my jeans. I realise. I struggle to sit up. I am struggling to get his hands off me, to push him away. I simply cannot believe what is happening. He is constantly repeating, almost pleading, "Come on, it's just pretend." I think I am screaming, "NO! Stop! Stop this. Don't! Let go of me!" I cannot tell if the screaming is all in my head.

He is stronger than me. Easily. I struggle as fiercely as I can. I still believe he will come to his senses and leave off. I feel a sudden wave of pain in my tummy. His knee? His fist? I can no longer keep up my arms. He fumbles at my jeans and pulls them down. He turns me over. His hand grabs my hair, presses my face into the bed. I scrabble for breath against the duvet, struggling. The fear is like a hot blade.

"So you wanna be a girl? Let me show you how that goes!"

I try to push him away. I try to close myself as tightly as I can. The more I struggle, the weaker I become. The pain is like nothing I have ever felt before.

I have no idea of how long it took. I have no idea if he raped me once or more. I do not even know what I said. I do not know if I ever told him to stop, or if I fought him in complete silence. What I do know is that my vocal chords were raw the next day. But that was just another pain amongst many. All I have are fragments.

I don't move, I don't make a sound. Perhaps he will forget I am there. Andrin is failing to fumble with his pants and open the door simultaneously. This detached thought going through my mind, "Dummy, you should have closed your pants first."

He finally has the door open. He takes a step back into the room, his face filled with revulsion, hate. He snarls at me, "If you ever tell anyone, I will make you wish you were dead!" I recoil even further. He lunges at me, "What? You wanted this, don't pretend you didn't!"

And then he is gone.

I grow aware of… … I need the bathroom. *NOW*.

I bolt for the door. Or at least that is what my head is telling me. Standing is not an option. Searing pain shoots though my abdomen. My legs give way. Why is my t-shirt on the floor? I retch onto my t-shirt. Better than being sick over the floor. Easier to clean. I retch until my stomach is empty. Then I retch some more. The dry heaves are excruciating. Any movement sends waves of pain through me, blotting out everything, making me sick again.

My next truly coherent memory is of finding myself in the bathroom. I was completely stripped. I do not remember whether I did that or whether he did. I checked if the door was locked.

Did I lock the door? Am I sure? There is something warm spreading down my thigh. Red. Am I going to die? Will I get an infection? I hope nobody heard. Or do I?

NO! No, I do not want anyone to see. I do not want the questions. I do not want to explain what cannot be explained. I do not want to look at what happened. Why it happened. Wha was I even there? It was my fault. I was stupid! So stupid. I should have kept my mouth shut. I should never have spent time with him. I want to go home. I want my Dad. But he cannot know. He can never know.

Not that I think anyone would believe me.

I need to get clean. I need this gone from inside me. I need him gone from inside my head. I need to be gone. Invisible. Just stop existing.

At some point, the water was hot. I sat in the bathtub under running water until the water was so cold, I could no longer feel my fingers and my ribs hurt. Or perhaps they hurt anyways? I tried my best to wash myself, to remove all of Andrin. At some point I stopped bleeding, or at least it lessened to the point where I dared crawl out of the bathtub. Slowly, carefully, I stood, locking my teeth against the cold and the screams, trying to stay as silent as possible. I wrapped myself in a towel and listened. Voices somewhere in the house, floors below. Conversation. Laughter. I hobbled over to the door to check again (fifth? fifteenth?) to make sure it was locked, hardly daring to breathe. I shuffled back over to the Bathtub. I turned up the radiator to the max, and sat myself down as slowly and as gently as I could against it.

I probably fell asleep there.

I barely remember how I got through the next days. I think I spent a lot of time, either in that bathroom, with the door locked. Or cuddling with Eirian, doing my best to be invisible. Or trailing Francesco like a shadow, never more than an arms length away. Today, there are bits and pieces of memory, how I crouch in the hall for what feels like hours, trying to be completely silent on stairs that creak, waiting for the coast to be clear. I was terrified that Andrin would find me again.

I remember no remarks, nor even any questions. No queries of what I am up to, what I am doing. My mother? My mind comes up blank. I simply do not know. I do not think she noticed. I am sure she was far too preoccupied with Eirian. I put in an astronomic effort to appear normal. To pretend nothing at all out of the ordinary had happened. Although, in retrospect I keep thinking, there must have been indications that *something* was off. Completely utterly off.

Andrin was gone. As if he had never been there to begin with.

...a few days later I was back on a plane. Back to My Dad. Back to my world of horses and people who welcomed me. Perhaps not as Nancy. But at least nobody held my face to a pillow.

Nancy broke on that bed that night. I found no way to console this girl that I was, never mind make myself whole. I had no way to cope with the pain and the shame.

Did I blame my mother? To some degree, I actually did. Unfair and irrational of me as it was. Blaming Francesco never occurred to me, perhaps because he was so...
...deferential. Always doing what my Mum told him, always going so far out of his way to appease her. Of course, Francesco was not to blame, but the plain fact that it never even occurred to me and blaming my Mum did, is worth mentioning. Not that it says anything good about me. Blaming my mother was just... ...easier. Sorry Mum, not your fault.

And nothing you could have done. I would not have let you.

More than anyone, I blamed myself. I remembered feeling the pique of curiosity when I watched the two teenagers making out. My mind wandering to my first experience of kissing. I felt I had betrayed Nancy's trust and I needed to protect her from the world. And I was utterly unable to cope with the guilt. Or the shame. Consequently, this part of me retreated even further into my imagination. I pushed what happened into the deepest darkest corner of my subconscious, I locked the door and threw away the key. In fact, I succeeded so well at this, that for the next twenty-eight years, I would barely think about it.

And yet, the picture I had of myself in my mind became a broken thing. Torn. A wrecked and tainted rag doll of a child, wandering like a wraith between worlds. Contrary to this, in my mind, this helpless, powerless child could change sometimes into a dragon, with an incandescent breath that would let steel and stone flow like tears… …unfortunately, it was nothing she could control. And while this is a very pretty metaphor, it also carries the fact that, as Nancy, I carried an enormous amount of anger.

Incandescent. Hell-bent. **RAGE**.

And most of this rage was turned inward. And more often than not, the fire consumed everything, including herself. Myself.

On the outside, I kept functioning. Smooth as clockwork.

The fear that I would be blamed. Rational or not, I was afraid of being sent away from my Dad. I think my absolute worst fear was, that my Dad would be as revolted and disgusted of me as so many others. That he would look at me the same way. Plus, of course, being sent away from him would have cost me my entire social circle where things were *good*.

All that kept me going. I continued to pay close attention to school. I put pretty much all my spare time into the horse community…

Loss

It might be, My Dad would have noticed. But as coincidence would have it, severe misfortune had also visited my family in my absence.

My brother Quiniso had in the meantime finished primary school at Gold Ridge, and was ready to go to high school. And since all of his school friends were off to Plum-Tree private college, that is where he wanted to go. I never understood, for the life of me, why anyone would voluntarily want to go to a boarding school. But whatever his reasons were, if it really was as simple as being with his mates, I realised quick enough that this really meant a lot to him, and gave him as much support as I could.

So I was still in Switzerland while my exams were being evaluated, while Quiniso and his pals were already at school when I went to stay with my mother. During his first week at school, there was a horrible freak accident. No one knew what had happened, nobody could explain satisfactorily how it was even possible. But fact remained that Quiniso had drowned in the reservoir pond belonging to the school grounds. To be honest, I suspected this to be a hate-crime. Plum-Tree originally was a high-end white school. Apparently, a hate-crime was ruled out with certainty? I still have my doubts about that today…

I was shell-shocked. And of course, I was still processing my own immediate past. My Dad was speechless with grief. And of course, Amahle was utterly beside herself. She had lost her youngest child.

And I learnt, that when somebody dies, you are left with all the ambivalences and quarrels with that person unresolved. There were not many. But there was one issue about a book we both loved where I wronged him, and I deeply, deeply regretted that. Regret.

Concerning Amahle, I actually believe the support she received from so many of the families of Quiniso's school friends contributed immensely to her getting through her grief. Maybe even through some of her prejudices. Most of the mothers who sat with her, spoke to her, offered comfort, or provided relief by looking after chores, most of the mothers of Quiniso's school mates were White.

For my part, from then on, I made sure to check in on Amahle when I returned home from school each day. I spoke to her as long, and as often, as she seemed comfortable with, watching her work at her sewing machine or embroidery, asking about what she was working on. And gradually, the ice between us melted.

Relationships

Gradually, gradually, things changed.

I was vaguely aware, that in a peculiar way, I must have been quite popular. Which was strange, because not many people really spent time with me. But I was approached by all kinds of people from school, and I did have all sorts of remarkable conversations, many of which were of a quite intimate nature.

Looking back, I suppose I had gotten rather good at reading patterns. Good at reading people. And while I did not have any personal or hands-on experience in relationships, I like to think I was observant and mindful, of what people did and felt around me. What they needed. And how this made them behave. And what kind of reactions that triggered in other people again. As a trans* gender, you learn to do this.

Henry and Josh had returned to Britain with their families. Instead, I got to know Emilio and Daniel, and to them I developed a rather close rapport. Not the only friends outside the equestrian community, but the only ones who actually spent time with me outside school. Their family had originally emigrated from Delhi in North India, via Lusaka in Zambia. They lived in Kwekwe centre, where their Dad practiced medicine as a GP. I remember their mother well, such a sweet and kindly woman, dressed in the most lovely of saris, colourful and bright. She was a fabulous artist of bakery, and her cupcakes and cakes were an inspiration for me to follow.

Emilio and Daniel were two really fine and thoughtful boys, mild mannered and considerate. The three of us played chess excessively, and we did a lot of studying together. Actually, let me rephrase that, Daniel was mild mannered. And better in physics. He regularly beat me at chess too. He was a great partner during practical physics lessons, an intuitive mathematician, while I was better able to support him and Emilio in chemistry and biology. Emilio was quite the outgoing smooth-talker, humorous, and *way* too handsome for his own good. Which might have been, why I found playing chess with him so enjoyable.

Emilio was also the first boy at school to trust me with talk about girls. Unlike Andrin (No, I never thought about him in Kwekwe). Unlike Andrin, Emilio was highly respectful, to the point of being slightly in awe, of the girls he found to be pretty or desirable. He was always polite, in both his language and his actually addressing people, very much focused on making a good impression. I remember being entirely surprised at his asking me what he should do about approaching the young lady that had captivated his attention. What I told him was a mixture of common sense, things *I* would have appreciated, and plotlines I gathered off rom-coms. Whatever advice it was that I gave him, it seemed to be the right thing, and he was very appreciative.

And possibly, this might have made the gossip. To my extreme surprise, I was approached by five or six further people in our year, seeking relationship advice. Funny how common sense is so easy when you are not emotionally involved yourself.

One of which was Winston. I rather liked Winston. We barely had anything in common, but he was one of the few prefects, who seemed to keep a level head, to not be seduced by the power and influence that came with being given a supervisory status and a badge. He was also graced with a mixed background, and I dare say, that made him mindful of how people treated each other. Not to mention that being captain of our school rugby team gave him a physique… …my mind always veered off those topics, the moment they actually involved me. But he had shoulders like Atlas, and I wouldn't have minded giving those pectorals a rub.

The refreshing thing about Winston was that he did not beat around the bush. He flat out asked. He said he was interested in this girl, and how he should approach her about this. I remember needing a couple of breaths to deal with the surprise. I mean, why on this great green earth was the potential head-boy, captain of the rugby team, asking me? What made *me* the expert? I was not exactly a Romeo (or a Juliette). Instead, I asked him to name me what it was specifically about this particular girl, why not another. Of course this took some work, but true to his nature, Winston took that head-on as well. Despite the fact that he was clearly uncomfortable with "talking to a guy" about his feelings. I summarised for him, and asked him if he would be prepared to tell her exactly that. Following that conversation, he always gave me a kind of minimal wave or a thumbs-up when we passed.

And then there was Shenaaz. With the pretty plaits that came almost to her waist. I have to admit, I was almost envious of her glossy hair: A deep, rich chestnut, so as to be almost black, perfectly matching her eyes, which sparkled when she laughed. I heard from the others, she was excellent at accounting and nutrition.

Shenaaz and three of her friends were waiting for me in the corridor after classes. She said she had forgotten her other bag in one of the classrooms. The one where we had had English. And would I go fetch it for her. From her body language, I interpreted there was so much more at stake than her "other bag".

However, the fact that Dalvinder was among the other three, tittering to themselves, made me instantly wary. Dalvinder and I had history. Actually, Dalvinder had history with quite a few people, namely that she was a vicious tease and a malicious gossip. I excused myself as politely as I could. Shenaaz seemed rather crestfallen. It rather worried me that the other three giggled even more at this, and I would dearly have avoided hurting Shenaaz's feelings or putting her in any kind of compromising situation, but I thought it best not to get involved.

I caught her on her own on the offside, some days later, and apologised and explained the best I could. I let her know that I had the impression that there was more than just a forgotten bag. Shenaaz blushed red ad a beet (Shenaaz was quite dark for an Indian and I had never seen an Indian blush this hard before. It was kind of curious). She sighed deeply, and said she had boy trouble. Apparently there was a boy she liked. *Really* liked. And apparently, sadly, he was not in her caste. It went through my mind, that if Dalvinder knew this, then Shenaaz and this boy could potentially end up in a world of hurt. Shenaaz's family belonged to the local ruling clans, and they were not to be trifled with.

What I asked instead, was, what she really wanted. Really wanted. Not just concerning this boy, but concerning her plans for the future, her ambitions, what she wanted to do for a living, her plans for family, what role her own clan played in all of this. How close or how independent she wanted to be from her own parents, and what she expected from any in-law family. When the bell finally rang for classes to continue, she was almost as flustered as when I first approached her. But she too, would always greet me cheerily, almost warmly after that.

Grace was friendly enough. Outspoken, focused and ambitious. We compared physics results in school, but other than that, she did not really show a reaction outside of classes. Actual conversations did not seem to happen, and I certainly did not push it. What did fascinate me that she was one of the extreme few girls that carried her Afro in the beautifully plaited and coiffed hairstyles, that were so common in Tanzania, but so extremely rare in Zimbabwe. In Zimbabwe, most women straightened and then permed their hair, something I simply failed to understand, because some of those Tanzanian hairstyles were (are) elegant beyond description. Grace absolutely lived up to her name and I am sure she grew into a very majestic woman.

And yet, at some point in physics practical class, Grace gracelessly lost her temper at Daniel. Apparently, Daniel had taken the set of optical lenses that she had had her eyes on, but he had simply been quicker. Grace said something about "All boys being such pigs!" which got me questioning, who the boy was that had behaved like a pig, because I was sure that it was not polite and soft-spoken Daniel.

I asked her later, whether she was okay. Grace jumped, almost as if bitten by a snake, and gave me a look. First a flush of surprise, turning into defensive anger. Finally, she became thoughtful. She took a deep breath and confessed that she had broken up with her boyfriend (Ohmigosh, all these people having boyfriends and girlfriends and here I am just wasting my time studying) because he had cheated on her. I do not remember exactly what I told her, but it must have been along the lines that she was absolutely right to do so, that any guy cheating on her must be an utter idiot, and that she deserved better. Better treatment and better boyfriend material.

A day later, I think Grace rather regretted her moment of confidence. But in the days and weeks that followed, I think she realised that I was not going to harass her, or take advantage, and she relaxed into a kind of distant but friendly "Hey, howzit?" (Zim. Slang: How are you, how is everything going?). We stuck to physics results, and every once in a while, she asked to use my calculator. Yeah, Baby steps...

Another point of contact was Andy. She was usually accompanied by Elsa, her younger sister, and Hope. The three of them would play double-dutch (a jump-rope game) during break-time. Like Winston, Andy came from a family of mixed heritages, and I know for a fact, that this made their lives rather rough (this is a polite British understatement. Zimbabwean prize winning author and filmmaker, Siphiwe Gloria

Ndlovu, wrote volumes on this topic). Regardless of this, Andy was a real sweetheart, and if you gave her the time of day, it seemed to bring the sun out in her world. Andy had a smile that positively glowed. By standards, she had so much going for her. She had a lovely light-copper tone of skin, loose curls with a reddish tint that framed a perfectly freckled face. And she really had a figure, all the right curves in all the right places, in fact she had everything that made a woman beautiful.

I like to believe Andy and I found an easy kind of kinship in that we both knew what it was like to be singled out and bullied. What touched me so deeply about her was, how she would be cautious, but still be so proactively friendly and accommodating. Despite how some people treated her. Today, the adult me recognises some of the underlying patterns. Of trying to be endearing and harmless in the face of insurmountable odds, to soften the blows of discrimination and transgressions. At the same time, I believe Andy is a perfect example of children learning from the role model of their parents. There really was a flame of courage burning in Andy, in her whole family. And I know she spent a lot of time looking after her junior sister.

Every once in a while Andy and I would share a quiet study break and a sandwich on the side. Or we would meet up at the supermarket and share an ice cream or something, looking over mathematics or English. We would talk of how school was going, which exams were up, which teachers were in what kind of mood. And I would try and bolster her self-confidence by emphasising how good the grades were that she was getting, and how she would surely do well for herself when she graduated. How proud her parents were going to be. When we spoke of that, she would get this dreamy look and speak of how she wanted to go to college and become a teacher. Or a scientist. And I told her how I would like to study biology, work in some wildlife program. Or go into engineering, like my Dad. We did not dream of becoming movie stars, presidents, or high-profile executives. It was clear to the both of us, that for every "superstar", there need to be several hundred thousand people just making a living. Raising a family. And if we were able to do that in peace, then that was already better than what we had dealt with in the past. We would say our goodbyes, shouting "Graduation! WOOOH!" and high-fiving each other.

Dave's rugby friend, Oscar, was studying accountancy at college. He was a little older than us, and he was also the one who got the rum-and-cola at the bar. Oscar was a regular at our squash-Fridays and he was *good* at it. He gave me tips in squash, on how better to aim for the balls, and it was from him that I learnt some killer serving techniques, that would drop that ball, literally, in my opponent's blind corner, and it would roll to a stop. I think Dave and Andrew rather hated him for that.

Whenever I think of Oscar, I am always reminded of Tom Selleck when he played Magnum PI. He certainly had the matching physique. He even sported the same base cap and moustache, the only thing missing was a Hawaii shirt. Boyish and mischievous, always tricks up his sleeve. By appearances, a playboy and a ladies' man, but I came to learn, basically with a good heart and earnest intentions. I was sitting, watching Dave (always energetic, if not graceful) chase the balls his brother Michael served him on the court. I noticed Oscar sat himself next to me, him with his spiked cola and me with my tonic water, and we watched the others go at it for a while. All out of nowhere, he asked me, "So do you think I will ever find a steady girlfriend?"

So, it turned out that this seemingly carefree playboy was in fact quite insecure and anxious about all the girls that seemed interested at first, but stopped seeing him after a while. I rather think that one of the reasons was, that he simply did not know how to express himself to begin with, and in the presence of female company, he became even more tongue-tied (yes, rather stereotype, but there you go). On rare occasions, we would talk about what it was that he looked for, and how to actually convey his hopes and wishes to the lady in question. He once told me, I had a calming effect on him, and that if he managed to remember the sound of my voice when talking to a girl, he managed rather better. Um. Okay Oscar, if that is what it takes.

Close encounters

In 1988, Michael, Andrew, Aileen, and I spent a week in Harare. There was an equestrian event that lasted several days, with dressage and show jumping competitions. All of us entered horses, Andrew entered his pony, Sue, while Michael and I shared Thor, Aileen with her Arthur, and finally me with piebald Anthony. Four kids, four horses, great days. We spent hours every morning, dolling up our horses, making them look as pristine as you can manage with bush ponies. And we took every possible chance at entering competitions, cheering each other on, or just relaxing in the shade on the side lines and talking, and assessing the competition. It occurs to me today, that we were so hopelessly outclassed by all the Harare thoroughbreds (peoples and horses alike), but we simply did not care. Taking part was everything.

Michael and Andrew spent the nights with their parents in a camper van, while Aileen had arranged for the two of us to have lodgings at her Uncle's place, who had a farm on the outskirts of Harare. She slept in the family's guest room, and I slept in a caravan, right outside the family home. I was quite taken by surprise at being invited into the family like this, and I hope I showed it too. I remember baking a cake and bringing that.

In the evenings, after we had both had a shower off the dust and the horse-sweat, Aileen and I would spend hours sitting in her room, talking. Reviewing the day, going over the events, which horses has performed best, which competition was toughest. This would then turn into talking shop about school, discussing books that we appreciated. We spoke of our respective families and people who were important to us. There were stacks of magazines in the guest room, and we giggled about how much skin was exposed in some of the ads. Or what the ads were for. We discussed what we would do after graduation, about what kind of field we would go for after that, what we expected from life.

I suppose Aileen asking me, what I expected from a girlfriend was kind of "in your face." (She knew there was no one significant.)

The fact that I was biologically male, that I was sitting on the same bed, across from an attractive biological female, never even crossed my mind. Yes, Aileen was pretty. Attractive even, if you like girls really slim. She did not have much in the way of feminine curves (sorry Aileen), but the way she carried herself spoke volumes. Every once in a while, this did in fact cause quite the conflict in me. Because that part of my body that was male, *did* in fact react on occasion to the accidental brushing of bodies in the tight confines of the stables, or the companionable hand on the arm. But the part of my mind and my heart that was a girl was completely thrown off track by these biological reactions, longing for a hug from Dave. Ultimately, I was not at a point of where I could deal with my attraction for anyone. And, Nancy is pretty much asexual. For all the obvious reasons.

So I simply blended those feelings out.

On that particular evening, I gave it a lot of thought. Obviously, the weight of the topic was not lost on me. I told her how I considered trust and commitment to be things I looked for in a relationship (yes, at eighteen) and how I would like to share my time with someone with whom I have a lot in common. Common life's goals. We talked of that for quite a while, and then switched to the topic of having children and what we both hoped for. I summarised, that for the time being, school was really in the forefront of my mind. And that I would most likely be going back to Switzerland for my vocational training, whatever that would be. And that under these circumstances, I really did not want to start a relationship with someone whom I would have to abandon after graduation. That I did not think that to be fair to either of us. I think I surprised myself with that insight, but it was the unmitigated truth.

She was very thoughtful at that.

What I did not go into, was, that I was so completely and utterly confused about what my body did, and what my mind wanted. Did I want to make out? Yes, I did, or at least a part of me did. Sometimes with girls, but just as much with boys. But I was absolutely not ready to deal with the fact that I was bisexual. As a result, I hardly considered myself relationship-material. And I certainly was not boyfriend-material. I was altogether too worried about hurting someone, or about getting hurt myself, to have considered just experimenting for the sake of making the experience. And. Blending out my body was something I was good at.

To Aileen, I might perhaps have appeared incredibly innocent or just plain stupid. What certainly did not happen, was, that I made any kind of advances. If, at all, Aileen expected anything. If she was disappointed at being friend-zoned, she never showed it. She remained a very dear friend and loyal companion, always cheery and full of appreciation. Spending time with her was fun, enriching, and the easy kinship and the trust she gave me was a gift like few others.

Rumours

Back in Kwekwe High School, life went on as usual, but somewhere along the line, there must have been talk. Possibly about Shenaaz and my private conversation with her. Fairly certainly about Aileen and me. One week. At that farm. The two of us alone. About what happened. About what did *not* happen. Looking back, I think everyone expected Aileen and me to become a couple. That in turn *not* happening, might have triggered an entire new flood of rumours about whom, and what kind of person, I would be attracted to.

In retrospect, this must have caused Dave quite some anxiety. I can no longer place the exact time, but I remember the two of us sharing sandwiches while working on a science project on snake venoms. He supplied the reptiles, and I supplied the protein biology. Completely in passing, he dropped the innocuous question of "which girls I liked best". In my mind, I went through the rather short list of girls that would actually give me the time of day. There was Aileen, obviously, right there at the top. I named two or three of the girls I more or less knew from riding, and who would have a conversation with me. I mentioned Shenaaz, because, yeah, she was friendly. And of course I mentioned Andy, because despite the fact that we did not meet often in private, I really liked her.

Being me, I don't just rattle off the names, but expanded on why the particular lady has made the list. Attributes, like being friendly, being kind, being pretty. Dave is making approving noises or supplying comments like, "yeah, she's a beaut" or "what, really?"

His eyes go wide when I mentioned Shenaaz and I can see his thoughts crashing and piling up like toy cars. Okay? So, fantasising about making out with my White best friend is okay? But thinking about a girl from an Indian family is not?

Besides, Dave, I rather want to make out with you. But I'm obviously not about to tell you that, am I?

I decide to skip Grace altogether (sorry Grace) and talk about Andy. Everyone likes Andy, right? I mean, she is so friendly, considerate, and helpful. And she has the cutest freckles.

Dave almost drops his sandwich, "Whoa, Dude! NO! She is scaly! (Zim. Slang: disgusting). That girl's a goffel! (Zim. Slang, *highly* derogatory: person of mixed heritage)."

I gently, but very pointedly, inform Dave, that perhaps Andy deserves rather better than that. Seeing as that she's a sweet and endearing person, sincere and straightforward. And that her skin colour really said nothing about her qualities or her personality.

He muses for some moments, taken aback at my reaction. "Yeah, I suppose."

I can see that Dave is making a sincere effort to see things my way, and that he is actually aware, in that moment, of the magnitude of his own bias. Nevertheless, I don't think he will ever consider dating a person of colour.

In retrospect, telling the story is partially funny, because it was just so stereotype. But it did bring me up short. It re-emphasised blatantly just how casually racist, homophobic, and prejudiced the people I was spending time with were. Even my dear friend Dave, on whom I had such a crush.

Come to think of it, it was probably a good thing that Dave asked me which girls I liked, as opposed to which people I liked. I can totally imagine myself saying something entirely thoughtless, and outing myself (again) by accident. I think that would not have gone well either. Aside from this, I continued to blissfully ignore all rumours concerning my purported homosexuality.

All of this came to some sort of conclusion some months later.

As it happened, Dave met Stacy, and the hormones just flew. Stacy was a very attractive blonde, intimidatingly so. Plus, she was from a rather well to do family in Harare. To be honest, I was cautious around people as attractive (or well off) as that. My own previous experiences had shown that that kind of beauty often went hand in hand with arrogance and depreciation. My own bias, right there. But Stacy certainly disproved this. She was genuinely friendly and genial, very eager to get to know new people.

Stacy came to Kwekwe to visit relatives. If I remember correctly, she and Dave were introduced to one another at a garden party, organised by Oscar's parents. Who had actually intended for *their* son to "meet" Stacy. I was not there, but Michael and Andrew were, and they filled me in on what I had missed. Dave could be a real charmer if he put his mind to it. He was good at telling stories and rounding them up with a punchline. And he had absolutely no shame in letting on, that every so often, the joke was on him. It was one of those things I, too, admired so much in him. So, yeah: talking was Oscar's Achilles' heel. Add rum-and-cola to the equation, and I have no problems imagining how the remainder of the evening went.

It took some weeks before Dave and Oscar could sit down at a bar together, without taking it apart.

Dave was cute when he was enamoured. Very much a love-sick labradoodle, he would talk about Stacy endlessly. All of a sudden, my manly Dave was all mushy and talking of feelings and needing reassurance. And advice. I had to repeatedly remind him how I did not know Stacy any longer than he did, and that I really did not know her taste in sweets, or what kind of gifts she would appreciate. But I like to think I supplied him with sufficient common sense while his brains steeped in hormones.

Stacy was curious about everything Dave did, accompanying us to squash, to the cinema, to the bush. She gave the impression, she had not been in such close proximity to "the outback" yet, and she seemed rather anxious. Just the right thing for a manly gentleman to help her over all the rocks and obstacles. It made me wonder if she simply put on a show, so as to give Dave a reason to touch her.

I did my best to give them space as a couple, but Dave communicated, he was glad I was around. When I asked him about this, he turned redder than I had ever seem him. He confessed, that I had a calming, balancing effect on him. That my presence made it easier to talk to Stacy (huh, déja-vu). And, that as long as I was around, he would be in less danger of Stacy and him doing something, that might have far reaching consequences. And he was not sure how he, still being a student and with no means of earning a living or supporting a family, would stand muster of her parents. I gently reminded him that there were other options, such as latex products to be obtained at the pharmacy. However, Dave seemed to think that once they had crossed a certain threshold, there would inevitably be "results", whatever those might be. Well, I was certainly not going to push him to do anything rash, so we dropped the topic, and on many outings, I accompanied the two. Or, she would accompany Dave and me.

What does stand out is one very thoughtful conversation we had, Dave and I. We were out at Sebakwe River, just the two of us, paddling though the water in a canoe, enjoying the quiet, watching the birds. He sat at my back, so I could not see his face and vice versa.

Dave paused in his paddling, and said, how extremely grateful he was, to have found Stacy.

I was genuinely pleased and happy for him. Considering how elated it was obviously making him and how he was more at ease. And how I was certainly not going to *ever* let on *any* kind of hints that I felt rather more for him than friendship. So I just agreed, that yes, this was indeed very fortunate, and that Stacy was doing him a lot of good.

Dave said that it was more than just that. He said, how *our* close friendship and our hanging out all the time with each other, had led to the rumours that "we were a couple of homos". I could tell by the tone of his voice, that this troubled him deeply. And it did confirm, how at heart, Dave *was* a bit homophobic (polite understatement). He continued by emphasising, how he really enjoyed my company, how much he valued our companionship, and how he "didn't give two sh!ts about the rumours." But that they were really starting to get on his nerves. Dave elaborated on how he was grateful that I seemed not to be bothered. How he was more than just pleased to have found a girlfriend. He explained how on top of that, he was so relieved by how his being with Stacy proved to the world the rumours were untrue.

I was glad he did not see my grin then, and all I said was, "Well, there you go, then. All good."

And it was.

Farewells

1989 was a tense year in many respects. For one, I was going to be writing my A-Levels in November (sort of equivalent to the Baccalaureate or Abitur). So I spent a great deal of time prepping for that. When I was not studying, I was working off surplus energy with the horses, or hiking through the bush with Dave. Or chasing squash-balls with the boys.

My Dad noticed more than me, that the political climate had gotten progressively rougher in Zimbabwe. More and more successful farms and businesses were confiscated and "nationalised". There were accounts of violent transgressions on isolated farmsteads, regardless of the ethnicity of the farmers. Although being White rather upped the chances of being targeted. Ndebele were more or less openly being discriminated, as were the people of Indian origin. Students and trade unions were openly protesting against the increasing corruption and mismanagement, only to be heavily castigated by the police. People began moving their wealth, or whatever passed for wealth, out of the country. By whatever means possible, since transferring currency was illegal. People began leaving.

I still spent Saturday mornings with my Dad, going shopping for groceries. He would tell me of his week, and I would tell him of mine. We would speak to each other about the things that moved in our minds and in our hearts. I think he was very pleased, comforted that I had managed to form such strong connections.

Among the things he told me of, was, how he was responsible for interviewing and choosing artisans who were going to work in his department to up-keep and maintain the factory he was currently working at. My Dad is strict. But fair. He tested his applicants, people who had graduated civil- or technical engineering with flying colours, for their technical understanding and haptic expertise. He completely ignored the grades and more to the point, he completely ignored the party-membership papers that were included in the applications. He employed those who performed best in his assessments, and those usually proved to be good engineers. Or at least passable. Pleasing my Dad took dedication and skill.

Fact was, sometime mid-1989, my Dad got a letter from the state office, revoking his work permit and his residence permit, stating that he and his family had three days to settle any affairs and leave the country. Permanently. Some five months before I was to write my final exams. Apparently, one of the people whom he had refused a promotion, had spoken to a person whose application he had rejected. And in turn, this person spoke to a third person at the party office, accusing my Dad of being a racist malcontent (a brazen lie) and being critical of the government (absolutely true. But then my Dad was / is a free thinker, and critical of *any* government). Perhaps we should be grateful he got a letter? Considering what happened in more remote areas, it could have turned out just so much worse.

The Mackays immediately offered me board and lodgings until I should graduate. Which permitted me to sleep again. But who really saved our family, was Mr Sithole, one my Dad's closest friends. He was also a work colleague, and more importantly, he had a cousin (everyone has a cousin). This cousin turned out to be quite the heavyweight, with connections into parliament or executive legislation. This cousin was able to pull enough strings on my Dad's behalf, so as to revoke the eviction. Instead, my Dad was required to extend his work permit on a monthly basis. Not optimal, not easy, but feasible. So in the end, I was able to continue studying in relative peace, and graduate without worrying about needing to up and leave at a day's notice.

And graduate I finally did. All of a sudden, the day, that had so far always been hypothetical, was now very real and final. My Dad had arranged for me to stay with his sister's family, on the upper end of Lake Zürich. OMG, I was going to be drafted.

And all of a sudden, I was really making my goodbyes to all these people I had come to be so close with, some of whom I loved dearly, from whom I had learnt so much. Tensions or no, disagreements or unison, I had met people here who were able to take me for all I was able to be. "A quiet, thoughtful boy, with a quirky sense of humour. With a warm heart, and a winning smile." That was how I was described by one of the Moms of our equestrian society in her farewell-speech. They actually threw a huge party. With a barbeque and more cake than was sensible, with music and lights, heaven knows how they had organised that.

And two short days later, my Dad drove me to the airport in Harare, thoughtful and melancholy. This was it. His baby was leaving the nest. Ten thousand kilometres.

For my Dad, the political climate kept getting more tense. It was clearly time to move on. He had already been looking for alternatives. This was still before South Africa was to achieve a miracle, and peaceful transition into a democracy (well, close to a democracy anyways). So moving there was as yet out of the question. It would be another two, almost three years, before the referendum that finally ended the Apartheid Regime there. My Dad and Amahle would stay in Zimbabwe for another year, before my Dad would take on a position in Blantyre, Malawi. Ultimately, they would move back to Johannesburg, Amahle's hometown, and buy a house there.

For myself and for Nancy, it was the end of another age. I had perfected the art of disassociation and stealth. Of living one life in the presence of others, while the actual person I was, lived another life within myself. Of remaining true (to a degree) to who I was, while doing my best to be a valued and contributing member (what a ghastly ironic pun) to society. I had gotten good at blending in. And good at blending the two people whose lives intertwined.

And I had gotten so very good at blending out anything that threatened the balance of my soul.

(4) Being a Man

Decisions…

…we are all flying blind.

All of us.

Doing our best.

To base our decisions on our past experience,

on our best educated guess, of what future probability will bring.

We all have decisions we are happy with.

Choices we would easily make again.

And we all have choices that haunt our dreams.

And shape our future decisions.

So much of growing up, is learning to live

with your past choices.

So just days before Christmas in 1989, I returned to Switzerland. I was going to stay with my aunt's family, Lisbeth and her husband Walt, and their two boys Urs and Remo. Urs is a year younger than me, and Remo is two years younger than Urs. At this time, I got along more easily with Remo, who was simply quicker and more extroverted. Urs and I did get along well, but I found being with Remo easier. I dare say, this was because I needed to make less decisions on my part, and was able to stay more in the background. Urs simply needed, and to some degree still does, a bit more time to process, so spending time with him required me to show more of myself. Always a little difficult for me. But in the long run, Urs proved to be the more sincere and loyal.

The family lived in their own home, rather the exception in Switzerland, where nothing is as scarce and as expensive as real estate. Lisbeth and her family made me feel very welcome, I got to have my own room, and I shared a bathroom with the two boys. Truth be told, sharing a bathroom with two boys barely out of puberty was not exactly easy on my comfort zone, but I then neither were camel spiders.

Both parents worked a full time job, Walt was in the upper management of a construction firm, managing acquisitions or something. Lisbeth was a kindergarten teacher specialised in speech therapy. Remo was still in school, and Urs had started training as an artisan precision mechanic.

And I got drafted…

Attention to detail

It is said that a son learns to be a man from his father. Others say, you learn to be a man in the military. And of course there is the usual bovine faeces about becoming a man when you have sex for the first time.

In 1990, military service was an obligation all "men" in Switzerland went through. The only exceptions were youths with chronic impairments or disabilities. There was (is) a voluntary service for women based around the non-combat units, the reasoning being that women cannot justifiably be exposed to the ravages of war.

But men can? No, please do not answer that.

I knew this was coming, but it still threw me off the rails. I knew for the entire last year in Zimbabwe, that the moment I should settle on Swiss soil after the year in which I turn twenty, I would get drafted into the army. The irony of the whole thing is, in the year *after* I had done my training, I got to vote, that young men could opt for a civil service instead.

The Swiss: loath to change and distrustful to new things. Yup. Good natured people, but slow to accept, never-mind integrate new ideas. For all the watches they make, they sometimes seem to want to make time drag its feet.

Being in the army did not do me good. First and foremost was the chronic and extreme lack of sleep. I (we) got about five hours of sleep per night, and that was pushing my luck. Considering how we were handling firearms with live munitions, and doing all kinds of things, sensible people only attempt when well rested, and with several dry runs, or better yet leave well alone, I am grateful we did not have more accidents.

And, oh hey! Yes! More uniforms and short hair.

The testosterone laden atmosphere was like constant sandpaper on my nerves. So many people. No, I need to rephrase, so many alpha cis* men. And so many of them with either something to prove, dominance to assert, or a chip on their shoulder. Or all frikkin' three... ...heavens have mercy! There were veteran instructors (Men? Boys? Emotional cripples?!?) who made statement like "*It's not a proper training course unless there is a suicide*". And they were sincere about it. Congratulations, boys! What a way to serve your country.

I mean, I get it. In an environment, where your worth is measured entirely by how much mistreatment you can survive, and still continue to function as a corpse-, Whoops! sorry, corps member, I understand that you are going to pretend to be proud of being expendable. Pride and ruthlessness are your only protection against ridicule. And the blatant accusation that you are committing an atrocity against humanity and yourself. And the realisation, that ultimately, all the "glory" and "honour" will not spare you from facing your own demise *alone with yourself*.

The result of this was, that I kept as low a profile as I could. I continued what I had been doing at Kwekwe High School: I followed the rules and got my work done. I said as little as possible. Which was not hard. Most conversations went straight over my head, because I had not spent the last twenty years with my ears to the Swiss ground and I had no idea at all what was èn vogue, cool or just basic cultural mainstream.

And, no. I never was a part of the "buddy" world of cis-het* men.

I was lost.

The horrifying thing was, it was just so… …easy. All you had to do, was do what they told you. And I was fairly good at following instructions. Strength was never my forte, but I was easily more agile and coordinated than two thirds of these city kids. All those years of climbing trees and riding horses paid off. And I was good at watching people. Reading patterns. And, oh yes! I was good at cleaning gear! The result of all of this was, that I was actually quite good at playing soldier. Apparently to a degree, that all my efforts to go unnoticed failed dismally.

So not only was this easy, I also got positive feedback from my officers. For a while, I think I simply put off making any kind of decision to go forward with my own life, because I was so intimidated and out of my depth by the sudden change and getting acclimatised to Switzerland. Climate, obviously, was not the problem. But standing on my own two feet felt overwhelming. And realising that despite what my passport said, I was culturally disconnected to any of these people. Furthermore, in an environment where people were apparently conditioned to test how far they could push someone else before they broke, my conditioned reaction to ignore taunts or bullying and *not* show any reaction did not serve me well. I was so used to this being the case, I did nothing to change the situation. I was caught in a feedback spiral.

On a side note, remarkable how my beard suddenly grew dark. As if the change of climate and sunlight had thrown a switch.

On the same side note, I was forced to look at my body. For the first time in fourteen years. I had friction burns, scrapes, and injuries in the most unspeakable and stupid of places. Walking sixteen hours in a downpour can do all kinds of things to your skin, regardless of how close or how loose the pants you wear. To make all of this perfect, showers were not always to be had. And in order to take care of myself, in order to remain healthy and to keep functioning, I simply found no other way that to inspect my body for injuries and treat them. I was *not* a happy camper.

It was a very good thing the training ended after eleven months.

Mountains

To be fair, not all of it was bad. In the savannah coastlands of Dar es Salaam and in the semi-arid shrub-veldt of Zimbabwe, what I had honestly, truly missed, were "real" mountains. Rugged, towering cliffs, with snow-capped peaks. And "real" forests, with ancient, mossy trees, multi-coloured greens and reds, fragrant pines. Some of my fondest memories of my paternal Grandma, are spending entire afternoons roving though bracken and heather, picking wild raspberries and blueberries by the bucketful. So. Faced with the inescapable requirement of military service, I volunteered for the alpine specialists, something rather unpopular, because it was rumoured to be physically so much more strenuous and demanding than other specialist troops.

About a third of our company were experienced hikers, climbers, and alpinists, and from them, I learnt a lot. By that I mean, I learnt stuff you could actually apply in your "normal" life. What I lacked in strength, I made up with sheer will and perseverance. I like to think, that quite got their attention, and I dare say, they respected that. Our instructors in these techniques were civilians, professional mountain guides and nature-reserve wardens. These guys lived and breathed the mountains in all their moods and weather conditions. Which was a huge alleviation, because they were usually quite mellow and easy going. Their primary concern was getting people through the mountains alive, not breeding ruthless soldiers. And as I said, climbing was in my blood, be it trees or rocks. I was actually quite proud, when one of instructors looked at me at incredulously, and asked if I had breakfasted on a tube of adhesive.

So, yes, I got to climb mountains, secure myself with ropes, ski across glaciers, climb frozen waterfalls, rappel down cliff-faces, rescue people buried by avalanches, do all kinds of cool stuff. I learnt all about the gear required, and how to use and maintain it.

And in retrospect, it was *this*, that permitted me to come to some kind of terms with this body of mine. I managed to accept, at least for the time being, that my body was not what I felt at home in. Had I been able to choose, I would still have opted for being equipped to bear children, without a second thought. But overall, I suppose, I was issued with a pretty versatile and serviceable (puns intended?) model.

Just do not ask me about showers. Seriously? Showering with twenty to thirty other naked cis* males? Or worse. Showering with three cis* males. The worst thing to happen is when you miss the point where most are done, and you are still rinsing shampoo out of your eyes. And all of a sudden, you realise, you are just one of four people. Perhaps it was my imagination, but I kept feeling glances and… …whenever I could, I chose to shower when everyone else was already done and dressed. Procrastinating was easy. All you needed to do was volunteer to clean extra gear. Which brought with it, that the water was usually kind of lukewarm to cold by the time I got to shower.

And of course, there were glances. Oh, hell yes! There were rumours. Because what I was *not* able to disguise, was my body language. The way I picked my way over rocks. The way I picked up equipment. Probably even the way I inched through elbow deep mud under live fire. Or perhaps it was my uniform? As the weeks went by, all my colleagues' uniforms had food spots, grease stains, mud splashes, grass burns. My commanding officer at some point got quite irate how my uniform always seemed so pristine in comparison, and had me crawl through puddles every once in a while, just to prove that he could. Wearing filthy clothes just did not sit with me. Never mind the fact that clean clothes actually kept in the warmth so much better. Well worth the hour of sleep I sacrificed to get clean again.

There was one incident that was odd. Looking back, the situation is almost comic, but I certainly did not find it funny at the time. We slept fifteen to a dorm. I was usually so fatigued that I simply crashed into my bunk, in every sense of the word, oblivious to the snores and other biological sounds of the others. It was one of those rare evenings that we had "off," as in, we were free to leave the grounds, partake dinner when and where we chose.

For most, evenings like these were an opportunity to have a supper in a restaurant, ensuring that food was not just edible but palatable. For many it was opportunity to drink themselves to the brink of being legless. For me it was a chance at a tranquil meal in our dorm room, and I did not have to wolf my food. And more than six hours of sleep. Bliss.

I wake up because there is someone touching me.

My mind is cloudy, and I just want it to stop. I need it to stop. I need to sleep.

But it doesn't. Ice cold realisation floods me. There are hands travelling over my body. Before I can react, a hand closes around my ankle and drags me straight off the bed. I crash onto the floor. A detached part of my mind thinks, "That's going to leave a bruise."

I feel myself being dragged in the direction I where I intuitively know the door to be. I am scrabbling to hold on to anything.

Yes. I *screamed* like a girl.

There are scuffles. Shouts. Someone hit the lights. I fight to disentangle myself from the blankets and I look up at my assailant. He is huge. Towering, and probably three times my weight. I am actually sobbing. I am trying as hard as I can to hold it together, but I fail. Any pretence of being a grown man is out the window. I am tired, I do not want to be here. I am frightened. Of this man. So I cry. Like a lost child.

It turned out to be a recruit from another group.

It's as if he wakes from a stupor. He has this kind of kicked-puppy-look as he takes in all the angry young men around him and me sobbing on the floor. He lets go of my foot. Despite my terror, it flashes though my mind, how completely at odds this expression is with his intimidating size. I can tell immediately, that he is drunk beyond rational thought.

He sways slightly. I catch how he mumbles, "Sorry. Go back to sleep." He lifts me bodily, like I weigh nothing. Like a damsel, one arm under my shoulders and the other under my legs, he carries me over to the bed. His breath reeks! Almost tenderly, he plops me onto the sheets. He actually pats me on the head and then shambles out the door.

Eggensberg and Schmid (two of my team mates) come over and ask if I am okay. I assure them, "I am fine, thank you." More than anything, I just want to be invisible. As if to prove everything is chill, I fetch my blanket which is still lying on the floor, and set about getting back to sleep.

And that was all there was to it. No apology, no explanation, not even an acknowledgement. Nobody spoke of what happened the next morning. I certainly did not report it. What was I going to say?

I saw the young man a number of times. He had either an authentic alcohol induced memory gap, or he concealed any kind of intentions or even recognition well. Regardless, I made sure to keep out of the way of him and his buddies. Luckily, they were easy to track. Their sheer size and the level of noise with which they were present, made them easy to avoid. And it might have been my imagination, but I had the impression Eggensberg and Schmid (Michael and Stefan?) took turns in looking out for me. That was an entirely novel experience.

A key moment

To understand this, you need to know that the Swiss federal railroads are an integral part of the culture. Switzerland has one of the best, most reliable and most extensive rail systems worldwide. The Swiss take this for granted, because that is what they grow up with. And, you need to know that the Swiss railroads and the military system are closely interwoven.

There is a marvellous thing about uniform. If in Switzerland you ride the public transport, say the railways, in a military uniform, you are *invisible*. I cannot say if that is still the case today, but in the 1990ies, that was certainly true. If you sat by yourself, you would be ignored so completely by all the other passengers, to the point that you melted into the background. Of course there were recruits that travelled in groups. These packs were (are?) usually accompanied by *loud* music and copious amounts of beer. So, no, of course that rule did not uphold for groups. But if you travelled alone, you became a part of the scenery.

It was one of the occasions, where I had the weekend "off," and I was travelling home to by rail, home in this case being my cousins' place. It was Friday night, after eleven, and I was finally on my last stretch. I used every opportunity to sleep, because regardless of how much sleep I got in the weekends, it was never enough.

This is one of those surreal scenes, that you normally only get on dreams or in movies. The train stops. People get off, people get on. The train is close to empty.

The wagons of the Swiss federal rail are divided into open compartments by double benches, back to back. Each compartment seats four. I was leaning against the backrest, with my feet in socks, stretched out across the gap on the opposite bench. I could have occupied just one bench, but then I would have had the armrest in the small of my back. This way, I could stretch out fully, more or less comfy, and it was way easier to sleep like that.

The train stops again. I wake. A couple enters, probably just a little older than me. Body language implies, they want to sit themselves on the bench where I have my feet. Wordlessly I shift, giving the bench free.

They are lost in their own little universe, those two. Do they even realise I am there? I watch for a while in the reflection of the window. At first I think, "Cute, fresh couple, new love." But after some seconds, I realise that, no, these two are too familiar, too much at ease with each other. And yet there is…

…I am so deeply, deeply touched. There is something so gentle and endearing, about the way he treats her. About the way he touches her. Always fussing, always caressing. Not sexual. Just… …caring. And she obviously feels absolutely secure in his arms, the way she relaxes into caress. Completely at peace. Happy. Radiant…

Okay, I should have caught that. How protectively he is caressing her tummy.

The moment passes. I let them have their privacy and I drift back to sleep. When I wake again, we are rolling into the station. They are getting up to leave. I check the station. Another half hour to go.

The complete serenity and the sense peace, the sense of fulfilment the two of them radiated, left a deep impression. Just *how* deep, I was to discover more than two years later. For now, I was happy to have witnessed the glow of their harmony, and just let it slip away.

Some months later, training ended.

Lucky for me, somebody decided I was not officer material. And you can take your pick. Whether someone thoughtful had recognised, that I was actually just going through the motions, that I would never actually scream at other people, because I had doubts as to whether crawling through the mud was indeed fortifying for the character? Or whether some someone decided that I was "gayer than a hatter's party" and way too much of a wimp to ever survive the rigors of officer training?

Whatever it was, I am grateful.

Self-determination

The first thing I did when I was discharged was that I let my hair grow out. This was actually the first time in my life so far, that I was able to self-determine anything. And I got my ears pierced. Both of them. No half-measured "left-is-right" (in Switzerland in the 1990ies, it was fashionable for men to wear a stud in the left ear. It was important that it be the left. Otherwise, you were gay). I wore a stud in both my ears, and I could not have cared less what that did or did not imply. Or did I?

That was the easy part. The hard part was, that this really was the first time I needed to rely entirely on my own wits and inclinations. Of course, my Dad and I had spoken about and planned what I was going to do. I was going to apply for techno-logical engineering (like him), but I was going to go into a different direction. What we also both knew, was that getting my A-Levels acknowledged in Switzerland was going to be a bit of a challenge. This was before the term globalisation had evolved to include education, certificates, and diplomas. Still, I applied at the Eidgenoessische Technische Hochschule (federal polytechnic college).

As it turned out, I was required to pass an entry exam. And while I might have passed mathematics and physics, I had never had geometrical-technical drawing in school, and so I flunked that. Pretty badly too. Lisbeth, my aunt, was helpful in that she encouraged me to broaden my options. And so I applied for both engineering and biology at the university of Zürich. And while biology was laughably easy, I flunked the exam in history that I was required to take. European history. I could have said some things about the colonisation of Africa, and how the construction of the railroad had contributed to that. But the routes taken by Napoleon, or the repercussions of Iron deposits in western Germany were a mystery to me.

Things went downhill from there.

Looking back I can see clearly how my dependency on Lisbeth's good will, and both our increasing frustration, led the deterioration of our communication. I think it was partially the way she worded it, combined with the fact that my own self-esteem and self-security were out the window. She had all kinds of expectations, I am sure she wanted to see me thriving and independent. Secure and settled. And yet, to Lisbeth, the entire concept of raising children by enabling what is good, instead of pointing out faults and flaws, was foreign to her. Fact was, Lisbeth was good at mak-ing me feel inadequate and useless. And possibly unwelcome. Today, I believe she was trying her best to get me "on the right track." But her suggestions of me going for the accounting and business sector had the feel of a "quick-fix" solution. And that led to my feeling depreciated and unaccepted. I imagine she too saw my retreat into my-self as something of a rejection.

I was overwhelmed by the shift in culture, and readapting just took longer than anyone was willing to give me time for. I believe, the biggest problem was, that I *looked* as if I belonged. I spoke the dialect. I passed as Swiss. But I was a foreigner.

The fact that my plans for university were not going to realise themselves did not improve my outlook. I had *no* friends. I had *no* connections beyond my aunt's family. Yes, there was Evangeline, but I could not just up and stay with her, that would solve nothing. Even I recognised that. On top of all that, the eleven months in the army had been really harsh on the girl that I was. I felt out of place. I was isolated. I felt unwanted. I felt trapped, my nerves were raw. So I did what I am good at: I withdrew emotionally. Of course, that did nothing to improve matters, but I was really not coping.

For a while, I entertained the idea of doing something with horses. I like to believe I have a natural talent for handling them, and riding was something I truly enjoyed. However, in Switzerland, owning horses was prohibitively expensive. This is closely connected to the fact that land is one of the most scarce resources, and if you did not inherit a farm, then you might as well hope in the lottery. Or be a CEO of a bank. Or better yet, be the significant other of the CEO, with infinite time on your hands and personnel to take care of your routine (yes, sorry, my own prejudice right there. But, based on experience). Riding was very clearly an exclusive and elite sport, only for the *haute volée*. And since I owned neither horses nor land, any way of making a living that way was an illusion.

Being a trainee

From sheer lack of visible alternatives, I got vocational counselling. I think the lady who spoke with me was just a little overwhelmed by the multitude of facets, influences (and neuroses) that I brought to her office. But she did seem to have a sixth sense, that I was emotionally at my limit, and that I needed some kind of outlet. Two good things came of this.

One: she gave me a phone number of a friend of hers at the Art College of Zürich. Policy of the Art College was, that if courses were not full up with regular students, then the vacancies would be offered up to public participation. This particular friend worked in administration of the courses offered there, and she got me placed in an evening class. Normally, these courses would have cost more than I earned with my entire trainee's salary, but being a trainee provided that I was able to take part to rates that I could afford. This was probably one of *the* best things to happen to me.

For the next seven years, I would be spending one to three evenings per week in varying art classes, where I came into contact with a wide spectrum of basic techniques and interpretive depiction. And of course, I met a broad variety of unique and extremely talented people, all of whom enriched my life immensely.

Two: the lady from vocational counselling was able to provide me with alternatives, perspectives on how to get my existence sorted out, and what to do for a living. She described and recommended several artisanal or medical professions I should look at, and provided me with pointers as to where I might apply for training. Carpentry I rejected immediately, I did not think I was physically strong enough.

Physiotherapy or being a nurse was something I could imagine myself doing, so I went and looked at those. From there, I happened on the profession of laboratory assistant in the medical field, and this *really* struck a chord. It reminded me of all the things we had looked at in school during practical lessons, the project on snake venom I did with Dave. And here was the chance to "do it properly." I applied for a placement in several clinics, but perchance, one of the placements was at the polytechnic where I had previously applied, and that turned out the stroke of luck I needed. I started training as a laboratory technician in neurosciences and molecular biology.

The department of neuroscience turned out to be a very good place for me. Maybe half of the PhD students were Swiss, perhaps a third German, and the remainder came from all over the world, Hungary, Britain, former Yugoslavia, several from China. Communication happened in a colourful mix of languages, and if that failed, hands and feet. I was passed around between a French post-doc, one German, and a US American. We were three trainees for technical assistance, Francesca, Tommy, and me. We got on like a house on fire, creating all kinds of mischief on the university grounds, going hiking together with some of the younger students, or going out together in Zürich.

It was Harper that I had the closest rapport with. He was a Canadian post-doc, with a sense of irony and dark humour, sharper that a shadow at high noon. Beyond that, he was a deeply empathic and caring man, devoted to his wife, Artemisia, and their two toddler daughters. We shared many coffee breaks, and even dinners, talking and sharing thoughts, particularly over people, relationships, and love. I remember a conversation between Harper and me on one of our coffee breaks. He was telling me of Artemisia, his wife, and how their relationship had grown ever deeper, "you know, it took time to find the right ways to talk. I mean *really* talk". Harper also painted in his spare time, and he encouraged me enormously in my pursuit of art, so that too was a regular topic.

Another close friend was Miriam, a PhD student. A lively redhead from Dresden, who prided herself on being an independent woman, wild, impulsive, and predictably unpredictable. Or possibly the other way around. At some point, we our conversations took a turn to common interests, and I let on that I was keen on dancing lessons, but never got around to going for lack of a partner. She straight up asked if we I would be willing partner up with her, simply for enjoyment and fun of moving to music. I was surprised, since I knew she had a boyfriend, but she simply explained that away with, "He doesn't dance". We went dancing together for about five semesters, getting really good at it too, and this firmly founded my love for dancing, particular to Latin music.

So yes, the multicultural environment was exactly the thing to permit me to feel at home, while the actual training itself proved to be the right mixture of requiring focus and accuracy, with creative adaptive thinking.

To give Lisbeth and Walt credit, they waited until I had a contract for training and some sort of income, before they asked me to look for lodging elsewhere.

Free falling

Gradually, I found my rhythm. Time I used to spend on horseback, in squash courts, or in the bush, I now invested in art school. Or in spending time with Evangeline and René, and their daughter Seraphina. Bern became something of a home away from home for me. Evangeline continued to be my safe place, the person I could go to if I was troubled or out of sorts. She was (is) observant and mindful of so many influences. A patient listener and an impartial mentor, providing her own view of things without imposing. She was and remains today, one of the few people capable of providing critical feedback, whilst still showing all her appreciation and love for a person. In this case, me, because as much as things fell into place concerning my immediate existence in this male role, the girl in me was very much discomforted and searching for ways to express herself.

Incidentally, René also played quite the role in my choice of profession. He was (now retired) a graphic designer / artist / musician and he is a patient and talented artisan. I was lost in admiration, of the care and devotion with which he restored an ancient cello to its former glory. Since I was rubbing elbows with so many talented people at Art College, I did entertain the idea that I could go in the direction of design or creating jewellery for a living. He was gentle and mindful, when he cautioned me, that being creative for a living did in fact drain much of the joy and satisfaction from the professions, and that it was a *very* hard road to follow. I think René realised how I disliked being dependent, and did his best to make me realise that talent, diligence and passion, were in no way a guarantees for success. He showed me how in the world of art, more than in most other fields, you were dependent on the whims and expectations of others.

Seraphina was every bit as much my sister as Eirian, and I loved (love) her dearly. I like to think she adored me at least as much, and we spent days making figures from horse-chestnuts, painting on paper, or each other, collecting pretty stones or just watching the animals along the Aare River that flows through Bern.

I spent not quite as much time with Eirian, despite the fact that Evangeline lived an hour's train ride away, and my Mum was more or less around the corner. But my mother was still my mother, always with multiple projects scheduled, and I still had problems finding common ground with her. This improved the older I got. The more self-assured and the more independent I became. The more I felt myself capable of drawing up my own boundaries and naming my own terms to which I would spend time with my Mum. Eirian was a sweetheart, and I like to think that she too, adored the person she saw as her older brother. We too spent hours in Francesco's workshop playing board games, or sifting through spare parts, admiring marbles, or drawing.

I came to genuinely love Zürich. It was so multicultural that I almost forgot that most people spoke Swiss dialect. There were expositions and performances, there were a multitude of cinemas, playing anything from mainstream to art-genre movies, there were concerts and events, platforms offering all kinds of exchange. Zürich was and remains today one of Switzerland's hottest melting pots with all the up-sides and down-sides that this brings with it. A conglomerate of traditional "olde-towne" dating back to before the romans, fused with an ultra-modern, so as to be almost cyberpunk.

As part of training, Francesca, Tommy, and I went to a vocational school. We were put on a class together with people training to be medical laboratory assistants, who worked in clinic laboratories. This also meant that a number of the professors who lectured us were medical doctors actively providing health services in hospitals, and I found that to be enormously interesting. Most of the things they taught us, I found to be a direct extrapolation of the biological background that I had acquired in my years at Kwekwe High.

There was a slight bit of friction between the scholars in our vocational centre. There was quite the competition between the different clinics, which had the best graduated, highest number of best performing graduates, etc. So we were kind of the odd ones out, both in the content of our training as in how we seemed to be treated by our supervisors. We did our best not to permit that to get any leverage, and every so often, we would go to the movies or cafés, some five or six of us. And that is how I got to meet Nathalie.

Nat and I got on quite well. She was a wild one, and non-conformity was a way of life for her. Quite the feat, considering how conservative and strict some of those clinics were. The fact that I openly questioned systems and organisations, made it easy to talk and spend time. At some point, I mentioned that I was looking for accommodation, and she suggested sharing a flat to split the rent. I was rather anxious about getting out of the situation with Lisbeth, which had gotten increasingly tense, so I agreed.

To be honest, I was probably not paying attention to the right things, or perhaps I would have realised, Nat had ulterior motives. I was completely taken by surprise when she seduced me. Looking back, it was a strange companionship. The simple fact that someone would not just accept me as a flat-mate and a friend, but also find me fun, attractive, desirable, whatever. It overwhelmed me with a flood of feelings that I was unable to stem or even properly identify, never mind deal with. On top of that was the complete and utter confusion, that this male body of mine clearly signalled, "oh WOW, is this cool or what! Can we do that again?" And I think Nat revelled in that too.

Despite this, despite the fact that outwardly I lived the life of a cis-het* male, Nancy was still very much present. And despite the fact that she was a silent observer, she influenced a great deal in my behaviour and in my choices. Particularly my choice of clothing. Shopping with Nat was an interesting and fun experience. Not that she was particularly helpful, but she seemed to enjoy watching me pick through clothes and choose for myself. I dressed myself exclusively in the ladies' departments. Not that anyone could tell. Everything I wore was unisex. But for myself, for Nancy, I knew it was ladies' clothing, and that sort of soothed my need for expression. Nat did not seem to mind, on the contrary, I think she found it to be delightfully subversive and non-conforming.

Nat shared a horse with a close friend of hers, and she went riding regularly. When she was not playing drums in a band. I got on well with one of her friends, but the remainder of the equestrian people were… …stand-offish. People, with whom I decided, I did not want to spend time with.

For about a year, this worked rather well. I was more or less free to plan my own week (aside from my vocational training, obviously). So I went to art classes regularly, and at least once a month, I would spend a weekend with my families. Nevertheless, Nat and I had lots of touch-points and we enjoyed each other's company.

That is not to say, all of this was always easy, or without episodes of tension. Non-conformist or not, Nat *was* jealous of any time I spent apart. Evangeline and Seraphina, Eirian and my Mum. Art classes, those in particular. Which is odd, because I never got to meet her bandmates or listen to a concert. She did not want that. Yes, strange, but she prevented conversation from going there, too. Every time I announced I was going to spend a weekend with either of my sisters, she reacted with withdrawal and passive aggression. Sometimes not so passive. And, yes, I did invite her along, which she declined. She asked about what I did at the Art College, but if I did tell her (and I was probably quite enthusiastic about it), she reacted with depreciation and belittlement. As impulsively fun and spontaneous as she could be, there were episodes where she was every bit as aggressive and vicious. Which in turn triggered my conditioned reflex to emotionally withdraw myself. My way of dealing with her passive aggression was to stone-cold ignore it.

Work was (mostly) fun, spending time with colleagues was cool and I learnt so much more than plain laboratory analysis. Time with Nat was sizzling. In good ways, or in not so good ways. Time with my Families in Bern (Evangeline's family) or in Zürich (Eirian) was soothing and sweet. Time at art school was so, so broadening and enriching. Life was, by and large, good.

Moments of truth

It was not a sudden thing. There was no flash of blinding light, more of a slow, gentle rosy dawning of warmth. Spending time with Seraphina and Eirian, watching the two of them marvel at the world. It permitted me to rediscover so much that was beautiful and miraculous about this planet of ours. Watching Evangeline with her Seraphina, seeing her hug her daughter and laugh, watching them play and learn.

Okay, I lied. Partially. The memory of the young couple on the train with the pregnant lady smacked me upside the head like a bucket-full of water. Warm, rose-and-lavender scented water.

I want this. For myself. I want to be a Mom.

I want a child of my own. SO VERY MUCH. I want someone to cuddle like that, to care for. Someone to take by the hand and guide first floundering, stumbling steps through the world. I want to have the opportunity to teach what I have learnt. And to show someone the beautiful multitude of miracles in this world. I want to make someone laugh like that.

And. I want someone (a man?) to touch me like that man caressed his wife / girlfriend. Someone whom I would trust unconditionally. To be able to lose myself in someone's embrace like that.

And of course, I realised.

That is not going to happen. NOTHING on this planet, will give me the gift to bring a child into this world. EVER. I will never feel life growing inside me.

The realisation and the acceptance, that I needed to *choose* between being a parent at all, or being myself, was something I hid from myself exceptionally well. As a result, there was never a moment of clarity, of looking in the mirror and saying out loud, "I am trans* gender, I need to face this." Instead, I kind of slid into the role of presenting myself as cis-het* until I no longer questioned this myself. My lives, that of Nancy and that of the man who wore my shoes, not so much drifted apart. In retrospect, it was more of a deference on Nancy's part. A realisation, that if she were to ever be a part of any kind of family, then she would have to step into the background.

And being in the background… …I was good at that.

Until there *WAS* a moment of clarity. Nat and I were experts at living for today. I forget how we came be discussing plans for a future. Probably, we started out with speaking of upcoming exams and, at some future date, graduation. The point is, I did ask her, what she actually expected from the future. And I indicated, that at some point in my life, I did in fact see myself with child. Better yet, children. I think Nat looked at me as if I had hit her. She made it absolutely clear that she would have no part in any plans involving children.

For a while, things went on as usual. But in the back of my mind, Nat's statement sat with a finality that brought me up short. And to be honest, the disdain and the disgust in her voice, as she said she would never have children, was something I projected onto myself. It is also possible that she did the projecting. Either way, justified or not, I was deeply hurt.

Until finally, we had a quarrel that simply exploded. As in the past, it started out with the time I spent in art classes, and the final trigger seemed to be, that I shut down if Nat got abusive. This time, it escalated to the point where Nat actually threw a bookshelf at me. How do you throw a bookshelf at someone? You start with the books, and when the shelves are empty, you throw those. That was the point where I decided that there was no future in this for me.

Within ten days, I had found myself another single room flat and I moved out. I am grateful beyond word for my Dad's (financial) support, without which this would not have been possible.

And this was an incentive, to focus on what I was doing. And for the time being, I rather enjoyed being entirely free in my choices. I took on one more art class. I went dancing with Miriam every Friday. Ours was completely platonic friendship and I appreciated her companionship immensely. Her boyfriend did not dance, but he did join our little group for movies and dinner every once in a while, and he did not seem to mind me going dancing with his lady. Heavens knows what she told him.

Looking back, I guess for most people I was a quiet, reflected young man. Dedicated to my training, getting top grades. Creative in my art classes. Appreciated by my friends. I believe a fair number of people thought I was gay (at the time, things like questioning, or fluid, or even bisexual, were not widely known options).

Skin off my back

There is a department store chain in Switzerland which offers all kinds of things, from foods through stationary, sports equipment, hardware, household appliances. And clothes. Mainly good quality for fair prices. It was (still is) one of my favourite shopping venues where I would get clothes. From the ladies' department.

I would wander through the department, checking out the clothes hanging off the racks and stacked on the shelves, looking out for tops and jeans that might suit me. I tried to pick times when there were few people about. The last thing I wanted, was to make ladies uncomfortable, or to make them think I was a creep. I would pick some items, check if I was being watched, and when nobody was looking my way, I would disappear into one of the fitting booths. Having Nat with me had been easier, because she would fetch another size if I needed it, but I was quite capable on my own. The cashiers might have had one or two quizzical looks, but they never questioned my choices. I was (am) particularly lucky in my size of shoes. While I require the more larger end of feminine foot-wear, my sizes are usually readily available. I always made sure that anything I chose was not too plainly lady-like or girls' clothing, and overall, I dressed in a way bordering on the unobtrusive gothic. With that, I had the impression, I was good at melting into the background.

Not so on this day, obviously. To this day, I have no idea whatsoever what precipitated events. I have speculated that I might have been observed trying on clothes that were clearly women's. Ultimately, it does not matter.

I am leaving the department store. My mind is still sifting through tops, feeling materials, weighing choices, deciding on which jeans to get. Calculating on what I can afford on my trainee's salary.

The summer dusk is mellow and inviting, the first stars are out. I unlock my bike and swing myself on. The sound of my tyres on the packed sand track and the wind in my ears is familiar. There are clouds of insects dancing around the lights along the cycle track.

I have not gone far. Barely out earshot from the main entrance. I see figures at the side of the cycle track. I pay them no mind, and deviate slightly to give them a berth.

It happens too fast for me to react. What is he doing?!? A hand reaches for my handlebars.

I fly straight over, rolling to prevent damage. I am confused. Angry. I raise myself on my hands, wanting to get up, wanting to shout at the man.

His boot catches me square under my chin. The sheer shock of it makes my ears ring. I curl up like a foetus.

"Schwuchtel, kranker Hurensohn, Arschficker, Missgeburt..." (fag, diseased son of a prostitute, arse-f*cker, freak)

All I see are combat boots. Each syllable is punctuated with a kick. There are three silhouettes, maybe four. I shield my face as best I can. I have no idea if I am screaming. I taste blood and acid. I try to crawl away and shield my face at the same time. There are hands pulling at my legs.

The world explodes in shreds of red melting white.

And stops...

The world is blinding light. The sheer intensity of it goes through my head like a spike of steel. Gradually my eyes adjust, and with it, I grow aware of a horrible weight pressing on my chest. Breathing hurts. The spike through my head dulls to a throb that pulses in my left jaw. There is a permanent high-pitched whine in my ears.

I am thirsty.

Voices. Swiss. Memory KICKS in.

I yank my arms up to shield my face. The movement drives a renewed spike right through my skull. The world re-dissolves in white.

At some point I was awake enough to properly take in my surroundings. The world was indeed white. I was prone on a hospital bed with an IV drip hanging from a rail. The weight on my chest were bruised ribs, possibly cracked.

A nurse, also in white, tried as patiently as she could to explain that I was in hospital, and that I should try not to move my jaw. She said it was lucky I wore a bicycle helmet. That I was fortunate not to have lost all my front teeth. That it was a happy coincidence, that I had been found by a couple talking a walk.

She said it would probably be a while before I would be able to ride a bike again.

Can you tell from the shape of a bruise what caused it? In movies, the detectives are always so deductive and intuitive. The hospital staff wrote it off as a bicycle accident. I never did anything to rectify that. I simply did not dare to. After all, what was I going to say? A number of men? The exact number of which I was incapable of narrowing down? Men whom I did not know? Who attacked me for reasons I could not rationally explain? Possible because they had seen me trying on clothes in the ladies' department?

I had no faith in any system to keep me safe. On the contrary, I was deeply afraid that the hospital personnel would recognise my clothes as women's. The fact that they failed to add up the dots that my injuries drew, made me feel even more alone and insecure. And my experiences, as a stranger in the country of my birth, cautioned me to silence.

Still, I needed to do something to keep myself safe. So that was when I started taking self-defence classes. And I became so much more discreet about when and how I shopped. How I presented myself.

And the woman I was, retreated another few steps into the background.

Choices

I graduated from my training as a laboratory technician, and that felt immensely good. And yet, I had acquired all this theoretical medical background in the three years of vocational school, to which I had no practical connection. And which I felt would go to waste if I did not somehow make the most of it. So directly after my graduation, I seamlessly started my next training to earn a bachelor's degree in clinical analytics.

All the hospitals I sent my application to declined, saying I was already trained, they did not see the need, they wanted to give younger people a chance. Ultimately, I applied at the faculty for clinical diagnostics of the University of Zürich, which was not directly part of a hospital, so that was not my first choice. It is deeply ironical how my military service contributed to securing me this training position. The professor who offered me the contract, confessed some two years later, that I was not his first choice either. Quite to the contrary.

The Prof in question was Swiss military old school. At my graduation, and after two glasses of champagne, he addressed our team in excellent humour. He told us, of how his first impression of me, with my ponytail, had been, that I was a "Weichei"

(German; lit. soft-boiled-egg. Work it out, it is not hard). How he had in fact forgotten all about my interview, and how all he had truly wanted, was to get rid of me as fast as possible. Nevertheless, out of pure politeness, he asked me where I came from, and what I had been doing so far.

So I gave him a very compact version of my school-years in Africa, and how I had trained as a Lab-Tech, and that I needed a trainee position in the medical analytics. This really got his attention, and he actually sat down to listen. It turned out, he had a co-op project running with people working in the Serengeti (Tanzania), concerning lions which were dying from distemper, caught off domestic dogs. When I finally told him, that upon returning to Switzerland, I had spent my first year in service, his jaw more or less dropped. He self-depreciatingly recalled, how he had thought to himself, that this young man with the ponytail could on no account be a "Weichei", particularly not since I had served with the alpine specialists. And that he decided there and then, that he was prepared to move mountains to secure a training position for me. I think this was the one time, that I profited from all the toxic male bovine faeces.

The department of clinical analysis was another cool and enriching place. Of course I spent some thirty hours a week, learning about routine metabolite and enzyme diagnostics. Aside from this, my previous training gave me the chance to assist one of the PhD students in his work, permitting me to get more in-depth experience in molecular biology, which would later prove to be highly beneficial. These were the years where HIV research was cutting edge. In the same department, there were projects running models for vaccines and anti-viral medications, and I got to contribute to those too.

On a side note, for the five, soon six years I had been back in Switzerland, I kept a continuous contact by mail to the Mackay family. (Yes, actual pen-on-paper mail. Private e-mail was as yet in evolution, Face-Book and WhatsApp were a generation away.) After a letter describing my enthusiasm for HIV research and how this would hopefully contribute to alleviating at least some of the problems in Africa, any return mail ceased. For a while, I continued writing letters, always slightly more sad about not getting any reply. Until finally, I remembered my conversation with Dave while we were working on the snake venom project together, and his asking me not to mention this to his family…

I was really upset about that, but it did make me re-analyse my feelings and my core beliefs. Again, I concluded that living conditions of *everyone* on this planet would improve, if more people had fair and affordable access to clean resources, education, equal opportunities. And medical care. People and, by proxy, animals. Take the existential fear and stress off people, take away the pressure of constantly scrabbling for resources. Give them an opportunity to develop freely and determine their own future. And they come up with the concept that *OTHERS beside themselves have rights too*. And it confirmed my conclusion, that my contribution to this was that I would do my best to find ways to improve medical care.

It was also in the department of clinical diagnostics that I met Rafet. Rafet was (is) a compact and highly energetic young man. Smallish (almost a head shorter than me) and beautifully muscular, with a buzz cut. He always gave the impression as if he had had at least five coffees in as many minutes. Able to talk faster than I could interject, contagiously cheerful. Behind the cheerful mask was a thoughtful, kindly, sometimes melancholy young man, who was deeply troubled by the requirements of his parents. Particularly his Persian father, who expected (demanded) Rafet to live up to his example of financial and social success.

He was a fellow student, and we turned out to be thick as thieves, working hand in hand, studying together, or organising reagents or hardware if they were not available. Goofing off during coffee breaks, Rafet and I shared our appreciation of ironic humour of the darker kind. There was always a newspaper available during breaks, and together with Susan, our other fellow student, we would study the movie line-up, or whatever else was on offer by way of culture and entertainment. We went to the cinema as often as five times a month, mostly just the three of us, sometimes accompanied by other colleagues. Usually we were unanimous in our choices, but every so often, we would go watch something that surprised us.

Also, Rafet and I would go hiking in the mountains occasionally, sharing our love for the great wide wild open and just freeing ourselves from any schedules and obligations. He was a good-looking boy, to grow into a good looking man, and every once in a while, I imagined I caught an undercurrent. However Rafet never acted on it, and I was not about to, not after what I had experienced. On the contrary, Rafet and I often spoke of girls, and I am sure he was (is) authentically drawn to women.

Another thing that became apparent in these following years. Not only did I find it rewarding and fun to teach trainees in lower years or supervise PhD students in their work. I was actually good at this. By all appearances, I found the right way to show or explain that made knowledge stick and engendered proficiency. I found empowering ways to motivate and encourage, which in turn earned me respect and appreciation. I like to think I was a good instructor and mentor.

Intersections and crossroads

In December 1995, Wiebke returned to the department of clinical diagnostics from a co-op placement in Davis, USA. She stood out from the other post-docs by being rather more assertive and outgoing, or simply more open to trying new things and going new paths. She liked to make fun of herself as being "the smart blonde." Quick witted and sharp tongued, Wiebke was a welcome addition to our regular trio for coffee breaks and cinema nights. At some point, it became a sort of a ritual that Wiebke and I would accompany Susan and Rafet to the train station after movies, and then from there, either walk or ride the public transport as far as the department of clinical diagnostics. We would talk of the movies we had watched, or discussing the implications of the science we were working on. And of course we talked about art. Upon reaching the department, Wiebke would put in a nightshift, and I would go on home.

Some five months later, spring was slowly turning into summer. We were the usual crowd of colleagues taking a coffee break, Wiebke had the paper, and read aloud the description of a theatre piece that had caught her attention. Something that sounded rather unusual, off the mainstream, challenging. I was the only one to volunteer any interest, and I offered to get tickets. She said, cool, then she would take care of dinner. Another month went by, and then the day came.

Dinner is fun, not to mention tasty. Conversation is sparkly. Wiebke tells of her time in the US, I talk of art classes. She displays open curiosity, asking about motives and ideas, materials and techniques used.

We leisurely stroll over to the theatre. The piece ("The Visitor" Éric-Emmanuel Schmitt) is better than any expectations, subtle, yet provoking, refined and on-point. Exiting the theatre, we are all exited, enriched, conversation flowing freely and easily.

From the theatre, we continued to the house of opera, where guests are exiting from a glamorous premiere. On a random wild idea, we enter the opera house. Wiebke tells me of a friend of hers that she bunked with, who works there sometimes. We go up to the rows of seats, admiring the view. We climb up to the stage, exploring the sets and try to make sense of the pulley systems.

By the time we get back to the main entrance of the opera house, the doors have been firmly locked. Even as we stand there, the lights go out. Giggling like teenagers, we backtrack behind the stage and from there, pick our way past the dressing rooms. Pretending we belong, we breeze past the cast who are still celebrating their premiere success in full swing. They actually wave cheerily, thinking us part of the crew, wishing us a good night.

It's well past one in the morning when we get back onto the street. Wiebke and I discover that public transport has ceased operating. It's a mild night, clear and starry. The streets are empty of traffic, suggesting a world apart. We casually set out for home on foot.

We don't make it all that far. Still immersed in our discussion of the theatre piece and its implications, we end up sitting on some stone steps of a small square of green at an intersection. Somehow, we don't want the night to end just yet.

Sitting for prolonged periods, watching the stars, does turn out to be rather chilly. So we inch a little closer together.

And that was when she kissed me.

She took me entirely by surprise. But since I was not involved in a relationship with anyone else, and since I liked Wiebke a lot, I was not about to protest.

She took it in stride that I was at Art College two evenings a week. And the fact that I went to dancing classes with another woman every Friday did not seem to bother her either. But then I did not complain about all the night shifts she pulled at the laboratory either.

Wiebke brought an enormous enrichment into my life. She was extremely enthusiastic and knowledgeable about art and antiques, something she was gifted with by way of family. Art, most particularly painting prints and objects, was a passion we would continue to share throughout the years to come, me rather preferring the more contemporary or Asian, while Wiebke would focus on the neo-classical to modern. So it was natural that she would be enthusiastic and supportive about everything I did at the Art College. Contrary to Nat, she was proactive and curious, which rather complemented my more timid and careful nature. I mean, I shared the curiosity, but I preferred to go with safety rather than all-out adventure.

But as contrary as this may sound, she brought out that in me, what I had learnt from my Dad: a gentleman obliges the lady. And so, if I was provided with the excuse that I was doing it for Wiebke, I was able to overcome my insecurities. We were (are) both enormously curious about cultures and love to travel. While I knew many places in Africa, Europe was very much a blind spot for me, and in this, Wiebke enabled me to find access to the Cultures that met and melted in my chosen home.

Also contrary to Nat, Wiebke appeared on good terms with her family. The entire idea of family, looking forward and having actual career goals was something she readily and happily discussed with me.

Truth be told, she was also just as direct and hard lined, in telling me that I was a spanner in her works. That she had taken on this placement as a post-doc to gather experience but that she had every intention to return to Germany. And from there go abroad. Be successful. Get a career. Build a reputation. Romance was really *not* on her agenda. And yet, despite all her agendas and plans, Wiebke seemed willing to make room for me in her life. Or perhaps, it was having a "gentleman" doting on her, that persuaded her that this was not all bad?

I made no changes in my shopping behaviour. Of course, Wiebke immediately clocked that I shopped in the ladies department.

We are leaving the department store. The air is brisk, the sunlight refreshing. Wiebke appears lost in thought. She asks what this means. That I dress in women's clothes.

For the first time in ten years, I speak about what I am. For the first time in my life ever, I actually use the term. I tell her, truthfully enough, that I am trans* gender. That I have identity problems and that the actual person that I am has more female attributes than male ones. I go on to tell her, that I have every intention of living this life as a man (the term cis* male was yet to be coined) *because I want a family. I want to have children.*

Her eyes grow wide. She looks at me, "You seem very sure." Not a question.

"I am."

I pause, ensure she is looking into my eyes. "I have made my choice. And I choose you."

That was the last we ever spoke of it. The next time I addressed this, would be more than seventeen years later. And by all appearances, she had forgotten that we ever had this conversation.

Gentleman or not, regardless of all that, I was anything but a showcase male. I like to think, she was attracted to the patient, unobtrusive and empathic sides of me. The fact is, that I could read into her moods enormously well and to some degree, I could almost read her needs or intentions. I firmly believe she *needed* somebody to be gentle and caring with her.

We had similar taste in food, art, movies, decoration, so it was rather easy for me to adapt if our ideas or desires did differ. Wiebke was (is) five years my senior, she had a PhD in medicine, she had good taste and she knew a great deal about Europe. And of course she knew her way around the whole administrative backdrop that you are confronted with when you "come of age." She had a most phenomenal memory for birthdays and dates. I came to trust her judgement in a great many things, where I simply lacked experience. In retrospect, I trusted on her memory to the point where I began to distrust my own.

The ambivalence of whether Wiebke did or did not want romance in her life was something that continued to be prominent in our relationship. I dare say, her continuous statements to the effect that she would rather be single, than compromise, did not exactly bolster my self-confidence.

I did love her. Very much so. To a degree, I still do. And I was certainly attracted to her. Wiebke was a pretty woman, not athletic but with a lovely feminine figure, and an open, cheerful face. And, yes, I was smitten by her boyish blonde bob, her clear eyes and her entirely kissable lips. I adored her humour, I certainly loved her laugh, and I appreciated that she put up with my very dry wit. Nevertheless, if I am entirely honest, gratitude that *anyone* would love a freak like me, did play a role in our dynamic. And I would be lying, if I denied that I subordinated some of my choices, simply to please or appease her. I really wanted to make this work.

Through thick

In the first year of our being together, I daresay, I was entirely more centred and balanced, more ready to challenge Wiebke's choices or decisions. Several things happened that changed that.

As mature and rational as Wiebke could be about navigating modern life, she had a very strong sense of pride, and that was one of the things she refused to compromise on. She was rational and analytical with other people, but in her own emotional world, she appeared less secure and self-assured. She could turn quite cold and distant if she felt wronged or neglected. As I said, I am sure that part of what drew her to me, was that I was empathic, sensitive to her needs. It is deeply ironic that this precise state of being turned on us. I was far too sensitive to her moods, too frightened of being rejected by this person who had accepted what I was.

We had been together for about eight months or so, when Wiebke was approached by a colleague from work. As Wiebke was a medical doctor, this was not entirely out of the ordinary, and she obliged. Things turned out that the colleague in question had contracted Mononucleosis infectiosa (also known as kissing disease because a lot of teenagers get it when they start experimenting). The colleague went down with the mild form of mononucleosis, which is unpleasant and stressful, with fever and flu-like symptoms, and it cleared up after about two weeks. Wiebke, never one to do things by half, went for the severe form. Four weeks of high fever, nausea, and pain-fully inflamed joints. Followed by twelve months of debilitating colics, and tongue-biting pain, caused by a spleen the size of a cantaloupe. A fatigue syndrome so severe, she barely managed a flight of stairs. For a year, Wiebke slept sixteen hours a day. Or more.

Since her performing household chores, or cooking for herself, were out of the question, I more or less abandoned my own apartment, to take care of her. I got up an hour earlier that I would have needed to, because it took me over an hour and several mugs (!) of espresso to get Wiebke to barely (and I mean barely) capable of taking herself to the office and look like she was propping up the desk. Four to five hours of this, and Wiebke would be so completely wiped out, that it was a miracle she got home, and when she did, she collapsed on the couch and slept until I came home from work. In the meantime, I had switched placements, and I was training at the department for haematology. Which was an hour one way, by train and foot. I would commute to be in the laboratory by seven thirty, and my day lasted nine hours. On my way home, I would grab some essentials, and see to it that Wiebke got at least some food into her. But during the week, that was all I had energy and time for.

Our social life ground to a halt. Of course friends were concerned and asked, but this was where Wiebke's sense of pride got in the way, and being seen as weak and vulnerable was a no-go. Needing help, being dependent on support was something she was not prepared to let others see. So either she brushed friends off, saying she was up to her eyes in work. Or she pulled together all reserves of strength and pre-tended she was fine. Only to collapse when our friends left. Rafet was one of the ab-solute few friends who kept showing up and who thought to check on us.

Trigger warning.

Gradually, gradually, Wiebke started to recover. That is to say, instead of being comatose for sixteen hours a day, she only slept twelve. And instead of needing a break after five or six *steps* of stairs, she was able to climb one storey. And carry her handbag by herself. It was a gruelling process, requiring immense patience and gen-tleness. But she still had a spleen the size of a cantaloupe and she still had bouts of colic every so often, that had her writhing in pain. She still needed more caffeine than was sensible or healthy to get on her feet in the morning. And I still spent so much more energy than I actually had, simply to keep ourselves afloat.

And then Wiebke became pregnant. Despite precautions.

I think she panicked. She had *dreadful* anxiety about splenic rupture and bleeding to death. And about how all the drugs she was taking for boosting her immune system, strengthening her circulation, and against the pain, would influence foetal development. We went to see two specialists.

The first specialist was horrified at the situation, saying the risk of losing both mother and baby was unacceptably high. Most particularly since an enlarged spleen would heighten the risk of thrombosis. Which would need to be countered with anti-coagulants. Which in turn again dramatically increased the risk of bleeding, be it the spleen, or the placenta. And that she recommended an immediate abortion, saying that we could try for children again, when a pregnancy would be safer.

The second specialist was horrified that we should even consider an abortion. While she admitted that there was a certain risk, she also maintained that she had never heard of any mother suffering a ruptured spleen during pregnancy. And since I was obviously good at taking care of Wiebke, she saw no problem.

And she said, that after all, this was not just the mother's decision.

I see the chance of having a child. Of being a parent. Maybe.

*I see the risk of losing the woman I love *and* with her, losing the child. Having to bury them both. Maybe.*

I see the chance of having child or children later. Maybe.

I look at Wiebke, her hand is clasping mine. She is deeply, deeply afraid, trying to look tough. And the past months of fatigue have drained her self-assurance. She has no strength. I can feel it.

I have no strength left either.

So I made that decision.

I still feel the scathing look of disdain that specialist gave me.

Wiebke forbade me to ever speak of it. Not to her, *not to anyone*. More than anything, she forbade me to ever mention it to her family. Or to mine. Of course, Wiebke was offered counselling. True to her nature, she refused that. Nobody thought to ask me. And I never dared ask. To be honest, it never occurred to me. And so, nobody ever knew. And nobody ever grieved. We both grieved, but instead of doing so together, instead of coming out stronger, it was a horrible painful and ugly scar, that we were both so ashamed of, that we did not even show each other.

We moved on. And yet we did not.

I only understood decades later, just how much that broke me. And how it crippled me. How it crippled us. And how the silence, the sorrow and the guilt paralysed me. It would be another twenty years, and five years of therapy, before I realised, that this was the moment I simply lost myself altogether. Trying to redeem myself by being there for others. This was the point in my life, where I abandoned the idea that I was worthy of living for myself, as well as for others.

But I am getting ahead of myself.

And Thin

I graduated, and for the time being, my curiosity for routine diagnostics was sated. Working in hospitals had been extremely rewarding and what I learnt from people, staff and patients, remains invaluable. Still, spending every morning in the identical processing of the six to seven thousand blood samples became a little monotone.

I returned to cutting edge science and found a position in a research group, looking at cancer pathways by way of genetically engineered cells, something that piqued my curiosity immensely. About a quarter of my time was spent cultivating HIV positive cells, researching DNA-based vaccines against the virus.

I was blessed with a really good lab group who treated me as an equal as opposed to someone who washed test tubes. (Ah, yes, the heady air of academia!) Our lab supervisor moonlighted as a dance choreographer in his spare time. Harper from the neurosciences and his family moved to Freiburg, something I regretted quite severely. Instead, I adopted Josephine, a pre-grad from Berlin, a perky Goth with a shock of bright red hair, into beer and hard-rock, skilled with her hands in drawing and modelling, and a talented scientist. Apart from the lab, I enjoyed showing her what I had gotten to know of Zürich. I taught and supervised the pre-graduates and PhD students in their laboratory work, showed them methods and gave tips. Apparently I did that well, because I earned a great deal of affirmation that I was a good mentor.

I was walking home from Art College one evening, something I enjoyed doing because it cleared the mind.

The sky is turning to lavender dusk. I am munching on a bun, lost in thought. From painting, my thoughts turn to Wiebke, the association is natural. OMG, I have a steady girlfriend. Wow.

I think of Rafet, who is "looking". My small but precious circle of friends. My mind drifts from my colleagues to my work. Working on getting an HIV vaccine. Working on understanding cancer. Working to improve living conditions for people.

OMG: I am actually doing what I set out to do: make the world a little better.

I am at peace.

The prof who was Wiebke's supervisor for her post-doc did of course register that her performance had plummeted. And despite the fact that she recovered and went back to her project with all her ambition, her contract was not renewed. I suppose we were not all that surprised. We knew the prof was old school and avant-gardists like Wiebke challenged his world view too severely. The problem was that her residence permit in Switzerland was coupled to her work permit, and with her contract running out, that too became dicey.

Ultimately, she found a position in a clinic in Ulm, Germany, as a medical doctor. She would have preferred to continue working in research, but then there was not really that much choice. By coincidence, Ulm also the city where her parents lived, Solveig and Torben. And while she was very ambivalent about moving back to "her old pad," it did have the advantage that she found her feet quickly. With a little reluctance, I started looking for a suitable position for myself, since leading a long distance relationship with a four to five hour commute one way was not something either of us wanted to do every weekend. At least not indefinitely.

At the same time, Wiebke's provocative claims of how I would be glad to be rid of her and "hook up with some dumb homely bimbo" (her words) did manoeuvre me into making the decision to leave Switzerland and follow her.

Ironically, as it turned out, positions for technical assistance were rather easier to find than positions for assistant MDs. Well, there were plenty positions for assistant MDs, but they simply did not offer a salary that would pay rent, never mind still leave money for health insurance and food. But fair working conditions for care givers is a topic *so* hot, you could power the internet if you could properly harness the energy lost there.

So, in April 1999, I once again uprooted my life and moved to Ulm in southern Germany. And I have to admit, Germany was (is) good to me.

Germany

The city with the highest (and IMO the most beautiful) church spire in the world. Ulm was a provincial village to compared to Zürich. A very beautiful village, mind you. The term "quaint" comes to mind. Ulm was lucky to get off comparatively lightly during the second world war, and large parts of the historic town are beautifully restored. The Danube River runs right through the city, dividing it into the Ulm, which is part of Baden-Württemberg, and New-Ulm, which is part of Bavaria. So, this is a very picturesque place to live, and the weekly farmers' market on the square in front of the medieval church still is one of my greatest joys, colourful and vibrant in its liveliness, while being grounded in an ultimately basic reality.

At the same time, Ulm still is a university city, so there are lots of student pubs and relatively cheap eateries, music clubs and amateur theatres. But it was and is so much less varied and diverse. As Vanessa says, it is "very German", by which she means, people are kind, and superficially hearty, but resistant to change or "otherness" and slow to open up. Vanessa is one of my closest friends, and she *is* German, so I guess she gets to say that. So, yes, I do partially miss Zürich. And I miss the ability to spontaneously visit my own family whenever I need some perspective or care. But Ulm is as close to "home" as it gets.

My new work group was focused on DNA vaccines against HBV (Hepatitis B), and immune modulation. They were a chill bunch, and I really enjoyed the creative freedom I had there. I was largely self-responsible. My supervising post-doc simply told me, what he needed, and I got to it. I continued to teach and supervise PhD students, and I enjoyed that immensely. At the same time, for reasons unexplored, we hardly ever did things privately. Each of the group was always very much focused on their respective personal lives, and somehow those did not mix.

Solveig and Torben, Wiebke's parents, more or less adopted me. With my Dad in southern Africa, my mother in Zürich and Evangeline in Bern, I was overall very grateful for this. Solveig was a very sweet, very gentle woman, originating from East Berlin. She was graced with some rather blue-blooded ancestry, and this expressed itself in her deep passion for modern art and antiques. She was an altogether gifted cook, and one of her greatest sources of satisfaction, was a full table of happy and content guests. She doted on her youngest. I think she was very much appeased by the fact that I went so far out of my way to please her daughter. Plus of course, she and I loved talking about food and recipes, cooking and baking. She was very knowledgeable about the different epochs of art and the furniture styles that went with them. We spent a great deal of time talking about painting and printing techniques, and sharing thoughts about art and inspiration.

Torben was (is) a Saxonian original, minted straight off the block. A professor in physics, and a patriarch to the core, he was very much submersed in his world. Torben was (is) on very good terms with several Nobel prize carriers, and he invited them to his home whenever they graced the University he taught at. I know that he was deeply appreciated by his students and his employees. I think he rather appreciated that I understood at least a hint of the science he talked about. And he too was an enthusiast for modern art. Aside from that, he had a passion for good food, Scottish whisky and for self-picked mushrooms (just the food kind). I loved going hiking with him in the woods, and he would often talk of his boyhood, before the great war. How he survived the bombing of Dresden, and how he was moved, to stay with remaining family in the countryside following that.

The both of them, Solveig and Torben were avid skiers, and they invited the entire family for a week's holiday once a year. So, they treated me with great courtesy and affection. At the same time, I was very much aware of my position as potential "son in law," and I did my best to blend in and live up to expectations.

Wiebke was rather estranged and disconcerted by my relationship to *my* parents, most particularly to my birth mother. She simply could not understand how I could be so distant and rational regarding my Mum. She completely failed to understand why I would have this rapport with my Dad, how we understood each other effortlessly. More than anything else, Wiebke was estranged by the deep emotional bond to Evangeline. I think this actually spooked her quite some.

I tried to tell her, in a way that would not make my mother look like a complete monster, how during my early childhood she had removed herself from our lives for long stretches, how my mother was somebody I was afraid of. I told her of how my Dad and I dawdled on our way home, when he picked me up from Kindergarten, and how we would sit on the bench under a tree, putting off the inevitable. She was deeply horrified at that story, and made me promise to tell her, if I should ever find myself sitting on that metaphorical bench again. I was deeply touched by the authentic sorrow she felt for that, and how she wanted things to be better for us.

Wiebke is the youngest of three daughters, each four years apart. Both of her sisters were already out of the house, married, and with homes of their own. Astra, the eldest, and Ditmar, lived in Dresden at this point, Torben's city of origin. Freyja and Marcus lived near Nüremberg. Despite the fact that I was doing my best to adapt and accommodate myself to their needs, I always had the impression that I was viewed as "the wild one." I got on well with my in-law siblings, but I did always get a subtext of, "ooh, what crazy and unorthodox thing will he do next?" But I suppose that went hand in hand with the fact that they became parents, while Wiebke and I remained more or less typical DINKs.

Wiebke made friends easily, and I was more the one to maintain and nurture those friendships. That is not to say I find keeping close contact easy. On the contrary, even with people I love, reaching out is sometimes a hurdle. But I do claim, I find it easier to hold a metaphorical door open, than Wiebke. Or maybe it is most accurate to say, I focus on the private connections for friendship, and Wiebke focuses more on her business networks. As a net result, a lot of our friendships revolved around her work colleagues. Strange perhaps, but I really did not mind. Most of my contacts were local people who were rather "settled" and conservative. Certainly more immersed in pre-existing social circles. While Wiebke's work colleagues were very often people who had moved from someplace else, who were automatically familiar with "not belong-ing," being more cosmopolite. And who were familiar with the need of re-establishing social circles.

One of those friends was (is) Darren, whom Wiebke got to know when she left work in the clinic to take up a more career-promising job of performing and managing clinical trials. Darren is a medical engineer, tall and lanky, fun loving, very good na-tured and easy going. Entirely devoted to his girlfriend, later to be wife, Suzy. She was a software specialist and web administrator for the Ulm college, a short and very sweet blonde, able to bring at least as much cheer and kindness to the table as her husband. Both of them raging technophiles, particularly so if whatever gadget lets itself be applied to the household. We spent a great many occasions together, sharing meals, rafting down the Danube, going to movies, each other's birthdays. They are the kind of people you simply need in your life. Their wedding was a smashing party that lasted well into the morning.

In four successive years, Freyja and Marcus had Linda and then later Melanie, while Astra and Ditmar were blessed with Nimue and Roman. I took great joy in spending time with my nieces and nephew, despite the fact that we saw each other only a few times a year. I undertook all kinds of outings with them, showing them more or less what my Dad had shown me, when I was their age. And so, we went trailing through the woods, carving hazels and watching animals. Or I showed them what I had learnt from Evangeline and in Art college, drawing or painting with them.

And of course, I joined along, when the whole family went skiing together for a week, once a year.

Every once in a while, Wiebke and I spoke of having children of our own, of trying for a baby. "When we are settled, when one of us has a secure job" was the argument that always came up. Both of us had six-month contracts at best, and somehow neither of us felt secure enough in our existences to "just go for it". In retrospect, this was stupid, but it was a hurdle we simply did not manage to take. There was an agreement between us, that Wiebke would "go for the career", while I would be the one to take care of the kid(s), possibly even as a stay-at-home parent. Throughout the years of our being a couple, I was primarily the one to take care of groceries and cooking. I cook like I paint: I check what is there and I see what evolves. Usually Asian fusion. Wiebke would cook occasionally, when we had guests. She was good at tackling menus the way she tackled management projects, with planning and strategies and multiple emergency contingency scenarios.

All this time, Nancy was alive, if sort of dormant, very unobtrusively active within me. I found an outlet for the woman I was, in relating to all the heroines and female protagonists in movies and books. And in computer role-playing games. Wiebke and I would stretch out on the sofa, our legs intertwined across and over each-other. While Wiebke watched her soaps and sit-coms, I would have my laptop across my knees, crawl through dungeons, explore cities, befriend monsters, battle baddies, and save worlds.

Another thing I thoroughly enjoyed, was accompanying Wiebke on shopping sprees. I became really good at advising her in what suited her best, which combinations were dash and daring, which were sharp and business-like, and which were luxurious and divine. And sometimes, a part of me wistfully let my fingers glide over the materials and imagine which clothes would suit me.

Very rarely, Wiebke noticed I was holding *something* back. When we were intimate. It was not that she was unhappy with how I made her feel, but that she had the feeling, I was not permitting myself to let go completely. Looking back, she was probably right. But it was nothing I permitted myself to look at, for what it was. And Nancy was not a part of what we shared.

Another thing that surfaced, was when we were talking of where we saw ourselves in future years. Career, position, influence were things that weighed heavily to Wiebke. As much as she downplayed her PhD, to a significant degree she measured her fulfilment by the plaque on her office door. The only goal I truly had, was to have a happy family, be a parent, have a circle of true friends. I was grateful for my job in developing vaccines, which enabled me to feel I was contributing something useful. That was important. But success was not something I ever measured by my pay cheque, or being issued a company car. More importantly, what others thought of us was of almost no import to me, I simply did not care for reputation or renown. Those parts of our life simply were not as important to me, and I was happy to let her take control.

What *is* remarkable, how Wiebke's taste in *my* clothing became progressively more conservative. When we met, I was still trending a guarded and cautious leather-and-lace gothic look. The longer the more, she pushed and coerced me to buy more male stereotype. Jacket, slacks, shirts. I always bluntly refused to wear a tie. Nevertheless, my wardrobe gradually filled with clothes that represented and reflected classical cis-gender, heterosexual status and success.

Peace

I have just picked up Wiebke from her night shift in the clinic, and we want to get breakfast in a café someplace in the old quarter of Ulm.

Things are good. As a matter of fact, things are great. Both of us have the weekend off, and nothing planned. Eternity is ours.

It is a beautiful, crisp morning, in late summer. The light has this special golden quality where you know the day is going to be s scorcher, but right now, there is fresh dew on the trees, and the birds are singing.

It is Saturday, market day, and the Minster-Square is chock-blocked with farmer stalls and people. There is a cheerful, up-beat feeling in the air as we pick our way through the crowds, taking in the colours and the smells of bountiful vegetables, plentiful fruit, and copious flowers. In this moment of time, life is nigh perfect.

"Where d'you wanna go?" I ask Wiebke.

"I don't know, where d'you have in mind?"

"Today's on me. Let's go to the café opposite the antique's place. They have the best coffee."

"Coffee…" Wiebke looks doped out on bliss at the prospect of fresh coffee. She breathes a deep sigh of contentment. The brisk air has brought a blush to her cheeks, and having the weekend off has put a shine in her eyes.

Everything feels right.

Flying entirely blind, I ask, "You wanna marry me?"

Wiebke halts in mid-stride. „Wait! What? Why?" And then, "Are you serious?!?"

I laugh at her shocked face. "What do you mean, "why"? Nothing "why". Yes, I'm serious. I love you. That's all the reason I need. Do you want to marry me?"

She cocks her head to the side, gives me a once-over. The sunlight catches a few strands that fall across her glasses. Those lips are so kissable.

"Um. Okay. Yeah."

We were married in July 2001. Of course Wiebke's entire family was there, Astra and Ditmar with Nimue and Roman, Freyja and Marcus with Linda and Melanie, plus a number of other of Wiebke's relations I did not really know. Harper was there to be my best man. My Dad made it, although I was really sad that Amahle did not accompany him. My mother was there with Francesco and Eirian. It was the first time that my parents met Wiebke's parents and that was… …interesting. It was the first time my parents met each-other after so many years. I was just anxious about the whole affair. Evangeline was there, with René and Seraphina. Rafet unfortunately could not make it, and neither could Josephine. Lisbeth and Walt were there.

In 2003, I left the university and became a full time learning coach and lecturer in a vocational training facility of an international company in medical research. This turned out to be the most fulfilling job I have held so far. Even if it meant giving up cutting-edge science, the human side of the challenge proved to be so much more intricate and fascinating, I have never regretted this choice.

I was gifted with four of the best ever work colleagues, Gerlind and Micha (Michaela), Stephan and Roddy. Or to use Micha's turn of phrase, my work-family. All of us individualists to the core, but with a common intention and ambition to provide school graduates with the best possible vocational training that we were able to provide. Despite the others having known eachother for some years already, I was welcomed for all the insight, experience, and perspective that I brought. We were and still are a great team, able to discuss hard lines and find good compromise, all the while maintaining our mutual appreciation, affection even.

Much to her delight and pride, Wiebke got promoted to project management. That really did her a great deal of good and bolstered her self-esteem.

There, she met Adrian, who was a controller and budgeted some of her projects. Adrian was at least as ambitious and driven as Wiebke, tall, very athletic, way too handsome for his own good. Krista, his girlfriend, was a petite redhead, who taught high school level, and she could cut vegetables with her mind. With her tongue too. She could easily keep up with Adrian, be it in her head or on her bicycle. Krista and I got on like a house on fire, trading stories and experiences of teaching adolescents. The four of us became quite close friends (Two more friends whom Wiebke met, and I maintained). We spent some really good times with them, cooking out together, watching movies, discussing politics, saving the world by proxy.

Eddie was another colleague in Wiebke's department. He was (is) a scientist, very successfully involved in managing research projects. But I believe his main focus and ambition was sharing the good life with his wife Athene and spending quality time with their two children. Eddie was (is) a lean, almost gangly hawk of a man, and his figure completely belied how much he was (is) a foodie. He could have made a career as a stand-up. If laser were composed of dark instead of light, that would give you an idea of how sharp his sense of humour was. Athene was (is) devoted to him, even if their playful arguments sometimes slipped into the serious. Athene is also a teacher, and a socialite through and through. She could be very diplomatic. But I deeply appreciated her perspective and her opinions. With me she was always straight and clear. Her exquisite taste always delighted me and the simple fact that she could be so impish and whimsical, it was easy to see how she and Eddie complemented eachother. They too were welcome guests of ours and I appreciated them deeply.

Regina, one of Wiebke's closest friends from her student days gave birth to Claire. She was a healthy and lively girl who seemed to be very much at ease with me when we visited. Regina and Knut asked me to become Claire's godfather. Deeply honoured as I was, I was also taken aback, because after all, Regina was Wiebke's friend. And truth be told, Wiebke was indeed a little bit upset about this. But For reasons only known to Regina, she and Knut, her husband, stuck to the decision.

Truth

The truth of the matter is, there *were* times when it was good. Really good. To say otherwise would be an outright lie. There were times when it was okay to have this body.

It allowed me to live the life of a person who brought joy, insight, and enrichment to the lives of others.

Be it as a partner and husband, who climbed street lanterns and danced with a rose between his teeth. Who offered an ear and a shoulder in times of under-appreciation. And who celebrated successes with all-out-no-limits sparkle. Or encouraged his wife to spend a ludicrous fortune on a dress. Or on paintings and art prints. Or, who escorted her through African farmers' markets and pointed out animals in far-away game reserves. A husband who kept surprising his wife, making her laugh to tears. Or gasp with delight. Or blush with passion.

Be it as a teacher who listened to things no one else had time for. Who offered you a hankie, and a safe place, as you wept for your boyfriend who has cancer. Or who straight up asked about those marks on your forearm. A teacher who taught things you do not find in any textbooks. Not even between the lines. A teacher who helped you find self-respect despite, or because, of having survived.

Be it as an uncle with a reputation for the flamboyant, or outright silly. Who pulled crazy stunts on bicycles and skis, that other grown-ups would never do. Or who stood knee deep in forest brooks, looking for newts and dragonfly larvae. Who showed you how to carve boomerangs. And joined you for teen-drama binge watching. Or encouraged you to travel internationally and broaden your horizons, against your parents' concerns and interjections.

Or be it as the friend in whose home you could count on a delicious meal, serious conversation, or witty words. Or who took time to offer empathic counsel or reflection on all the myriad crisis that people might have (My friend-sight was perfect. Still is, I think).

There were times when Wiebke and I were on a good stretch of our relationship and our personalities complemented each other in all the right ways. Where we shared ideas and ideals. Where we travelled and marvelled together at all the things we saw and the wonders we learnt. Where we worked hand in hand. Where we supported and upheld each other in the face of challenges and injuries. There were times when being with each other was fun, joyous, passionate, sweet, loving, peaceful, creative. There were times when we both trusted the other to have the best possible intentions, even if things did not work as planned. There were times when my relationship with Wiebke worked and I had the unconditional trust, *that we *both* really wanted this to work.*

There were times, where I was at peace. At peace with myself. Of a sort.

There were times when I *wanted* to be this man for Wiebke. Where my love for her was fulfilling and rewarding. Where I saw myself being appreciated and *seen* for what I was giving. Where I felt respected. Where I felt loved. For that which I was. Despite, or because, of all my flaws and shortcomings. Despite being a freak and an accident of nature.

And it was times like this, when it was almost okay, that I was born biologically male. I even learned to relinquish some of that iron control that I held over my anatomy. And I permitted myself to experience my body.

Keeping it steady

There were subtle changes. Wiebke slowly but steadily guided me away from my casual goth / androgenic athleisure wear. Instead, she encouraged me to dress more stereotype male, and of course I did not find those in the ladies' department. Overall, she became more and more focused on building a career, until her working hours devoured most of what time she had.

I was also aware of the extreme discrepancy between time spent with her family, and time spent visiting mine. I was aware of these things, and more. But I really wanted to avoid tension. It had been a while since our last "cool period", and I put in considerable effort to prevent us from sliding into another conflict. Considering how Wiebke's episodes of shutting herself off continued to progressively grow longer, I was authentically worried about how many weeks the next one would last.

In 2007, Wiebke finally got a contract that permitted us to plan more than six months ahead. She was exuberant about this, this was the recognition and the affirmation she had desired. And we finally permitted ourselves to stop taking precautions. Although she made it clear that she expected me to "take care of things" should we have children.

Being who I am, I was extremely perceptive of her body. So much so, that I think I knew her body better than she did. I noticed her moods and her weight. I noticed changes in her skin, in her water retention, changes in her breasts. I was aware of her biology, and I knew before she did, when her days were due.

There were three instances, May 2007, September 2008, and February 2010, when I was (am) convinced that Wiebke was pregnant. If she was, she never acknowledged that to me. Each time, I asked as cautiously as I was able, if indeed she was expectant. Which she playfully denied, why in the world would I think such a thing? I was dreaming things up, my wishful thinking influencing my perception. Or she absent-mindedly brushed it off, saying she had a lot on her mind and that work was overly stressful.

If she was pregnant, the child never stayed past the fourth month. I would notice how her body changed and how her cycle skipped several beats. And then suddenly it would resume, and all the "normal" expressions of her cycle and her body would re-establish themselves. Again, I would ask if indeed she had lost a child. But she denied and deflected the questions in the same manner, distracting me from following those thoughts.

The doubts never really left me. Neither did the impressions of how her body had responded and changed. How my perception of Wiebke had changed in those months. But since I got no reply or resonance other than my own intuition, and since I was always slightly unsure of myself, I just left it at that.

And the steady rhythm of our every-day would sweep us up again.

And, overall things were good.

I do not know if my father taught me "how to be a man". But he certainly was, and remains, a most educative example of being human.

(5) Being Equal

You would think,

We are all alike.

After all,

we all have the same basic needs.

What a colossal error in judgement.

What a fatal mistake.

What a fortuitous state of being.

What an incredible chance…

…what limitless opportunity.

To be better together.

This is a look at boundaries, cultural, sociopolitical. Musings and reflections, on all the myriad excuses we humans make, to justify gratifying our immediate urges, to justify our transgressions...

In Germany, there was recently (2019) a man whom I will describe as shallow and sort sighted, as ignorant and lazy. Possibly even as vain and cruel.

He once asked his followers, "Do you want to be sheep? Or do you want to be wolves?"

This man was in Germany. And he was White. But then a great many people are White in Europe. And this man might as well have been on *any* continent of your choice. With *any* colour skin you like. Inciting hatred and righteous rage has ever been a very human trait. Against the unbelievers, against the capitalists, against the infidels, against the eggheads, against the homophobes, against the OTHER. Tell me I am wrong, I dare you!

Back on topic. Naturally, confronted with such a basic metaphor, reducing the world to two choices, his followers declared that they would rather be wolves. Certainly fierce, supposedly proud, and in the minds of some, noble. Certainly more noble than sheep. And I understand. Of course I do. Given the choice between being a victim and being a predator, then the predator is the obvious one. You avoid pain and loss. On the contrary, you exercise power.

You have control.

Well. I say, I will be neither sheep nor wolf.

I will be a shepherd.

But the entire metaphor is too simplistic to convey the entire spectrum of what it means to be human. And what we require to thrive. It blends out everything that sets us apart from animals. It reduces everything into a simple equation of devour or be devoured.

There is nothing more dangerous than a small mind.

We humans are economic creatures. We like simple answers. Our brains are geared to reduce the world into simple choices. For all our intelligence, we are not a rational species. We are rarely guided by contemplative planning and careful premeditation, not as a collective we are not. Very often, we react. Steered by our most immediate biological impulses and primal urges, pure blank basic. Fear. Hunger. Procreation. There is nothing more vicious and dangerous than a mob of humans.

But the world is complex, and being human can express itself in forms and variations so far from what we are accustomed to, what we grew up with and what we have been conditioned to believe in, that we sometimes forget to look for the humanity in other people as well. People who are different from us.

And yet, they are still people.

And another thought that is easily lost or ignored in the fight for the moral high ground, is, that the followers of this "wolf" are themselves diminished in their freedom of choices. They too are disempowered. The saddest thing, the most perfidious thing is, they probably never noticed.

So now that I have basked in the glow of my own superiority, I will get off my high horse, before I pass out in the thin air.

Make no mistake. I make no claim at perfection. I feel these urge too. The difference is, I am well aware of my inner primal Lucy. Even more so, having grown up in places, where being stranded on a dust track might mean your death by exposure. Or predator.

So, yes. Deep down, I too, desire to be invincible.

It is probably a little late to say so. But if you believe, that being feared is better than being respected, loved, you might want to put this down and read something else.

Human rights

I am aware that in so many ways, I have grown up entirely privileged. Pampered even. And yet, the vulnerability of the human state of being is not lost on me. Not my own. And most certainly not that of other people.

The universal declaration of human rights was adopted by the general assembly of the United Nations on 10 December 1948. In the aftermath of two world wars, humanity across the globe saw the necessity to make a common statement of what unites us as humans. As people. It was the first time that we agreed on a comprehensive statement of inalienable human rights.

- That all humans desire, need, and have a right to dignity, liberty, and equality before the law. To be free to express our thoughts and opinions, to be free in our self-expression of identity and belief.
- That all humans desire, need, and have a right to a self-determined life, free of oppression and cruelty. That we have a right to a standard of living that enables us to live and thrive in health, to pursue prosperity and enable us in living with our kindred.

It is remarkable, not to mention worrisome, that the declaration of human rights explicitly states, that no human can own another as property, and that slavery is prohibited. But in the face of how commonplace slavery is (yes, is), and considering how many cultures have founded their achievements on the backs, and corpses, of other human beings, it is perhaps not surprising. And necessary.

Side note to modern slavery (2024): just to name two examples, have a look into working- and living-conditions of young women from the northern African states, who work as domestics in the Arabic nations, and Indonesian women who work as domestics in Hongkong.

Melanin and Genes

Siphiwe Gloria Ndlovu, Zimbabwean prize-winning author and filmmaker wrote along the lines, that, politicians and peoples of influence encourage people to think about differences in the simplest terms. Ethnic group A versus ethnic group B. Black and White, as it were. But, she says, that is a misrepresentation. A lie. Because the truth, the true succession of events as they unfold, as opposed to history as it is recorded by those in power, this authentic history is messy, and complicated. Often brutal, violent, and ugly. And she goes on to state, that when ethic groups meet, both come away changed.

She also states, that is it a human condition, to desire simplicity. But that in doing so, we deny ourselves the honesty and clarity we need to meet each other at face value. Eye to eye.

I need to say this. And I need to be direct. Racism is a huge trigger topic for me.

History is implacable. The colonisation of so many continents by the European nations remains a basic fact. The subjection and humiliation, the exploitation and ravaging of the cultures found there, by people who shared my tone of skin, an undeniable truth. The fact that humans were enslaved and treated with unspeakable disrespect remains an immutable disgrace. And we are still trying to grow beyond the clinging, clutching, devouring repercussions of that today. So many of mankind's "achievements" were only possible because *many* were (are) oppressed by *few*.

Fact.

Having said that.

I spent fourteen years in Africa. I met a great many racists. Most of them were, in fact, not White. I spent my childhood, my formative years in Tanzania and Zimbabwe. As a "privileged rich white boy", because that is how I was perceived. I was naturally termed as the "Mzungu" by the indigenous Tanzanians, and this was the contemporary norm. What the US-Americans with African heritage called me, is something else again. I spent those years being singled out for the colour of my skin. The lack of pigment in my skin led to my being accused as being discriminative and callous, as being ignorant and cruel. As a matter of course. My geographic origin automatically caused a great many people to treat me like some officious clerk or a miserly shopkeeper. Someone you needed to put yourself on good terms, but a person whom, in your heart of hearts, you hated. I met people who thought it was okay to cheat me, or help themselves to what was important to me, because after all, I was richer than kings. And after all, I deserved it did I not? After all, it was my ancestors that had (insert your favourite grievance here). So, please forgive me if I grow defensive, when my opinions are disregarded, my criticisms are discredited, by means of accusations of being motivated by racism.

What I mean to say is that I am extremely familiar being met with prejudice and bias, simply on the grounds of pigment content of my skin, or the shape of my nose.

At the same time, I grew up with a parent who *lived* with people, as a matter of course. To my Dad, people were colleagues or employees, neighbours and friends. And they were such, entirely regardless of their ethnic, cultural, or geographic origin.

My Dad worked with these people. Hand in hand. He (we) had supper with friends, in their or in our homes. He went jogging with them and he played tennis with them. Or volleyball at the beach. To my Dad, all that mattered, was that his friends were honest and dedicated, authentic in what they presented and what they did.

What my Dad did *not* do, was treat indigenous Africans with the patronising, well-meaning pity, so common in a significant number of ex-pats. Which also meant that he was far less easily manipulated by means of guilt, or coerced by emotional pressure. Which, ironically, often led to his being accused of racism, when he failed to comply as expected, and the people with manipulative intent did not get what they wanted. These people unaware of their own bias and their own prejudice.

I am inclined to say that racism is a disease. And the deep underlying irony is, that just as diseases go, racism does not discriminate. It will infect everything it touches, and lay entire countries to waste, if you do not meet it with the appropriate measures.

I will go one step further.

I will respectfully point out, that wanton cruelty, absence of compassion, are not patterns that are reserved for old white men. The inherent cruelty and complete lack of empathy we humans are capable of, independent of ethnical heritage, remains surprising. And deeply frightening. We humans are so very capable of utterly atrocious behaviour. It sometimes raises the impression, that we humans hate and fear nothing quite as much as other humans. That if given the excuse (and we are highly creative in finding these), we humans can *and will* treat each other with utter disregard for common ground, or dignity. Even if our skin tones are more or less identical.

Take a glance at *any* history of tribal rivalries, *any* culture on *any* continent. Tell me I am wrong, I dare you. It is a very, very human trait to separate, to *discriminate* into "US" versus "THEM". We do it all the time.

I say, there is no "them". There is only an "us". Any "them" is a construct. It is a conditioned reflex. We have been raised to think of "us" and "them" by traditions dating back to when we still glowered at each other with envy and distrust over the embers of a campfire. The earliest campfire is dated some 790'000 years ago.

Time to do better, don't you think?

Chimamanda Adichie, Nigerian author and activist said, "Power is not just telling a story of a person, but to make it the definitive story of that person". Meaning, every time you reduce a person to one single parameter, you are neglecting all the potential that is also there. And you are robbing this person of the opportunity to bring their whole self into play.

She reminds us that it is *in our power* to support, or hinder, another person, in how they contribute to society. Our society. She goes on to suggest, that we need to listen to all the stories, to see the sum of a person. And I wholeheartedly support her in this. We need to see people, and societies, for everything they are, for the whole truth.

Knee-jerk reactions

We humans require drawers into which to sort information. There was a time, when our daily existence was threatened by sabretooth squirrels, and being stomped on by woolly mammoths. Not to mention plain simple starving to death. These drawers root back to our ancient reptilian instincts, to be able to make split-second decisions between "dangerous" versus "food", between "sex" versus "boring". It was quite a while later until our brains learned "useful," never mind "interesting", or "pretty".

There is a theory developed by neuroscientist Paul D. MacLean, about our brains being divided into three regions, as they evolved along with our species. The oldest and most original region being the protoreptilian cortex, which is responsible for our instincts. It is incapable of actually *learning* anything and does not enable any kind of social cohesion. It is very good at survival though. And fighting. The paleomammalian complex, which is responsible for emotions and affective reactions, is guided by our biological prerogatives. It is capable of learning. It is also the seat of our memory. And finally, the neomammalian complex, which actually enables us to analyse and rationalise. And it is this which enables us to reflect, that *what is true for us, is likely to be true for others as well*. The theory of the triune brain has been hotly debated. Nevertheless, it has contributed to many psychological, psychiatric insights, to explaining human behaviour and patterns of social interaction.

In a nutshell, evolutionary biology has ingrained behaviour patterns into our biological prerogatives. Dating back to when resources, food, and skills were the kind of scarce, where trusting the wrong hominid meant the demise of your own tribe. The death of your progeny. The failure to propagate your DNA.

For all our intelligence, we are not a rational species guided by contemplative planning and premeditation. We are beings steered by our gut feelings and emotions, pure blank basic. The drawers are still there today. And while our drawer-cabinet has grown larger, more complex, we still categorise information as a matter of course. All of this has been imprinted into our brain by our upbringing in our families, by society, and by our very own personal experiences. Our perfectly normal unconscious bias.

And this programming provides us with the perfect excuses to overstep our inhibitions, and ignore the fact that we are de-humanising each other. In literature, films or television, videogames, we are surrounded by the ever-present narrative of survival. At any cost. There is something seductive about it. About the violence. And how violence is justified, because we are after all protecting what is whole (holy) and good.

We learn that violence is such an easy solution. And there is no real consequence. We never talk about how violence doesn't really solve anything in real life. We don't stop to consider the collateral fatalities, we do not consider repercussions down the road, or the consequences of what it does to *us*. Because disregarding these things is what it takes to discriminate and deface another human being. It makes you hard. To the point of where you lose your own humanity. And of course we ignore that. In the meantime, we, as a species, are capable of destroying ourselves quite thoroughly.

Can we at least be honest about the whole affair? And address the central screaming issue?

That this is all about *whose genetic offspring get to drink at the waterhole !!!*

I have heard people say, that things like moral values, ethics, or having a conscience, are simply attempts of the weak to control the strong. Well I say, that is the talk of people who are empty. People who have no purpose beyond gratifying their own ego, feeding their primal biological urges, and masturbating their pride. People who cloak transgression as the exercise of free will. They care only for themselves, contributing nothing to the future of a community. They abandon what makes us human: the ability to care. They are alone.

Xenophobia is present in *every* culture. The fear of the "other."

And incidentally, so is misogyny. Noteworthy, is it not?

Belief

I believe in the inviolability of human dignity and self-determination.

I believe that there is something divine in, and about, every human being, that goes above and beyond the biological clockwork of the body, and the finite existence of a human life span. And I will happily call this the soul. And, yes. I believe my soul to be female.

And I believe that there may indeed be a greater benevolent consciousness, that enables and guides us. To some degree. I imagine this "being" like a parent. Sometimes nurturing and protective, sometimes delighted and possibly even amused, sometimes sad, sometimes frustrated. Affectionate, caring. Expecting us to *grow up and sort ourselves out*. Expecting us to mature into beings that are capable of sustaining ourselves, *ALL* of ourselves. Even those that deviate from the norm.

Having said that.

What I do *not* believe in, is religion.

As Bertrand Russell, analytical philosopher, said, religions are based primarily upon fear. Fear of the arbitrary elements. Fear of our own fragility and mortality. Fear of running out of resources. And therefore, fear of other people. Fear of failing to secure the continued existence of our genes. It is only a human who is *devoid* of all hope, devoid of all promise of prosperity, devoid of a sense of security, that comes up with an idea like strapping children with explosives. Or teaching a five-year-old to shoot a gun.

I have come to believe, religions have lost their way. They have lost themselves in self-preservation. In worshipping the ashes. They have failed to be what they originally were: a guide to how we want to treat one another, and a summary of what we hold dear. Furthermore, I believe religions have focused far too strongly on the Darwinian survival of the most ruthless, the irony of which is just bitter.

My years in Tanzania and Zimbabwe, and even later experiences in Britain, Switzerland, and Germany, have led me to believe that religions are overall power-political organisations which serve primarily themselves. My travels in Malawi were educative and devastating in the extreme. My observations and interactions led me to these conclusions; that *ALL* religions, *are rampantly corrupt*, that they wilfully bend their own rules *to serve their own ends*, in complete disregard of what we term common sense, integrity, or decency.

I find religions to be controlling, manipulating, and disempowering. Exercising power through intimidation, guilt and shame. Downright disrespectful of human dignity. Incursive into self-determination. In far too many cases, transgressive and crippling. Sometimes even cruel.

All religions are DIVISIVE.

And, yes, this is my own personal prejudice. I am biased on this account.

To be fair, I have met many highly motivated scholars of different scriptures. People of exemplary integrity and compassion, who devoted their lives to aiding and empowering the people in their care. I am inclined to say, they performed their self-designated duty *despite* the belief system they represented. Not *because* of.

What remains essential, is that we respect each other's belief systems. And that we recognise the humanity in one another. Despite different belief systems. That we make a conscious effort to do so. It all boils down to respect and compassion. What do we want for our next generation?

Evolution

In real life, there is no failsafe, no saving-point, no safety net and no such thing as a second chance. You live with the choices you make, and you deal with the consequences. Or they deal with you.

Perhaps it is time to reassess our place in this world? Time to reconsider what we need to do, to keep this planet in a state so as to continue to be supporting of life? All life. Time to rethink how we treat each other?

Violence is no solution. On the contrary. It only makes things so much worse. It suggests to the victims that they are "in the right", that they have the moral upper hand, and that any response is justified. Violence only ever engenders counter-violence, provokes retaliation, and it escalates a conflict. To this day, I believe and maintain, that nothing stands to be gained from aggression or retribution. Hate and revenge are signs of weakness, symptoms of an inability to cope in a constructive way.

Yes. I could rant about this all day. Because, on my bad days, I am reminded that we humans as a collective, can be stupid. Terminally so. We can be lazy. Ruled by fear, ruled by base biological urges. We can be utterly blind to the obvious. And we can be terminally bad at learning from our past.

What my past *did* leave me with, is a very deep sensitivity for respect and fairness. Or the lack of it. And how important it is, to meet every individual with appreciation and courtesy.

We, humanity, are waging a constant war. Against ourselves. And it is plain and simply stupid. We need to break the cycle of survival. Considering what we produce and create on a global scale, considering the resources, the skills and the means at our disposal, *there is quite simply no need*. There is no longer a need for this constant competition, this urge to out-perform other nations, other social circles. If the only thing people strive for, is to be better than their neighbours, humankind will never amount to anything, and we are going to destroy ourselves in short order.

On the contrary, we need to think about fairness. And population distribution. Most particularly, population distribution versus resource and wealth distribution. Beyond national borders. We need to offer solutions. We need to offer a way out. It is our responsibility.

Which brings us back to the triune brain with its protoreptilian cortex. And how we all are still very much geared towards making heart-beat decisions between friend or foe. Normal and natural, yes. But *outdated*. In today's day and age, where we produce enough to feed the planet, in a day and age of smart-devices, is it not time we did better? How can it be, that struggle of survival depends entirely on where you were born, and to which parents?

One: It is more important than ever, to be *aware* that we are using these drawers. Be aware that we are selecting and prioritising our input, according to our own personal preferences. According to schemata that we were given by our parents, our social circles, media, and our schools.

Two: We need to ensure, and we need to enable, people across the globe to live without fear. Without fear of starvation, without fear of repression or violence, without fear of famine or disease.

Yes. That is a tall order.

But frankly, we have the means at our disposal.

We do.

It is our *failure* to think of humanity on a global scale. It is our failure to *empathise* with people on other corners of the globe. People beyond our doorstep, or out of our comfort zone.

The resources on this globe are finite. And yet, we have more than we need. Or, more precisely, some few have so much more than they can possibly, sensibly consume in more than one lifetime. If the immediate survival is secured, free of oppression, then people have the capacity, and surely the curiosity, to learn *more* than what is immediate necessary for survival. What is required, is that the "first-world" relinquish its jealous hold on resources. What is required, is that we learn that enough is sufficient. What we need, is to learn, that excess delivers only an illusion of security. I do not believe, *I refuse to believe*, that we are incapable of coming up with a model of distribution, that ensures the prosperity of humanity on a global scale. A method of ensuring, not just the survival, but the comfort and the well-being of people next door.

Access to sustenance, to medical aid. Access to technology and information. Those same resources, and the same information.

And neither do I believe that such a distribution model will lead to the collapse of the global economy. Yes. It might lead to there being less people, who have lavatories of solid gold. But it might also lead to there being less of a compulsion to amass superfluous resources, only to have them go to waste. Some people argue that a person who no longer needs to exert themselves, in order to survive or thrive, will abandon any kind of purposeful perseverance, decaying into complacency and self-indulgence. But to say that humanity is so slothful, so lacking aspirations or ambitions, that we as a species, will fall into stagnation and ruin, is to deny our brilliant creativity, our variegated ingenuity, and our plain resourcefulness.

We humans are better than that.

Well. We could be...

Education

It is my conviction, that one of the main contributors, to developing solutions to engender *equity*, is education.

From what I have seen and experienced on different continents, in different cultures, the raising and education of children works by *discouraging behaviour that is undesired*. Very often with a smack on the hand. Or in some cases, a bamboo cane to the rear. Another very efficient, well explored and widely applied method, is public humiliation, and shaming. Or any combination of these.

I suppose, it is not entirely surprising that we humans should have learnt to teach this way. From infancy on up, this is what we experience, it is the behaviour that is modelled and preconditioned by society. To make matters worse, evolution supports and enforces this. If you fail to fit the requirements, you are unfit. Wrong. A mistake. And Darwinian selection will see to it, that you drop out of the gene pool.

Is it not time that we outgrew biology? After all, for us humans, capable of imagination, capable of thinking and envisioning beyond our horizons, there is no such thing as "wrong".

All there is, is *a learning opportunity*.

By extension, showing vulnerability is a strength. Letting our guard down permits us to meet on an entirely new level of understanding and connectivity. It is only in recent years, that educators and learning coaches (and parents) have begun to focus on a non-violent approach of teaching. An approach that focuses on looking for solutions, instead of eradicating mistakes.

And that is the precise point. These new teaching and training methods focus on *appreciation*. They focus on respect. They focus on people facing each other as equals. Not on the same base of knowledge, obviously, since one is an expert and one is a learner, but humans who show sincere mutual esteem and courtesy. They permit learning to happen in an environment that is safe and welcoming.

And these kinds of solutions, when applied to human conflicts, enable win-win outcomes. Because they focus on common ground. On fulfilling the needs and the requirements we all share.

Again, education is a basis, for enabling us humans to be better than we were yesterday.

So, yes, worldwide, independent of their geographic location or place of origin, independent of their heritage, I would like to see people be secure in their existence. And being secure, they no longer need to send their children to work in a quarry or a textile mill. Instead, they children could go to school and learn. About language and mathematics, surely. And about science. But also, about other humans. And about what humans need and desire. About the meanings of respect and appreciation, and why they are so important.

Learning is key. We grow, when we are confronted with things outside of our previous horizons. It schools the imagination, it enriches the mind, it broadens the focus. Enabling people, enabling humans, all across this globe, to make educated, informed decisions. Enabling people to experiencing new things. Beyond gratifying our own immediate impulses. Across geopolitical borders, beyond cultures, spanning the full possibility of what it is to be human.

Enabling people to empathise.

Experiencing that it is safe to do so.

And in turn, enable decisions beyond ensuring the security of our own comfort zone.

One in nine

Many different studies show that men are more inclined to aggression than women (this peaks to an extreme extent, if their gender identity, or their sexual orientation, is questioned). The hypothesis to this readiness to aggression, is, that in our prehistoric past, it has proven to be a survival trait for our species. Key-word, prehistoric, we are back at our campfirc, 790'000 years ago. (*Study Anger, Violence, and Masculinity, Duke University, 19.March 2021*)

We are human. We want to have sex. We just do.

- We are biologically hardwired to do so.
- Sex can be a most beautiful thing to share.

Will you *PLEASE* stop pretending it is not so!

And more than anything else, will you stop telling your children that they will be damned eternally for entrusting another human being that they have feelings for this person? Peoples, seriously!

Our biological prerogative powers a drive that sometimes is strong enough to overrule even our instinct for long term survival. All societies I know of have such bigot and self-contradictive relationships to sexuality. Yes. All of them. I know of *no* so called "natural" belief systems, that are free of taboos and ridiculous restrictions, any more than your greater world religions. How we relate to sexuality is devastating. We have turned it into a moral conflict and a tool of control through guilt, intimidation, and coercion. And yes. Again.

All of this boils down to *whose genetic progeny gets to continue existing*.

More knee-jerk reactions

Wikipedia defines emancipation as, "any effort to procure economic and social rights, political rights or equality, often for a specifically disenfranchised group, or more generally, in discussion of many matters". Another very interesting word in this connection is heteropatriarchy, a descriptive term evolved from heterosexual and patriarchy, meaning the world is dominated and oppressed by cis-het* men. And one of the ways that men have erased women's accounts of their own realities, is by treating misogyny as a joke.

I currently live in Germany. A so called first-world country, with excellent infrastructure and educational facilities. A stable democracy, with a multi-party system that balances out, more or less, and offers political diversity. An environment that truly provides for the evolution and exploration of freedom of expression.

In Germany, one in three women experiences violence or sexual violence. This number is based on a study in relation to human rights in 2014, and more recent research continues to confirm this. South Africa, sadly, has one of the highest crime rates today (early 2020ies), with the official number of women who have reported a rape being forty percent.

In 2006, Jacob Gedleyihlekisa Zuma, South Africa's then-vice-president, was acquitted of the charge of rape. The same man, that was later voted into office of presidency. Despite his long and bruising history of (alleged) sexual violence, mind-boggling (purported) corruption, and utter (rumoured) disregard for decency, common sense, or any sense of integrity. Fezekile Kuzwayo showed exceptional bravery and moral fibre, because accusing the vice president meant drawing upon herself the wrath of the monopolising ruling party, the African National Congress (up to and including the ANC Women's League). In the face of escalating death-threats, she went into exile in the Netherlands. Considering the ANC's history, the irony of that is so bitter, it could eat its way straight through the African bedrock.

Ms Kuzwayo and Ms Mathabela, together with many others, founded the "one in nine" movement. They support women who take it upon themselves, to bring rapists to court. In an environment, where blaming the survivors is a natural knee-jerk reaction, they do their best to raise awareness, and bring about a change in the general state-of-mind of South Africa's societies, to enable and strengthen women's rights and ensure their safety. They do their best to educate and empower women about exercising the rights they have. The movement is titled so, because in South Africa, there exist statistical evidence, that of nine women to be raped, only one will actually report it.

Forty percent. One in nine. Do the maths…. To quote Margaret Atwood, Canadian author and poet, "Men are afraid that women will laugh at them, women are afraid that men will kill them."

Dudes, boys, guys, men.

Can you please, please *OWN the fact; You are going to catch a boner, REGARDLESS of whether a woman wears a bikini or a burka.*

A woman can wear a burlap sack, and you would still check out that ass. Boys, it is what you are *hardwired* to do.

And yes, I get it. As a matter of fact, *I probably get it better than most girls*. The fact, that your penis has a life of its own, is disturbing. The fact, that the thought of a wriggling female body makes you lose all self-control, is frightening. Add to that, that you were raised to be strong, hard, mean, invincible… …yeah, losing control like that confronts you with the utter paradox of being very mortal and very vulnerable.

And on top of all of which, women have this singularly blessed gift to bear children. Yeah, I get it. Women are intimidating.

And true to basic biological *and* social preconditioning, you lash out. You attempt demonstrate your superiority, you attempt to control what frightens you. Failing which, you obliterate it.

Face it, worldwide, the absolute majority of cultures are severely misogynistic. And frankly, boys, *this is not right*. It just is not.

And you know it.

So. You want my respect? You want me to treat you like a man?

Get with it. Grow up. *Grow a pair*.

But guys, you are truly quite awesome too. And lovable. And desirable. And necessary. You are overall stronger, on average more competitively goal orientated, you are generally better able to rationalise. (Ladies, if this were not true, we would not be in such a mess). Stereotyping? Yes. Exactly. Stereotyping. Because stereotypes exist on a law of averages. Because it is normal. And because variation from the norm is normal too.

Unfortunately, in our past as a species, these differences have led to women being treated like livestock. Dating back to when resources were so scarce and valuable, that a child not of your bloodline was considered a liability and a waste of food. Tribes, clans, raiding each other's territories, killing all the males, all the male children, and all the infants. Taking the livestock, because that was valuable. And the women. At least those of an age who would continue to bear offspring. And apparently, the human females' way of coping with this was, on average, mute endurance and submission. In fact, we women are altogether too frikkin' good at enduring. Because it ensured our survival. And on the broader scale of Darwinian biology, it ensured the survival of the species.

To the point of where women have internalised being disgraced per default. To the point of where we women reduce, restrict, and subordinate ourselves. Become people-pleasers. To make ourselves less than we are. Less threatening to men. You can draw a direct line from all this. From following fashion trends that magnify our vulnerability, straight to female genital mutilation. *We even do that to our own daughters!*

Today, we are still trying to overcome so many generations worth of conditioning.

I believe, all of the above does play a strong part in why the genders are so riven. Why males feel such an intense need to cast down, to depreciate, to *CONTROL* women. I imagine men feel controlled, intimidated, subordinated, and conquered themselves. By their own primal biological programming. Face it, *no* human being reacts well to being subordinated. Particularly not the archetypal hunter... ...and all of it leads to fear. And, possibly, men still bear a traumatic heritage, a deep seated grudge, that males should be killed by conquerors, while the females would be spared, and thereby betray their erstwhile mates. In the face of "honour"-murders, femicides, and the roles and rites that are upheld in the machismo- cultures, I believe this still plays a strong influence today.

Why do I talk of this?

The narratives of the subordinate woman; of the woman who exists as an extension to the male identity, and subject to his whim (libido), is still being propagated globally. The trial of Jacob Zuma is exemplary for the off-hand and matter-of-course way that sexual violence is trivialised by institutions of the law. It is exemplary of how sexual transgression is considered a peccadillo, and how that in turn is a direct reflection of the station and value of women in society. It is a clear illustration of how the availability and the *disposability* of women is taken for granted. It makes women basically faceless. Invisible, ineffectual, and powerless in their traditional status in the "tribe". The only influence women exert in the "classical" families, is indirect. It reduces and devalues any contribution a woman makes to society or economy. And in the same breath, it displays just as clearly, how males are reduced to this warrior-provider role, with no other options or alternatives for self-expression or creativity. And basically expendable.

Because even in a "first-world country" like Germany, we still have a long, long way to go, before we humans stop looking at one another, with constant appraisal of how to gain an advantage over each other.

My mother and her sisters-in-mind, spent their entire adult lives, working for the betterment of how women are recognised and treated. In Switzerland, in Germany, in Israel, in Palestine. My mother's generation needed to be guerrillas. They fought with bitter trench warfare, of flat-out violent protests and blunt refusal to be a part of the system that was. And they won. To a degree. Women have voting rights in all of Switzerland, something that was not to be taken for granted right up until 1990.

Nevertheless, when I look at my mother's generation, this victory came at a high price. What I miss in my mother's kind of feminism, is how it leaves no room for the soft and sensual side of being a woman. No room for acknowledgement that there *are* men who are great to have around. My mother robbed herself of that entirely. Any boyfriend of hers I ever met, was treated with a volatile mixture of grudging adoration and bitter, generalising recrimination, for all the grief my mother and *her* mother had endured.

For my mother and her comrades, women's emancipation *remains* synonymous with an ongoing war. Today. My mother has never been able to free herself of the ever-present anger and injury. In fact, a part of her type of heroism is entirely self-destructive, hinting at some very vicious monsters locked away in the dungeons of the subconscious. So many of her friends and comrades have never been able to cast off the "guerrilla mode". There is no resilience there. Just brute strength. It colours their perception of every project they embark on. And *it rules any relationship* to any partner, *male or female*. What I find so sad, is how there is no room for any greatness. The kind of greatness that reaches out across borders and offers support. The kind of all-encompassing love.

And. Much as I love and admire Francesco, my Mum's husband, he is not what I would want any partner of mine to be. Too meek, too deferential. Far too lacking any healthy self-esteem (As I type this, Nancy smirks challengingly in the mirror of my soul). I am convinced, despite all his creativity and energy, Francesco is not a happy man at heart. And despite all her achievements, neither is my Mum a happy woman.

Toxic conditioning

"Toxic masculinity" describes and encompasses the expectations societies place on cis-het* men. What we might describe as the epitome of stereotype manhood.

- Real men are hard, tough, mean, ruthless, strong,
- Real men are ambitious, driven, successful
- Real men don't cry
- Real men don't show (have) feelings beyond hunger or thirst. They do not tire.

The list is endless, pushing the concept of the "real man" into something bordering on the mythical, the herculean hunter-provider. Invincible, a one-man-army.

But also, unfeeling. Unable to show (feel) compassion or vulnerability. Maybe able to love, but unable to show it. Even showing simple things like joy or sadness are very strictly regulated. Expressing sexual release is a taboo (and if you think I am wrong, I suggest you watch standard cis-het* porn: watch for *where* the focus is, and *who* shows which reaction). Simply expressing sympathy, or attesting to common ground, or a common purpose, becomes a complicated, awkward ballet of hints and metaphors, of implications. Accompanied by embarrassment, unease, and fear of losing face.

Why, in the nine cold hells, does showing *you care*, cause you to lose face? Are we as a society really that broken? That afraid? Of vulnerability?

The result, the outcome of toxic masculinity is devastating. On the one hand, I am convinced, it bears a central contributing factor to the ever pervasive, and seemingly global misogyny. But it also causes biological males to be utterly overwhelmed. Either, when their own perception-of-self deviates from this herculean ideal. Or, if they find their body reacts to males rather than to females. Or if they witness this in other males. To the point of where they react with unspeakable violence and staggering cruelty. While at the same time, this kind of masculinity is infinitely fragile. It is entirely dependent on conquest, on victory of some sort. Usually over another human being.

I do not believe Andrin was homosexual. I am convinced that his impulse had nothing to do with desire or attraction. It was simply a short-circuit reaction over being caught in a situation, where he was overwhelmed, and unable to cope. With his vulnerability over being aroused by the teenagers, and his feeling threatened in his self-assurance as a male. Loss of control, loss of self-esteem, loss of picture of self. His reaction was about re-establishing that control.

Homophobia. Most people believe, this means "a strong dislike of homosexual people". But I think what the term truly means, is a fear-of-self. A fear of those aspects of your personality and desires, *that you supress*, because they challenge the belief systems that define the comfort zone you were conditioned to accept as "proper". So, strictly speaking, there is no such thing as trans* phobia, there is only suppression and denial of your truest needs. Denial of those aspects of your identity, that are ambiguous.

On a side note, I believe *every* male has homoerotic tendencies. Or more precisely, I believe *every person* thinks it is cool and rather delightful, to be sexually excitable. If not, I imagine you would be asexual.

I have *not* come across the term of "toxic femininity". The concept certainly exists, though. Too bloody good at enduring, remember? On top of which, we women have evolved our own tools and strategies for surviving under hostile conditions. And, like men, we are equally good at looking out for what is closes to our skin. And preserving our comfort zone, or securing what happens to be convenient. Equally good at tearing each other down. And to pieces. And we are equally good at being cruel. And deluding ourselves, that we are doing it for the greater good. We just go about it differently. Considering how a great many of us pride ourselves in being more empathic and more integrative, we have accepted the concept of "us" versus "them" all too easily, and we apply it all too readily.

No, ladies, we have no fewer reasons for pride, or shame, than men.

Roles and rules

To me, it is clear. Outright confrontational revolution is not the way to go.

We have redefined the meaning of "Queer". We need to redefine "emancipation". And we need a new way of bringing about change.

Make no mistake. I will clearly say; the classical narrative concerning the roles of men and women is a dead end. The traditional state of inequity is unacceptable. Inequity of gender, of ethnicity, of identity, of orientation.

NOT ACCEPTABLE.

We need new definitions for what it means to be a "man" or a "woman". And all the other people that identify themselves in a place somewhere, orbiting these binary poles. I do not mind "male" and "female" being the twin suns. After all, they *will* remain the biological centres of gravity, to which our species are bound. But to place a higher "value" on one of these poles, or on any of the orbiting clouds of designations, ethnicities, and identities (and please note: clouds, not planets. There is no absolute), is to discriminate and depreciate *all* the others. And that is a crime. It is a transgression against humanity.

It is vitally important to be aware, what we integrate into our personalities; that what we term as male and female, are social constructs. They are titles of roles that arise from how your cultures evolved from around a campfire, with females gathering and looking after children, and males doing the heavy lifting (and apparently that is a myth. Not true).

We need to rethink and reinvent our expectations, our inner portrait, the narrative of what "men" or "women" do in society. We need to free ourselves from the restrictions that we were raised with. Assumptions of what we think people are capable of performing and fulfilling. Or more specifically, not capable. This starts with "Who does the dishes", "who minds the kids?", continues on to "who can be a leader", and ends with, "Who am I? What can I offer?" In the same context, what stops us from growing beyond the need to out-perform each other on the field of commerce or co-operation? Do not tell me, you are not as tired as I am, about the constant bickering and the battling. The manoeuvring for power, an edge or an advantage over another person or community. Striving for greater things, and visionary ambition, is possible, without there being a loser.

Time to let go of ancient patterns, and redefine who we truly want to be.

If we can accept that raising the next generation of human beings is the responsibility of *everyone*. Moreover, if we can liberate ourselves of biological prerogative to need to exterminate the competition. Then possibly, we can free ourselves of this yoke of moral-code with which we have shackled ourselves. No, there is nothing wrong with the classical family of Mom and Dad raising their family. But there is more to being human than this single truth. Again, to reduce our view, our options to this dogma, is an incarceration of our creativity. It is a crippling of our potential.

We need to look at those drawer cabinets that we have inherited. We need to realise that these pieces of furniture, practical and reliable as they might have been in the past, they are vastly outdated. In today's day and age of cloud computing, where is the problem of freeing our minds, and our roles, from a cage? And permitting our *self*, permitting our *identity* to have attributes that belong in one drawer, along with attributes that belong in even so many more other drawers? A single individual, a coordinate in a multi-dimensional spectrum of personal evolution and the summary of our life's experiences. But instead of isolating ourselves in a new drawer, with its fixed spot and its precise label, how about we simply permit this identity to exist. More importantly, to contribute. All of its assets, all of its strengths. Instead of locking it away.

We do not need a world in which "exotic" minorities need protection. And thereby our locked little niche. Our reservation. We do not want pity or special attention. We are human. We are a part of humanity. We want to share what we are and make this world a bigger and better place for it.

We need new definitions of what it means to be committed to another person (or persons) in love, in unity, in friendship or in parenthood. Just as sex is more than bare "penis penetrates vagina". If we permit ourselves to face the truth, that what we term as ethical-moral, and particularly what we term as sexual-moral, all boils down to *whose children deserve to sit by the campfire*, whose children get to drink from the water-hole. *Then we can address the underlying needs*: to keep our children safe. And to ensure the next generations' prosperity. And if we can open our hearts, and our minds, to include not just our own children, but those of our neighbours' as well, then we have taken a step into a richer and brighter world.

Do not dare tell me, there is not enough to go around. If that is what you truly believe, I challenge you, to open your eyes and look at what we, humanity, have so far carelessly discarded. I challenge you to look at what we are truly, truly capable of.

Pride

Germany is a good place to be Queer*. The constitution recognises different states of being. You do not (no longer) get arrested and sent to "the institute" for re-education if you are gay. And you do not get sent to the secluded ward for conversion therapy if you are trans*. And there is in fact a law in place that forbids discrimination on *any* grounds.

There are a great many cool people here. Humans who recognise the potential in diversity. Who welcome people, regardless how different they are. And who celebrate the enrichment that a larger, more colourful crowd brings. And let it be said clearly, there are Germans who truly know how to party!

But I do not wish to pink wash too brightly.

Despite what laws dictate, just as there are countries where outing yourself as Queer* can cost you your existence, there are places in Germany where you do *not* want to be waving that rainbow flag. Ulm is in the heart of southern Germany, and in many ways, it is archetypical conservative. That is to say, people are hardworking and studious, dedicated to raising their heteronorm families in prosperity. But most prefer to go about their lives untouched by things that raise questions about what they take for granted.

More specifically, I have a great many friends, who are okay with what I am. In the sense that, as long as I pass as cis-het* female, they are not truly touched or influenced. I do not endanger their comfort zone. I do not provoke any deep confrontation of their core beliefs. They are not required to acknowledge my being trans* or bisexual in any way.

And most importantly: *they do not have to expose themselves* in public as persons, who are associate with "a Queer*".

But if faced with my being politically active, faced with my being a part of awareness programs, faced with my bringing up the topic of my background in conversation *in the presence third parties*. That is when I observe body language changing, friends becoming uncomfortable, perhaps wishing they were someplace else. Or them wishing, I would shut up, go away.

Them wishing *I were normal*.

Despite my being an absolutely marketable attribute to my employer, a proud statement of diversity to advertise. It remains rooted deeply in so many cultures, the German culture is no exception there. How important it is to be "proper" (yes, in the very sense of purity). And. How important it is to be a "Real Man". In fact, this latter has taken a turn for the worse in the past years, a change that can be at least partly related to an influx of migrants with cultural backgrounds where machismo, or fundamentalism are the norm. I view this development with unease, and I believe it is going to be a challenge we need to be highly mindful of, to not escalate things by resorting to instinctive exclusion and discrimination of these cultures.

Critical thinking

I will be blunt. I have always viewed pride to be a singularly destructive and disruptive emotion. To be proud always requires being-better-than. Having one-upped someone else.

What precisely is there to be proud of? To be homosexual? To be Queer*? To be trans*? To have lots of Melanin? To have blue eyes? To be born with testicles? To be born with a womb? But that would mean, being homosexual, or being a natural blonde was an achievement. And that we have achieved it *by choice*. But there was no choice involved. There is nothing we can do to change to change the biology we are born with. The family and the heritage we are born into is beyond our choice.

I am going to postulate, that *everyone* who was ever in any way "different" from the majority, wished, possibly prayed to be "normal". Ethnicity, geographic origin, Queer*, religions…

Of course, the true source of pride is not dark skin or a requirement for same-sex relationships. But to hold you head high in the face of discrimination and adversity, and be true to yourself and who you are, regardless of how other people depreciate you and how they mistreat you.

Pride. Perhaps the more adequate term ought to be "dignity"? But then Pride has everything to do with overcoming shame, and Queer* peoples *are* taught that they are shameful.

Another thing that disturbs me. Much like the "feminist sisterhood", the Queer* community is… …anything but a community. And. It is a sub-society, that is just as much dominated by cis* males as any other culture. Unsurprisingly, it remains a perfect reflection of society as a whole, with intellectuals and ignorami, with open and intolerant people. With humans, brave, wise and welcoming, respectful. But also, with just as many people who are short-sighted, ruled by impulses and fears, people who are downright unpleasant. Or even dangerous.

And a great many people who are a little bit of everything.

I do not have that much experience in "scene bars". In the early days of founding our support groups, we used to sometimes hang out at the bar specifically for homosexual clientele, mainly gay, and some lesbian. Marie, who was more or less our lead founder, had a great many friends and connections there. Her claim being that she feels less exposed, less endangered of being hassled or heckled by cis-het* men. And she seemed to be of the opinion, that most of our group would be more comfortable there. Oddly enough, it contradicted with my experiences. Personally, I had the impression, that rather more people stared at our little group, than in "ordinary" cafés. Nevertheless, in my early days, the two of us would spend companionable evenings over drinks along with two or three other trans* girls, talking shop, exchanging tips and experiences. Support group at the bar, if you would.

There is a subtle, but significant power struggle, between all the little clouds of subcultures in this minor arm of the galaxy that is humanity. Without wanting to overemphasise this, I have caught more flack in Queer* pubs, either in Ulm, Stuttgart, Munich, or Frankfurt, than in any other "normal" clubs. I have no idea why that is, either. I thought I was minding my own business. I certainly was not "looking" for anything. Perhaps I should not have taken this to heart, and just let it slide off me, but I felt unwelcome. And since not-feeling-welcome is part and parcel of being trans* in the first place, I decided I no longer need to expose myself to that.

Fact remains, the nebulous and transient borders (pun intended) between cross dressing, role playing, and transitioning, exposes trans* people to some of the most extravagant and exotic fetishes. It just is. It just happens. Today, it is an entertaining anecdote, funny even. But at the time, I was almost paralysed with fright.

The place is packed.

I am standing at the bar, alone, waiting for my order to be served, so I can take it back to the table our little group has taken. I am very much self-conscious. I feel scrutinous gazes crawl up and down my body like warm spiders. Curiosity gets the better of me, and I look around.

The man is twice as wide as me (Why is it always the big ones?). *Is he really wearing a leather harness, with chaps? Wow! And, gosh, that thong must really chafe badly!*

My eyes must have lingered a fraction of a second too long, because his face lights up with... ...interest. He rumbles at me, "What? You caught a boner, girly-boy? Wanna go out back and show me? Maybe I'll show you mine" To make sure I catch his meaning, he makes the appropriate gesture.

I am sure I've gone as white as the wall. I consider myself exceptionally fortunate that my mind goes into auto pilot.

"Haven't got that anymore."

His expression turns into disgust and frustration. "Well fu*ck, why d'ja do that? Ruins all the fun. P!ss off, freak!"

Make no mistake. I do not take offence at his offer. It was an honest proposal. He thought I was looking for something, and he thought he could provide. Thank you, but no. Most certainly *not* in a back-alley. And *NO FRIKKIN' WAYS* in a toilet cubicle. But as long as he leaves me with the option to say "no", why would I take offence? And I get it. Metaphorically speaking, he was caught with his Mr Twinkie out of his pants, and now he is shocked that instead of "getting some", he is confronted with a person, who not only identifies as female, but has the matching parts. And he thought he was in for a good time with a dude. He was confused and insecure.

Nevertheless. I take offence at his tone of voice. At the depreciation in his body language and the implication that I am filth. I take offence at his dismissal as my being less than human. A freak. So, I am good enough for a quick f*ck in a restroom stall (my skin crawls at the thought), but if I out myself as trans*, then he proves himself as just another cis* guy, complete with preconditioned homophobia. Trans* phobia. Whatever.

This encounter was harmless. But I frequently got misgendered at gay bars, and that never happened in "normal" places. On top of which, I routinely got offers for a quick tumble, at a time where this was most unwelcome. I realise, that is *my* problem, not theirs. Nevertheless, some offers came over as a just too insistent, people getting quite irate when I declined. That pushed me way out of my comfort zone. So, I will go to a gay bar with friends, but I would not choose it myself.

As a trans* person, I found myself either being a "fake lesbian", or failing to have the "proper tackle" for the gays. Even gays belittled my gender dysphoria as a fetish. Or I was outright accused of cowardice, of being a *"closeted gay who would rather cut off his own d!ck, than admit he is gay"*. I kid you not.

I also found being bisexual seems to spook a lot of people, homo- and heterosexuals alike. I have had so many generalising accusations thrown at me. Again, of being cowardly and dishonest, of being secretly gay but not wanting to out myself. And of course, the standard, *"Oooh, you're bi? Fancy a threesome?"* Um. Nope. Thanks. One reoccurring generalisation is, that bisexual people are unfaithful. Which is outright atrocious, and ridiculous. As if sexual orientation had anything to do with being capable of trust, commitment, and integrity.

A significant topic in the Queer* world is, how exclusively, how visibly, and how assertively (aggressively) you identify as Queer*. Even trans* peoples amongst themselves clash occasionally. I have repeatedly been accused of being too "stealth". My lack of being visibly Queer*, my lack of being visibly trans* was defined as a deficit by these people. A betrayal even. I have been charged with being too "mainstream", too cis*-friendly, too normal. Trans* acquaintances declaring "Eeew! How could you?!?" on learning of my cis-het* partner. If irony were sparkles, I could enchant the world…

And finally, on a very personal note, I was deeply hurt by some of my Queer* friends. When I suggested, I introduce them to David, my cis-het* partner. Instead of seizing the opportunity, to meet a really cool dude and make a new friend, they said, *"He's cis-het*. Why would I ever want to meet him? What would I even talk to him about?"* I was deeply disappointed by the lack of self-reflection and the prejudice evident in those statements. And what does that imply about those people themselves? That being Queer* is the only content to their life? How small, how empty is such a world?

For all the colourful diversity, it is evident that even the Queer* are "just" ordinary people, and not automatically better equipped to deal with challenges to their world view, or their comfort zones. And all of this is exemplary, of how all people, including Queer*, clash every once in a while. How *some few* individuals manage to make a lot of noise, jealously self-segregating and proactively working on raising borders between the different subcultures. And how cis-homosexual people are still cis* people, and how some of them feel just as threatened by what I am. And that all of us are terrified of being singled out, of facing discrimination, ostracism, and transgressions. And as a consequence, all of us react in ways that are plainly guided by our selfish reptilian instincts for asserting dominance and securing our comfort zone.

We Queer* also sometimes tend to forget, that we are a part of the global community. We blend out that we share this world with the cis-het* people some of us so condemn so easily. That too, is something I would like to see change. In the same way that my cis-het* friends automatically close ranks *to stand at my side*, when I get discriminated, I would like to see the same kind of reaction from Queer* peoples. That they, too, would come to the defence of any cis-het* person, when they witness this person being depreciated for being "straight". I would very much like to see the Queer* community evolve to where we permit ourselves to drop our guard. And approach each other with more trust and more appreciation. To where fairness and moral fibre means being fair to *everyone*.

Academic discussion will not bring about change. Neither will a revolution. *We *need* to be a part of society*. We need to be visible. We need to be approachable. We need to be real.

I feel ambivalent about Christopher-Street-Day-marches or Pride-Parades.

On the one hand, I actively contribute to raising awareness and educating people. I am open about my being trans* in my work environment, as an educator of youths and young adults. I want them to have a positive example of who and what Queer* is and what self-determination can mean. And I am openly and visibly active in our network of Queer* peoples in the science world. Incidentally, in a lot of countries, I would not be permitted to teach. By law. I would not be permitted to convey any kind of knowledge to youths or young adults. Because I am trans* gender. Because I belong to the Queer* community.

So. I will clearly state. That it is necessary. It is *vitally* important that the Queer* community insist on its right. Not just to an existence. But as a natural part of humanity. Respected and appreciated by the cis-het* world. It is so very necessary that countries, which outlaw and persecute Queer* people, are sanctioned by the global community. Worldwide, there are too many Queer* peoples who do not have the foundation, never mind means and the liberty to live their lives as they would. Never mind that flaunting their queer* side would land them in hell's kitchen. It is not okay, that violence against Queer* people, is not only sanctioned, but incited by so called law-keepers. It is not okay, that Queer* people are justly concerned about rejection and ostracism. From their families, by their friends, from their communities of belief.

It is not okay that Queer* peoples are being thwarted and crippled in building fulfilling lives.

NOT OKAY.

At the same time, I feel misrepresented.

If Christopher Street Day (CSD) and Pride Parades boil down to crowds of rowdy, raunchy boys in leather, or transvestites portraying blatantly cis-het* male pin-up-dreams of what women should look like. Neither do I believe, trans* peoples parading their naked bodies, will achieve any change. *Shocking is not the same as making a statement.* You want to party? Fine. Party! Nevertheless, I find it highly hypocritical, if those same peoples complain, that the heteronorm society perceives and portrays Queer* as excessively stereotypical, and hyperbolic cliché types of all kinds of cross-dressing or fetish cultures. Sweeties, if *we reduce ourselves* to these clichés, then we forfeit the right to complain.

And *we lose credibility*. And that, my dears, could be our downfall.

I know. In know that there are plenty trans*, gay or lesbian peoples that are indistinguishable from your average ordinary cis-heteronormative jane and joe. They have their jobs, they pay off their mortgages. They ruminate about what to have for supper, and they loaf on the couch in sweatpants. But that is not how Queer* people are portrayed by the media. Of course, that is the medias' responsibility. Nevertheless, it is not helpful to engendering openness and inclusion, if we ourselves confirm and fortify the very clichés we are trying to dispel.

What I mean to say is, it is a thin line to tread, to find the best possible way to engender equity and inclusion. To further understanding and enlightenment. Without antagonising or alienating the cis-het* world, or even other parts of the Queer* family. Or risk not being taken seriously. We all are a part of this world. *Visible*. And apparently, we *want* to be a part of this society. Or at least I do. And if we are going to celebrate events like Christopher Street Day in public, we need to come up with ways to make it a party for *everyone*. We want things to change, but we really need to remain mindful about how we go about his. So many individuals are fighting so hard for their individuality, possibly, they tend to forget sometimes, that we do not need to fight everybody.

For all those birds of paradise. For all those peoples, whose outward expression involves breaking the mainstream, crossing boundaries, pushing limits in such a way, that it SHOUTS! Well, honeys, you are asking to be seen, are you not? You forfeit the right to be surprised that you are singled out. What you share with trans* gender, is the necessity for a thick skin. And a truckload of patience. Trans* gender invariable go through a phase, of where their exterior is *visibly incongruent*, thus they are predestined to be targeted by media, greedy for sensations. What I have found to be extremely helpful, is to learn to differentiate. Between people who express surprise or even curiosity (be honest, this is a natural and legitimate response). And people who are veritably derogatory, transgressive, or depreciative.

So. I apologise if you feel like I am kink-shaming. Maybe I am too timid. And perhaps I do need to lighten up. Possibly it would do me good to get showered with champagne dusted with sparkles at the next CSD. However: I feel ambivalent about the way we queer peoples are representing ourselves. And I believe a little more empathy and mindfulness would do us good.

Affirmative action

There is a seriously heated discussion ongoing, about how trans* people in movies should in fact be played by trans* people. And not by cis* actors. For the record, I think Eddie Redmayne did a rather good job, as did Felicity Huffman. Strangely enough, it is the actors that catch the heat. As if they had much to do with the decision, of who gets the role. That they auditioned at all? But it is their job, right? They are actors.

On the one hand, all the arguments are extremely convincing. Yes, of course nobody knows more about gender dysphoria, than someone who suffers from it. Furthermore, trans* people are amongst the most marginalized. In many countries, they are systematically excluded from society. To the point of where their existence is not even legally recognised, and they are not protected by the law. So, yes, having more trans* people in the limelight, would be a great contributing step to engendering more awareness, and offering better and more subtle political leverage.

Trans* organisations state, that trans* people themselves are still sorting themselves out, still working on defining who they truly are. And this rings true in my books. As a matter of fact, I am of the opinion, *they will never be done*. Because part of being trans* is to be continuously evolving. But that is my opinion. Nevertheless, I find it hard to accept the argument, that cis* people get it wrong, the portraying a trans* person, that is. If trans* identity has not been defined (and how can it?) that how can anyone get it wrong?

What I do get, where I do wince, is when trans* women are portrayed by a cis-het* male in a bad costume. Because this truly reinforces the very persistent idea, that trans* women really are just guys in drag. And that their identity, and the struggle, is a hoax. A game of deception and allure. And yes. This is where I truly take offence. Because this is the absolute core of what trans* people are fighting to get into cis* people's heads: this is not a fetish. This is not about sex. This is not about getting it on, or with whom we want to get it on, or what we wear when we get it on. It is about *who we are*.

(Made so much harder by the fact that there is an entire branch of the sex-industry catering to fetishes of cross-dressing and trans* vestism. And that far too many trans* people outside Western Europe do not have access to legal protection or proper health care, and are thus forced to prostitute themselves.)

Nevertheless, I expect *ANY* actor to deliver a convincing performance. And to exclude cis-het* actors from queer or trans* roles, is just as discriminative as firing an employee because they have announced to undergo a transition. Or favouring the artwork of an artist of colour, simply on the grounds of their racial background. Or to have a woman in a leadership position, solely because she fulfils a quota. I understand that in today's day and age, it might be tempting, and even affirming, to make allowances for marginalised groups to be given tactical advantages. But *that can only ever be a temporary solution*. I will not accept people trying to bend a situation to their advantage, to make up for lack of talent. There is no fairness in that. I have met so many artists, trans* gender or otherwise "disadvantaged", who were not able to cope with being awarded second place. Even if it was clear, that the project that took first prize, simply outclassed the entire contest.

It remains a healthy practice to keep looking in the mirror every once in a while. To keep a critical eye on our own prejudice and our own capacity for bigotry and discrimination. And that goes hand in hand with the ability to accept criticism. The ability to do so, is a matter of maturity. Please bear in mind, I say accept. I do not say integrate or agree with. That decision is always the individual's.

And, to give pandora's box its moment of attention. At what point does self-expression turn into "I-don't-give-a-f*ck", and transgression? I do not mean safe-sane-consensual kink, or the more exotic birds of paradise that the Queer* has to offer. I am talking about disregarding the rights and the dignity of other people, in order to gratify one's own ego, and calling it progressive self-actualisation. Committing atrocities, and excusing the crime with the blatant hypocrisy, that the victims will be stronger and better off for it. Or disguising cruelty and hate, or the desire for retribution, by glossing it over with a veneer of political activism, or the guise of a statement of personal freedom.

NOT ACCEPTABLE.

Political correctness is a thin line to tread, and I worry about where it is taking us. If honest concerns or valid points of criticisms are cancelled, by means of an accusation of racism or homophobia. There is nothing inclusive or progressive about that. People of influence, placing thinly veiled homophobic statements in key places, spreading racism and hate. Undermining women's rights to self-determination. Disguising their venom with sophisticated arguments, or resorting to populistic tactics, emotionally derailing fact-founded debates.

The topic of affirmative action and quotas always reminds me of the experiences my Dad made in Johannesburg, after the referendum that gave the oppressed Indigenous Africans the right to vote. They were quick to pass laws to the effect, that all positions of power, economic and political, should be filled with Indigenous South Africans. Which led to companies, enterprises and infrastructure being administered and directed by people with neither the economic experience, nor the technical or financial knowhow. After all, the vast majority of the population had never been trained to cope with this kind of responsibility. That people were placed in offices of power, on the basis of their position in the hierarchy of the ruling ANC party, or their connection to families of influence, did nothing to improve matters.

And this is what *truly* gets my knickers in a twist.

There are altogether too many polit groups, members of polit groups, who exist entirely to serve their own ends. Constantly lobbying for a position of power. Each of them negotiating to ensure the greatest possible advantage. Complaining about life being unfair. But what they actually mean, is, that *they want life to be unfair in **their** favour.*

Which to me is proof that we, humanity, are still scrabbling for one-up-man-ship on the Darwinian playing ground.

And ironically, that may well cost us our survival on this jolly little globe.

In Germany and in the western European countries, there is an ongoing debate about quotas of women in leadership positions, positions of influence and power. And, yes, we absolutely need *fairer conditions* to which people of *any* gender or identity are imbursed, promoted, and empowered. Globally, not just western Europe or the so called first world countries. We most certainly need better and more farsighted means, to choose people *whom we entrust with such a responsibility*. But having a quota can only ever be a makeshift, a transient solution. The requirement for any person in a position of influence, be it social, political, or economic, should be *that they do a good job of it*. A decision based on talents and aptitudes. Regardless of ethnic origin, age group or gender.

The tragic thing is, that positions of power and influence appear to attract the entirely wrong sort of people. I believe it is vital, it is necessary that these leadership positions become vastly less attractive. Leadership may not, *cannot* be a trophy that provides privileges. Leadership must be a vocation. A calling.

A leader must be a servant and a provider.

One way to do this, would be via financial remuneration. Imagine if a CEO of a bank earned enough, to live comfortably, and send their kids to a good school. But not more than that. Imagine if states people and party officials were offered the kind of compensation, that permitted them to fulfil the duties and responsibilities with which we entrust them, and to take adequate care of their loved ones. But *not* rake in seven-figure stipends, and still be exempted from taxes. Not five villas, no yachts, not three cars for every child at all of the twelve condominiums. No bank account on the Caimans or in Lichtenstein.

It is a basic human need. To be supplied with sufficient food. To be warm. To have shelter. To be part of a group, and to receive affirmation from this group. This tribe.

Perhaps if we, as a society, get to the point of where we can ensure each other's existences? A state of coexisting, where the fear of losing everything is not so real anymore? Where we humans are in a position *to acknowledge, but ignore,* our preconditioned gut-reaction to always want *MORE*. Perhaps then, we can actually empower ourselves to point of where there are no more people who run out of ideas of how to burn their wealth. And no more people who have no idea of where their next meal will come from, or if the piece of cardboard on which they sleep will still be theirs, when the sun goes down.

Perhaps then the tone of your skin, and how you define your gender, will be less important?

Hope.

Hope is in the form of my Dad, a *Caucasian male on the far side of seventy*. And hope is in the form of Khanyisile, a sweet Zulu lady of similar age.

My Dad's relationship to Khani simply developed and grew. Contemplations of culture or ethnicity were not involved. Two people meeting at eye-level. Finding common ground. Permitting themselves vulnerability, and finding a readiness to share.

My Dad tells me of his long talks with Kahni. Books they read, movies or soap-operas they watch, newspaper articles they discuss, how they reflect on the struggles and development of South Africa. My Dad speaks with sadness and blank disgust, of how some men view women. And how such kind of men, make him feel ashamed for being a man at all.

And my Dad discusses with me, his daughter with a trans* background, what we need, what women need, what people need, to thrive. And be mindful and respectful of one another.

Another person who appears entirely untouched by hatred, or the need to divide the world into "US" versus "THEM", is Evangeline, my godmother. All she sees is a person, a human being in need. A parent, wanting to raise their family, and being helpless in the face of odds, troubled by transgressions and trauma of the past. Or in the face of a governmental administrative apparatus that is unyielding and callous to people who are already struggling with adapting to language and culture.

She is not oblivious to the fact that a father from Eritrea is going to feel challenged by a white female social worker in *his* house, telling him that our society expects his daughter to go to school. Telling him that noncompliance is *not* an option. And naturally, she is sometimes confronted by situations that have the potential to bring grievous harm. But the fact remains, she addresses the man as a father and as a provider. And she always shows respect, even if she is in disagreement. She always goes out of her way to provide solutions that enable people (patriarchs) to maintain face.

And she expresses her genuine appreciation on her next visit, when she discusses the daughter's homework supervision with the proud parents.

Hope is in the form of my direct supervisor and my colleagues, who continuously proves themselves great-hearted and open for change. People who recognise challenges and are willing to work on their own comfort zones. To accommodate people from all walks of life, and permit those people to feel welcome and make a new home away from their point of origin. People who engender and promote continuous learning as a way of life, and who have the bigger picture of an inclusive society in mind. People who are true to their beliefs and authentic in their way of being role models.

Hope is in the form of invitations to Queer* symposiums. Or to community of therapists and counsellors. Being welcomed as an affiliate, being appreciated for my contributions and my insights. Meeting so many cool people, who are capable and willing to look beyond their own immediate comforts and agendas. People who are ready to meet the world, *ALL of it*, at face level. People ready to step out of the shadows, and challenge themselves to be leaders and role models. People ready to learn. Ready to teach by example.

Hope is in the form of my students. Youths and young adults, who are interested and curious, keen as razors. Soaking up knowledge like sponges and relishing the vast abundancy of experiences that life has to offer them. Science, yes. But so much more. Eager to learn from all the people whose lives they touch, accepting opinions, reflecting on states of mind. Shaping their own form, their own person. Stepping up eagerly, gladly, proudly, to the responsibility of shaping this world's tomorrow. Making a home for themselves in a society that is welcoming. And mindful of the necessity, to care for our home. It gives me hope when I catch my students talking politics amongst themselves. And openly questioning the roles their parents have foreseen them in. Late teen and early tweens in earnest discussion how they cannot fathom how the world is full of injustice and neglect. Actively deliberating changes that are within their reach. Envisioning a future for themselves where heritage, identity and biological sex does not limit what you contribute to society.

Hope is in the form of my friends and loved ones. People who have whole-heartedly embraced Alice, and welcomed me into their hearts and into their homes. People who are always looking for ways to strengthen the community and empower other people. People to whom it is second nature to look further than their own comfort zones.

Hope is in the form of watching children, when I travel. In Germany, in Switzerland, France, Britain. In South Africa, Lesotho, Mauritius, in Malawi. In China. I have not yet been to the Americas, but I would love to. Hope is in the assurance that the joy of children is the same everywhere. Any continent, any skin tone, any culture. Children squealing with wild enthusiasm, chasing butterflies and each other. Children who approach each other with no expectations other than, "hey, wanna play?" Marvelling at the world with curiosity and a thirst for knowledge. Children are the same everywhere.

And hope is in the form of parents, all parents, who want nothing more, than see their children grow up to prosper.

Equity

Obviously, achieving a society that is balanced in maturity and enlightenment requires change. This is going to frighten a great many people. Because change implies, that something will be taken away from them.

There is something seductive about victimhood.

I should know, I have been there often enough. It automatically gives you the moral high ground. And it relieves you of responsibility. Providing you with the perfect excuse to go right ahead and do things you would normally not ever even consider. And the more "they" apparently hate us, the more we hate them. So, we are safe and secure in being justified in our resentment.

Having it hard is not a qualification. Having experienced discrimination is not a free ticket. It is a cycle of hypocrisy.

Sometimes, force is the only way that is immediately apparent. It is important to be aware of how easily violence comes to us. If you look at the world down the barrel of a gun, all you will ever see, are enemies. It remains a very deeply ingrained neural response to anything we perceive as a threat. But nobody is going to be willing to cooperate, nobody is going to accept you for who you are, if you are being rude and offensive. It seems, we forget too easily, that we are more likely to be accommodated, and our needs respected, if we actually show some respect in return.

We cannot afford to give other people any kind of excuse, to disqualify our demands for basic human rights. We cannot afford not taking the time, or not making the effort, to understand other people. Or to show them our appreciation. We *make* people judgemental and reluctant to change, by living up to stereotypes and prejudices. We need to remember, to give others a chance to understand us.

What we need, is a gentle change.

We need to impress people. We need to make them think, "Oh Wow! How cool is that! I want to be a part of that!"

And a part of that is people who in some way stand out being out and being visible. Being present in society and being seen as contributing their talents and resources. Whether it is Queer*, people with disabilities, sensory restrictions, or differences in culture, differences in skin tone. People who are "different" are recognised and appreciated for their input. It simply does not do to segregate and isolate. And neither should we wrap people in the toxic cotton candy of political correctness. Society needs role models that defy the norm. Examples that defy the streamlined, efficient socially-unobtrusive, well-adapted, and conform. *Alongside the well-established, tried-and tested, heart-of-the-oak*. People who step up and take on responsibility. People who care.

The beauty of the declaration of human right is, that it was developed on the basis of what every human needs and requires to thrive. Independent of origin or biology.

So, yes, I would like to see a cultural evolution that goes far beyond political and geographic limits. A change in how we perceive being human on a global scale. We need leaders who are ready and capable of putting pressure on ruling structures of those countries and cultures, that continue to that live off unjust profits, skimmed off the fruits of oppressed, the victimised, and the deceived.

We need to show people *that* we have learnt, and *what* we have learnt from our experiences. We need to make it clear that we are ready to share, to contribute to this world. For everyone. Being gentle takes more strength, takes more fortitude and self-confidence. Being gentle takes everything you have, to turn away from those reptile instincts.

In order to have that particular, special kind of strength, *each and every one of us needs to be their best possible self*.

To quote Martin Luther King, "I have a dream".

If we manage to provide an environment, where who you are is defined entirely by your choices, your actions, your talents and what you bring into your community? An environment where it is irrelevant that you are of mixed ethnic heritage, where the degree or lack of pigment in your skin is of no concern or consequence. But where your roots and your experiences are welcomed as a benefit and a resource. An environment where your self-designated gender or identity is only important to the person or persons you love. But your insights, your experiences of exploring yourself, testing your own limits, and relearning your own versatility, where those things are taken gratefully as a gift and as an enrichment.

An environment, where the only necessary restriction to personal development, is that you do not transgress.

Because you can offer something outside of what other people bring to the table. And "other" is accepted as being constructive, as being valuable.

We do not need to be equal.

We are not the same.

All of us, each and every one, we are individuals, singular and unique. And all of us gifted with unique talents, strengths, insights, wisdoms. What we need, is to be respectful. Mindful. We need to be open and inclusive. Together, we are more creative, more innovative, better equipped to what life, and the universe, throws our way.

Together, we can surpass, what we were yesterday.

(6) Being Guilty

Decisions…

…some break you.

Sometimes, there is no right *choice.*

So

You choose,

what you think you might live with.

And you spend the rest of your life, trying to make it right again.

And sometimes, you don't.

Looking back, you could think it was the harbinger of a storm drawing together on the horizon.

In 2008, Ella, our dear friend and neighbour, was diagnosed with ovarian cancer. The screaming irony of it was, she was an abdominal specialist surgeon herself, and she knew the exact stakes. She withered away over the space of two years, right under her husband's caring hands. She left him and their ten-year-old twins bereft and confused.

Before she died, and she knew she would, she spent almost a year looking for the right child minder and housekeeper for her two boys and their dad. And she made just as sure, that the young lady knew *exactly* what Ella expected of her; that she had *three* men to take care of, and ensure their healing, solace, and fulfilment.

Such is love.

Lisbeth, my aunt, came down with lung cancer. She fought very bravely for a little over a year. I visited her shortly before Christmas 2009. I would be that last time that we were to speak with each other.

I am so very grateful that we were on good terms when she died.

Beginnings

I was always highly perceptive of Wiebke's body. I think I watched her more mindfully, than she did herself.

It was November 2010 when I first noticed a subtle change in Wiebke's right breast, that worried me deeply. I urged her to get herself checked by her ob-gyn. In January 2011, we noticed something like a mild relapse into her fatigue syndrome, Wiebke was overly tired and exhausted. In March, I finally managed to persuade her, to get herself checked. The first standard examination came up blank, so I insisted. I remember Wiebke's ob-gyn being entirely incredulous, asking how I had managed to detect the anomaly. Without minute examination, she said, she would have missed it.

However, the breast tumour alone was not a sufficient explanation for the fatigue. As a consequence, Wiebke got herself checked by a neurologist as well. And he diagnosed a non-identifiable object blocking one of the ventricles leading past the cerebellum to the spinal canal. This would later turn out to be a glioma. Both tumours needed to be surgically removed as soon as possible, requiring a mastectomy and open brain surgery.

I still remember walking out of that doctor's office, the metallic taste of anxiety in my mouth like a foreboding wave. Putting on my bravest face, and hugging an ash faced Wiebke.

April 2011. The surgeries are performed within two weeks of each-other.

On two occasions, I find myself sitting next to Wiebke's bed, waiting for the narcosis to wear off. The smell of nitrous oxide is strong on her breath, metallic. I am holding her hand, her fingers almost as pale as the sheets. With my other hand, I dab at the blood oozing from the punctures left by the fixators that held her skull.

It is unusually warm for April. I have brought the first available strawberries, red as roses, their fragrance fills the room and makes the nurse smile when she enters. Apparently, the scent is strong enough to drive away the fumes and penetrate Wiebke's fog. She opens her eyes and smiles at me drowsily. Speaks my name with a voice like stones sliding over each other.

I am so grateful.

That she has woken at all. That she recognises me.

June through November 2011, Wiebke went for chemotherapy. I tried to be with her as often as I could.

Because two thirds of the lymph nodes were removed, she required lymphatic drainage massages. Twice to three times a week, she went to a professional therapist, but in order to support her healing, I had the therapist teach me the basics, so I would be able to perform this at home as well. I tried to move Wiebke to take the offered onco-psychotherapy, to support her in her recovery, but she flatly refused that and asked me not to mention it again. She reasoned that she was a doctor, and she knew exactly what she would be asked, or what she would be told. Insisting seemed to create more stress fer her, than the chemotherapy. So I dropped the topic. For now.

In the past, Wiebke had worked in a haematology / leukaemia ward. There, they had lost more patients to infections during chemotherapy, most particularly to invasive Aspergillosis, than to the actual leukaemia themselves. As a result, Wiebke was anxious, to the point of being obsessive / phobic, of catching a bacterial infection, or worse, inhaling spores from mould. Fact was, we were living in the five-room attic apartment of a beautiful house, some hundred and twenty years old. Dust and spores were a fact of life. As a consequence, I vacuumed our apartment daily and damp-wiped it three times a week. The kitchen and bathroom I wiped down with disinfectant on a daily basis. This would be something I continued to do until Wiebke returned to work eighteen months later. I cancelled a skill enhancement training, in coaching and change supervision, in order to be available to make sure Wiebke felt safe, despite the fact that I had been planning to take this course for almost two years.

I suggested a number of things to change in our apartment to make things easier, I came up with designs for supportive pillows so Wiebke' scars would not be strained, and she would retain less water in her arm. She outright refused those, getting really upset that I had picked up the topic at all. I remember being entirely nonplussed and hurt by her rejection.

To my utter dismay, Wiebke isolated herself completely. She told her family to stay away. I think in the entire time she was in medical care, she saw her Nimue, Linda, Melanie and Roman once. She forbade friends to come around.

To avoid catching an infection, was the reason she gave. Although, I rather suspect, she did not want anyone to see her in her weakened state. To make matters even more complicated, she forbade me to speak of her breast cancer. All anyone was permitted to know was that she had had a brain tumour. There were two or three friends who simply ignored Wiebke's instructions, and I dare presume, she was grateful for those visits, despite herself. But concerning her family and our other friends, I felt caught between the hammer and the anvil, making thin excuses. And I could feel how confused and estranged Astra and Freyja were by their sister's behaviour. I spent a *prohibitive* amount of energy *not* saying anything concise, without outright lying. Comforting Wiebke's family, without actually sharing any information.

I really wish Solveig would just stop asking. Of course, she is going spare with worry and grief for her daughter. I am running out of things to tell her. I no longer know how to comfort this mother. I spend nights just crying.

Damned if

One of the friends to visit us, despite Wiebke's prohibition, was Rafet. 2011 was also the year that he turned forty. The two of us had been talking of taking a road trip to Scotland, like, forever. And I had wanted to gift him with a ticket for his fortieth. However, considering that Wiebke was in the middle of chemotherapy, I was not about to up and leave.

Wiebke, however, argued that I desperately needed a break. That I needed time to myself, and that a holiday would do me good. She emphasised that Rafet and I had been talking about this for fifteen years or more, and now was the perfect time to do it. Wiebke actually kept up this line of argument for over a month, through two cycles of chemo. Again, I suspect that this had more to do with her needing to be invisible in her weakness. With her being conditioned to putting on a show of being independent and capable, that everything was okay. She became that insistent, and that irate, to where I appeared to be causing her more distress if I was there to take care of her, rather than if I gave both of us a break. I suppose I understand to some degree. She really did not want to be responsible for my missing out on something we had planned for so long.

At some point, she wore me down.

With *severe* misgivings, and a heavy heart, I set off for Scotland. The road trip itself was a mixture of exhilaration and disaster. Every day I checked in on Wiebke, to see how she was doing. I could tell over the phone that she was using her "I'm being brave" voice.

Scotland showed itself from its absolute sunniest side. Rafet and I went hiking on the moors, we toured so many ruins and castles, we climbed "mountains" and smiled our secret Swiss smile to ourselves.

And Rafet came down with a kidney-colic. He was in so much pain, he was delirious. I had to find him a hospital, where he spent three days. They gave him as many painkillers as they safely could, and I carted him off to an emergency flight back home. So, change of scenery, yes. Colourful and enriching, yes. Restive and regenerating? *Not by any means.*

When I returned home, Wiebke was largely silent, tense, cool to the point of being abrasive. In September 2011, she accused me of having abandoned her. She no longer tolerated *any* kind of proximity. Sexuality had long been gone; neither of us had felt the inclination since before the surgeries. But now she no longer permitted *any* kind of comfort, or even moral support. She no longer permitted me to perform the lymphatic drainage massage. Whenever I accompanied her anywhere, she was terse, passive aggressive.

I was devastated. This was more or less what I had been afraid of. I spent months not keeping my supper, although I was careful not to let her know this. The guilt and frustration ate at me like acid.

Wiebke spent most of her nights on the couch in front of the running television. For a few months, I stayed up until she was sleepy enough, and then tried to encourage her, to at least sleep in our bed, so she would not ruin her back. I slept in my office on a fold-out. At some point I simply could not keep up the useless persuasion, and I let her sleep on the couch.

December 2011 through May 2012 Wiebke underwent radiation treatment.

On several occasions, when I though she was in a receptive mood, I tried to approach the subject of her getting some form of counselling to deal with the fallout of cancer. Or to find somebody we both trusted, who could mediate between us to rekindle some kind of spark in our being together. To both, she said she did not have the energy. She radiated a permanent anger, she was callous and abrasive. And there was nothing I could do to remedy the situation. I started feeling cold all the time. I was so tired at times, I could have slept a year.

I began spending a great deal more time in my own head. My strength and my perseverance were growing thin. A great deal of both came from the satisfaction that I drew from the fact that I *was* a good teacher, and that I *was* appreciated by my colleagues. That kept me upright. That gave me purpose and rhythm to get up in the morning. My immediate colleagues did in fact register that I was deteriorating, and said as much. I spent hours after work, talking things through with Micha, who at the time was also having a rough patch with her husband. Gerlind, more than anyone I know, is able to keep private from business, but there were a number of times where she gave me a squeeze and offered me a hankie. All I could tell them was that I was doing my best to keep it all together and that things would surely start to improve at some point.

Of course, Darren and Suzy were among the people who regularly asked after Wiebke and how she was holding up. They were also among the few who noticed that I was slowly losing my grip. Or more to the point, they were among those who had the interest and the backbone to cut through all the "I am just a little tired, things will get better soon". And Darren asked if I would like to go indoor climbing with him on a weekly basis. Pre-mediated or not, this was something I was *good* at and I gratefully took him up on his offer. It provided me with an alternative for driving myself beyond the point of exhaustion, but instead of draining me further, this was the exhilarating kind.

In the same December 2011, Solveig, Wiebke's mother, was diagnosed with a pancreas carcinoma.

Watching this kind and gentle woman wither away under so much pain was heartbreaking. Gathering all her resources and strength, Wiebke arranged a ten-day trip to the seaside in Spain, and she persuaded, more or less coerced, her sisters Astra and Freyja to accompany her and their mother. In April 2012, Solveig needed to be hospitalised. She spent days in a state of semi-coherence. I spent hours at her bedside, reading to her, so she would know someone was there.

Later in the same month. Solveig exists in a world of pain. When she finally loses consciousness and her breathing lags, the doctors decide to turn up the morphine. And withdraw life support. All the adults are gathered at her bed. Astra and Ditmar, Freyja and Marcus, Wiebke and me. Torben kisses his wife a last time. I do not think I have ever seen anyone so distraught as Wiebke and her father.

In this moment of time, it goes through my mind, clear as glacier water. We are finite. It does not matter who stands at your death bed, it does not matter who holds your hand. It does not matter who reads to you.

And anything unlived thus far, will never be lived.

Ends

In September 2012, eighteen months after the surgeries, Wiebke was able to begin a reintegration program to get back into her job.

She was focussed entirely on her work, on "getting back on the horse", her own words. And, "This is all that she has left now". Hearing her speak those words, was like swallowing a razor blade. She still treated me like something you might find, very flat and slightly putrid, at the side of the road. In fact, she treated me as if I were directly responsible for her cancer. She still slept on the couch, in front of the running television. I still slept on the fold-out, in my office. In the morning, I would brew her the strongest coffee I could, and try to get her out the door on time.

Christmas 2012 was the first we spent without Solveig. The entire family was staying at Astra's and Ditmar's home. It was a melancholy and dreary affair, of rather forced cheer, and everyone trying to put the braves face possible on things. I did my best to keep the children occupied and distracted.

Something happened to upset Wiebke to a degree I had previously not experienced. She cursed me with language she would normally not ever even approach. I was rendered completely speechless. When she had calmed down, I asked what exactly had happened and what I had done to that she was so upset about. That only triggered more of the same. I think that was the first time I actually raised my voice. I asked what exactly she meant by all this. She became vague, until she finally turned her back on me.

I never learnt what precipitated that, or what it was all about. Of course I speculated, to the point of where I lost most of my meals. Somehow, I kept going.

Two weeks later, I approached her again and tried to talk it through. But all she said was that if I did not know, then I would never learn. And that she meant all those insults she had called me. That I fully deserved them.

On several occasions, I tried to open a discussion about us. Whether or not I was the only one who missed the warmth in our being together? About how I felt alone even if we were together, and that I had the impression she did too. About how we want to be with each other. About how I caught myself looking for ways to spend time apart, taking long walks on my own (thinking of my Dad and me on a bench under some trees, dawdling on our way home). About how we need to look forward. Wiebke either deflected the topics by saying she was tired, she lacked the energy, there was too much going on and she needed to focus on getting her feet back first. To the point where she became hostile.

I do not even know where I got my energy from. Work and weekly climbing remained those things where I could actually draw sustenance from. I still took care of the household, and I did my best to keep some form of contact upright to all our friends. When I think of those months, all I see is grey.

The fact was, that all of my immediate colleagues commented with concern and worry about how I appeared exhausted and lacked concentration, how my condition had deteriorated. A fair number of friends did too. I related truthfully enough that we were (I was) in a rough spot, and with everything that had happened, it was costing me more than I could come up with. All of them said I should take care, and take it slow, which I faithfully promised to do. Albeit with no idea of how I would actually achieve that.

Trigger warning.

Solveig and Torben had overseen the construction of their house themselves, when their two eldest were of schooling age. Solveig had a room to herself on the top floor. This was where she would write letters, work on her patchwork-quilting, or do her book-keeping. It used to be Astra's room when she still lived there, and now it doubled as a guest room since Astra had long moved out.

It was early February 2013, almost a year after Solveig's passing. The entire remaining family, both Wiebke's sisters with their families including the four children, Wiebke and me, and of course Torben. They were gathered around Torben's dining table to discuss Solveig's will and testament, the distribution of what Solveig had left as heritage. They discussed what Torben would keep, what which of the children would like to have. What they would donate, what they would toss.

The winter in Ulm is one of the harshest in many decades, with prolonged frost. Our thermometer shows 15°C below zero or more. In our home, which has old windows, there are beautiful frost flowers on the panes. It is too cold for snow. Any precipitation that falls, is in the form of fine powder, swept through the streets like dust that gathers in piles and dunes. The trees are laden with thick coats of crystals, glittering and pristine in the grey blue winter light.

I have failed.

I have failed as a friend. I have failed as a partner. I have failed as a husband. I have failed to be a man.

More importantly, I have failed at all my attempts to improve the situation. I see no way of redeeming myself. Of making good.

I am empty. Worthless.

I am exhausted. Drained. There is nothing left. All I want is to sleep.

I am in Solveig's room. There is a muted hum of voices downstairs from the rest of the family. I have excused myself, saying I am tired, I need to take half an hour. Instead of stretching out on the couch as I sometimes do, I am going through Solveig's things that sit silently, gathering dust.

Pancreas carcinoma can be one of the most painful ways to die. Solveig's doctor had given her pills so she could sleep, despite the crippling agony. Just one would take out an elephant. Or so I imagine.

The plan is to go for a long walk.

The plan is not to take a whole handful. The plan is to take two.

And just sit on a bench under a tree. And let the snow cover me.

I contemplate the pills. I have never taken sleeping pills before, so these should kick in just fine. Should be easy.

The face of my Dad goes through my mind. Tears. The vision of him standing beside my grave. Bereaved…

The room goes away, and I am… …somewhere.

My legs no longer support me. I cannot do this. I cannot do this to him. I cannot cause my father grief this way. I simply cannot. It would break him.

And I cannot do this to Eirian or Seraphina. I cannot make them think that this world is so cruel and devoid of love. At twenty-five, they deserve better.

The same goes for Nimue, Linda, Melanie and Roman. I cannot make them live in a world where someone they love should feel such a despair.

So I choose to live.

The room comes back to me. I am sitting on my heels, shivering, sobbing uncontrollably. Tears are streaming down my face, my hands blurry, the room distorted. I am fighting to keep silent.

Okay…

…now what?

After forty years, it was clear that I could not continue this way. Yet the fact remained, that I had no clue of how to go on.

(7) Being a Ghost

Denial…

…is a decision too.

The hardest thing about paralysis,

is the feeling of disempowerment.

The world keeps turning.

Going back is never a choice. We humans are not made to do so.

But to realise, that some things do not need to be endured.

And to realise, that in stepping forward, we can shape our path.

Proactively.

That is life.

Picture a palace of thought. The metaphor for the sum of all our experiences, learnings, and our core-beliefs. The library of our soul. For each of us, our palaces look different, each entirely individual. What they all have in common, though, are places that are open and airy, inviting and peaceful. Places that are filled with life and flurry, with colour and vibrant harmonies.

And what we all have, is a locked section. Sometimes, just an unobtrusive line of cabinets of books, that just happen to be in an out-of-the-way side corridor, the cabinets discreetly and tastefully locked. And sometimes, the proverbial dungeon of our soul, complete with walled off passages, and cells like vaults, lined with lead. Populated by wraiths and spectres.

Picture this palace on fire. There are places that are untouched, where apparently nothing is out of the ordinary. Not even smoke will mar the scenery. And there are places where the fire is raging out of control, consuming entire wings, the monsters running unchecked.

Fire is contagious. Smoke blackens. Sparks fly. Flames lick.

I believe, no therapy is ever a straight line. Certainly not when you are addressing a biography as heterogenic and motley as mine. I rather think, therapy is like trying to rescue such a palace of the mind from this fire. There are places that burn more visibly, where the pain is greater. So that is where we concentrate our efforts, where we focus our attention. And by the next session, it is possible that we need to address another topic entirely, even if the first fire has not yet been properly extinguished. But to ignore the new blaze would be so catastrophic, it would be ruinous to spend attention and energy on the first issue. Any firefighter will tell you, there is a significant difference between cosmetic damage and structural damage. But all the fire needs to be put out, or it will consume everything else.

Sounds straightforward, does it not? See fire, turn on water, problem solved. Except *this* fire is alive. Very much alive. It comes fully equipped with an instinct *honed* for survival and it is intelligent. The sole purpose of this fire is in fact to prevent the forbidden library from being read. Ever. So the fire might instigate multiple smaller conflagrations simply as a distraction. But it will, if all else fails, do its level best to burn down the library. Simply to protect us from being reminded of our own painful past.

And so it was with me. I started out addressing the most pressing issue. That I actually needed to find something to live for. Everything that followed, evolved from there.

The next breath

The entire remaining family is still gathered around the dining table. Torben, Wiebke, both her sisters, with their husbands and children.

Everyone else is still engrossed in the discussion of what to do with Solveig's belongings. And if Torben will not, after all, accept a domestic to help him with the huge house, since Wiebke and I are vastly outnumbered by the dust-bunny population. I think even Wiebke is beginning to realise, that the two of us are not up to the task of keeping Torben's home in shape, even though we have begun to spend two to three evenings a week, taking care of what is most obviously necessary.

It's as if my existence has been fractured. All of a sudden, the world has an edge, it cuts reality into pieces. Or. Maybe, I am finally aware of the break that has always been there…

I need to return to the others. I am not prepared to share this with anyone. I wash my face, tidy myself up. Remove any trace of the schism. And make my way back downstairs to the dining room.

I think Nimue caught some vibe.

Nimue smiles as she sees me coming down the stairs. She gets up from her chair to make room for me among the adults. However, sitting down and pretending to follow the discussion I have no stakes in, more than overstrains the resources I have.

Instead, I do what I'm good at: I function.

I smile back at Nimue, but instead of sitting down, I start clearing plates and dishes off the table. Wordlessly she joins me, as the others keep discussing, and we busy ourselves about clearing the table. In Solveig's tiny kitchen, where the light is not so good, and we are both busy balancing plates and dishes into the dishwasher, I permit myself to relax a little.

Nimue talks about how she loathes *the entire discussion about Solveig's things and how it is picked over like… …she hesitates. Sorrow is obvious in her face. Conflicting with the love for her family. I give her a brief hug, and tell her, that this is unfortunately the way of things. And does she not think it is better to see things continue to find use, instead of just sitting there, waiting to be cast aside?*

We talk of her school and how things are going. We talk about friends, hers, and mine. I speak of my students, about Darren and climbing. We get into the discussion of what she wants to do when she finishes school. She asks about my time in Dar es Salaam and Kwekwe.

Astra, Nimue's mother, shouts from the dining room, do we want to go for a walk? Get some fresh air?

Fresh air sounds good.

The cold is so sharp, it could cut glass. The sky is crisp and clear, the air pure as new snow.

Ashes

A few days and a lot of phone calls later, I realised just *how* hard it is to get a timely appointment with any kind of counselling specialist or therapists. Today, now that I offer counselling myself, I have an overview of the situation. It is entirely frightening how badly overburdened professional (and less professional) counselling services are.

I got lucky.

About the same time we buried Solveig, Adrian had something of a mid-life-crisis. He bought himself a vintage Porsche and found himself an affair. Krista found out about the affair, of course she did. (To give Adrian his due credit, he manned up in so many ways, and for a time, he seemed to be winning the fight against his inner demons). The two of them had quite the fall-out, upon which Krista turned to me for moral support and empathy. We spent hours in cafés, talking through her turmoil and feeling of depreciation, triggered by Adrian and his need for "more". The long and the short of this is, that Krista was one of the seven people (Darren, with whom I still went climbing. Rafet, who found his way from Zürich. Plus, my four immediate colleagues, Micha, Gerlind, Stephan and Roddy) who actually addressed me, and asked, *genuinely* asked, how I was doing and what I needed in the way of support.

So, Krista gave me the phone number of the clerical social welfare services, and the name of the counsellor who had managed to sort out the crisis in her heart, and the crisis of her relationship. She said to ask for Ms Steyr, and to go to no one else. When I phoned them up, I must have either sounded desperate enough or pathetic enough, because the lady in administration came up with an appointment someone else had cancelled in very short order. I told her I would take it, I would cancel all my other responsibilities, I would be there.

Ms Steyr was (is) a kindly lady, elegant and cultivated, always neatly groomed and well dressed, soft spoken and discerning. Her therapy room was brightly lit, with a view into an interior yard. One wall was taken by a shelf, abundant in books and toys, and whatever other props she required to help her clients find the right metaphors for their lives. I am entirely sure she could be tough as nails, if she thought it would help her clients. And yet, with some very few exceptions where she became insistent, she always treated me like something very fragile, ephemeral. Which I suppose I *was* when we first got to know each other.

In our very first session, she showed how she wasted entirely no time and cut straight to the chase. Just as she proved how experienced, and empathic, she was. I really appreciated her for that.

She asks me to relate what brings me to her.

I can see her mind working as I speak, aware with all her senses. I tell her how Wiebke and I have our good times, and our not so good times. That I expect this to be normal for any relationship. I relate to her step by step, the sequence of illnesses, debilities, and recovery, of miscommunications and reciprocal hurt feelings, that lead up to the present. How Wiebke accuses me of having abandoned her. I tell her how I lack any perspective, any options. I feel powerless to make this right again. How I no longer feel anything except fatigue. How my strength is gone.

I tell her, that I simply do not know how to carry on.

She is silent for a few breaths. "Wow, that's a lot. Even considering what I hear in this office every day. And you carry this all by yourself?" I appreciate her acknowledging that. But all I am capable of is shrugging my shoulders, trying to keep myself from falling apart completely.

"I've stepped away from the abyss. But I don't know where to go from here. I see no path. And I cannot go back the way I came. I cannot. There is nothing *there anymore."*

She asked me directly, if I had considered or attempted suicide. Which I confirmed. If there was a danger of my doing so again. Which I denied, truthfully.

We spoke of what I expected from coming to her. Where I saw myself in five years. What exactly I wanted, and what I thought her part in that was. And I told her how I needed to regain my strength. How I needed to get myself together again and have some kind of path to follow for myself, before even being able to think of what I wanted in the next six months, never mind the next five years. I said, I needed to get back to where Wiebke and I would be able to draw strength and joy from being together. I needed to find a way to fix our relationship.

I told Ms Steyr, if I was going to keep my marriage together, I needed to find back to having something to live *for*. That continuing like this would kill me, either by my own doing. Or because I would suffer a cardiac arrest or develop cancer, simply because my body did not want to imprison my soul any longer. And I said I needed her help in showing me things I failed to see. I needed her to reflect what remained in me, remind me of my resources. Show me options and enable me to make choices, actually see a path. And from there, I could speak with Wiebke about where we were going to go, together.

I think she was surprised, even pleased, that I recognised that she was not going to offer me quick-fix solutions. Or do any of the work for me.

She asks me how I came to her. We speak of Krista and Adrian. And I relate how Krista recommended I ask for her specifically. Something in her body language tells me, there is still something on her mind. She makes a decision.

"Tell me, Mr Oehninger, is there a chance that you have fallen in love... ...outside your marriage? And perhaps... ...inside your gender?"

I am startled.

In a heartbeat, I make a choice. If I truly want help, then I need to be honest. This is as much an admission to myself, as it is a clarification for Ms Steyr.

"I have barely been capable of feeling joy, never mind feeling passion in the past two and a half years. Besides, I would never betray trust. It is not who I am. As for gender, I am not gay. I am trans* gender. I am a woman."

I will not forget the look of forthright surprise on her face. However, she never misgendered me again.

Baby steps

For a year, I visited Ms Steyr in her office every two weeks. Sometimes even once a week. This was also the time I began writing long letters to Evangeline, relating what I was going through.

Wiebke made no indication that she might have thought it strange that I would seek counselling all of a sudden. After all, she knew nothing of how close I had come to suicide. Ironically (I find it ironical), Wiebke expressed a great deal of affirmation to the effect that she thought "it would do me good." Although she never specified what changes she hoped it would effect.

For the next twelve months, Ms Steyr patiently, mindfully, kindly helped me reflect on my achievements and my strengths. We went through all the things that I had brought about or enabled, that were good in my life. We reflected on the things that were important to me, that motivated me, from which I drew strength and self-esteem. And we re-established where I needed to be, in order to feel good about myself.

It took me a year of therapy, to go from saying, "I cannot do this to my Dad," to being able to say, "I cannot do this to myself."

And since you are probably wondering, it would take me another four years of therapy to be able to touch the hotplate of my soul, that was the child I chose not to have.

Tutoring and coaching my students was enriching and rewarding. I saw no reason to stop doing that, although I *did* see, that my work had become a replacement for any appreciation I was getting from my private life. This simply could not continue at the present level of dedication. Even Stephan, our team leader and supervisor, spoke earnestly about how he was concerned about my health. How I needed to keep an eye on my working hours and respect my own stamina levels. I was going to need to reduce the amount of time and energy I invested there if I was to have anything left for myself.

So. I had the will to survive. But I still required something to live for. Gradually, gradually, I began to rebuild some form of idea, of what I wanted to do with the remaining years that I might or might not live to see. I began with those that were easy. To begin with, I clung to the security of my relationship to Wiebke, such as it was. And to the love that had once warmed me. I clung to this persona of the perfect gentleman, catering to Wiebke's wishes and trying to earn her respect and affection.

Ms Steyr and I went through my past with Wiebke, what had brought us together. Most particularly, what had kept us together. We explored where I saw the strengths in our relationship. The common ground. And what either of us contributed to keeping us together. What were patterns that required strength. Patience. Ms Steyr was gently adamant and meticulously mindful, at guiding me through the network of guilt and sense of duty that I had gotten myself trapped in. And she was caring but implacable, in pointing out what she perceived as my being toxically dependent, in an environment typical for an abusive relationship. And that, also typical for the situation, I was enabling Wiebke in her gaslighting.

So, we set about coming up with tasks and way markers, to try and bring back some life into my marriage, and to bring about a shift in balance, where Wiebke and I could share a more transparent and appreciative exchange. I did not see myself capable of doing that on my own. To me it was clear, I would need someone to counsel Wiebke and me, who would have an unbiased and independent take on how we communicated and how we enabled each other. And who would prevent Wiebke from shutting me down. I felt unable to communicate in a way where I would not be misunderstood, or my intentions misread.

I tried to effect once more, that Wiebke and I would talk to somebody we both trusted. To see the common good intentions, and guide us back to where we could actually communicate about the things that wounded us, and caused us to retreat so far. I needed to find a way to resolve all this contrition. I needed to find a way to achieve forgiveness for having abandoned Wiebke. Find a way to permit her to heal. Or so I thought.

A fragment of time, another episode of us sitting across from each other, on the sofa in our living room.

I am appealing to Wiebke that we need someone to help us talk to each other. "Look, I want us to be good. I love you and I want us to be good with each other. Good for each other. But I feel overwhelmed and frankly I feel intimidated. I really think we need someone to mediate".

She looks disgusted. "Don't tell me you love me. Not ever again".

And so, I didn't. I found other ways to express my affection and my loyalty. But the world had grown several degrees colder.

I offered Wiebke that she could choose whomever she wanted, as long as we actually started talking again. Not about how stressful work was. Not about whom to invite for supper, and what to cook. Not about shopping for food or clothes. But talk about the things we wanted from life. And from each other. From this relationship. This she blankly refused, by saying, it would bring nothing. When I queried what she meant by that, she stated that I (me) would never change, and that she would gain nothing by having an outsider there.

I did my best to intensify contacts to friends and even rekindle some contacts to people who had grown distant. I had the impression, Wiebke rather appreciated this, and did her best to give the overall impression that everything was good, everything was normal. Adrian took on a contract in Boston, so he and Krista moved to the USA for two years. I was very sorry to see them go, and unfortunately that did make keeping in touch less matter-of-course. I tried to reach out to my family in Bern and in Zürich.

But the fact remained, I barely had the energy to actually look people in the face, so travel to Switzerland was a daunting prospect. Instead, I spent long hours on the phone with Rafet, Evangeline and Eirian. I spoke with my Dad as often as I could. I phoned up my mother every once in a while.

In complete contradiction to what I just said about my energy, I renewed my interest in photography and art in general, doing my best to keep an open eye out for expositions and curiosities (This was easier, I didn't have to lie to loved ones in the face about how I was doing). I went to art galleries, I made sure Wiebke took time to go visit an art fair with me. And I encouraged plans around travel and exploring culture. To the effect that we took shorter weekend trips to Dresden, to Stuttgart, several trips to Munich.

We still spent enormous amounts of time with Torben. We spent three evenings a week with him, cooking for him and cleaning what we could. I did not even dare raise the point, that Wiebke seemed unperturbed to clean her father's house. She seemed to see it as her devoted daughter's duty. But if confronted with our own household, she suffered from anxiety about mould, her recovering immune system and pneumonia.

In these months, I grew aware of how I made room for other people's choices, particularly Wiebke, of course. How I deferred to other people's convenience, in lieu of my own. How I was conditioned to do so. Ms Steyr helped me see and analyse my behaviour patterns, particularly those cost me far more energy that I got any appreciation for. I behaved as was expected of the role of the perfect gentleman, that I was playing. I no longer shopped in the ladies' department. Wiebke would have been mortified.

Of course, I realised that I could hardly turn back time and make everything "good" again. Over the course of many sessions with Ms Steyr came the realisation, that the identity of this man was gone. And I quite simply no longer wanted to be this person. There was still a love there for Wiebke. But it was weighed down, buried under guilt and sorrow, for which I had no solutions. I no longer drew joy or even comfort from our being together. I do not remember having ever been so cold in my life. I remember Wiebke irritably reprimanding me, telling me I looked ridiculous. It was a chill I could not shake, even if I wore pullovers and long-sleeved shirts in the middle of summer.

Of course, Wiebke expressed curiosity as to how my therapy was progressing and what it was that we were discussing. Hesitantly, I told her of how I struggled with finding any joy. I think that was when she realised, just how far gone I was. And I told her how I my energy was drained, how I had found motivating myself more and more difficult.

I tell Wiebke of how I struggle with my identity. I tell her how my idea of self, in this role as a man, has gotten lost. And I can't find it anymore. I simply don't know what to do.

I tell Wiebke, how a great many attributes inside me are female, not male. That I am trans* gender, and that somehow, I need to acknowledge that.

To my surprise, Wiebke says, "Yes, I know". Maybe she does remember our conversation twenty years ago? Or perhaps this is a blooming of tenderness and compassion?

I tell Wiebke, how I really do not want us to continue this way. How I want to work on finding common ground. But that we needed a fresh start. I needed a fresh start.

"I know you have forbidden me to say so. But, I love you. I still do. But my love is buried under all this grief. And guilt from your feeling abandoned by me. I want us to work out together, what it is that we really want from each other".

Again, I try, "I really believe we would benefit from talking to someone with an outside view on this. Someone we both trust. Someone you trust. Someone who can help us get through this".

Again, Wiebke refuses, "No. I am not the person that needs therapy. We will figure this out somehow".

I was through one of these discussions that we planned our travels in China.

In November 2013, we took a round tour trip to China. Witnessing the Forbidden City, and the changing of the guard on the Tiananmen Square. Strolling through the Hutongs of Beijing, taking in the food markets and the art galleries. Climbing the steepness of the Great Wall, as it winds its way through the mountains of Badaling. Visiting the terra-cotta legions of Xi-An, wandering through the old city, mingling with the citizens. Browsing through the food markets of Guilin, being paddled down the Li-River on a bamboo raft, between surreal towering chalk pillars. Climbing the rice terraces of Longsheng, breathing deeply of the brisk mountain air. Marvelling at the secret zen gardens and the thousand bridges of Suzhou, drinking in the wonder of millennia of human aesthetics. Having my breath taken by the towering skyline of

Shanghai. Diving into its deluge of smells, colours and lights of the pulsing cyberpunk nightlife. And the total contrast, dancing a meditative waltz, together with the street dancers under ancient trees, and the soft glow of distant streetlights.

And. Observing families, sometimes parents with children, sometimes four generations. Some proud and extroverted. Some lost in tender appreciation and gratitude of being given the gift of sharing each other's lives.

Being wrapped into spontaneous dialogues and haggling over artworks, possibly priceless, possibly worthless, but certainly a keepsake. Picking my way through food stalls, following my nose and my intuition, being adventurous and free of inhibition. Speaking with so many bright and hopeful students and young adults, relentlessly curious, profusely friendly, and eager to test their language skills. It was in these conversations that I truly understood the term "laowai", as in, not old in years, but old in experience. Well-travelled. Exchanging stories and insights with these people, relating hopes and experiences was such an eye opener. Such a blinding realisation of common ground and shared dreams.

It was a most, most beautiful journey, and one of the most enriching experiences of my life. I learnt so incredibly much. Most importantly, it was a reminder that other cultures are collectives of people, with lives to live and families to raise. And it confirmed, that regardless of what political parties enforce, all these people truly desire, is to watch their loved ones thrive in peace. To see their children grow up safe and happy. And I was reminded of my school days. In an environment, where non-conformity is sanctioned with ruthless brutality, then resistance comes at a prohibitive price. And as an adult, is something you can only afford if you have no loved ones or dependants.

The journey certainly fulfilled my desire to learn and experience new things, see new places. But at the same time, it was a distraction. And while it certainly gave me inspiration and new impressions, it did little in the way of opening communication between Wiebke and me. On the contrary, I was acutely aware of just how much time I spent outside myself, looking at this man, touring all these magnificent landmarks, fabulous historical sites, and beautiful places.

The journey also required four weeks of close proximity to Wiebke. As I had hoped, it enabled something to give and shift in the way we lived next to each other. When we returned to Ulm, she actually asked me to move back into our bedroom. Not that this meant we were talking. And it certainly did not mean we were intimate. After all, she still spent most nights on the couch. In fact, I was relieved she did not make any attempt at seduction, because I was absolutely not in the mood. Nevertheless, something in that change gave me some kind of hope.

But the man whose life I had lived, remained gone. Nancy had, if you will, stepped in to fill his shoes. And the longer this in-between state lasted, the longer I lived and breathed like the woman that I am. And the more strongly, it felt like *me*. I suppose it was by this, that I realised, that not only *was* I a woman, but that I would need to acknowledge this and bring it into my life. My real life.

Even if my body language had never been a stereotype male, I think in those months, it changed again radically.

Bridges

May 2014. Little had actually changed. Wiebke and I still lived alongside each other. Every so often, we would invite friends for dinner. We would discuss what to cook, what needed to be bought, who was going to take care of what (I still took care of cleaning). Ironically, despite the pretence, I was really enthusiastic about these evenings, because Wiebke made every effort to present a perfect exterior, and her tone with me was so much more pleasant and easier to take.

After Solveig's passing, we spent two evenings a week, or more, at Torben's house, to keep tabs on Wiebke's father. I came to dread these evenings. I simply did not have the energy to devote to cleaning yet another living space next to what I already invested into our own apartment. The house smelt stale. For a while, Torben refused a housekeeper, as a result of which the house was always musty.

To be fair, Torben evolved enormously following Solveig's death. He learnt the basics of preparing a warm meal and laundering his clothes. And yet, there were altogether too many bottles of wine, whisky and vodka in places that were almost-but-not-quite hiding places. He never spoke Solveig's name. I pitied (pity) Torben. Such a proud man, so creative and strong in his profession. When he spoke of his field trips as a youth, I could still see the boy he was at heart. Now so broken, in ways he was not even capable of articulating. Nobody had ever taught him how.

It was strange, the dynamic between Wiebke and Torben. I was (and remain today) deeply anxious and disturbed by how Wiebke had taken on role her mother had formerly fulfilled. From what I know, she still does so today. Looking after Torben's daily needs, looking after his house, managing his social contacts. And by strange irony, put herself in the exact same position of casual depreciation and disregard for the effort of making a home, about which she was (is) so angry. I raised the point as gently as I could, but it was nothing she was prepared to analyse, never mind question. My raising the issue at all was not something she took well, so that caused even more friction.

So I did my best to support her in the only way I knew how: I made myself useful by making dinner or cleaning. To prevent us from spending entire weekends at Torben's place, I insisted on inviting him to our place for Saturday dinner.

I felt myself torn between fatigue from lack of self-care, and supporting these two people for whom I felt love. And of course my ever present sense of duty, and not being worth anything, unless serving others' needs.

I still went climbing once a week with Darren.

If we were alone, we spent the evening on our respective ends of the sofa, our legs not touching. Wiebke would watch her sitcoms, and I would play some RPG on my laptop. At some point she would fall asleep. I would make sure she was tucked in safe and snug, and from there I went to bed. I slept in our bedroom, and Wiebke slept on the couch.

I admit, I was stuck. I was still waiting for some form of enlightenment as to precisely how I wanted to continue living. I knew I was a woman. I felt that now very clearly. But I found no way to integrate this identity into the life I was living. Not without causing mayor disruption. Other than focusing on RPGs and casting wistful glances at pretty tops and dresses if I accompanied Wiebke shopping.

One of the most disturbing questions at this point was, what did I gain from upholding the status quo? Because obviously, things were not improving. The fact was, I was afraid. Plain and simple. Afraid, that if I actually admitted to being a woman, and if I was consequent about it, then I would be ostracised, anathematized, vilified by the people I loved. I would lose my home, my family, my friends, my job, my existence. I was afraid of change.

And. I was afraid of the fact, that I was not alone to blame for the predicament Wiebke and I were in. And to solve this, I would need to confront her. I realised I was genuinely frightened of that prospect. So much so, that I was almost more inclined remain in my current role. Not at all fair towards Wiebke. But it was, at the time, beyond my abilities to change.

At some point, I think Wiebke plain lost her patience, that I was "not getting any better". She demanded to know what I intended to do about myself. I tried to explain how stuck I was. That I had no idea of how to rebuild our trust. How I did not know how to resolve the double bind of my identity. She seemed extremely disgruntled at that, "So this is not about you abandoning me?"

What was I supposed to reply to that?

Of course that accusation was the push that had originally upset the balance and sent me over the edge. Of course it still contributed to the overall mess I was in, contributed to my feeling unworthy and guilty. But I had promised myself I would do anything I could, to prevent this from degenerating into a match of reciprocal accusations. And I had sworn I would not guilt trip Wiebke into anything. Not knowing what else I could say, I simply broke down in tears. Which caused her to lose her patience entirely.

I waited for what I thought was a good opportunity. Some days later, we had come back from Torben's place where we had cooked lunch for him. Wiebke had taken her usual place on the sofa and was about to switch on the television. I asked if she had the mind to talk.

I tell her that I cannot find my way. That I feel lost. Lost in my lack of identity. Lost in our relationship. I tell Wiebke that I need to find a way to resolve of all this guilt and shame I am carrying. Because it's making me blind to any joy in this life.

I tell her that I want to make this work. Our being together. But that I cannot do it alone. And that it will take some trust and compromise on her part as well as mine, because I simply do not have the strength to continue like this.

And I tell Wiebke, that I cannot find this man anymore. He is gone. And I do not know if he will ever return. I tell her that the me that is left, is a woman. And whatever that means, I need to find a way to bring a balance to myself somehow. A balance of who I am and who we want to be.

Wiebke looks at me with blatant disgust and impatience, "That's your problem. You will have to sort it out with yourself."

I am too stunned to react. A part of me is outside myself, watching me sit on the sofa. Frozen. Watching the two of us.

Wiebke mutters, "Oh for heaven's sake, stop that." and reaches for the remote control.

I have no idea how long I sat there. In my mind, the moments stretched out to eternity. But it cannot have been more than a few heartbeats.

I left the living room and gently closed the door behind me. I heard the television come to life.

I fetched my blanket from the bedroom and brought that to my office. I fetched some foldable laundry baskets and piled in my basics. Jeans, t-shirts, underwear, socks, sweaters.

And I never went back in that bedroom.

As a bird

Or in other words, nothing left to lose.

I remember Ms Steyr being *LIVID*.

And she was surprised that I was not, like her, furious with disappointment. She reminded me with absolute certainty, that the promise of marriage went both ways. And that in her opinion, I had more than fulfilled my fair share of the union. She followed that up with, that she had counselled so many women in abusive, toxic relationships, and that the same was clearly the case here. And that she would give me the same advice, as she had given all those other women; that I would do best, to get myself to safety.

But I was just far too numb. I was shell-shocked into paralysis.

So. Now what? What did I want to do? Who did I want to be?

The fact was, *I no longer felt bound to the promise I had once given*. I still followed the routine of my male character, obviously. But now it really *was* just a role to perform. A duty. And it chafed horribly. I no longer wanted to be this person.

It was not that I no longer loved Wiebke. I did. I wanted (want) her to be well. Safe. But in my mind, she had made it more than clear, that I was not the person that made her happy. Not the person she needed at her side. And she had, with absolute certainty, withdrawn any mandate that I might once have had, to care for her. She had made it clear she no longer trusted me.

All of a sudden, making a decision was easy.

In the early summer of 2014, in the absence of any remaining commitment to male identity and any desire to uphold this role, I did something I had not *ever* done before. I made plans without ever informing Wiebke. It was easy. Wiebke was "back on her horse," and her calendar was liberally freckled with business trips. In the absence of any limitations, I tried out what it really felt like to move among people as a woman.

Within her world, Ms Steyr went out of her way to ensure I was safe and well cared for. She spoke with her hairdresser and sent me his way, recommending him as a worker of miracles. He was in fact the first non-medical professional to whom I disclosed myself. It took all my available courage, but I told him of my situation, and asked him if it were possible to have my hair cut in a feminine hair style, but to be able to gather it together in a "man bun".

He looks at me intensely, his forehead creasing, his eyes concentrated behind his glasses. Like a specialist studying a rare butterfly. Or an artist contemplating an empty canvas, envisioning... ...I am acutely aware of my palms turning damp and my breathing growing shallow. I am scared. And exhilarated.

He mutters, more to himself than to me, "Ah, you're Ms Steyr's friend. She said you'd be coming."

And then he transforms into this humorous and buoyant caregiver, beaming at me with genuine cheerfulness. "I know just the thing! Leave it all up to me."

And I did. He took great care to make sure I was at ease, taking over an hour to cut my hair. We spoke a great deal about stereotypes, gender roles and societies' expectations. And he treated me with such ease and matter-of-fact-ness, something I had not yet experienced before. Even in professional circles, this is rare. He is and remains one of those specialists who has my deep trust and with whom I share more than just perfunctory "hidey and howdy."

But a haircut alone was of course not enough to diminish the male signals my body was broadcasting.

There are people, mainly professional transvestite artists, who specialise in doing up other people, mainly men, and let them experience the other gender role for a few hours. After all, for grown-ups, this takes a little more effort and hardware, than simply putting on different clothes. I invested a little extra. After all, I did not just want to get myself made up, I wanted to learn how to do it myself. Properly.

I had not used make-up in twenty-four years. Despite of what I knew myself to be, seeing this woman in the mirror required some serious getting used to. I needed to find out if I could deal with my erstwhile reflection and look past the face that my mind had been conditioned to see.

Still, I am a quick study, doing my make-up was something I got the hang of easily. I started plucking my eyebrows and shaved my legs on a regular basis. And over the summer and autumn, I spent several days in Frankfurt, then in Zürich, and in Munich. I did what I had dreamt of my entire life: I went shopping. Strolling through the aisles, sifting through the clothes, trying on anything that caught my eye. Who would have thought that spending money could be so liberating?

Although, to protect Wiebke, I never did so in our hometown of Ulm. And I made sure her family never caught wind of it. There had been some instances, by some twist of fate, where conversation at Torben's dinner table had somehow ended up revolving around Queer* people. Some of those statements had not been pretty. "This is so disgusting", or Torben literally asking how "there must be something modern medicine could do about those poor wretches?". Astra and Ditmar are not precisely role-models of inclusion either, when I think of discussions revolving around adoption rights. It was another of those instances, that I was glad not to share Wiebke's surname. It made protecting her so much easier.

In those days abroad, I was only ever openly misgendered once. An elderly lady with a keen eye, and a lot of pluck, asked me if I was in fact a man. She was sitting opposite me in the Frankfurt subway with a grocery bag on her knees. She was simply curious, and as polite as you can possibly be when you are uncertain about somebody's gender. Everyone else simply walked right past me.

None of the ladies (or the few gents) who attended the clothing stores ever remarked anything or even raised an eyebrow. What a surprise that was! And it gave me quite some confidence. On the contrary, one of the cashiers actually reprimanded me, for wanting to pay "with my husband's credit card". I simply came clean. I straight up told her I was trans* gender, and that the card was mine. She reacted with total surprise. Once she had recovered, she was entirely sweet and respectful, complimenting me for following my designated path.

I felt so incredibly liberated.

The realisation that I had in fact found my path, that I had found a way that lead out of the despair, was such a flood of joy and empowerment. And above all, *hope*. And if I am honest, telling a complete stranger and earning respect and dignity was such an incredible adrenaline high.

Not to imply that any of this was easy. Stepping out into the street "in drag" as it were, was not something I managed on a full stomach. There were moments, many of them, where I would have been promptly sick from the sheer tension. I was *acutely* aware of every casual glance and look in my direction. It cost me extreme amounts of energy, confronting my anxiety, trying to remain mindful of the difference between getting looks of actual depreciation and ordinary "men-look-at-anything-with-legs" looks. And outing myself to somebody, like to the lady who checked my card, took every shred of nerve I had. And while it left me flooded with adrenaline, as I imagine a bungee jump would, it also left me utterly, utterly wiped out.

And regardless of how much or how little time I spent dressed as a woman, leading this double existence, feeling myself to be a woman whilst upholding this male role to society drained my strength seemingly twice as fast. I think I spent days more or less sleepwalking, doing my best to keep all the balls in the air.

Every once in a while, I dropped one. Or even several. Things slipping past my attention, or in some cases, I simply gave up and let things crash. Supplies did not get bough, be it for home or work. Papers did not get marked, important discussions were neglected, appointments were forgotten. I put immense focus and effort in keeping myself together at work, because I felt this was my only thread to continue existing. But still, I know for a fact that my reliability and my productivity suffered. Even the awareness, that any fall-out would only add to the overall stress level, failed to pierce the leaden fatigue I experienced.

Along with this, deciding to follow my path opened an entire new line of questions. To begin with, I thought it would be the natural thing to do, to call myself Nancy. But that did not feel right. Nancy still spent most of the time hugging herself and weeping. Or she was consumed by silent, but utter vitriolic rage. Directed mainly at herself. It was going to take another year of therapy, but in retrospect, it is blatantly clear. Nancy had quite simply had enough. Too much violence, too much grief, entirely too much rejection. She made it clear, that she would have no part of the world of the living. And perhaps she had never been truly a part of this world...

Another strong contributing factor, that only became clear in hindsight, was, that Nancy is asexual. And I am not. I think Nancy burned all that away, together with so many other things. Lucky for me, she never burned away her empathy. She may be cynical and impulsive, possibly even hard. But at heart, she remains a person of kindness.

Either way, I needed a new name for myself.

This is another of those episodes, where I can truly no longer differentiate between virtual and reality. In those days. In those months of frozen solitude, sitting on the same sofa, but in different worlds. While Wiebke was watching her sit-coms, I was immersed in my laptop, our legs no longer intertwined. I was playing a game that relied on a great many elements of Lewis Carroll's "Alice in Wonderland." ("Alice: Madness Returns", developed by American James McGee, published through Electronic Arts by Spicy Horse).

I will not go into the game, but as in the original book, the Cheshire Cat plays an important role, acting as a kind of mentor. In the game, possibly even a therapist, goading and coercing Alice through the labyrinth of her own psyche, as she deals with her past of abuse and transgressions. He is not altogether nice, this Cheshire Cat. Rather, he seems to gain a sadistic pleasure from watching Alice struggle with coming to terms what she has done in order to free herself from her tormentor. But he is undeniably helpful.

The game is interspersed with cut-scenes, which are always crucial to the plot and offer up key insights on how exactly Alice came to be here, and why she is even going to all this trouble.

I have a memory of one of these cut-scenes.

Alice has just successfully navigated a "level", and her triumph is ridiculed by the Cheshire Cat, who sees right through her attempt to procrastinate looking at the *actual* memory that torments her.

"Aah, Alice, do you really want to spend the rest of your life in your imagination?"

*That single sentence. That solitary question flashes me so completely, that I forget everything else. That query neatly summarises **everything** that I have been doing.*

In my memory, I still see the exact way he preens himself, twirling his whiskers as if they were a waxed moustache. I have since played the game again. Twice. I never found the cut-scene again. I had no way of telling whether any of it was real, or whether this was another fragment of a dream that snuck into my conscious. In fact, research tells me, the line is not from the game at all. My memory is a construct of my own subconscious. A dream.

And yet. Since then, I have borne the name Alice. And I dare say, it is appropriate.

Realisation

A great many things followed, evolving in parallel, very often being inter-dependent. Finding an appropriate and qualified therapist, getting my name and gender legally changed, finding an endocrinologist, finding a surgeon for my GRS.

I have never been someone to do things half-heartedly.

One of the earliest things I set in motion, early July 2014, was the official fact of my name and assigned gender. The entire odyssey around getting a legal change of name and gender just mocks all description. What this was going to cost me in terms of nerves and other resources is irretrievable. I started out by inquiring at the Swiss consulate if they were able to offer some guidance. But even then, it was clear, I was going to need professional help.

If I was going to finally live my life as a woman, I needed someone who would enable me to transition. I needed to find myself another therapist, ideally somebody who was experienced with trans* people. And qualified to actually do something to help me. In other words, write a psychiatric evaluation to achieve changing my name. And convince my health insurance that I needed hormone replacement therapy and gender realignment surgery.

For all her experience and qualification, Ms Steyr was not a psychiatrist, and she was certainly not accredited by the health system. By means of the internet (thank heavens for the modern internet. In the early 1990ies this would have been nigh impossible) I informed myself about support group meetings in Munich and Stuttgart. By sheer lucky coincidence, I met Marie. She was looking to set up a peer-group in Ulm, and I happily assisted her with that. At the time, Marie was still studying to become a professional counsellor, with her mind set firmly on opening an office catering to the special needs of trans* gender peoples. Together with Franco, we held a monthly support group for grownups, and a second group twice a month for youths. I was quite surprised at the numbers of people who would show up for our meetings. Naturally, some of them grew to be valued and trusted friends.

Those meetings proved to be of inestimable value. What stand out, were the experiences and recommendations of where to go for which services. Which therapists were good, which endocrinologists' practices had trans* friendly staff and which surgeons were best for the different kinds of changes. Again, I was so extremely fortunate that there were in fact two of Germany's most experienced therapists practicing in my chosen hometown.

So, it was through the recommendations of Marie and others from our peer group, that I got in touch with Dr Chamberlain. Ordinarily, his calendar is booked and then some. Again, by sheer luck he offered me an appointment just two days away, because somebody had cancelled. I immediately took it, well aware that people sometimes wait more than three months for an introductory interview. I remember being so nervous on the phone, I was feeling physically nauseous. I told him that I would not be in a position to come to see him "èn femme" because I would come from work, and my present situation did not make that possible (There was a time, when the prerequisite to proving you were indeed trans* gender, was, that you performed your perceived gender role for three years *prior* to even being admitted to therapy). He comforted me immediately, saying that was not at all necessary.

Lighting a candle

Dr Chamberlain turned out to be a cheerful and good-natured man. Usually dressed in faded jeans, a chequered shirt, and well-worn loafers. With kind and humorous eyes glinting behind round, horn-rimmed glasses, his tousled dark hair almost boyish. I was later to learn, that he is an avid cyclist and takes great enjoyment from long tours. He also has a sweet tooth, which I find entirely endearing.

I also learnt (not from him, from the support-group) that the vast majority of Dr Chamberlain's clients were trans* gender like me. And while opinions amongst his clients were and are unanimous concerning his being extremely forthcoming and conductive to transitioning, the opinions tended to differ sharply concerning his professional competency. This still surprises me today. As if telling the difference between somebody deep in reflection, and somebody nodding off, were that difficult. I learnt very early on that he was (is) a highly attentive listener. He rarely interrupts his clients. Instead, he dips into deep meditative pauses. Only to come up with a pin-point question that neatly cuts to the heart of an emotional barrier. And he gently and safely brings you face to face with all your inner monsters. Yup, the man is terrifying.

I began regular therapy once a month in mid-summer of 2014. I recounted to Dr Chamberlain the events leading up to my seeking his counselling, up to and including my therapy with Ms Steyr. I feel it is important to point out, that he, too, reassured himself that I was not suicidal. We started out by going over my biography, and the highlights of where my gender dysphoria had shown itself most clearly. Alongside this, we talked about what next possible steps could be and where to inquire, whose help to ask for.

Overall, I might have impressed him to a degree, with how structured and reflected I was. I am sure a contributing factor was the time I had already worked with Ms Steyr. Thinking back to the newspaper article I had stumbled across when I was eleven, I was expecting to spend at least a year in psychiatric supervision. Instead, soon after we had begun regular therapy, Dr Chamberlain brought up the topic of hormone replacement therapy, HRT.

We had been discussing how I entertained the idea of a transition when I returned to Switzerland in 1990. And all the things that lead to the decision to lead a life as a man. Wanting, needing to be a parent.

He asked me if that wish had changed, a question I had already given quite some thought. No, the wish to be a parent was still there. However. I explained to Dr Chamberlain how I was approaching my mid-forties. And how, yes, I could have continued living as a man in the hopes of being a parent. But kindling a relationship with another woman? If she was my generation, then bearing a child would come with exorbitant risks. So the lady who would have to be considerably younger than me. Would *she* want a family with a man so much older than herself? And *I* would want to spend time getting to know each-other. As in, two or three years. Because raising a family is not something you jump into. And it would mean, that I would be approaching seventy, when my child or children graduated from school.

I simply could not see that.

Besides, I really did not feel ready for any kind of relationship, never mind that any woman dating me would be getting a wreck of a deal. He chuckled gently at that, remarking, that I excelled in cutting myself down. But that, yes, he understood my line of argument, and that I was probably being realistic in my appraisal. He continued by asking, whether I had given any thought to hormone replacement therapy, HRT. Well of course I had. After all, that was part of the reason for seeking professional psychiatric supervision.

Dr Chamberlain asks me, when do I think would be a good time to begin?

Well, what kind of a question is that? I tell him straight up, "Um, Yesterday?"

Contrary to any expectations of mine, he laughs out loud, long and heartily. I would have thought he heard that line countless times before. Even more contrary to any expectations, he says, "Well then, let me write you a letter of recommendation for the endocrinologist. Give me a moment, will you?"

He gets up to sit by his computer, asks for my birthday to make sure he has it right. He hits a key, saying, "I've printed an extra for your health insurance, you're going to want to let them know."

And just like that, I am holding a professional psychiatric recommendation for HRT in my hands. My first official document stating that I am trans* gender. I realise there are silent tears running down my cheeks. I look at him and tell him, "I don't want to hand this to any doctor. I should frame this and light a candle in front of it."

Tentatively, gently, he reaches over and gives my shoulder a soft squeeze.

Together with the letter of indication, Dr Chamberlain gave me an excellent pointer regarding where to go for endocrinological supervision. Considering how a vast number of his clients were in need of HRT, his connections and his experience with other doctors and with authorities was very broad and well founded. Something I was immensely grateful for.

Summer sun

By pure chance, my Dad had chosen that same time to come and visit me, and of course his remaining friends and family in Switzerland. I picked him up from Frankfurt Airport, and he stayed with us for a few days. Despite the tension, I was overjoyed to see him again in person. I did not need to warn him of the permafrost that had taken hold of our apartment, I had already written him that things were not going smoothly between Wiebke and me.

He was deeply saddened by our loss of trust in each other, saying that we had always given the impression, that Wiebke and I were devoted to one another in kindness and love. But even he caught the undercurrents, despite our best efforts to make his stay as easy as possible.

For me, his visit was a true blessing. How else would I ever adequately communicate that he never really had a son?

I asked him whether he would make time for a very serious discussion? And would he accompany me into town?

We sat ourselves down in a street café. I do not know why I chose this environment. It just felt natural. And I think in the back of my mind, there was the idea that a public setting would inhibit any kind of outburst or transgression. Of course, if I went through my thoughts rationally, I expected neither form my father, but I was so tense, I could barely drink my coffee. And the setting avoided being interrupted.

My father is a very sober, very rational person. Quite the stereotype engineer. If it has wheels, grease it. If it has an engine, fuel it. If it has a gear, I can fix it. So far, discussing emotions with my Dad had not been all that easy. I think it was something he was simply not used to doing. I know he caught the gravity of the situation. He certainly caught my discomfort, and did his best to put me at ease, saying that he understood that I was in a hard place, and that after all, he too had decided to end his first marriage rather than continue exposing the two of us to any more abuse.

I tell him, that over the course of her medical treatment, Wiebke has withdrawn herself completely, but even her getting better has not led to *our* healing. Even though I repeatedly asked her to get marriage counselling. I relate to him, how she has, in my mind, made it clear. That I am not, or no longer, the person to fulfil her needs. So, yes, I am going to leave Wiebke.

And I tell him, "but that is only half of what I need to tell you." My voice shakes. I take a deep breath and try to still my trembling hands.

"Since I am no longer Wiebke's husband, there is no need for me any longer to keep up any pretence." I swallow the lump in my throat. "Dad, I am trans* gender. I have never truly been a boy or a man. I am a woman. This body says something else, but I need to continue this life as my true self. I am going to live the remainder of my life as a woman."

There it's out.

My father considers for some of the longest seconds of my life.

He looks up at me, thoughtful. "Well, I am sure you have thought this through long and well. What can I do to support you?"

The sheer magnitude of what my Dad said, the easy, matter-of-course acceptance and the love that spoke through his simple words took my breath away. I remember fighting to stop myself from crying.

He looks at me with a chuckle, "What? Was that so bad?"

I suppose my father's reaction was further testament to how he saw me as his child. How my neither my biological sex nor my gender identity defined his love for me. How could I tell him of the forty years of fear of rejection (not his, but rejection regardless) that I had needed to overcome to entrust him with this?

242

All I manage to say is, "Well, I was scared. This is important."

He gives me a moment to wipe my face. "So, what's your name?"

Even in the moment, I was awestruck by how thoughtful and clear-minded my Dad appraised the situation. How he immediately realised, that the name he had given me at birth was no longer suitable. So I told him the name I had given myself, Alice.

"Oh, that's a good name." He smiles. "Alice. A clear name. Strong. Very appropriate."

I told him my full name, Alice Claudia Oehninger. This did in fact provide my father with a soft moment, where he reacted with more emotion than usual. He was deeply, deeply touched by the fact that I kept the name he had given me, as my second name, even if in a slightly changed form. Perhaps it was for him, a kind of confirmation, that I remained his child? That the love and the bond between us remained intact. That he had not "made any mistakes to make me be this way."

We continued talking for a long time. We spoke of my mother, of how they had gotten to know each-other, and how he had decided to go his own way. He told me things I had guessed at from filling in the gaps, or that I had constructed from how I watched things develop.

We spoke of my childhood. He remembered very well how I had been ostracised and teased both in kindergarten and in Dar es Salaam. Curiously, he seemed to have forgotten the dresses, the shawls, the clothes I made for myself. He did remark how he had always thought it interesting that I never really showed any serious interest in girls. We spoke about Aileen in Kwekwe, whom even my Dad remembered. And of course conversation turned to Dave, and I was finally able to confess my crush to my Dad.

I suppose it was natural that our conversation turned to my Dad's junior years, the time he spent in New York City, and his friendship with the young man who turned out to be homosexual. I knew the story, but I did nothing to interrupt my Dad. It was so rare to have him talking about himself and his feelings. I felt so fulfilled, so *secure*, basking in the light of his love. For the first time in months, I felt the warmth of that summer day.

I ask him, "why strong? Since when am I strong? I rather feel I have failed in so many things."

He reflects for a few moments, and then says, "One of the things I have always admired about you, is, that once you have committed to a decision, you don't mess about. You follow your path, and you stay your course, come what may. It was that way with Nat. It was that way with Wiebke. And you have done the same now. You always find a way to make it work with the people you love. And if you find that they no longer love you, then you are not afraid of change. Even if it means changing everything."

It was surprising to have my Dad reflect that to me. Strong would have never been a term I would have used to describe my past self. But I suppose he is right. I do not do things half-heartedly.

Gradual changes

Over the course of the summer, I had managed to schedule several appointments with my new endocrinologist to perform all the necessary tests to begin my hormone replacement therapy. It was October when I finally was able to begin taking my prescription.

Taking testosterone-blockers was like breaking up through the surface of water into clean, fresh air, and taking my first deep breath since puberty. The world seemed crisp and bright by comparison. Any and all emotions were suddenly so vivid, almost surreal. I learnt what it truly means, that hormones are psychoactive substances. Another side effect that I noticed after one a surprisingly short while, was my chest becoming *extremely* sensitive. As in "going jogging or taking stairs at a trot has me doubling over in pain" sensitive. I say chest, because aside from the increase in in sensitivity, there was no noticeable change. I did however order myself sports bras for developing teenagers, which I wore consequently. That helped to some degree.

Taking hormones was a fist mayor success in realising my goal. One that I kept that entirely secret from Wiebke. My intuition told me, she would have resisted this change with any means at her disposal, and I simply did not feel equipped to deal with any more emotional coercion. I did however feel obliged, by plain fairness, to tell her that I was in regular therapy with a psychiatrist, that I had gotten myself checked by an endocrinologist. And that I was looking for accommodation of my own. She seemed to take this in stride, remarking only that I should watch out for myself.

Fact was, I barely had the energy to go to work reliably.

Following several letters and emails with the Swiss embassy, they informed me that were unable to provide me with guidance. It was beginning of winter when I discussed this with Dr Chamberlain, what I could do to get my name and gender legally recognised. He recommended I try to appeal to the Ulm civil court, with whom he had a lot of experience.

I know I spent the Christmas days with Wiebke and her family, but to be honest, I have little memory of who was there or what we did. I was subdued those holidays, even more so than usual, spending those days in a haze of fatigue. I know I spent as much time as possible in the kitchen. That way, I was out of people's way but making myself useful at the same time. It was as close to being invisible as I could get.

I took five days to go to Zürich, to speak with my birth mother and with Eirian. Wiebke made it clear that she disapproved, but for possibly the first time, I made it clear that I was going to do this with or without her approval. I think that gave her quite some food for thought.

My mother was relieved that I had come to some kind of conclusion, anything was better than turning circles in the dark. She was sceptical, though, about my being trans* gender. Not because she could not see my feminine attributes, but because she could not remember me being miserable in my childhood. And I think even then, she was deeply suspicious and renunciative, that I had entrusted myself to orthodox scientific medicine. She would spend the next thirty months imploring me to find "gentler" ways, find a way to deal with my feminine side with a homoeopathic shamanistic approach, make changes in the mind but leave the body untouched. Sorry Mum, yet again. Not happening.

Eirian was the complete opposite, wildly enthusiastic, totally exuberant. Making lists of which shops she wanted me to accompany her to, which was totally cute, because Eirian was, at the time, absolutely not the "shopping-queen" type of woman. I am not sure she even owns make-up, and if I went "èn femme," I was of course heavily reliant on foundation and powder. Eirian was already dreaming up girls-outings and making a list of friends she wanted to introduce me to. And she was already planning witches' covens and female chakra meditations. Yes, it runs in the family.

I also managed to meet Rafet and bring him into the picture. He was, I believe, quite dismayed. He had followed the decline of my marriage with sorrow, and I think he anticipated our separation. I believe he had been seriously hoping that I would return to Zürich, and that we would relive our easy going, work-hard-play-hard days of our early adulthood. But returning to Zürich, quitting my job was not something I wanted to risk, seeing as finding an equivalent in terms of salary and fulfilment was in my mind nigh impossible.

I was devastated that I did not get to see Evangeline or Seraphina, but they were away. Once I was back in Ulm, I spent long hours on the phone instead, explaining to Evangeline what I was going through. To my initial surprise, she was rather cautious. But she immediately explained, that she had made rather questionable experiences with another person, who described themselves as trans*. From what she tells, it involved a fetish, rather than an identity transition. Nevertheless, she assured me of her unrelenting trust and support.

Forged in fire

Also back in Ulm, I renewed my efforts to find a suitable flat. And I set about pushing for alternatives of litigation, concerning my name and the gender in my passport, since it looked like that was impossible in Germany. I explored all possible avenues and alternatives with Dr Chamberlain. Whether I got my name changed in Switzerland, or in Germany, regardless of which court processed my request, I was going to need two independent psychiatric evaluations or appraisals, attesting my being gender dysphoric.

On top of this, should I need to process in Switzerland, then the Swiss law stated (still states today) that I should be made "zeugungsunfähig" (Ger: neutered, sterilised). From a rational point of view, I could not have cared less. After all, having children of my own was something I had accepted as not happening anymore. And getting gender realignment surgery, GRS, *was* exactly what I wanted. The sooner the better. However, from an emotional, psychological point of view, the Swiss law is so *malignantly* inhuman and depreciative in its wording, it virtually reeks of a frame of mind, just barely risen from the ashes of World-War-II. Nevertheless, since the choice was out of my hands, I needed to deal with the real possibility that I would have to go to court in Zürich. Crying about it was not going to help.

In preparation of getting the psychiatric evaluations, Dr Chamberlain and I set about going over my biography in greater detail. And he referred me to Prof Aedelfrid, a long-standing colleague of his, who had contributed volumes to revolutionising the way the German judicial system goes about providing for trans* gender peoples.

So with both of them, I analysed when and where my female identity was most clearly defined. And where it was anchored in my psyche and in my memories. It was the first time *ever* that I spoke of the transgressions in my past.

The intense and detailed illumination of the past brought another, quite dramatic change. I began having vivid nightmares. Sometimes about Jeremy, or about Joey's older brother Martin. Often about the children in Kindergarten in Zürich, sometimes about the other kids on my way to and from school in Dar es Salaam. Often about the men with the combat boots behind the shopping centre in Zürich. But the most visceral dreams were of Andrin. There were nights I relived that scene several times, sometimes observing from the outside, powerless, screaming at myself I should run, fight, or I should flee. Or just as powerless, flailing against his strength, his weight, struggling for breath against the bedcover.

I began having flashbacks in broad daylight. Memories being triggered by sounds, smells, most particularly invasion of personal space. I became very sensitive about violence. Not the blatant, in-your-face Hollywood action. The subtle kind of violence that goes unnoticed by most people, even as it happens right there in the midst of society. Threats communicated by a grabbed wrist, a hissed word, or a person being crowded and intimidated. The subliminal kind of transgressions that leave you feeling lost and abandoned even within your own family, because it seems so… …ordinary.

Dr Chamberlain walked me through the experiences with great mindfulness and security, trying to instil in me the ability to defend myself. He even suggested I place a kitchen knife next to my bed. But the idea of the knife somehow failed to "click". He and I spent many sessions talking through these episodes, and how best to deal with the panic attacks. I had more success with breathing techniques, self-centring, and awareness exercises, like the 54321-grounding technique, but I still felt powerless.

I am walking home after one of my sessions with Dr Chamberlain. We have been talking about my nightmares. How I feel disorientated when I wake up. Forsaken and helpless. The session has been draining and terrifying. I am thoroughly shaken.

I am walking home, and I am thinking of Nancy. It dawns on me: in my entire life so far, every time I was truly myself, the only times I truly and openly declared myself as *female*, every time I was really *in* my state of being the girl that I was. Each time, I was with someone whom I trusted. Sometimes more, sometimes less, but I trusted. Each time, my trust was broken. Each time, my disclosure was met with ridicule, rejection, depreciation, emotional and physical violence.

These are the only memories I really have of my female past.

I think of the wraith of a child, wrecked and tainted, sad and afraid. And angry. A child with an incandescent breath that would make flesh melt off bones like tears. Very often her own...

And it comes to me. The problem with cleansing by fire, is, that all that is left, are ashes.

This insight brings me up short. Despite the fact that I am walking over a square filled with people, I am sobbing. Any thought of control is gone. I grow aware of shoppers casting me inquisitive and irritated glances.

I sit down on the stone steps opposite the supermarket. The third one. Grey granite. I take note of the grey-blue sky, reflected in puddles on the pavement. The intense red colour of the bricks, red as the few leaves that still cling to the trees. Two trees. I look up. The smell of wet leaves and the promise of snow on the wind. And I wait for the turmoil to subside. It's okay. I am alone. I am safe.

And it comes to me, that it has been two years. Maybe not to the day, but close enough. Two years since I decided not to take those sleeping pills. Not to go for that walk. Not to go sit on that bench under a tree.

When I sit in the cold today, it is also by choice. A choice to live. A choice to live in *this world*, not in my imagination.

And despite the fact that all three, Ms Steyr, Dr Chamberlain and Prof Aedelfrid, all three have told me, that I am a survivor. That I made it thanks to my strength. Because of my will to get back up and keep going. Today, sitting on these stone steps, is the first time that I grow *aware*.

Today, I feel it. My spine of forged steel.

I am alive today, I am still breathing and feeling the cold February breeze in my face because I was able to live through all the hate and the transgressions. Because I was strong enough to do so.

And in the same moment, I realise. If my being a survivor is to lead anywhere, then only living this life as *myself* will fulfil me. And only doing so will make this second chance worthwhile.

And if my life so far as a woman was filled with sad and terrible memories, then it was time to make new and better ones.

So that was the point where I grew to realise, deciding not to die by degrees, is not the same as deciding to live.

Separate ways

Every once in a while, Wiebke still asked me how therapy was going, and If I was making any progress.

Early on, I was quite open in my relating what I was going through. About addressing my female identity. About dealing with the fact that I was gender dysphoric and that I needed to find a way to integrate my personalities. She responded by saying, that, all I had ever been, was a man. And that that was all I would ever be. And I should focus on other things, like getting back on my feet. From there, she steered the conversation to how Torben, her father, was doing, and the support he needed. And how her work was going, and how she needed to focus on proving she was good enough.

As I progressed in my reflections and my insights, I became less and less open in what I told Wiebke. I had no desire at all, telling her about my exhumed memories. I had no faith in that she would even believe me. And I certainly said nothing of the dreams that followed. What I also did not speak of, was how the requirement to appear male was seriously beginning to grate on my nerves. And on my health. I was honest and direct insofar as that I made it clear, I no longer saw myself capable of upholding this role of the man who shared her life. And that I no longer desired to live my life as a man at all anymore.

She dismissed that by saying, that I had let myself be talked into being trans*. That perhaps I was not a typical alpha male, but that I had been brainwashed into thinking I could be a woman. She said, verbatim, that I would never be a woman. That I was being ridiculous. And that I would do good in removing myself from the influence of these people, who were obviously unprofessional and misguided. I did not really know what to reply to that. Every time I had tried to speak about my past, or communicate how far back my gender dysphoria could be traced, she had derailed the conversation.

Finally, I found a suitable flat. I let Wiebke know, that I would be moving out. I think it took her quite by surprise, that I was actually going through with it. And to give Wiebke credit, she made several attempts to show some affection for me, being a little softer and gifting me with tokens of appreciation, possibly in the hopes of changing my mind. But to be bluntly honest, my heart was no longer in it. I no longer trusted her. And while I dearly would have liked to prevent her being hurt, I was not capable of... ...of what? Staying? Pretending to be a man I whose role had become painful? Above all, I was no longer capable of going back to this co-dependent existence.

To save us both a lot of heartache, I timed it such that she would be on her skiing vacation with her family, while I would be packing my stuff and moving it to my new pad.

I took time to inform Astra and Ditmar, Freyja and Marcus. I told them that Wiebke and I had grown too far apart and that I had lost all touch with the person they had gotten to know. That I was in for some radical changes. I told them my name. I think Marcus and Freyja were none too surprised, they had always been the more sober and rational of the family. Freyja even said something to the effect, that I had always been very effeminate. Dietmar and Astra, particularly Astra, were quite dismayed though.

I spoke with Torben, asking to meet him in a public place, giving him a slightly watered-down and softened version things. I was very unsure of how he would take it, and to be honest, I would not have put it past him to become… …irate. Fact was, I think I rather shocked him into speechlessness. So much so, that I felt sorry for this man. How he appeared so helpless and lost. But I no longer saw myself responsible.

I hired three university students along with a minivan. Another very noticeable side-effect of my hormone therapy was, how my muscles changed. I was no longer able to lift things which I had easily shifted in the past. Lifting boxes of books or baskets of clothes had become a challenge, never-mind lifting furniture. To make matters perfect, I developed a fever of forty-something Celsius in the five days I had planned to move. My body was telling me, I was way, way over my limits, and I was ever so grateful to have three pairs of hands which I could direct, while I barely managed the three flights of stairs.

But move I did.

I think that was when I stopped being a ghost.

(8) Being Gender Dysphoric

Fear…

Is always there.

…so much of life, is about conquering it.

We are social beings.

We bask in the warmth and the reflection of other humans.

And so much of life, is about developing patterns,

following rules, that make you part of a group.

Break those rules…

…and you break the world.

And sometimes, precisely that, is what it takes.

To be yourself.

This is a closer look at being trans* gender. Some thoughts on what trans* peoples, and/or their loved ones might need, in order to cope. Perspectives that might be helpful...

All of us, each and every one, we are unique. Each life, every existence follows its own path and spins its own tale.

By the same rule, no two trans* gender biographies are the same. There are of course parallels and similarities. There is common ground, even between male to female (mtf) or female to male (ftm). People who define as non-binary. What we all share, is the dysphoria.

Most trans* gender describe it as an innate knowledge, that their gender identity deviates from the one they were assigned at birth. That it deviates from their biological sex. Think of it like having a female soul in a male body or vice-versa. In a great many cases, we know who we are from between three and five years old, when all children form a gender identity. For others, it remains a diffuse, intangible feeling that *something* is wrong. That *they* are wrong. We grow up with our families and friends expecting us to behave in a particular way, and we are socialized according to the gender identity that we have been assigned with, but we intuitively feel this to be wrong. Moreover, we learn very early on in life to hide our true identity, so we can fit in and be accepted.

I had two therapists, Dr Chamberlain and Prof Aedelfrid who certified my gender dysphoria before court to have my name legally changed. Prof Aedelfrid once asked me, if ever I assumed a reason for my being trans* gender. We spoke of this at some length; about how possibly my innate need to win my mother's love might have made me refuse my own gender, in order to make myself more acceptable in her view.

And yet, I personally do not truly believe that. I never believed there *was* a cause. Even today, I still do not.

Prof Aedelfrid is one of the most experienced psychiatrists in the field of gender dysphoria and the concept of identity not coinciding with biology, and he is a globally recognised expert. He affirmed, that while the reasoning behind my hypothesis certainly bore a credible and ready logic, he *did* agree and emphasise that there is *nothing* that has ever proven that gender dysphoria has any direct causes, predispositions, or that it can be provoked by any kind of external circumstances. If you are trans* gender, it just *is*.

Above all, he made it clear, that being trans* is not a debility or an illness. And thus, that it can *not* be "cured". It cannot. Just as homosexuality has no triggering cause. It simply is a state of being, with which individuals are born.

Being trans* gender

There are way, way too many taboos surrounding these topics, and there are too many misunderstandings and wrong impressions flying about.

Gender and body dysphoria have gotten quite some attention in recent years. On the one hand, this is entirely constructive, positive. Because we trans* gender desperately need a lobby to engender acceptance, and improve conditions under which a transition is possible. I believe Germany does have room for improvement, but overall is veritable decent. And the positive thing about gender studies is, that I can truly see how this contributes to societies evolving, and becoming more welcoming to people who do not identify with heteronorm standards.

The sad part of this sudden publicity is, how there is so much focus on all the challenges and hurdles, all the trauma involved. And we are offered profuse reassurances of sympathy. But my experience is, that far too often my fears and concerns are belittled. They are turned into a cute. We are an exotic curiosity. An interesting subject to study. And all of a sudden, we are objectified. I have met both students and graduates of gender studies, who utterly failed to realise that we are *real* people with *real* problems. Not abstract hypothetical concepts over which to muse and debate.

We do not need a reservation. Pity and curiosity are not helpful. They keep us in a state of victimhood. And that is entirely unhealthy. I am aware that this is kind of self-contradictory, because I also complain about people who say, "suck it up already, your nothing special". At the same time, the basic concept is the same.

We need to be taken seriously and at eye level.

We spend a lifetime, defending and justifying ourselves to others. Trying to let others see what we intuitively feel and know to be there. Sharing a world to which the remainder of humanity seems to be blind. It is vexing. It is frustrating. It is so utterly draining.

And please, please; do *not* tell us, we chose this. Or ask us, "isn't this what you wanted?"

Yes, we choose. We choose, to go to utter extremes, to live according to the identity that we have. Because there is no other way. *Because NOT doing so would kill us*, one way or another. However, we do not choose to be trans*. Being trans* gender is not a choice. Only war survivors show suicide numbers that approach those of gender dysphoric people. Roughly two thirds of all trans* gender have considered suicide, more than half have attempted it. No human being with a healthy sense of self-preservation undergoes a transition by choice. And thereby risks losing family and friends, social networks and status, employment and security, health and life.

How do you know?

To Torben, my former father in law and professor of physics, reality was (is) anything that he could measure with his apparatus. Reality was founded and anchored in hard, tangible facts. It might have been only when Solveig died, that he realised just how deep into the non-physical our inner universe reaches. And how each person's reality is far, far more, than the ground we walk on.

We call the sky blue. But who says it is blue? Moreover, who is to say, that we all have the same perception of what we term "blue"? How does a left-handed person know they are left-handed? How does a medical specialist determine in how much pain a pain-patient is in? The specialist will ask the patient to describe their experience, and they will try to place it on a scale in relation to other sensations, but finally, ultimately, it is entirely in the world of experience of the individual. And how do you convince a health-insurance carrier, of how crippling and debilitating an agony is, that cannot be measured physically or biologically?

As a cis* gendered heteronorm person, you might find puberty to be tedious and stressful. You might find that the body feels odd and that you are out of sorts, not at ease. You will certainly rebel against your parents and their values, you will rebel against society. However, all of that is part and parcel of finding your way in life. After all, puberty is the stage in life, when we are all questioning and finding our way into adult life. Finding our identity. And building our own characters, finding out what is important to us and what defines us a person.

Nevertheless, at some point, you find what you are looking for. Often enough, coupled with the first erotic experience (or self-experience) and you forget you were ever troubled. Problem solved, collect two-hundred credits, proceed to deal with the next challenge that life throws at you. Overall and within limits, you are comfortable with your body and happy with your assigned gender. More to the point, you are oblivious to the fact that there could possibly be anything out of order. Probably, you take that for granted.

And, you might say, why shouldn't you?

The question whether you prefer people of the opposite binary sex or of the same sex for fun and / or partnership does not even come into the equation at this point. We are talking about *who you are*.

Again. A great many people will feel discomfort during puberty as their body changes. But I claim that *nothing* an "ordinary" pubescent cis* teen goes through, compares to the complete wrongness of the body you feel as a trans*gender. Your skin does not fit, the movements are wrong. Your soul feels imprisoned in a body that does not respond as it should, that does not experience the surrounding environment as you intuitively think it ought to feel. You feel stunted and limited in encountering and interacting with this world. You feel impaired and gagged in the dialogue with yourself and everyone else. You are imprisoned in a shell that does not empathise with you at all, and you have the innate sense that this is all wrong. That there was a mistake. A huge, irreparable fault-line in reality.

And it is made so much worse, by the fact that nobody else sees this. *You are alone.* Everyone else seems to see you as someone whom you are not. The world expects you to suck it up, and be grateful for this wonderful body you have. After all, there is nothing biologically wrong with you. And so, we are forced into a social role that imprisons us like an ill-fitting corset. Various therapists and specialists, for example Dr Preuss and Prof Rauchfleisch, have voiced, that this socialisation into the wrong gender roles, is akin to ostracism, abuse, and love-deprivation. The result is a severe traumatisation of these children, and they need to be treated as such. (*„Transsexualität – Transidentität, Begutachtung, Begleitung, Therapie" by Prof. Dr. rer. nat. Udo Rauchfleisch. „Geschlechtsdysphorie, Transidentität und Transsexualität im Kindes- und Jugendalter" by Dr. med. Wilhelm F Preuss*).

Dysphoria does not up and go away. There is no "healing" or therapy that can make it go away. The only way to improve matters is to face it head on. Do something to accommodate your identity in a social role that enables you to thrive and bloom. In most cases, this means not only changing your gender expression, but adapting your body as well, and providing your soul with the appropriate home. Or as close to appropriate as possible.

And, no. We are not doing this, because we crave attention. The idea of that is so preposterous. The accusation is so unspeakably vile, so devoid of empathy and warmth, it is staggering. There are safer ways to get attention. And they cost less too.

Less effort and less resources. Less fear and distress. Less risk of losing everything, including life.

I am very well aware that there are a multitude of reasons why people, particularly pubescent or post pubescent youths, resort to self-harm as a means coping with the stress and the strain of coming to terms with the demands placed on them by family and society. And, yes, there are those that seek to blind out their despair with drugs. Studies in 2015 (*Clark et al. International Journal of Transgenderism*) showed, that among trans* gender the rate of self-harm was 46%, as compared to cis* gendered people with 4.1%. Or opposed to 10-20% (horribly inaccurate) of gay, lesbian, and bisexual peoples. Sadly, but unsurprisingly, numbers rise dramatically when focusing on suicide rates of trans* peoples of colour.

Particularly interesting is another study in 2015 (*Reisner et al. International Journal of Transgenderism*). They performed a survey of youths seeking support in a generic health centre, comparing trans* gender youth with cis* gendered youths. They found rates of self-harm trans* 30% versus cis* 8%, suicidal contemplation 56% vs. 20% and suicide attempts 31% vs. 11%.

When trans* people disclose their gender identity, the reaction they face is very often one of scepticism and disbelief. Of belittlement, or ridicule. And far too often, downright aggressive. Trans* women are seen as men in a dress, at best, confused with trans* vestites, people with a kink or a sexual penchant. At worst, we are turned into creeps, predators, and psychopaths. And trans* men are cause for confusion, because they are virtually invisible and unknown to most people. But basically, societies' declaration is unmistakable. Your identity is not valid, a disguise. You are a joke, you are a threat. And until you have been "fixed" by therapy, you will be cast out of society and out of your family.

Connectivity is a fundamental part of being human.

Being a part of society. Being a part of a family. Being loved. Being important to someone. All that builds the core in which our humanity lies.

Being connected

I do not know whether this need be said, but here goes. Of our youth support group, the overwhelming majority have years of history, as inpatients in youth-psychiatric wards, years of experience with heavy psycho-stabilising drugs. *Years* of experience. In Germany. In a society that is generally accepted as being progressive and open. And we are talking about teenagers. You would not believe the heartrending tales they tell. Of being cast out of their families. Their parents telling them verbatim, "You are not my child", "I hate you", "Why are you doing this to me? To your family?". And always, always, "What would the neighbours say?"

…as if they had a choice…

We are social beings. It is the quintessence of being human. To be part of a tribe, part of a family. To be connected to people. We care what others think about us, we are dependent on their being benign and sympathetically aligned. If we lose our place in our family, if we lose the love of the people we identify with, then we lose our hold on reality.

I am grateful I got away without harming myself. I am so, so grateful, that I got away without ever having resorted to drugs. My only forms of escapism were books, and single player RPGs. And of course, an imagination that was fathomless, that turned over endless universes, just to avoid facing what I was. As a child and as a youth, the reliability and the continuity of support and the love provided by my Dad, was paramount to keeping me stable. Just like the environment provided by the horse-riding people in Kwekwe. And later, as I transitioned, having a steady job, having colleagues and friends who had my back, who offered sympathy and took an active part in my life, were essential. People who made me feel *connected*. A part of society.

And. *This is why trans* people are pushing so hard to be heard.* Because we are systematically being excluded form society. On account of what we are and who we are trying to be.

Never underestimate the importance of making people feel welcome and appreciated. *It is key to being human.*

Anatomy

…and then there is this thing. It is attached to you, yes, but it does not really belong. It is apart. Repulsive and loathsome. And yet, like a toothache, you cannot just leave it alone. Everything focuses on this… …thing. Your own private little black hole. But instead of being silent, it constantly wants to be fed. It leeches energy off you, constantly, permanently, incessantly, demanding attention. Treacherous and licentious. Sometimes whispering, wheedling, cloying, coaxing. Only to turn around and scream, howl, wail. Deluging your other senses, making what you were working on a chore, blinding you to anything else. Radiating a permanent, all-pervading static, that disrupts your thoughts and sabotages your creativity. The one thing I found to be among the most invasive, to be the most **unbearable**, was the *Fremdbestimmung*, the other-determination of how my body grew to shape, and grew to respond to other people. The development of sexual desire, the urge, the desire was triggered by things that my mind, my self felt entirely... ...alien. Not me.

I felt betrayed and violated by my own body.

And yes, in the months of my transition, I made sure my anatomy was invisible. Really? Are you sure? Google "tucking". And do not say I did not warn you.

Ianto, an ftm friend of mine, described puberty as having their body annexed by a jellyfish. Wobbly and vitreous, a cancerous growth. Surreptitious, almost intangible at first. But irrevocable, dominating. Disfiguring, distorting and alien. Strangling, and above all, poisonous.

As a trans* gender, you are not at home in the body you were born into. It is a feeling of wrongness that chafes like an ill-fitting skin, and rubs the soul raw. We do not like being looked at, we do not like interacting with other people.

Because *everything reminds us of our predicament.*

I knew, when I was four years old. And to me, it was entirely clear what the problem was. But I do know of others, who were confused and disoriented until their fifties, and who started out on their endeavour only after *their* children were grown and leading lives of their own.

Yes, there are children that go through a "phase". But usually, that "phase" clears up within months, or even weeks.

My "phase" of not looking at my own body lasted fourteen years. And it ended, only because medical necessity required me to examine bruises, and take care of injuries. From the childhood age of six years, right up into early adulthood of twenty, I completely refused to look at my own body from the chest down. No glancing down at myself, no self-examination, no mirrors.

You are wondering if, and how, I discovered my sexuality as a teenager during puberty? The wonderful thing about self-exploration is, it all takes place in your mind. It is the ultimate proof, that sex is what happens between your ears, not what happens between your legs. You can be anyone, or any*thing*, you want to be. But I will remind you, this is sexuality. For cis-het* peoples this issue never arises. Nevertheless, sexuality remains independent of your identity. Who you love is not dependent on who you are. This is a vital distinction.

You are asking yourself how I dealt with my married life in my role as a man? The same applies. And, yes, there were times, where I was as close to peace as I could possibly be in that state. In fact, there were incidences where I did things, or acted in ways, that were textbook stereotype male. As long as I felt loved, desired, welcome, that was all it took. Which, incidentally, is partly why my entire identity construct crashed and burned so fast, when I lost hope of ever redeeming myself and rebuilding the relationship I was living in.

Not-doing in a doing-kind-of-way

Even procrastination is a decision. Of a sort.

I spent years avoiding facing myself. I buried myself in work. And if I did not work, I made sure I was so caught up in organising some project, following up on people, keeping tabs on art. Oh, and of course I read. I drank books. Libraries. And at some point, I got into role playing games. And of course, I married someone who seemed to know what they were doing, the perfect excuse.

I am going to permit myself a generalisation here. Trans*gender are experts at denial. And procrastination. We are so entirely capable of existing in a semi-state of being. But it is not living.

I believe being honest with yourself is a process of several steps. First off, it needs to be clear, what precisely it is you want or need. Even if you are clear about being in the wrong body, then obviously you need to decide, just how badly dysphoric you are. Whether or not you can live with what is there, or whether you need to change it.

So, even if you know who you truly are, you still need to deal with the unspeakable terror, that you are breaking what most people (falsely) take for granted, the immovable, unbreakable dichotomy of biological sex. That's the thing about trans*gender. It questions the very fundamental *given*, that one plus one is two. Because, all of a sudden, a human with a penis is not a man, and a human with a vagina is not a woman. And you are intuitively aware, breaking a core taboo like that is not going to sit well with people. People you love, people who love you, people on whom you are dependent, might turn on you. Expel you from their midst. You could lose your social circle. You could lose your source of income. You could lose everything that enables you to exist. People you love could suddenly reject you. Hate you even.

There is no getting away from dysphoria. After all, you cannot escape from yourself. Of course, we try. After all, there are lots of means to escape reality. Ranging from science fiction, fantasy worlds, movies, or games. Right up to hard drugs and self-harm.

But at some point, there is a key-moment. The pressure, the pain simply becomes too great. Something breaks. And this is where a choice is made. And you realise, that things cannot get any worse. If the present situation continues, if the present state of things does not change, *it will kill you*. One way or another.

What can I tell you?

It gets better.

It is worth it. So very much.

But to get there, you need to find out *what you truly want.*

Being kind

Please be patient, please be kind to trans* gender. We really have enough to worry about without cis* people giving us a hard time.

Having a loyal circle of friends in *invaluable* in a transition. Having a steady job or school environment that is accepting and supportive is essential. These are prerequisites if trans* people are to come through a transition in a way, where their faculties, their personalities, and resources intact, being contributing members of society.

Also, dear fellow trans* peoples. Please be kind. Be patient. With yourself. But also with cis* people.

My experience with myself, and with so many other trans* people, has shown.

- We tend to isolate ourselves. For all the obvious and excellent reasons. Nevertheless, this is very unhealthy.
- We are *reeeeally* good at being co-dependent.
- We tend to obsess. And overthink. No, not just me.
- We excel at denial, and at procrastination. Heavens, do we ever.
- We fall into victimhood far too easily. Even more unhealthy, we tend to cling to victimhood. More so than others.
- Every so often, we take ourselves far too seriously. Sometimes, we are just way too sensitive. And we are too easily provoked. We have been in survival mode so long, we forget what it's like to laugh at ourselves.

- ...and every once in a while, we enjoy talking about ourselves way too much. After all, we are discovering so many cool and new things about ourselves, life is just so terrifyingly brilliant!

One of the greatest problems with coming out to the people around you, about your being trans*gender (or being any kind of Queer*), is, that, for you, this is an issue which you have been aware of for a very long time. Basically, by the time a trans*gender person gets around to where they are ready to entrust other people with this very sensitive and personal piece of information, they have already gone through several significant steps of change.

It is essential to keep this in mind.

Because, *for everyone else, this might be BIG NEWS*. For a vast majority, this is going to be a surprise. This is going to be disconcerting and worrisome, needing some adjustment and accommodation. And for some, this is outright terrifying and unspeakable. A breach of just so many taboos and social structures, that they would prefer this piece of information not to exist at all in their world. And by extension, they would prefer you not to exist in their world.

Families and loved ones, significant others, and partners, often have it the hardest when coming to terms with a person coming out as trans*. In my experience, the closer the people, the harder it is to cope with such a fundamental shift in the world. It is not entirely surprising. Their emotions are so much more fragile. That is part of what love is. It makes us vulnerable. And just as we, as trans* gender, are hesitant, to confront our loved ones with things about which we are secretive, uncomfortable, or downright ashamed. They too are insecure about what such a vast change can mean. *Because we all fear rejection.*

The difference is, if your loved ones, if your friends, love you for being yourself, then they will accommodate the "new" you in their world, and they will welcome you.

And if they do not... ...then that is a very sad sign. That they loved only the reflection of *themselves* that your "old self" projected. And that the discomfort, of needing to readjust their world view, is more important, than offering you comfort and support in your transition. And that they do not truly care for *your* wellbeing. And that perhaps, you are better off without them.

Of course, for some of your friends and loved ones, this is not going to be news at all. Because they can see the writing on the wall. And they might possible have been aware of "something being in the bush" before you even sorted out what you truly want to do with your life.

I think one of the hardest parts about being trans*, is how strong you have to be. And I do not mean just swimming against the biological dichotomy of sex versus gender, or surviving the socio-moral and legal gauntlet. No, what is hardest, is keeping your social circle intact. Keeping your friends, your family. Keeping your job. I have come to find this works best when the person in transition appears strong. Secure, unshakable. For a lot of cis* people, watching a loved one go through a transition, seems to be highly stressful. Yes, the irony is not lost on me. Please bear with me. My point is, that the better we trans* people are at showing cis* people, "Hey, look, everything is cool. I am trans* and this is perfectly normal. I may look a little unusual, but it is perfectly okay. I am perfectly okay. And you are too". The better we are at offering reassurance and giving a show of stability and unerring purpose, the easier it is for cis* people to just follow and accept changes. And to include these changes into their lives as normal.

The challenge of course is, that we trans* people *are* insecure. That we sometimes do not know what we are doing. And we are frightened. And we do doubt and worry and obsess. Which is why it is good to have a therapist you trust.

Finally, being kind to yourself is a mind-set. And this includes your bearing, your carriage. Never underestimate how much influence your body language, and your stance, influence your mental wellbeing. And. Being kind to yourself begins with making the decision to do everything you can, to enable yourself and feel good about yourself. So, yes, HRT is part and parcel for this, but so are basic, everyday things like hygiene, self-care and surrounding yourself with the right people.

Gatekeepers and enablers

I am extremely fortunate in the specialists that look after me. They are authentically empathic and supportive. Even my endocrinologist, whom I have dubbed Sushi.

If you are a trans* woman, my advice is: do not go cheap where your hair is concerned. Actually, scratch trans*. If you are a woman, and you value your hair. The buoyant effects and the positive enforcement of self-esteem of a proper good haircut cannot be overemphasised. Find yourself a good hairdresser, and stick with them.

I meet far too many trans* girls who refuse to wash, never mind blow-dry their hair regularly. The reason being, they say, that it damages the hair, and they want to grow it out as fast as possible. What they completely neglect to take into account, are the detrimental the effects of having unwashed, unkempt, possibly smelly hair. Not just on the individual, but on the social circle as well. It is a reoccurring topic in families, who struggled severely with being supportive to their transitioning child. Because to them transitioning appears to have everything to do with self-neglect and possibly self-harm. And the fact is: with dysphoria, the line *is* blurry and ill-defined. Depressive episodes will make you forget or ignore self-care, and that, in turn, is a direct feedback system for your depression. Good self-care reinforces your morale and confidence like little else, and it gives you a glow. That, in turn, will make you so much more approachable by your friends and loved ones, building trust, and enabling understanding.

Of course there are women, trans* or otherwise, who have massive problems with lack of hair. Fact is, hair and hairstyles are deeply rooted in femininity, and self-expression of what is accepted to be female. If lack of hair is the case, I urgently recommend spending a small fortune on a good wig. A friend of mine owns several, depending on her mood. Or. Flaunt it! Show off that beautiful skull of yours. There are so many ways a woman can look good with a shaved head. But do not make it even harder for yourself, by doing things only half-way.

My gynaecologist is entirely sweet. I appreciate how he is mindful and on point, that he makes no pretence that I am cis*. At the same time, he offers generous reassurance and moral support. The impression he conveys, is that he, too, appreciates that the body is a most wonderful thing, in its ability to adapt and regenerate, and that he takes genuine happiness and optimism from how well I am doing. When I chose to seek out an appropriate gynaecologist for myself, my heart wept at the thought of sitting in a waiting room, full of happy expectant mothers-to-be. I am happy and grateful for all my friends who get pregnant. And I will eagerly carry your bundle of joy on my arm and smile at them burping up on my t-shirt. Just, please do not invite me to baby showers. I can only take so much.

So. My gynaecologist is not an ob-gyn. He is an oncologist.

I sit with women, who come regularly for their chemotherapy. Women who have lost their wombs, or their ovaries. Who are maybe considering mammary-reconstruction. And I feel quite welcome there. I can empathise with these women. Some who, like me, are dependent on HRT. Who needed a cosmetic surgeon. Who require regular check-ups. And who require a specialist, one who *knows exactly* how the body and the soul react to hormonal imbalances. And what happens to women, bereft of something that previously defined them as female.

Litigation and infrastructure

This is Germany. Say what you want about the Germans, much as they are ruled my bureaucracy and red tape, much as they can sometimes be stubborn and narrow minded. This is a good place to be trans* gender. There are laws in place that acknowledge and safeguard. The state recognises that people whose sexual orientation, and people whose gender identity is other than heteronorm, not only exist, but that they (we) are "normal" human beings with the same rights as everyone else. The condition of being gender dysphoric is legally recognised. There are processes and provisions for people who need to change their life, in order to align their gender identity with their gender expression. And obtain legal documents that support and reflect this.

There is a support system, social services and there are networks. There are people who will counsel you, offer you therapy and provide you with information and help you keep an overview. There are therapists who are caring and proficient, experienced in matters of gender dysphoria. There are specialists that offer expertise and provide care. From basics like endocrinologists, that provide and supervise hormone replacement therapy (HRT), surgeons that offer gender realignment surgery (GRS). Speech therapists for mtf ladies. And enough variety in cosmetic studios and beauticians to permit finding someone, who is not freaked out by a woman sporting a five-o'clock-shadow.

In a great many countries, trans* people find themselves faced with the almost insurmountable hurdle of needing to pay for their transition. Either for lack of any health care system, or even worse, lack of legal recognition of any such thing as gender dysphoria. In Germany, there is a state governed health care system in place, which, for the greater part, works. As a consequence, there is basic care provided and paid for.

In Germany, few trans* gender need to prostitute themselves to fund their transition. And please note, I say "few". Because they, too, exist. I have met two people who have fallen through the cracks in the system, usually as a consequence of their dysphoria. No health insurance is going to pay for your HRT if you have a history of severe self-harm or drug abuse. These people are forced to sell their bodies, simply to survive, and make an attempt at self-determination.

And despite there being a healthcare system, a transition still remains a ruinous enterprise from a financial point of view. Even more so, if the trans* people concerned are cast out of their families and fired from their jobs. This being Germany, there are a great many people who own real estate, who *build themselves a home to live in*. Some even own multiple houses. In the countryside, it is the stereotypical "done thing" for young couples to obtain a plot of land, usually with the help of the greater family, and build a house. Or buy a flat, if you live in the suburbs.

I built myself a body to live in. I am currently free of debt. Once again. But then, I have a steady and well qualified job. But none of those three things are to be taken for granted. Even in the remaining "first-world countries".

Ianto, a very dear friend of mine, had lived in Wales and England for a time. They greatly enjoyed the overall freedom of thought, the open mentalities, and mind-sets they met at Cardiff university. Ianto tells me that socialising and generally coping with day to day life as an Queer* person was so much easier and smoother. And yet, they returned to Germany, because remaining in Britain was out of the question. The legal system was flat-out overwhelmed with other topics, so that requests for change of name and legal gender had waiting lists of five years or more. And Ianto would have had to pay for their own HRT and GRS.

I remember reading *"Always Anastacia, a Transgender Life in South Africa"* by Anastacia Tomson. Unfortunately, she never mentioned how she funded the steps she undertook. She was (is) from a privileged background, so it could be, she was able to pay for them herself. My mind balks to think, of how other trans* people in South Africa fare.

Or the Latin American countries.

Hooray for support groups and crowdfunding, I guess?

Surgery and consequences

Choice of surgeon is something trans* people *agonise* over.

At the risk of making myself immensely unpopular; if people took the same care, to pick their therapists, I am convinced, there would be overall less stress, less sadness, less anxiety.

Obviously, surgeons with experience in GRS come in variety. Please forgive the horribly bad metaphor, but GRS is like Swiss watches. You can opt for the 1550€ watch in the supermarket, and be done in ten minutes. Metaphorically. Or. You can put your name on the waiting list, and wait three years or more (yes, I am entirely serious). And you get yourself the 85'000€ chronometer from the specialised GRS vendor in, say, Thailand. Or in Iran, curiously enough. And the next thing to consider; in a country like Germany, health insurance will cover a GRS. Obviously, they will not mind, if you go for the 1550€ cheap watch, but if pushed a little, they will also spring for the metaphoric 35'000€ timekeeper (semi-realistic numbers). If, however, you insist on the exclusive, then you will be paying it out of your own pocket. And you will have travelling- and accommodation expenses on top.

As a friend and working colleague of mine says, *"there comes a point where I can no longer tell the difference between the excellent and the exorbitant"*. But yes, I understand that this is not a watch, where you can own one for every weekday. This is a one-time, life-changing decision, and I fully empathise with people who will grasp at any illusion of security sold. But. The metaphor stands. And. I find it important to bear in mind, there is in fact a highly lucrative business behind all the medicine.

Whatever you do, decide on a surgeon whom you trust. And if you do, trust them, stick with that. There is nothing worse than second guessing your own decisions, the insecurity and anxiety that causes, is disastrous. I think one of the things that engendered the greatest trust in me, was that my surgeon outright told me, the less "work" he did "on me", the better. And that convinced me, this was a person doing their absolute best, *to enable me, to be the best possible me.*

Today's gender realigning surgeries border on miracles.

As do our biological bodies, in terms of what they are capable of re-structuring, re-forming, re-pairing and re-developing. As my gynaecologist will happily and very respectfully confirm. Years ago, my chest area used to be kind of bland when caressed. Today, my breasts are amongst my most sensitive zones, and they are most certainly erogenous. You surgically remove the testes and you more or less invert the penis, you supply oestrogen, and voila: the body needs a little time to readjust, and then responds by forming a perfect vaginal canal, mucous lining and all. And, yes, internal pelvic muscles are just *the coolest thing ever*, I am so grateful for mine (try saying that without blushing).

Nevertheless, none of this should be taken for granted, and I believe it to be wise to be conservative in your expectations.

These are real risks. If you supplement hormones, you *will* have a significantly increased risk of thrombosis. And cancer. You are informed of this in your interview with your endocrinologist or your gynaecologist prior to HRT. You sign that you undergo HRT in full awareness of these risks. For me, it was absolutely clear. Going without HRT was not an option. In my mind, the risk of breast cancer is significantly smaller, than, without HRT, the risk of relapsing into severe depression. And thus developing a heart condition, cancer, or some other terminal condition.

When I made the decision for surgery, it was clear to me that there were serious risks involved. I had two worst-case scenarios. The first was that I should lose a limb or a vital organ through complications via thrombosis or something. The second was that I should suffer neural damage, and thereby lose control of bladder or bowel functions to a degree as to severely infringe my movement and social interaction. However, these were the only things that I evaluated as putting me in a *worse* position than I would have been If I went without surgery. And anything else *I would learn to live and deal with.* I was fully aware that this was a potentially life-threatening surgery, but to be honest, that did not bother me that much. After all, if I died on the operating table, I would be no worse off than before.

Drastic? Yes. But in my opinion, *this is what it takes* that makes a person decide to undergo HRT. Or have their genitals surgically altered.

If you opt for surgery, you can die. You can suffer a critical lack of oxygen to the brain or limbs. You can be crippled or maimed. You can lose all and any feeling in your lower abdomen. Or, you can be pain ridden and plagued with restrictions of mobility and biological function. There are, of course, less severe complications, but they are not pleasant either, ranging from the necessity of a temporary alimentary-canal exit to severe pain syndromes. You are made aware of this in your interview with the surgeon prior to your surgery. And you sign that you have been made aware of these risks. This is the very reason they ask you one final time, right then and there on the operating table, *"are you going to go through with this?"*

Of course, nobody truly expects to suffer any of these complications. But they remain very, very real indeed. And I find it vital, that people realise, that the process of informed consent is more than just a formality.

Oh, and please: do not neglect aftercare. You will bitterly regret it if you do not dilate your newly healed mumu regularly. There are some things that can only be done once, regardless of how good the surgeons are. You will need to re-learn hygiene. Obviously, you are not going to need tampons or period supplies, but you are going to need panty liners. Furthermore, most people born into a biologically male body go through life, never experiencing a urinary tract infection. No, the human body is not a sterile entity, and yes, the body comes with natural bacteria. But trust me, UTIs are a very real thing. And left undetected or untended, they can turn very nasty so very quickly to the point of becoming life threatening. You will need to learn to take care of that mumu of yours, or she will make you one very stressed-out camper.

On a side note, concerning period supplies: buy some tampons and pads anyways. Always carry one of each in your handbag, or backpack, or whatever. Trust me, you are going to meet someone who will be grateful.

Hormones are psychoactive substances. You *are* going to have mood swings. I am told, the high from testosterone is so epic, it may as well be illegal. But coming down packs such a punch. As for oestrogen, every emotion is just unfiltered. Even more so if combined with progesterone. It really takes getting used to, to sift and differentiate between what is true distress or enthusiasm, and what is just hormones messing with the amplitudes. Neither exactly help getting through the phase in your transition, where you are between places and identities. All the more reason to have a good network, and a supportive therapist.

And finally, even if we trans* girls do not bleed on a monthly basis, my experience with myself, and with others, shows that our moods come and go in cycles. Accompanied by cramps, headaches, possibly acne, sometimes nausea, maybe bloating, and super sensitive or sore breasts. Regardless of how big or small those happen to be. So, yes, by all means, equip yourself with a hot water bottle and painkillers, because you are going to need them. And download a period tracker on your smart device, they are downright useful to have.

I have spoken with many trans* peoples who went through a troubling phase of disorientation and unease. I know trans* women who had hugely distressing phantom sensations, needing time to readjust to the new layout of their anatomy. I am certain, this was as confusing and disconcerting as it sounds. I consider myself lucky I did not have to go through that. Nevertheless, on the whole, your body will respond differently, and this will take getting used to.

Give yourself time.

Psychosomatics

I know more than one person who had trouble with proper oxygenation of tissues because the blood circulation had been disrupted or reduced. One of my friends from our support group developed severe and crippling pain in her genital area, weeks after the surgery, causes unknown. Maybe an inflammation of nerves? Maybe scarring and retraction of tissues? The pain was so bad, she was no longer able to walk, never mind work. While this is strictly speaking a biological cause, it does make me wonder what role self-love, self-acceptance plays in the development of such complications.

To become even more concrete: what I believe noteworthy, is, how many gender dysphoric people develop autoimmune disorders. Too many for this to be coincidental. I suppose there is a bitter and cruel logic to this. The soul is caught in a circle of rejection and self-loathing, because the body does not fit, because ethe soul fails to feel at home, feels betrayed by biology. And so, the body rejects itself. Which translates itself into an overreaction of the immune system, creating disorders like extreme allergies, Morbus Crohn, coagulation disorders, general digestive problems, or kidney disorders. Or it translates itself into chronic pain disorders, ranging from acute discomfort to agony, all seeming without organic cause.

Another lesson that some trans* gender come to learn in a cruelly hard way, is that surgery does not solve all problems.

I know several trans* gender or gender dysphoric people who developed health problems or malaises, not only before, but *after* they were "done with everything". Meaning, they had their name and legal gender changed, they had successful GRS, they healed, and they got on with their lives. Or so one would expect.

Personally, I am inclined to believe, that somewhere, deep down, there are issues as yet unresolved. And possibly it would be a good idea to find a trusted friend, or an adequate therapist, to talk to.

In connection to that. What I find deeply, deeply disturbing, is how a significant number of the trans* people I have talked to, do not trust their psychotherapist. In our support groups, there are always some people, who tell me, with a sly kind of pride, how they skimmed some of their biography, how they bent the truth just a little bit, how they exaggerated just a tad. All to paint themselves as utterly, irrefutably trans*. No ambivalence, no insecurity, no second-guessing.

I fail to understand this.

Well okay, that is not true. To some degree, I do understand. *Your therapist is your primary gate keeper.* Your therapist decides, ultimately, whether or not you are eligible for HRT, eligible to have your name changed, eligible for GRS. So: yeah, I get it. You are stone cold frightened as hell of this person. They could say "no". And then you would really be up the Amazon without a paddle. Most particularly, if you have this nagging little voice at the back of your mind, which implies, that you might be dysphoric as f*ck, and a danger to yourself. But you might not be trans* sexual. And HRT might possibly not solve your problems…

It does sort of explain why some very few people end up with reoccurring depressive episodes *despite* that they legally changed their name. Or they develop extreme psoriasis, even if they had their GRS.

I will repeat; I am shocked at the number of people with whom I have spoken, that distrust their therapists. I am unsure if this lack of trust is a statement about the quality and qualifications of the therapists that are about. When I think of Dr Chamberlain, I find it hard to find fault with him. But then I am aware, that he is booked into the next year, and then some. And I am aware of some of the reports from some of the other trans* people, of their therapists. Reports which, even if taken with a generous pinch of salt, are hair raising. Or if all this is testimony to how trans* people are so troubled by their pasts, and slow to trust due to their experiences with society. Or how they might be projecting their own insecurities and fears onto the person whom they are supposed to confide in. Seriously, peoples. You want to be yourself, right? Your best possible self? How do you hope to achieve that, if you do not trust the person who is supposed to enable you?

It is just sad.

I have met people who expressed utter surprise (and alarm) at being asked about their past by their therapist. I have met people who avoid therapy, avoid confronting their problems. Because that will face them with the plain fact, that we do not have control.

Fact remains, if we ignore our problems, we are obviously not in control. And if we do not put the effort into sorting out our issues, they *will* end up controlling us.

Several things come to mind. We are a part of *this* world. I find it necessary for trans* people to be mindful, that we are a part of the humanity whose basic rights we are struggling for. That our change is only possible because we live in this society. It is possible because cis* people have recognised our plight, because they have gone out of their way, to enable us and empower us. Do remember to show some appreciation for this.

Also. Yes, it is unfair that cis* people get to make decisions that impact our lives, our wellbeing. It is unfair that cis* people have the power to constrain us in our self-actualisation. But. I find it important to differentiate. Between the hetero-patriarchal prejudice and the earnest exploration. Differentiate.

Between gatekeepers who are still stuck in a mindset, where trans* gender was a novel discovery, where there were sincere debates of whether this was a mental disorder to be cured by means of conversion therapy, and you had to spend half your life under utterly humiliating conditions, simply to prove you were indeed sincere. Or Predators in the guise of self-proclaimed demigods, who satiate their egos and their fetishes by having trans* peoples strip their souls bare.

And between experts and scholars who truly care. Humans who authentically wish to enable trans* peoples to evolve into their true selves and support them in their way to living their best possible life. There are a great many truly cool, truly empowering, truly lovable cis* people out there. Have courage. Have hope. Go find them.

It is worth it.

The underlying mindset is vitally important. If you view yourself as a victim, then obviously all and any questions you are asked will appear an intrusion and a transgression. An attempt at disempowering you. If on the other hand, you view yourself as empowered, then a therapist (or a loved one) challenging a concept is not a threat. On the contrary. They are helping you. They are gifting you with an outside perspective on something they find puzzling. And they are permitting you to analyse this. And come out stronger and clearer than you were before.

Sexuality

By extrapolation of rule thirty-four of the internet. Regardless of who you are, regardless of how you identify or self-designate, entirely regardless of whom you perceive yourself to be, and how you express yourself: *someone* in this world will be a total fan of you and will be entirely prepared to make out with you.

Question is of course, whether you desire the same of this particular person and whether you happen to be compatible at all.

Straight up

The twentieth of November is trans* gender day of remembrance. An annual day of mourning and commemoration of those people whose murder can be directly connected to their being trans*. And in a disturbingly high percentage of the cases, murder is far too a harmless word to use. Humans are capable of unspeakable things…

What is even worse, is that most of the particularly gruesome and excessive crimes against trans* people can usually be traced back to family. Honour murders.

Other than that, I am inclined to believe, that sexual encounters (or potential sexual encounters) are among the chief triggers for trans* phobic violence and crimes. Trans* women are particularly vulnerable and susceptible to this. I am sure that in turn is connected to "normal" cis-het* male roles and societies' expectations of how a "proper" man should behave and react. This seems to be confirmed by fact that both the numbers, and the *extreme excesses of violence* are focused in geographies and societies (Latin America), where male roles are traditionally anchored in "machismo", and therefore cultures where homophobia is a matter of norm.

Let me be clear. I am not implying that victims of trans* phobic violence had sex in mind before they got murdered, much less, that they are to fault. But if you are presenting as female at a club (or at the supermarket), and you happen to have legs and top-girth, then chances are, you are going to be chatted up by a cis* guy with intent. Add to this, that outside western Europe, a significant number of trans* people are forced to prostitute themselves in order to finance their transition. In an environment that the majority of societies view as morally grey at best, and for which there are no safety provisions. So when that cis* guy finds out you are not what he expected, then his world comes crashing down. And that is not something a lot of cis* males cope well with on any part of the globe.

Western Europe is not spared from this, even though numbers are comparatively low. Regardless of this, it is wise and sensible, that if you are trans* you are heading out to the club or disco, then keep it safe. And if you intend to encounter cis* people for sex, then you should have your act down pat. And a backup plan. And a friend (not the cops), who knows where you are. On speed dial.

I strongly recommend being proactively open and honest. It might not keep you from rejection. But at least it should go a long way to prevent you ending up in the ICU with bruised ribs and a cracked jaw. Or in the morgue. Or several morgues. You think I am joking?

I am aware that my anxieties about this seem ridiculous to a great many trans* sisters here in Germany. Nevertheless, even here in Germany, there does seem to be at least some underlying tension. Another taboo, that is rarely addressed or even implied. As a matter of fact, I have a hypothesis, that many trans* gender peoples seek partners among other trans* genders themselves, for precisely that reason: the fact that they are assured understanding and acceptance for their dysphoria.

What is it like?

Sexuality is one of *the* central taboo topics. This gives rise to a labyrinth of some of the wildest hopes, the strangest myths, most exotic fetishes, most extreme desires, and utterly misplaced priorities.

I have spoken with a great many trans* women. Thankfully, most had ideas that were grounded more or less within the boundaries of reality and the feasible.

I have, however, met trans* women whose sexuality played a very prominent part in their lives, predating their transition, and who were *bitterly* disappointed (and surprised) by loss of sensitivity, lack of response following the GRS. They were completely overwhelmed and overstrained by their requiring so much more self-awareness, mindfulness, and patience. A truly frightening aspect would be to regret the decision to have had surgery, so of course every available defence mechanism is called upon to deny that, possibly, surgery might have been a mistake. "Is it better than before?" is a question that seems to be often at the forefront of many of trans* peoples' minds. Still caught in the notion that we need to justify to others (and to ourselves) that we are now "healed". Placing an enormous burden expectations, of needing to prove that now, "everything is so much better".

Some of the hopes I came across, bordered on the plain ridiculous. Nothing, no kind of hormone replacement and certainly no surgery will transform you into a cis* woman. Nothing on this earth will change your bone frame, your basic body-build and limbs. Your body will *not* react like that of a cis* woman. Something surgically realigned and healed will never be the same as grown and evolved from an embryo, regardless of how proficient and nimble the surgeon, regardless of how many years you have to let your body accommodate. The more surgery you have, the more you run risks of complications. And: the less your will feel.

Counselling people like that always leaves me deeply disturbed and anxious. In my imagination, their biographies can go one of two ways. The first is, that they will intuitively know that they are deluding themselves, but in order to protect themselves from such extreme disappointment, they will forever procrastinate any actual decision to change anything in their lives. And they will not transition, spending the remainder of their lives in misery. The second alternative is, that they will actually transition, but be forever disappointed by the results. So they go for the next surgery. They are likely to forever keep chasing their illusion, never actually living a life grounded in reality, and remain deeply unhappy with their fate. Again, the risk of depression and self-harm is immense.

I know very few trans* gender who were honest enough and clear headed enough to acknowledge that their sexual fulfilment took such an importance in their lives, that they opted to keep their anatomy and be women with a penis. I have immense respect of these women, even if, to a high degree, it baffles me. It is certainly nothing I could ever do, but regardless, I do believe that gender is in the mind, in the soul.

Another sensitive topic, is how deeply you expose your partner to the particulars and specifics of transitioning. I have met trans* people who expressed surprise at their cis* partner being weirded out. Particularly when going into medical details. During pillow talk. No offence, peoples, if you are going to do that, then I am not surprised that trans* people are confronted with the accusation, that being trans* is a kink. Regardless of how cool your partner is with your being "different", show a little sensitivity and tact. And pick the times and the topics you share with your partner with care. Particularly if they are cis-het*. But even if they are trans* or queer*.

Yes, but...

...you want to know if trans* women can have penetrative vaginal sex?

Well, duh. That kind of *is* the general idea behind surgically constructing a vaginal canal.

...you want to know whether or not they can achieve a climax? "The big O", as my friend Vivienne puts it.

Yes, we can.

Or at least, most trans* women can. But. There is no guarantee. And count on it, it will be utterly, completely different. Again, as Vivienne puts it, for some it is kind of "meh", while others swear upon travelling the cosmos, her words.

Although, bearing in mind what some of my cis* friends have shared with me, the cosmos statement makes me slightly sceptical. And a quiet part of me furrows her eyebrows and contemplates on how much we sometimes need to protect ourselves from disappointment, when reality fails to match our expectations. Another, equally quiet part of me, gently admonishes the first part, to not be so cynical, and reminds me that stars are stars, right? Whether they are celestial nuclear fires or CGI projections of our brain. Cold, sober statistics say that *more than 80% of **cis-het*** *women do not achieve climax from penetrative stimulation alone*. 80% seems a little high, but that's science for you. Nevertheless, I think it extremely healthy to keep this fact in mind, and not let ourselves be misled by pornography or fictional depictions of sex.

...you want to know if a partner person can tell the difference?

How the hell should I know?!? Who cares? Stop thinking. *Feel*!

...you want to know what it feels like?

Get lost! None of your business.

Or... ...Kiss me. *And mean it*. And maybe you will find out...

...Although currently you are out of luck. That privilege is exclusively held by a very charming gentleman, and I believe he is quite serious about maintaining the status quo.

Seriously though

When I opted for GRS, I was fully and entirely aware, that my entire body consciousness would change. And naturally, I expected my sexuality to change. The entire function and feeling. When I opted for GRS, I lay down on that operating slab with the crystal-clear knowledge that I might never feel anything again. *And I was okay with that*. If sex would turn into something I would only ever share with a partner for *their* sake, without ever actually feeling it myself, then so be it. If getting rid of my penis, if having a vagina meant giving up on orgasms, then that was the price I was prepared to pay for peace of mind and freedom of self-expression. Anything I would feel, any pleasure or fulfilment, would be a gift.

Extreme? Maybe.

The upside of my mind-set, pessimistic as some people might find it, is that *I do indeed view today's life as an absolute gift*. Every day I get to live in my own identity, unhindered and unlimited in my expression, is a renewal and a liberation. And I am thankful for the peace and the equilibrium that I feel within. Being able to not only share my passion with a partner, but feel it as well, is the absolute icing to my cake. In fact, words fail me to express adequately, just *HOW* grateful I am for my life today and everything it entails.

If you are trans* I recommend you not pretend to be cis*. And I will cautiously point out, that vaginism is a thing. I put a lot of effort into maintaining my new anatomy, to make sure I would not be hurt. It paid off. Lubrication is another such topic. Yes, penetration is hypothetically possible without the help of moistener. If your partner shows the patience of an angel and takes extra care with foreplay, then anything is possible. But again, that cannot be taken for granted. And there is no shame in reaching for a tube of gel or lube. On the contrary, make it into a game. Show your partner that you appreciate.

Yes, it might come naturally. And it may be fun. But you cannot ever take that for granted.

You are going to need to re-learn sexuality.

From the ground up. Your body will need to move differently, and you will need to learn. The feelings, the sensation, the response, everything is new and different. And, no. We, including cis* women, we are not all as supple or as limber as porn stars. Give yourself a frikkin' break, it is not a competition, you are supposed to be enjoying this.

Above all, take your time.

And if your partner does not take their time, well, perhaps they are not the right one for you?

Finally, this is another thing I cannot emphasise enough: *your most vital primary sexual organ is between your ears*, not between your legs. It works most easily if you actually love yourself. If you *feel* sexy. And if you can completely relax into the moment of being *here*. And relaxing means you need a partner, with whom you can let yourself go. *Whatever that means for you.* Like I said, you will most likely need to re-learn from scratch what it is, that pushes you over the brink.

Feel the rhythm. Feel the life! Dance!

Gender expression

For trans* people, it is essential to "pass".

That is, to have an outward identity and appearance, that is congruent with society's expectations of what that gender should look like.

Yes, this is an entirely cis-het* binary dogma, but truth remains, that is what the majority of society portrays and expects. No. This has nothing to do with fairness, or inclusion. This has everything to do with *avoiding* being singled out by a pack of neo-Nazis, or a gang of hot-heads steeped in testosterone and machismo (homo- or heterosexual). Or, incidentally, by a murder of TERFs. We still have a way to go, before people who strongly differ from the "norm" are naturally treated as "normal".

This is a very real matter of safety.

And, yes, many cross-dressing people, trans* or otherwise, dress them-selves in highly stereotype, over-the-top, reduced-to-stereotype kind of clothes. I would assume, that this is an attempt to fit in, to fit into a picture that we grow up with, that we are socialised with. And as many feminists point out, maybe the reason is, that they are trying to compensate that they have been socialised in another gender. But I ask you to bear in mind, every cis* girl goes through a phase of developing her identity, of finding her own brand of stye, of adapting her look and her outward expression. Usually, this is called puberty. And I will remind you, that most parents of teenage girls will tell you, that their daughters wear *way* too much makeup and show *way* too much skin. And if you look at any trade brand of body-care-products, or fashion labels, then tell my how they are not emphasising and reinforcing stereotyping, I dare you.

Being perfect

It is a topic that comes up every now and again with my cis* friends.

Yes, women are raised to think, we need to be perfect. Permanently perfectly styled and clothed, perfect people living perfect lives with perfect bodies and perfect faces. Media, ads, fashion- and lifestyle mags do nothing to alleviate the burden or correct this misconception. Not even the so called "alternative" scene, even they are ridden with the "proper" way to dress, the eco-friendly and organic way to look your best. Well of course they do, they all want to sell you something.

Acceptance of imperfection and deviation, for change and for ambivalence, is being lost. The acceptance of being normal is lost. Obviously, in so many things that touch our lives, it is so much more important to actually make the choice and *DO*, rather than aim for perfection.

Nevertheless, I will maintain that the situation of trans* people, particularly of trans* women is more exposed, more extreme. Not just by degrees, but by magnitudes. Because there *is* such a thing as a gender stereotype figure and expression. And to be misgendered is incredibly painful and depreciatory. Because your own perception of self, and more importantly, your own perception of worth, is something you are already struggling with.

I remember a time when compliments were always something very ambiguous for me. Take a remark like "Hey, you're looking good". Which is a compliment at heart. And probably, the person complimenting you, is truly trying to be good to you. Be supportive. The problem is, if you are trans*, there are many levels in this very simple statement. There are so many implications, that, if you are gender dysphoric, is immensely hard to free yourself from.

Depending how good I felt about myself, I would hear different things.

- On good days, "You have an athletic figure". "That shawl looks lovely on you, it complements your eyes. You picked well".

- On not so good days, "Hey, for a guy in drag, you look pretty decent".
- On bad days, "You show yourself in public like that?!? F*CK! You're brave!"

Trans* men have it slightly easier on this front. Not many people argue about your gender when you are sporting a beard and voicing a baritone or deeper. So much so, that trans* men are close to invisible, once they are developed. But. You have to get there first. Just as trans* women need months or even years to get rid of their beard, and grow into the shape. Grow into the role. And dysphoria still does things with your mind, I know that much from myself as well as friends.

The global trans* conspiracy

There is a huge fuss about restrooms. Public toilets.

Because people with a vagina are regularly targeted by people with a penis. Plain basic fact. At the same time, people who feel they are men, would like to use the "men's room", because this feel appropriate and affirming. But if they happen to have a vagina, and if they are misgendered, this could go sideways very fast and very badly. And. There are women who would like to use the "ladies' room", because that is what girls do, and when you gotta go, you gotta go. But if they happen to have a penis, or a five-o'clock-shadow, they might be facing accusations of assault and/or violation.

There are some women, who would like to ban trans* women from the ladies' room. Even those trans* women who gave up their biological water works. They say people like me use the ladies' room, because we are voyeurs and predators.

Personally, I do not see cis-het* male sexual predators cross-dressing to go lurk in ladies' restrooms. Somehow, in my mind, that contradicts with them being testosterone driven sexual predators that prey on women. But. I am aware, that is a dangerous assumption. Nevertheless, I am going to speculate, that a predator will not have the body language of a lady. But that of a predator. I am convinced, that the body language of a predator will be blatantly different from that of a cis* woman, even a butch. Or a trans* woman, with or without anatomy. Or even a cis* male transvestite portraying a woman, with no predatory intentions. And. Even if I have not data to back up this claim, I am going to say that you will not find many trans* women (or cis* lesbians) who masturbate in public.

But.

I am aware *that is very thin ice.*

And entirely beside the point. Because to people who are afraid of being preyed upon by predators with a penis, to them it is neither here nor there whether the predator wears a dress or trousers, and whether they self-designate as male, female or queer. Survivors are afraid of people with penis. And, yes. That is discriminative. But please bear in mind, they have good reason. I too, do find the idea of a cis-het* man in a "ladies' room" to be disquieting. Very much so.

But, to cut the entire discussion short. What all of this boils down to, is:

There are people that need a safe place.

Some of them menstruate. And some of them do not. And some of those that do not, sport a penis. *But they still need to be safe.* All of them. And that is the common ground.

So yes. We do need public rest rooms that guarantee the safety of the people that use them. Personally, the easiest way would be to build them in such a way, that only one person can use them. And build them in a way, that stalking is not possible. No more multiple cubicles, no more corridors where someone can be mugged. I am sure that there are solutions.

And. We do need safe houses for rape survivors and survivors of domestic violence. And I am inclined to say, such a safehouse is not the best place for a woman with a penis to go to. Or even a trans* man.

And yet. Even women with a penis, even a trans* men need a safe place.

Where things really escalate in an ugly way, is when (self-proclaimed) feminists discriminate gender dysphoric people on grounds of their socialisation and upbringing. They say, people who were socialised and raised in a cis-het* male environment, can never be women. There are feminists who invalidate my existence, by saying, my self-expression is the sum of a patriarchal and heteronormative upbringing. That we are all fakes, that we are all predators.

This is where everything I am, is reduced and contorted into a kink and a lie.

And this is revealing. Because I get the impression, the entire discussion is not about protecting women from predators. Or about who uses which lavatory. It is about exclusion. About devaluation. About US versus THEM. About people who are afraid of having something taken away from them, and it has nothing to do right to inviolability. Do they realise, they are permanently, *totally* reducing males to sexual predators? And women to perpetual victims?

Small minds and hard hearts… …sort of like predators.

What is entirely alarming, downright macabre, is how so many TERFs are highly eloquent and well-educated women. Well off in their material needs and secure in their role in society. Curiously, often in positions of influence and power. Not at all the victim type. So… …what has gotten your knickers in such a twist?

For the record, I am not here to control your life. Or to take away your child, or your SUV. I don't want to be treated as someone or something special. I don't want to be treated as an exotic exception. I don't ask for extra privileges. I am not your better, I am not a conqueror, I am not your replacement. I do not take anything away from anyone. My existence does not threaten anyone else's.

I just want to be treated as a human being. I wish to be treated with the same respect, dignity, and appreciation that every other human desires deep, deep down.

And.

I will not suffer my struggles to be reduced to a choice of restrooms.

Or my identity to be reduced to a fetish.

Trigger words

Another argument that is often raised, is that "our children need to be protected against the brain-washing of the global trans* conspiracy, because the number of de-transitioners is skyrocketing".

I kid you not, "global trans* conspiracy", get out your tin-foil hats, peoples. As hard as it is for me to keep a straight face when confronted by such infantile, one-tracked, and plainly paranoid accusations, they need to be taken seriously. To ignore them would be fatal. And after all. Misguided and irresponsible as these conspiracy ideas are, I am going to give people the benefit of good will. And I will assume that they are drawn up by loving parents. Confused, insecure, and ignorant, but loving, nevertheless.

As opposed to obtuse, insensitive, and self-centred parents. Who would sacrifice trans* children, even their own, rather than acknowledge that their world views and their core beliefs are outdated. And yes. Those too, exist.

- Fact. The numbers of people of any age, who register and pursue therapy for gender dysphoria, is rising.
- Fact. The number of youths, who voice a need and desire for transition, initiating HRT up to and including GRS, is rising.

- Fact. The percentage of teenage biological females, who describe themselves as questioning, as trans* men, as non-binary, or queer, is disproportionately high.
- Fact: If absolute numbers of transitioners rise, then absolute numbers of de-transitioners will also rise.

Sweden performed a 50-year survey with close to 800 trans* gender people, which they published in 2010. According to which 2% of those who had undergone GRS, experienced regrets. The centre for trans* gender equality in the US conducted a survey in 2015, with close to 28,000 trans* people. 8% of the respondents said they de-transitioned (reversed their transition). Of those 8%, 62% said they detransitioned *temporarily*, due to pressure from parents. I remember speaking to Prof Aedelfrid in 2018 about this, and he puts the number of people to detransition at 2%. I have no idea whether that is Germany, or western Europe. I assume he meant people whom he counselled.

From my experiences with counselling, from my experiences talking to youths, talking to parents, I will say this. *All* the youths in our youth group are dysphoric. *All* of them suffer from depression in varying severity. *All* of them suffer from problems with self-acceptance with their bodies, with their gender roles, and with their gender- and sexual- identities. All of them.

Nevertheless. My intuition says, for a small, but significant number of our youths, transitioning and HRT will *not* make them feel better about themselves. They are dysphoric, certainly. Confused, feeling unloved, and supremely at risk of self-harm. But not necessarily trans* as in trans* gender or trans* sexual in the "classical" binary sense. And I wonder if they feel a kinship with all these other highly dysphoric youths, who very much feel themselves as victims (as teens do), misunderstood and oppressed by their parents and society. And it makes me wonder if, for some, the idea of GRS is a "quick fix". An escape from something else, a replacement. I question whether there are other tensions and disharmonies, which will not be solved by removing primary or secondary sexual characteristics. I ask myself if those few of our youths are not simply lost. Possibly due to the utterly toxic demands, dictated by outdated gender roles, maybe being forced into marriages. Or quite simply because, in some places, the plain fact that you are female *makes you available*, even if you are not yet of child-bearing age.

There is a hugely volatile "discussion" ongoing, that trans* people should be interviewed and evaluated only by peers. To ensure a fair hearing, by people that understand what it means to be gender dysphoric. Therapy for trans* sexuality does have a long and *heinous* history, of being completely at the mercy of bigots with raging delusions of self-importance. Transition used to involve conversion therapy, inhumanly humiliating obstacles, and utter invalidation. You were more or less co-erced to debase yourself completely, to the point of destitution and exile. Suicide by degrees. Nevertheless, I find myself becoming very cautious when confronted by ar-guments like that.

On the one hand.

There is the demand to reduce the age limit before GRS can be approved. The thought of fifteen-year-olds getting GRS gives me the shivers. When I think of my students, they sometimes barely seem capable of making life-directing decisions. So, I do shrink at the thought of a human, whose development of personality is not yet completed, should make such a far-reaching decision. I feel even more apprehensive when I think of a small but significant number of our youths, whom *I know* are not honest with their therapist. Or honest with themselves.

I have met trans* people in counselling functions, who have indiscriminately, en-abled *anyone* who claimed to be gender dysphoric. Their own struggles, their own histories overshadowing their clarity and perspectives. Unable to distinguish be-tween their own past, and the biography of their clients, trying to save the child *in their own subconscious*. Thereby irresponsibly providing youths with access to treat-ments that have irreversible consequences.

And. I have met cis* people that were clearly biased *against* enabling trans* peo-ple. Counsellors, judges, medical specialists, *Gatekeepers* who hinder, hamper, con-found and prevent. With a seeming malevolence, culminating in a purposeful spite-fulness. And whose true motives probably lie far from "helping" or "protecting" anyone, other than protecting their own comfort zone. Or securing their heteropatri-archal privileges.

On the other hand.

We *are* dysphoric. And most of us have the scars to prove it. And being dys-phoric is a state of being that will kill you in the long or short run. I *know* that the majority of youths, children even, *are crystal clear about who they are* and what they want from life. Their behaviour and their personality are *consistent* throughout. I empathise that gender dysphoric youth *need* access to treatment that delays the body development of puberty. Because undergoing the development of secondary sexual characteristics is unnecessary. And cruel.

The path to self-determination is hard. Self-determination is such a deep, basic need. A fundamental right. And to be invalidated by thin arguments and bureaucratic side-steps is humiliating and degrading in the extreme. Even today, it is seemingly controlled and governed by gatekeepers and bureaucrats. All of them cis-het*. A great many of them males. Not traditionally, stereotypically, the best clientele for explorations of deep feelings, balances of feminine and masculine attributes. So, I understand the call for gatekeepers who are trans*.

And. There are cis* people, humans, who *are* guided by compassion and the desire to enable fellow humans to become their best possible selves. And who go several steps beyond what they are legally *required*, to help. When I think of the judge that enabled me. Or Dr Chamberlain.

Being clear

My answer to all these queries and ambiguities is: there is no simple answer.

There is not.

Life is complex. Answers remain complex. And need to be re-examined for every individual biography. There is no such thing as a universal procedure. Not concerning body dysphoria, not concerning trans* gender. No two lives will ever be the same. Just as no two people, not even identical twins, will be the same. My friend Naomi is the best possible example of this. She is a successful young woman who is trans*, and she has an *identical twin* brother, who is perfectly happy with his life and his body.

Changing a name and gender expression is easy (aside from the bureaucracy). It is reversible. Without devastating repercussions. HRT has irreversible effects. GRS can be done once. After that, it all deteriorates into patchwork and repair. And it cannot be undone.

So, yes. I *do* believe that trans* people should continue to be required to undergo a psychiatric evaluation. Before any irreversible treatments are administered, I do think it is a good idea that two independent specialists are involved. The question remains. When someone decides over the fate of another, what guides that decision? The need to protect a privilege, or a comfort zone? Or the genuine empathic desire to enable and empower another human being. To be human.

I am often disquieted, by the amount of peer pressure trans* people in general exert amongst themselves. The amount of heat and aggression I have caught over this discussion is staggering. I am faced with a huge amount of opposition, when I imply that there might be other options. Or that deeper (and therefore longer) therapy would be beneficial. If I raise this topic amongst my colleague counsellors, I am accused of being a traitor and a heretic. But then I have generally found trans* people to be hugely defensive, and be very quick to lash out, if their transition is threatened. Not entirely surprising, I suppose.

And it is so important to bear in mind. The moment political agendas are involved, all empathy and common sense are out the window. These decisions do not belong in the jurisdiction of any political party. Which is difficult, because we need political pressure to further the right to self-determination.

It is a very fine line to tread. The number of people who regret their choices are marginal. Despite so much in this book being about people on the margins, I cannot condone trans* gender being prevented from exercising their right to self-determination, to supposedly protect the extreme few *from themselves*. People who fail to be honest with themselves, or with their counsellors.

Again, it comes down to a matter of trust.

The only person who truly *knows*, is that person themselves. For all other people, family and therapists alike, however well-meaning, all of them are trying to evaluate a situation in which they are outside observers only. Involved only by proxy, and dependent on experience by proxy. Ultimately, I would think, the operative word here is "consistent". If a person truly has shown a longer and coherent past of gender dysphoria, then chances are, they are trans* gender. And they are not going to up and change their mind. And, self-determination has everything to do with self-responsibility. And while parents obviously need to guide and support their children, the choice of transition is one they will need to trust their child with.

Angels in clouds

I observe it in our youth group of gender dysphoric people so very clearly.

I hypothesise, that the reason for us having more and more youngsters who are gender dysphoric, is that today, these topics are actually spoken about. Our society is stepping out of the dark ages, and lifting the taboos. And there are words for them, there is a vocabulary to name the feelings of unease or displacement, there are terms and adequate descriptions for the alienness, for feeling like a Cheetah trapped in a Labrador skin. And, there are people who prove, you are not losing your mind. This is real.

But that is "outside". There is also an "inside".

Another thought that comes to mind: the majority (estimated greater 70%) of our youth group were ftm trans* boys. The majority (same) of our adult group were mtf trans* women. One ready explanation would be, that, like me, the older trans* peoples transition later in life because they have realised, any transition will make having a family with children far more difficult. And when I spoke to our trans* youths, all the ftm boys were screamingly dysphoric about their female biological body functions, and having babies was a topic so far off the grid, it was unimaginable.

Another explanation paints a more encompassing, a more social portrait. That to-day's societies place youths under extreme pressure. Making inhuman demands. Concerning looking perfect, being immaculate, out-performing everyone else, excel-ling in every way. And with rising population numbers, with increasing competition on the academic and job markets, this is not showing any inclination of decreasing. On top of which, the media and advertisement industries have recognised a target group that is easily manipulated and intimidated. Add to all that, that particularly young women are exposed to the requirement of being permanently attractive, al-ways sexy, and by implication *available*. But not under any circumstances biologi-cally functional. To be more concise: having a period, the possibility of pregnancy, the risk of getting an infection, even worse, catching an STI. All of these are non-topics. Taboos. The word "Purity" has come to represent an entire system of denial and re-pression of both *sexuality and identity*, to the point of where in so many cultures, sex has become something entirely shameful and filthy. The perfect Freudian schizo-phrenic setup.

Add to all of this, that in complete contradiction to the foregoing, young women are pressured into wedlock, because it is the "proper" thing to do. And because it secures the continuity of the tribe, the assures the prosperity of the family. It enables the proliferation of the genes (deliberate choice of words). As if that was not enough, in far too many places, girls are considered fair game, simply because they happen to have a warm orifice. Yes, Girls. Not just Women. All of which raises the question in my mind, to what degree do societies' structures and world-view contribute to rising number of gender dysphoric people? To what degree do the demands of society con-tribute to young women distancing themselves from ideals and roles of femininity, that they cannot identify with? Cannot exist with?

No, I am not trying to find "causes" for being trans* gender. There are none. Nev-ertheless, the overall impression I get, is that, trans* and cis* alike, our youths feel driven to explore and redefine. Not just in Germany. Not just what roles "men" and "women" fulfil in society, that too. But also, what it *is* to be "man" or "woman". And that those two are by far not the only choices. Even redefining what it means to be lesbian or gay. I hypothesise, that our youths are setting their sights on the next step of evolution, not so much biological, but spiritual. An evolution of the mind. Of the soul. That we are so much more than binary male and female, and that our identities are free to evolve into an entire cloud of possibilities, exploration into several dimensions. In the same way that language shifts and develops according to our technology and our needs, who we are is beginning to adapt, to readjust. That our souls are *growing*. Possibly to step up, to fulfil our next greater task of founding a global society that can coexist in peace. Without permanently competing for the moral high ground. Or some advantage over another human, or group of humans.

There are remarkable parallels and similarities in internet subcultures across the globe. Be it my students and trainees in Germany, Indonesian domestics in Hongkong, or girls of northern Africa that serve in the Arabic states. Entire parallel universes in which people rediscover and redefine themselves. Live out entire existences online, because that offers the kind of private life and the quality for self-expression not found in "reality". A world in which they find solace and support, even love and intimacy.

On side note. People ask me how I like movies like "Danish Girl" or "Trans-America". And, yes. They certainly are emotionally moving. And yet, I am not of the opinion, that they truly or adequately portray what it means, to be confronted with the kind of changes, that require both the person AND society to change their perception, of what it means to be human. These truly are stories. Entertainments. They are melodramas that tell of heartbreak and perseverance, but they say little of who these people are, and what drives them. They timidly touch on the limits that are met, and which concepts need to be reinvented.

Depictions that truly impress me, movies which I personally find far more appealing, and more true to the actual core topic of *transformation*, are "Blade Runner" or "Alita". And my favourite, which I think really expresses the core concept of human evolution, is "Ghost in the Shell". Souls giving up their hitherto fixed form. Dissolving. Breaking apart, yes. And this is the thing that frightens the people anchored in the binary dogma. But water cannot break. Fire cannot break. It simply takes on a new form. And fills whatever space there is. It fulfils the purpose it was designed and destined to. And you become the person you were meant to be.

I further hypothesise, that this is by no means just a thing of trans* people. I see this reflected even in my very "normal" students in vocational training. They question. They experiment. They break taboos, they push limits, they challenge traditions. Not randomly, not carelessly, but with hope and with purpose. And in many ways, I think they are freer in the mind, more creative, than my parents' generations, when those struggled for an end to wars and an end to gender oppression. So, even cis-het* youth are testing the limits of what a male or female identity can be.

As they should. It makes me hopeful.

Make no mistake. I am *not* implying that the solid and well serving model of binary soul and identity are obsolete. Or wrong.

But we are more than that. And we need to permit ourselves to be more than that. We need to look beyond our own horizons.

There is a complex system of needs and fears behind the drive of youths to rebel "against the system". Ironically, I believe the same is true of the parents' so vehement rejection of trans* children and what they view breaking of rules. A primary and simple aspect of this is, there is of course a parent afraid of "losing" a child. The parents themselves afraid of being rejected and unloved. The primal hurt child deep within the parent themselves. I am inclined to believe, this fear is easily assuaged, if you reflect on the fact that ,the only way to actually lose your child *is to reject them yourself*. If you enable your child, if you offer affirmation and strength, if you ensure that there is the family remains a safe-zone and a place of solace and support, then regardless of what changes your child will go through, they will always come back to you.

What is perhaps more difficult, and certainly more complex, is the structure of how family-tribes are historically (and biologically) about securing their continued existence in an indifferent environment, or an environment that is potentially hostile. Pick any culture on any continent. The concept of arranged marriages, of securing of resources, of strengthening of allegiances and of eradication of potential threats, all these are as old as humankind. Incidentally, so is the concept of the rebel couple who absconds in search of true love and self-determination. The stuff of legends. And depending on *who* tells the tale,

- It will end with the rebel couple breaking over their hubris, the realization, that the parents were right all along and how much safer and better it is, to listen to the elders' council, and that the young peoples may have been meant for each other, but safely under the watchful care of their elders and betters.
- Or, it will end with the overthrowing of the council of elders, the breaking of traditions, and the vindication of the young rebel couple, and how they grow to be wiser and better leaders than their ancestors ever were, leading their new tribe to united prosperity and founding a new way of life.

Either way, it ends with someone breaking.

So basically, that which we have identified as an inalienable human right, the right to self-determination, might even be in direct conflict to what tribe-tradition requires for it to assure continuity.

What if the truth to all this lies somewhere in between?

So. What is required, is that the existence of a family (tribe) is secured. In other words, what we need is a society, in which the prerequisites for the assured continuity of, not only survival, but of prosperity, are given. By society. All this implies the importance of there being an inclusive society. Which welcomes and includes different people as an opportunity for growth and extraordinary contribution, as opposed to being a source of friction and cataclysm. And if we build a society that welcomes the individual for their differences, for the richness and diversity of their background, then I claim, that individual will in turn be all the more motivated and dedicated to bringing themself into play with all their energies and resources.

Summarily, **being your best possible self**, regardless how "far from the norm", will make an inclusive society better and stronger, more productive and safer. A good place to feel at home in.

Ultimately, we need to bear in mind, that identity is singular. Yes, you can be gender fluid. But you are still you. Each of us. Each and every one of us is a single individual. Unique. Biographies may share similarities, but they are never the same. And each of us is valid. Has a right to exist. In peace, in dignity, free of oppression.

My hope is, that it is this precise state of being, that draws us humans to each other. Why we feel so connected. We all feel the vulnerability and the singularity. While at the same time basking in the glow of kinship.

So, it is okay to be confused, when you encounter a person that does not meet your expectations. Bur how you deal with the other person, and how you deal with your expectations, is a matter of your own self-security, and a measure of your heart. It is okay to be worried. It is okay to be thoughtful and critical.

And it is okay to be human.

But I ask you to be mindful. And kind. **I require of you**, to recognise the humanity in the person opposite you. Offer them a hand in kinship, and in trust. You might be so, so positively surprised.

Afterthoughts

I like to believe I am aware of my privileges.

Even in Tanzania, even in a country at war, my family was always materially so much more secure than so many of the peoples. I know hunger, but my life never depended on my next meal. In Zimbabwe, I was protected by a community. I was blessed with education. I had access to resources. I was blessed with *awareness*.

*And the pure and plain availability of **choice**.*

In my life in Europe, I was (am) safe. Within reason. One of the reasons for moving back to Europe. I passed as a cis-het* man. I pass as a cis* woman. Within reason. I never had to face a line of riot-police. Or justify my existence to a bigot apparatchik. Or a religious zealot. Under the looming threat of conversion therapy. Or at knife-point. And I was never expected to marry for wealth, security, or influence.

I have never needed to struggle for my voice to be counted. Others had struggled in my stead before me. In the pure random chance that I was born with light skin, I grew up with the privilege of my voice being given more weight than the voices of others.

But most of all, I am supremely privileged to have the unwavering love and support of my Dad and Evangeline. A steadfast circle of friends. Regardless of how bad things got, I intuitively knew they would always be there for me. They might question, they might challenge, but I had the trust, that they did so out of love. Out of care.

And in the face of antagonism, *I could rely on them to have my back.*

The remarkable thing is, priceless as it is, that kind of love and compassion from a family is something that ought to be natural. A given. Unaffected by of geography or culture, regardless of belief or skin-pigment, independent of education or affluence. Independent of identity or sexual orientation.

It is something I would wish for all people to have. To be able to rely on as a given basic provision.

To be surrounded by people who care.

(9) Being Patient

Consequences…

…sometimes cost more than you have to give.

The hardest thing about patience,

is that it can feel longer than you have endurance for.

And sometimes, all that keeps you going forward

is the hope

and the trust

that tomorrow will be better.

How wonderful then,

if it is.

I moved into my new home to the first of April 2015.

It was a first step, for everyone except me. After all, I was already well under way with my HRT, and committed to transitioning. What I did not yet know, was, whether I would be able to do so in my present environment. The memories of Zürich preyed on my mind, and the fact that trans* sexuality had cast off its status of being a taboo topic, did not comfort me in any way.

I must admit, the idea of going stealth, cutting all ties, and starting with a completely clean slate did have its very seductive lustre.

But the fact remained, there were so many people in my life whom I loved. After all, it was precisely the love of these people which had kept me from doing myself harm. I enjoyed what I was doing, I thought it was (is) a meaningful contribution to society. And in the face of being childless, it remains a chance at being able to pass on some of what is important to me. Finally, as I said before, not all memories were bad.

And so, I set about preparing all the people for the changes about to happen.

And negotiating with the legion of gatekeepers.

Learning to dance

The first thing I did after recovering from my fever, was to speak with Stephan, my team supervisor, and our head-of-vocational-training. If I did not have their backing, then I might as well have gone stealth, and looked for job opportunities in other cities. Or gotten myself a really good employment attorney. As it turned out, our chief of vocational training made it easy for me. He clearly stated that vocational training was *the* place where young people learnt by example. And where better to integrate that life is diverse, manifold and complex, than in our department?

Truth be told, there were times where I was unable to differentiate between my supervisors doing what was legally binding (in Germany) and politically correct. Versus doing what they truly felt to be right and good. Our head of department had it easy, he never needed to really deal with what our team went through. Nor did any of the HR peoples.

However, Stephan did not accept my change all that easily. Rationally speaking, he was fully aware that this was a part of life and a part of being human. Or, in his words, within the range of what God gives us, in terms of challenges and opportunities, to learn and grow. Reflection and reminder that we are not born into the same world, even if we tread the same earth. And rationally speaking, he was entirely aware, that he had no way, legal or otherwise, how he could avert or avoid what I confronted him with.

Emotionally speaking, my transition challenged him. Probably more so than he was willing to admit even to himself. Particularly to himself. I believe his patience was already slightly strained by my slight but steady decline in concentration and output over the past three years. And I also believe that, while he rationally *knew* that people who suffered from gender dysphoria existed, being confronted with the reality of witnessing the transition severely challenged his inner world with which he was raised. There were times when we challenged each-other's comfort zones quite thoroughly. I think he needed time to adjust to my change in exterior, particularly in the phase when it was still incongruent.

On top of which, there were times when I was simply *unable* to deal with the turmoil of emotions, and it all broke out of me. He was clearly overwhelmed by that. I believe he finds it overall challenging to show vulnerability. Or lack of knowledge, and thereby insecurity and weakness. So in the face of my lack of emotional inhibition, I think he felt extremely overburdened. Ill equipped. And probably, he felt it was not within his job-description. I understand that he probably felt, that I should leave my emotional turmoil at home and deal with it like a professional adult. But that is precisely the point: *I was unable to do that.* In retrospect, it makes me wonder how he dealt (deals) with his own daughter's mood shifts. There were times when we were both at our limits and but neither of us able to pinpoint how and where we had been injured in our sensibilities.

Nevertheless, Stephan *is a fine man of exceptional integrity and loyalty.* In fact, one of his defining characteristics is that he *acknowledges* the necessity to readjust his own standpoint and he *is* willing to do the work. Over the course of the following two years, we both managed to present our respective needs and talk through how we could achieve what was best for the both of us, best for our students, and best for our team. And the bottom line remains, Stephan is a man whose faith is rooted in the love and respect for the human, in all its variegate splendour and fragility. And he outright acknowledges that I often challenged his comfort zone. I still do. But he freely agrees that this was always the first step to his personal growth, and that he has grown more firm in *his* way of meeting the world because of it. Because of me.

I like to think that our mutual respect, and even affection, has regrown firm and solid since then. In fact, I believe we are both a little proud of how we readjusted and found renewed trust and confidence in approaching one another and even challenging each other. We permit each other our weaknesses and support one another all the better for it.

As I expected, Gerlind and Micha were extremely supportive. Gerlind was her usual reserved and self-effacing self, but she still communicated clearly how pleased she was that I had made the decision to be good to myself. Micha was her usual delicate but exuberant self, and she made sure to let me know how welcome I was as Alice. In fact, she went out of her way to make time for me, and we often sat in her or my office, sharing a coffee and talking things through, my challenges and hers.

I was unsure of how Roddy would react, since he too is a man deeply immersed and alive in his catholic faith. His open joy over my development and his appreciation for the token of trust I offered, by coming out to my colleagues, quite took me by surprise and overwhelmed me. As a matter of fact, Roddy has been one of my staunchest supporters at my workplace, and a sympathetic shoulder to turn to. He was far better able to cope with my needing a minute, or even five, to collect myself and wash the tears out of my face.

Looking back, Roddy and Stephan contributed a great deal to my reconciling with the idea that religion can be more than blind dogmatic faith, which exerts control by guilt and intimidation.

I called a staff meeting for all my colleagues from the other faculties and informed them that they would be getting a new colleague. I was touched, by how moved and how supportive they were. I called together the three current year-courses of trainees, and gave them a brief summary of what they could expect within the next months. The year for which I was supervisory teacher was ever so sweet. They went to the trouble of getting me a flower bouquet, and a voucher for the most expensive hairdresser in town. To be honest, I was rather worried about what our trainees' parents would say. After all, we work in a small town and the social structures are still very much anchored in tradition. And there are countries, which forbid people like me contact to "fragile and impressionable youth". But our chief of vocational training and Stephan were unanimous on that: none of anyone's beeswax.

With my continued employment and existence secured, I permitted myself to truly commit to living in my new home. And setting about informing my circle of friends, one by one setting dates to meet or issuing invitations. Since all my friends and colleagues knew what had been going on the past three years, my moving out was par for the course, no surprises there. My being trans* gender did however elicit quite some exclamations. It is curious and remarkable, how some friendships grew to become so much more profound. I suppose, when considered how much of myself I had shut away so far, it is not altogether surprising.

Darren and Suzy continued to be true and loyal. Darren needed some time to readjust the pronouns he used for me. It was interesting how he only misgendered me in the third person (three years, no longer so today). But we continued to go climbing together, right through the time when I was feeling blatantly incongruent, and he encouraged and supported me on my worst days, where I would have liked to crawl into a drawer. Or peel the skin off my bones. In fact, it needs to be said, Darren stands out as exceptionally supportive. It is a clear statement toward his being at peace within himself, that he was able to be there for me.

The friendship to Athene and Eddie grew rather closer after I disclosed myself as Alice to them. I remember Athene's reaction very fondly, proof of her empathic and sensitive nature, "You're a woman? OMG, that explains *everything*! And we always thought you might be gay. Of course we noticed how troubled you were, and we were so at a loss of how to help you. So you're going to transition? Yeah, good for you! Let us know if you ever need anything."

I went to see Harper and Artemisia, who at the time were making a living near Freiburg. Our contact was (still is) rare, but very precious. Harper looked at me a little awkwardly, and confessed, that at the time when I introduced Wiebke, and I had asked him to be my best man, he had had long discussions with Artemisia, "Why on earth is he marrying a woman?"

Three months after I moved out, I put into effect what I had set out to do. I gave myself a new birthday.

And from that day forth, I never pretended to be a man again.

Missteps

Of course there were other reactions too.

Some friends grew distant and non-committal. When we spoke, when I told them about upcoming changes, they made a show of support, telling me that no, of course they were not bothered. After all, this was perfectly normal, right? It happens. But I never heard from their side again. If we happened to bump into one another, it would be just weird and awkward with shallow conversations and empty promises to get in touch.

Incidentally, one of those friends was Regina. And by default, Claire, my godchild. I console myself that there were a lot of dynamics involved, including torn loyalties about "whose friend" Regina felt herself to be. But I think what *really* hurts is, that Regina failed to have the backbone to tell me to my face.

Claire was eleven at the time, frank and sober (too sober for her age), vastly intelligent and inquisitive. I kept in touch for some years, doing my best to visit, keeping contact via phone calls and gifts. Looking back, it was always Knut who picked up the phone, Claire's Dad. And it was always he, who passed on potential birthday gift ideas. There was one visit that left me feeling entirely out of place and, despite Knut's best efforts at conversation, I felt plain unwelcome. I never called again. I just did not have the strength. And nobody ever called back.

I guess another thing that really hurts, is that Claire is in the meanwhile well past her puberty. Has graduated from school. With a smart device, with a functioning WhatsApp contact and with the self-sufficiency to reach out of her own accord. But, I suppose that is unfair of me. Children acquire what they get passed on from their parents, and Claire's mother cut those ties. A quiet part of me has the hope, that someday, we will be able to talk this through. And then again, for whose benefit?

There *were* people who did *not* recognise me. And who fell out of all kinds of daydreams when I spoke to them. Most of those meetings were in fact positive and affirming. And to be honest, the fact that they did not associate me with my former image felt good.

There were also people who did their very best to treat me like air, pretending they did not know me. And the once or twice I addressed them, there was this typical heartbeat-pause of decision. Before they pretended not to have heard me, not to have noticed that it was *them* I was greeting, and walk straight past me. I never tried a third time. No need to set myself up for that kind of rejection.

I do not know what is worse, the people who pretend they do not know you? Or the people who meet you with leering grins? The kind of ghoulish smirk that implies, they know some unsavoury and filthy secret about you.

And of course, there were (are) those, that change the side of the street they are walking on, if they happen to chance across me in town. Those that whisper in voices just loud enough for the whole room to hear. Yes, those people really exist. And as ridiculous as it is, I dropped out of a dance sport group because of that. You get *so* sick and tired of justifying your existence.

Breaking the chains

Nevertheless, my change opened new doors. Being a vocational trainer meant I had a great many contacts within our firm. After all, we had (have) twenty-four trainees every year, all of whom needed three different placements. Add that to all the trainees that had already graduated, and who were still with the company, and you come up with well over four hundred faces. So, when I "came out" at my workplace, I sent a declarative e-mail to a great many people.

Vanessa and I were acquainted. She was, at the time, press and public relations officer for the company we worked for, so whenever vocational training did anything spectacular, she would report on it. We had been amicable, but never friends. In retrospect, Vanessa says, there was something about me she could not place. And that consequently, she had kept her distance. I knew, being in the works council and being press officer, she would get wind of the whole deal, so rather than let her be misinformed via the grapevine, I put her in the mailing list.

What followed was an invitation to share lunch in our cafeteria. I was unsure what to expect, but it turned out, we hit it off extremely well. We talked well over an hour and a half that first time, and from there, we slid into talking regularly, both of us opening up a little more each time. Vanessa is the stereotype modern cowgirl, blonde, slim, and intimidatingly pretty, plays an e-base for a country band. She has a mind like a welding arc, on-point, good at bringing things together and making them stick, but sometimes leaving scorch marks.

I told her about being the queer white kid who did not like soccer in Africa, and she told me about being the wild tom-boy, in tradition-steeped southern Germany, who loved soccer with the boys. I told her about culture shock in Switzerland and cosmopolitan university environments, and she told me of racial tensions she experienced in her student days and finding roots in country music in the southern USA. I told her about my crash-and-burn with Wiebke, and she told me about the challenges of being married to an Iraq-veteran. I ended up spending a great deal of time at Vanessa's place. And I grew to love them like my own family. Her husband Bart, a hard-working, hard-playing bundle of muscle and modesty. And their pride and joy, John Ray or J.R., a lanky basketball enthusiast with a teenager's natural predilection for anything with a screen.

This was around the time when I was experiencing heavy fall-out from my psychiatric assessment. And in connection to the experience in the commune in Zürich, or with the skinheads, I was seeing Dr Chamberlain every two weeks. Vanessa contributed measurably to my being able to ground myself and overcome my anxieties. Her lending me her baseball bat offered me a lot of solid comfort. And simply by being there for me, she allowed me to feel connected and secure.

Vanessa is the kind of friend you really need in your life.

Red tape

I grew to loathe the legislative bureaucracy with a vengeance.

Concerning my legal change of first name and gender, I had written the first letters to the Swiss consulate in early summer 2014. I think it was late summer, when I received a brief and entirely unhelpful reply from the Swiss embassy, stating that they had no experience with the legal status of trans* gender people. That I might be best advised asking the civil court, either of the place I was living now. Or of the last place I had lived in Switzerland. But they really did not know.

I discussed this with Dr Chamberlain. Considering that I had been living in Germany for over fifteen years, and considering that in his experience, the Ulm civil court was overall benign and cooperative when asked to process transition requests, he recommended that I write them a formal request and just see what would happen.

The civil court of Ulm got back to me in early autumn 2014, saying that unfortunately, they could not help me. Since there existed in Switzerland a law regulating the change of name and gender, and since I still had Swiss citizenship, then it was hypothetically possible for me to achieve a legal change in my home country, and therefore German law could not be applied to me.

Letters to the sent to the Zürich registry office and the Zürich communal court at the close of 2014 came to nothing. The Zürich central civil court finally answered in Mai 2015, stating that since I resided in Germany, they saw themselves not responsible to effect any changes.

I followed that up with several letters back and forth. To start with, to the Ulm civil court, to see if they had any advice. But all they did was repeat what they had already stated: that I would have to litigate in Switzerland, since there existed a law to follow. And for as long as there *was* a legal possibility for a ruling in my home country, then German law could not be applied. As a consequence, I requested a reassessment of the legal situation by the Zürich civil court, giving them a copy of the denial from Ulm. I got a brief and rather terse reply, saying that unless I was to move to Switzerland, they were not in a position to do anything for me.

Since I had moved house, I was strictly speaking no longer in the legal district of Ulm. I made myself believe that this might be fortuitous. Knowing that any German court would deny my request on account of a ruling being hypothetically possible in the country of my birth, I requested letters of declaration, that the Swiss courts were in fact *not* in a position to do anything about my name and gender. That took more than one shot, because the first statement was fraught with spelling mistakes, the second had the wrong date, and the third letter finally stated that I was unable to legally proceed in Switzerland.

Dr Chamberlain encouraged me to write a request to the civil court of Ravensburg. But he was very cautious, knowing that the judge there had, by all accounts, a personal prejudice against trans* gender peoples. As a matter of fact, by way of my activities supervising and counselling in the adult and youth support groups, I knew for a fact that requests to change name and gender were denied categorically. Consequently, several of our youths had in fact relocated from Ravensburg to Ulm or Munich, because moving house proved to be easier than attempting to push for a legal breakthrough in the face of what looked like an unsympathetic judge. This is one of the most vivid examples of how one person's prejudices in a seat of civil responsibility actively hindered several other humans from determining their own lives.

As predicted, the judge in Ravensburg denied my request. The reason given was, again, that for as long as Switzerland's law was in place, she could do nothing for me.

Despite my providing an official letter of declaration, that the Swiss courts had their legal hands tied.

In the meantime, it was November 2015, and I was growing desperate. And depressed. And naturally Dr Chamberlain registered that. I got in touch with the embassy once again, checking if they had any advice and whether it was possible to get a court hearing in Zürich if I still resided in Germany. They did not and I could not. This was the point at which I consulted three different lawyers, all of them experienced in Queer* issues. One of them in Switzerland, and two of them in Germany. But none of them able to really help me. I actually remember naming the Ravensburg judge to the German lawyer lady on phone. She gave a mirthless laugh and said, I was better off moving to a new home. However, moving again so soon was not something I had the energy for. Getting German citizenship might have been a possibility, but that too, was both expensive and arduous.

What did console me was that I was rather more successful at organising my gender realignment surgery GRS, and for a while, I concentrated my efforts on that. In April 2016, Dr Chamberlain gently prodded me, if I did not still want to get a proper passport with my right name on it? Well of course I did, after all, I wanted to go see my Dad and Amahle, who were in the meantime living in Johannesburg.

My suspicion is, that Dr Chamberlain had made a confidential phone call. After all, most of his clients sooner or later request to have their name and gender changed in the Ulm civil court. And being requested for his professional opinion on a regular basis, Dr Chamberlain was bound to *know* people. He suggested with more than his usual emphasis, that I should call up this one particular judge, and tell him of my predicament. Ironically, it was the same judge that had denied my first request in the summer of 2014.

We spoke for quite a while on the phone, this judge and I. And I recounted to him the whole ridiculous odyssey. He was extremely patient and kind, however all he said in the end, was that I should send him the entire stack of letters. And that he would see what he could do.

And this is when I learnt that, while a judge is bound to follow the law to the letter, it is in their human judgement of how they see fit to apply this law.

The next I heard from him was by mail. It was an official summons to a court hearing in August 2016, deciding on my first names and gender. I was flooded with such *immeasurable* relief and joy. And with the realisation, that all it took, was for one person to make a decision. A decision far from red tape and paragraphs. A decision to step up and take on responsibility. A decision entirely compassionate and human.

Shiny and chrome

And so, in August 2016, I dolled myself up, donned my best business suit and appeared before court for the first time in my life.

I do not know what I really expected, but not a relaxed and amiable gentleman. Early fifties, clean shaven and athletic, in suit-sans-tie under a traditional robe, and with an open, inquisitive face.

"You're the lady from Africa!" He is beaming, "How on earth did you end up there? Forgive me please, I am so curious to hear all about that."

I brain registers "Lady". My heart takes a LEAP!

What ensues is a half-hour conversation about my very colourful biography. The schools I went to, the different cultures that congregated there. Returning to Switzerland and meeting love, moving to Germany. The only things he really askes about, is whether I feel adequately represented by the two psychiatric evaluations, and whether I am happy with the names I have chosen for myself.

He proceeds to relate, that it was extremely fortunate, that I had applied in Ulm right back in summer 2014. This way, there was a case for him to reopen. And since I was able to supply a legal document that litigation in my home country is not possible, he was able to apply German law to my situation. He goes on to explain what will happen next, how his ruling will be reviewed, and that this will take a little time.

And that's it. I am dismissed.

I think I walked around Ulm aimlessly for about two hours, completely lost to the world in bliss and doped out on exuberant joy. It is probably a good thing nobody offered to sell me twenty laundry machines, or a piece of real estate in the Antarctic.

It took another five months and several phone calls until the court ruling was reviewed and legally binding. I spoke to a very helpful gentleman, who was hugely apologetic that this was taking so long, *"I really don't get it myself, after all, your file is comparatively thin and it has been on my supervisor's desk for sixteen weeks now, all it really needs is his stamp and signature to be on it."* Fact was, I was vastly anxious that for some absurd and arcane reason, the ruling would be challenged and declared not legitimate. But days before Christmas, I actually received the document declaring me female, all biological evidence to be disregarded, valid with stamps and all.

I barely took the time to scan the paper, before immediately sending it on to the Swiss consulate. They in turn sent everything to Bern in Switzerland to be checked and processed. It was March 2017, when I was finally invited to the consulate in Stuttgart, to have pictures taken for a new passport and ID card.

Under my down coat, I am wearing my business suit again, freshly ironed blouse. My palms are sweaty. I am on time. I am valid. I am prepared. All is good. Why am I even anxious?

The waiting room in the consulate is much like some of those of a prison in the movies. There are cheap looking tables and chairs in the visitor area, appearing almost as if they had been donated by a school, complete with Formica tabletops marked by generations of bored students. The personnel of the embassy sit in a completely separate room, behind a counter shielded with armoured glass. The only way of communication is by way of intercom. There are small deposit boxes that can be shuttled back and forth. There is a subtle smell of peach scented cleaner, underscored by the sharp tang of antiseptic.

I try to steady my breathing and cool myself after the brisk walk.

There are two people aside from me. Some kind of athlete? If the body build under the tracksuit is any indication. With his interpreter? The fact that the athlete neither speaks any of the Swiss languages (ergo no German either) nor even English, clearly vexes the lady behind the counter. The fact that his papers are not complete do little to improve her mood. Or the mood of his interpreter. Tension raises the hair on the back of my neck...

The lady calls me to the counter. Through the triple-reinforced glass, she is radiating frustration and impatience. I can see that she has all my documents. There are all kinds of stamps on the court ruling and birth certificate, proof that they have been to the Swiss capital and back. All she needs now is my old passport. I place it in the steel box, and she pulls a lever. All business, she double-checks all the documents once more, as if checking for forgeries.

I can taste my own tension.

"New passport and identity card we need to take a contemporary biometric photo and fingerprints in the booth you will find an adjustable seat please adjust the seat by rotating clockwise for up counter clockwise for down until your eyes are level with the white line smile but not too widely after that we are going to scan your fingerprints place both your index fingers on the reader when I tell you first the left and then the right when we are done sit over there until I call you."

She rattles this off so quickly, I am completely unprepared. "Forgive me, *where* do I go for the photo?" I try a smile to soften the mood a little. She wordlessly points me to narrow grey door that I had missed, let into the wall behind me.

After the photo, I sit back down on the salvation army like chairs and wait. I am alone now.

Some minutes later, she waves me over. Without losing a beat, she declares, "Biometric passport and ID card." A statement, not a question. "That will be 170.- Euros in cash. I trust you have brought the amount in cash? If not, there is a bank right close by. If you exit the building through the..." Obviously, she has a great deal of experience with people not reading the instructions.

I give her my warmest business smile and bringing out my wallet, I interrupt as politely as I am able, "I have the appropriate cash." This is the first time she perks up a little.

I count off the amount and place it in the shuttle box. She pulls her lever and recounts the bills, then sets about printing out a receipt. "You will receive back your old passport, now invalid of course. Your documents will remain with us. Passport and ID card will be sent to your provided address via insured mail. Delivery will be four to six weeks."

She places my invalidated passport and the receipt in the box and shuttles it over to me. Six weeks. After what I have been through to get this new passport, six weeks is laughable.

I thank her. Lost in thought, I shake my head. More to myself than to her, I say, "Over two and a half years of red tape coming to a close."

The lady behind the counter undergoes a complete and magical transformation.

Gone is the austere demeanour. Gone is the border-security-officer body language. Gone is, in fact, any pretence that she is clueless of what this means to me. Instead, she graces me with a tender and cautiously hopeful smile. "Yes. But it was worth it, wasn't it?"

I barely manage to supress tears of overwhelming relief. I grin back, "Oh, hell YES!"

Now she veritably beams at me, gives me two thumbs up and declares, "Well then go! Celebrate! You have so earned it!"

Four days later, I have a shiny new passport in my letterbox.

After almost three years of largely futile correspondence. Three years of being made to feel in-visible, non-existent, un-desired and in-valid. Four days! I have *NO* idea what strings were pulled or what phone calls made, to make that possible.

Once again, I was humbled and awed by what we humans are capable of, if we are mindful and appreciative of one another.

Unconditional

The very same day I had my passport in my hands, I emailed my Dad to finalise plans to visit him in Johannesburg.

In the same year, November 2017, I stood in immigrations at Tambo Airport, fretting about my appearance, horribly anxious about being targeted by some officious customs officer with a grudge and a need to prove how powerful they were. I was as nervous as if I were smuggling live kittens armed to the teeth.

Finally being able to hug my Dad in the reception hall released so much in me, it defies words. Three years after I had disclosed myself to him, I was finally able to present myself as the child I truly felt to be. I think he was a little overwhelmed by my emotions. I rather think he was unaccustomed to witnessing such depth of feeling first-hand. He welcomed me with is usual understated cordiality, quiet affection twinkling in his eyes.

Less happy was the fact that Amahle had suffered a second stroke in early 2017, and her condition was such that she needed to be cared for in a clinic. For most of my visit, we spent three to five hours a day, just sitting with her and going through her exercises to retrain her faculties. I have no idea who she thought the "young" white lady was, who accompanied my Dad, but I am certain she made no connection to the youth she had once accused of being a racist. She veritably blossomed when she saw me. I seemed to be able to motivate her like no one else. I spent hours drawing fruit and vegetables with coloured crayons. Mostly, she refused to speak, obviously embarrassed by her severe impediment, but she was very appreciative of the time we spent with her.

Also, it was an opportunity to spend time with James, the older of my two brothers. The only one remaining of my step siblings. Despite his busy schedule, he made time to drive me to meet his remaining family living somewhere in Soweto. He occasionally brought his daughter by to spend time with my Dad after school. And of course we met regularly at the clinic.

Most of the clinic staff was very friendly, and obviously touched to see how my Dad looked after Amahle. They also did their best to look after him to some degree, reminding him gently, that he could only do so much without jeopardising his own health. Something he took to heart, despite all the seriousness and his devotion to Amahle. My Dad made time and we spent a wonderful five days hiking in the

Drakensberg and another couple of days in Kruger park, which was beautiful and thrilling.

I drank in the one-on-one time with my Dad like the waters of life. Having breakfast together, cooking supper together. Talking of how Amahle's treatment was going and how he had coped so far after her first stroke. Talking of the challenges of dealing with the insecurities of urban life in Johannesburg. Talking of politics in South Africa and how we both hoped for a brighter future for the growing generations.

Talking of his past with my mother, and of my ended marriage with Wiebke. Contemplatively drawing parallels. Talking of our common past, and looking at what we had experienced together. Talking of decisions we made, some for partnerships, some for self-care.

We are sitting in the bright, sunlit winter garden of his home in Johannesburg. It seems to be my Dad's favourite room in the house, aside from the kitchen. We are sharing a sumptuous breakfast of coffee, fresh Papaya, whole wheat bread and cheese.

The Papaya brings back memories of our days in Dar es Salaam.

I tell my Dad how I am so grateful for our time together there. And how I had always felt so secure and welcome when he was there. That I was grateful for all the experiences in Africa, even if some were very challenging. How I was grateful to have grown up as his child, and how I always felt free to make my own choices while in his care.

I tell my Dad, how things were sometimes rough (I do not go into *how* rough) but that I am happy and at peace with the choices I made, to get me to where I was, here and now. That I would do it all again if I needed to decide.

My Dad looks thoughtful. Without preamble, he says,

"You are the best thing that has happened to me in my life. I am so glad to see you content and safe."

Thank you, Dad. I am proud, yet humbled, but more than anything else, happy to be your daughter.

A matter of biology

The first my health insurance learnt of my gender dysphoria was that I applied for reimbursement of my therapy sessions with Dr Chamberlain. That was followed in rather short order, with my being treated and supervised in regular intervals by my endocrinologist, and all the bills that generated.

I think at that point, they realised that, whoops, this was going to step up my cost intensity as a client quite drastically. And pretty soon after, my monthly premiums went up. Considerably so.

I asked around in our support groups for names and places of recommendations surgical clinics, setting things on track for a later GRS. At the same time I took on the name Alice, I regressed to my routine of not looking at my body from the neck down. I could ignore my biological sex on most days. You learn to blend it out, and tucking my anatomy away helped considerably.

But blending out facial hair?

Not to be done.

Ever since puberty, I have shaved myself as closely as I am able, without taking off too many layers of skin. There was a time when Wiebke tried to encourage me to grow a beard. I did not try to understand why. I humoured her for about three weeks, and then it just *had* to go. Regardless of whose role I was living at the time, and who I was living it for, I could *not* deal with having a beard.

Camouflage and powder

My mother has skin cancer, so I get my skin checked regularly by a dermatologist anyhow.

The moment it was certain that I had an apartment, the moment I had a date set that I would move into my new home, I made appointments and addressed the topic of epilation of my facial hair. And from Spring 2015 onwards, for the next thirty-two months, I would go to see my dermatologist on a monthly basis, and get my face and chest treated with an Intense-Pulsed-Light IPL device. A close friend of mine describes it very adequately: like having an elastic band around your face. Then somebody pulls it away, and releases it to smack your skin. Hard. Followed by sharp heat and the lingering smell of singed hair.

After the first eighteen months, my health insurance became reluctant to continue carrying the costs, but with gentle nudging by a lawyer, they agreed to fund another year. I say gentle nudging. But what it involved for me was weeks of restless nights, fraught with plain, pure panic and hyperventilation, obsessing over how I was going to come up with the funds necessary to pay for the ruinously expensive treatment by myself.

On ordinary days, I got up half an hour earlier than I would normally have needed to, simply to give myself a full facial makeup with concealing foundation and powder, so as to hide any trace of my beard. I spent months obsessing over how people saw me, saw my face, whether or not they saw a woman or some freak (yup successfully internalised homophobia right there). Except on days where I would go for epilation treatment. On such days, I was not permitted to wear makeup, nothing was allowed to be on my skin. I dreaded those days, not wanting to look up, not wanting to lift my head, not being able to show my face to anyone without veritably dying inside. And still earning my keep by teaching.

Until my first gender realigning surgery. But more of that later.

I am blessed with light skin. And I was extremely fortunate to have a quite dark beard. The best possible prerequisites for successful IPL treatment. Needless to say, I was unhappy when the health insurance refused to continue permitting me to have IPL treatment. But truth be told, after two-and-a-half years, my really dark beard growth was largely gone. What remained were patches of blonde to reddish stubble. And that was not responsive to IPL. And so I bid my dermatologist erstwhile farewell, and promised to be back for my annual skin check-up. I think she was rather sad to see me go. Of course she was, she had earned a fortune by way of my treatment.

I found myself a friendly and skilled beautician, who performed needle electrolysis epilation. This is when you stick a needle into the hair follicle and then heat the needle by means of an electric current, in order to cauterise the hair follicle. The art of this is, to be gentle enough not to raise blisters and scar the skin permanently, but persistent enough, to burn the hair root so as to reduce the growth. It takes many passes, once will not do the trick.

So for the next three years, I went to see my beautician on a weekly basis. And for ninety minutes, she would work over my face, particularly the corners of my mouth and the upper lip, all the while humming along to the soft ambient music, or chatting with me happily about whatever was on her mind. My health insurance does not cover this, and the thought of what I spend on epilation veritably shorts out my mind. But then I really should not be complaining. I have a steady job, and considering my qualifications, it pays rather well. I am extremely fortunate to be doing this at all.

In the meantime, I have allowed myself to reduce the treatment to once every three weeks. But having cats' whiskers in the corners of my mouth still sets my teeth on edge and makes me want to take my skin off. Even more so, that nowadays, I have somebody who enjoys kissing these lips. Ironic that having a partner triggers rather than soothes my dysphoria in some situations.

Tight strung

Of course there were many clinics that perform gender realignment, but some have less favourable reputations in the close-knit community trans* genders. The choice is something each person with gender dysphoria agonises over during transition. The costs and the length of the waiting list being directly proportional to the reputation the performing surgeons. But what it all reduces down to, is a matter of having the trust and the confidence that the surgeons and the staff enable you to live a life as close as possible to that which you envision for yourself.

There were four surgical clinics which I took into closer consideration. One I ruled out as too far away. It would complicate getting there, and more importantly, getting home. One was quite simply too expensive, because the surgeon was known to require an "extra" fee, something I could simply not afford. And I was already on tense terms with my health insurance. And ultimately, with the remaining two, it was a matter of where I was able to get a date scheduled earlier.

About six months after I moved into my new home, I managed to get a preliminary interview scheduled with the surgeon. I was grateful for the work on psychiatric assessment with Prof Aedelfrid and Dr Chamberlain, since the assessments were a vital part of convincing my health insurance that I did in fact require gender realignment surgery GRS. And that they should pay for it in order to maintain my psychological health. Every time I received a letter from my health insurance, I would first empty my stomach in the sink out of sheer anxiety (Always be sick in the sink. No need to bruise your dignity even further by kneeling in front of the toilet. That will make you feel even worse. Trust me on this.)

There was little truly notable about that preliminary interview. I was well prepared, having spoken with the other girls in our support group. I knew all about the possible complications, all the myriad things that can possibly go wrong during and after surgery. Being under such close scrutiny was absolutely not my idea of fun, and having my male genitals palpated made my skin crawl. But then, I was presenting myself to this specialist in the hopes of being rid of self-same genitals soon. And I needed the preliminary, in order to be issued with a cost estimate for a GRS, which I needed to hand in to my health insurance. All the discomfort and dysphoria aside, I was encouraged and reassured by the fact that the personnel were indeed very mindful and polite.

What does stand out about the entire two years during which I underwent my different surgeries, is the constant state of *tension* under which I existed. The moment I had both my psychiatric assessments, I sent them to my health insurance and applied for cost coverage for a GRS. With my psych-evals in hand, I was confident (within a given frame) that I would be permitted to transition. Nevertheless, I was *permanently* obsessing that something should go wrong at the last minute, that my assessments would be revoked, that my cost coverage would be denied, that I would be hindered by some wild coincidence or prevented from having surgery by some ludicrous chain of events. That I would be declared plain and simply psychologically unstable, unfit and unsuited to teach youths. Or even worse, that I would be declared an ordinary male just suffering from a silly mid-life crisis. Or that I would catch a stupid common cold, and the clinic would declare any surgery too risky.

I had taken to skyping face to face with my Dad on a weekly basis. I did my best to keep my ups-and-downs from him. And yet, the overall the quality of our exchanges evolved into a whole new world. He opened up about all the myriad challenges and worries that troubled him. We spoke of the unrest and corruption in South Africa, citizens severely disappointed by their leaders. We spoke of Amahle's condition and her struggle in regaining her faculties. Of course I let him know about my impending surgery, but I made sure to worry him as little as possible.

Apart from Vanessa and Darren, Athene and Eddie were amongst those who regularly asked how I was progressing. I ran into Eddie at work every so often and he always made time for a chat, regardless of how stressed out he was, conveying Athene's inquiries and regards. Evangeline kept close tabs on me. I think she was quite anxious about my state of mind. We corresponded in lengthy e-mails and WhatsApp texts. And she sent me a collection of homeopathic therapeutics which she herself had made excellent experiences with when she had had her caesarean.

My colleagues were entirely supportive. Stephan of course ruminated about how we would manage to bridge my anticipated six weeks absence, but Gerlind said, if push came to shove, she could at least teach the cell-culture part of my courses. And all of them, Stephan included, wanted to see me back on the job as my best possible self.

Free to breathe

There was a heavy fog and the fields were soaked with dew. Darren, my climbing buddy, was deep in thought as he drove me to Munich on a very dreary Sunday in March 2016. I was so very grateful that he would take it upon himself to drive all the way and back again, simply to do me the favour of accompanying me safe and sound to the clinic. We took a break at a petrol station and he invited me to coffee and croissants. I remember the smell so intensely, fresh and crisp, deliciously buttery.

I remember being admitted to a room that was cold as a stone. It being Sunday, there was only a minimal staff on the ward and the nurse was clearly stressed out. She said she would be back later and that the anaesthesiologist would also check on me, so I should stay put. Darren got back on the road, so he would still have some of his Sunday to spend some quality time with his family, and I was left with my own thoughts.

There was a strange kind of peace in that ward room. The fog never lifted that day, and there was a soft twilight coming through the half-lowered blinds. I had forgotten to turn on any lights. The world outside was cloaked in a deep, grey shroud, only half-real. For the first time in months, possibly even in years, I was able to just sit and breathe. I contemplated all the things that had brought me here. I had brought all these changes into effect, and they were actually realising themselves. And at the same time, my sitting in this ward, waiting for time to pass, it was such an analogy of my transition. A state in between, neither here nor there. Waiting for things to become real. Waiting for myself to become real.

For a brief while, reality stepped back in, in the form of the anaesthesiologist. He was a cheerful and vivacious young man, alarmingly good looking, so much so, I was glad he did not take my pulse. He made sure that all my entered data was correct. "Any know allergies? Any known problems with coagulation or healing? Take any painkillers in the last few days? When was the last time you ate? What do you weigh? Yeah, I know, one does not usually ask a lady." And I wondered to myself how often he used that line.

The anaesthesiologist was followed by another nurse. She took a blood sample to check for coagulation and blood group. And she brought me a cleansing solution to empty my system, and provided me with a razor to shave myself. I was glad that I had already done so in the comfort of my own bathroom, considering that there was no kind shaving lotion or anything. She left, telling me, that I should drink nothing aside from plain water until morning. I spent most of the night doing just that, barely sleeping, going to the bathroom at regular intervals.

And I realised, for the first time in a very long while, I was at peace. Yes, I still had some basic anxiety, that for whatever wild reason, the surgeon would be incapacitated or there would be an emergency and the operating theatre would be needed for other, more life-saving surgeries. I even managed to dismiss the thought that my permission would be revoked, or my health insurance would rescind their cost-coverage. I no longer cared about any of that.

I was there. This was going to happen. I felt free.

Which was an odd way to feel. Because in few places in the world are you as intimately inspected, closely constrained, or meticulously monitored as in a clinic.

Self determination

I was up with the first light, awake long before the nurse came to fetch me.

I was surprised that I was not permitted to walk. The effort of carting me around in a bed seemed ridiculous when I could have just tagged along with the nurse and climbed on wherever they needed me. Instead, I watched with bemusement and just some few nervous butterflies in my tummy, as the corridor lights flitted by overhead. Okay, so maybe being rolled around in my clinic bed did have its upsides. I realised at some point, I was horribly cold, and my body had nothing left to metabolise into energy.

The staff changed. People in surgery-greens.

This is where things got real. I was asked to tense up as well as I could, as two nurses lifted me bodily off my bed and place me on the mobile operating slab. My mind was doing overtime, my curiosity assessing my environment. Slab was entirely appropriate, a slim, multiple-jointed construction of pre-formed stainless-steel plates. My Duvet had been replaced by a sterile cotton blanket of bleached green. My skin cringed at the cold and I started shivering so hard, my breath came in ripples. The nurse told me his name, but I was preoccupied by the cold presence of the IV-port he skilfully placed above my left wrist. He politely apologised while he lifted the sheet and placed adhesive electrodes on my chest. I felt extremely self-conscious. It was so weird, being completely nude with all these fully clothed people with their facial masks walking and working around me. He kept talking to me all the while. I remember thinking distractedly, how mindful he was to divert his patients from their anxiety. Between clenched teeth, I told him that I was not at all scared, but if he would provide me with a second blanket, I would be ever so grateful. Smiling, he provided me with the best thing ever. He placed the tube of an air-heater right under my blanket, carefully tucking in all the corners, and I was bathed in a soft, cosy halo of warmth.

And suddenly my chief surgeon is there. He greets me warmly, asking if I am okay. I tell him, truthfully enough, that I am doing great, just a little chilly. He nods and checks my heater.

"So, Ms Oehninger? Are we going to do this?"

In a heartbeat, so many flippant or humorous answers go through my head. But ultimately, they all summarise the same feeling.

"Yes, we are. Please go ahead."

He nods to his staff. The anaesthesiologist comes over and gives me a friendly "Hello again." He places a breathing mask over my face, explaining everything he does. "Now, this might smell a little metallic, and you might feel a bit nauseous, but don't worry. I am going to be right by your side the entire time, monitoring your vitals, taking the best possible care of you."

Nauseous? Not half! I feel lightheaded, disorientated, almost as if I am falling. I am grateful I have nothing to throw up. I realise I am hyperventilating and try to consciously steady my breathing. The room is spinning. I grab the anaesthesiologist's hand to steady myself.

All the while, two nurses are working. I realise, they are strapping me to the slab. I hear the throb of a blood-pressure reader and feel pressure on my right arm.

The anaesthesiologist says, "In a moment, I want you to count down together with me. Can you do that? I am just going to turn up the anaesthetic in your IV, and then when you're asleep, I will…"

Breaking the surface

Funny thing about doors. Sometimes, instead of leading into the next room, they truly lead into another world.

I was never truly worried that the surgery would go wrong and that I would suffer complications.

I had two worst-case scenarios. The first was, that I should have a thrombosis in one of my legs, causing mayor tissue damage through lack of oxygen and which would require an amputation. The second was that I should suffer damage to nerves and muscles in my lower abdomen, leaving me incontinent to such a degree, that I would not be able to pursue prolonged work. Or spent time with friends. Or travel. But other than that? *Everything else I would deal with.*

I was completely unafraid that I would die on that operating table. After all, if that would happen, I would simply never wake up and everything else would be somebody else's problem.

True. My Dad would be massively upset. But then my committing suicide in the short term, or my dying of heart failure or cancer induced by depression in the mid term, what difference would any of it have made?

I wish they would change the lights.

You wake up to cold, harsh fluorescent tubes. They hurt the eyes, driving spikes of light through my brain. And the place is loud! Mechanical pumps, beeping monitors, clicking valves, humming ventilators, intrusive intercom announcements. And I wish the nurses in the wake-up area of the ICU had better bedside manners.

But then being kind is not their job. Their job is to make sure you do not forget to breathe. But I do remember being quite exasperated at the attendant. It cannot truly have been that long, but after what felt like hours, the Nurse finally seemed satisfied that I was not going to quietly expire, and she let me sleep.

When open my eyes, I am in a tiny ward room, lying in my solitary bed. There is a rosy evening light coming through the foliage outside.

Vanessa is sitting in a chair next to my bed. She looks tired. Anxious.

She becomes aware that I am awake. "Hey, Honey." Our customary greeting. I give her the best smile I am able, but my "Hey" comes out dry and scratchy. My throat is still sore from the intubation.

My tough-ass tom-boy-in-pink bestie is close to tears, and it dawns on me that I have just survived what was potentially a life threatening surgery.

I know that Vanessa was not as cool as I was about my surgery. As a matter of fact, she was deeply worried about complications, and whether or not I would be safe. Whether or not I would make it at all. She understood that I needed this surgery. As much as other people need a heart-transplantation. She just never understood why. The miracle of Vanessa is, that despite her knowing me for years, all she ever truly saw was Alice. And to her, Alice was whole. Or as close to whole as a human with my past can be. I tried my best to comfort her in her worries. At the same time, I believe her being so worried permitted me to simply accept that it was out of my hands and that I trusted the surgeons to do their best.

"How long was I under?"

"Little over seven`n half hours. Doc was here a few minutes ago. Says everything went just perfect! You're now officially a member of the swim team."

"Member?" I feign horror. "I hope not! If they gave me a second one, I am going to have serious words with the surgeon!"

Vanessa gives a little hiccup as she makes a split-second decision between laughing or crying. She opts for both. "Oh, God! British humour. After an eight-hour surgery. Only you could pull that off!" She gets up and gives me a very cautious bear hug, rocking me like a child, and I can feel the tension fall off her.

She continued telling me how she left Bart and J.R. outside with their campervan, and that they were going to check out this pizza place. I knew Brad had (has) a strong disinclination to clinics after his brush with a suboptimal repair of his arm. And the fact that he almost lost his wife during J.R.'s birth. So I was not surprised to see her alone.

We continued talking for an indeterminable length of time. I was dimly aware, that I was drifting in and out of sleep. At some point, we seemed to come to an intuitive unanimous agreement. As we so often do. She rose from her chair and declared that she would head back to her family now and leave me to get some much deserved and needed sleep. And that she would be back the next day.

Uphill work

The first thing I noticed, was, that I could not use my right arm. At all. All I felt in my fingers was the characteristic tingling of when a limb "falls asleep." And I recalled dimly, how the anaesthesiologist told me, how he would be monitoring my blood pressure every five minutes to make sure I was safe and sound. A surgical procedure lasting seven and something hours. Blood pressure every five minutes… …that is a lot of measurements. More than my anaesthesia-addled brain was capable of calculating right then.

Trying to drink a cup of water with my left turned out a severe challenge because the IV was still in place. Never mind that I was not my usual coordinated self. More than anything else, I was thirsty, even though the nurse made sure I remained hydrated intravenously. Metamizole is wonderful stuff. And while it kept the dull throb in my lower abdomen at bay, it did nothing for the sharp knot of discomfort that was beginning to build in my spine.

I really failed to develop an appetite. I was not allowed much solid food, and the "light diet" was far from my normal choice of sustenance. I would have done something drastic for a fresh apple, so I was ever so grateful for Vanessa that she smuggled in some fruit for me. But regardless of what might have been pain or discomfort, I more or less slept through the first two days.

Day two brought a change of bandages, which made me ever so curious, after all, this was the first time I was permitted to witness my new anatomy. My chief surgeon emphasised that he was very pleased with how things had gone, but he warned me against disappointment: it was going to be a while before it looked pretty. And indeed, I had an *epic* haematoma, reaching right around my pelvic area. I think he was just a little disquieted by *how* soaked the bandage was, and I caught him requesting the nurse to check my haemoglobin (oxygen transporting protein contained in the red blood cells).

Closely related to this: another thing nobody prepares you for are anti-coagulants. They give you these as a prophylactic measure against thrombosis from spending most of your time in bed. But what the anti-coagulants also do, and what none of the medical staff seems to be mindful of, is that they also make you bleed rather more.

And how your bruises turn so dark, your skin looks like it is one step over the brink of necrosis.

It was post-op day three when I was permitted out of bed the first time. I knew from friends who had gone through the same procedure, that such a long wait was not customary, nor was the fact that I still retained my IV-port. Some of my friends bragged, that they walked to the bathroom and back one day following the surgery. My right arm was almost back to normal, with just the tingling sensation remaining in the fingers. But otherwise, I my arm was fully mobile again, for which I was intensely grateful. In the company of my junior surgeon and two nurses, I placed my feet on the floor, a nurse on each side, and very slowly levered myself upright.

Upright lasts for all of six or seven breaths. I manage to say, "Nope." before my vision tunnels out and my knees give way.

They must have caught me and put me back to bed. The junior surgeon was visibly disquieted. She asked me *not* to make any attempt at getting out of bed by myself under *any* circumstances, but emphasised that I really needed to get back on my feet, or my low blood pressure was going to be even slower to recover. She explained that I had lost rather more blood than usual (my hb-level had dropped from a healthy 14,6 to 6,7), but it was not yet at the point where they would want to give me any concentrates (red blood cell concentrates from blood donations) since it was always the better way to avoid any potential complications.

It is Friday before I finally to shuffle to the bathroom, with a very careful nurse, watching every step like a hawk. I finally get to brush my teeth.

Sometimes, heaven is a toothbrush.

What improves my mood even further, is the shower I am permitted to have two days later.

I think I healed quite quickly. The iron supplements they fed me with helped. And once I was back to eating more complex foods, my vitality returned to some degree. In the next few days, I challenged myself to visits to the bathroom, accompanying Vanessa to the door, until almost a week later, I finally graduated to walking the length of the corridor. It was to be yet another week before I was able to take a flight of stairs, a prerequisite if I was going to be able to get to my apartment at all.

Soul work

I am not going to go into the details of the surgical procedure. If you are curious, there are plenty descriptions and even videos to be found online.

What does remain significant, is the fact that the surgery requires a stent of some kind. A placeholder. To shape the newly formed vagina, and to keep the body from closing, what at first it perceives as a wound. There are different options for a stent, but the one used for my surgery was a slightly pear-shaped object, possibly metal, about the length and diameter of my stretched hand.

Obviously, at some point, that needed out.

The presence of the junior surgeon together with another colleague *and* two nurses made me anticipative and alert. The two doctors delicately peeled away the bandages, closely appraising the healing. The surgeon seemed pleased, reaching a conclusion. She explained that she was going to remove the placeholder, and that it would be very beneficial if I concentrate on my breathing.

One of the nurses takes my hand, her other hand on my shoulder. The surgeon patiently counts breaths with me. The way she is focused on my body brings to mind the parallels to a delivery ward, and for a heartbeat, the idea goes through my head, that this is my own birth I am experiencing.

"Okay, big inhale on three. Ready? One, two…"

It's not really painful. Well, not that much. But it is… …visceral and intimate in a way that I have not ever previously encountered. And for the first time in my life, I become aware of having a vagina. I am overwhelmed. Completely. I distantly register the surgeon appealing to me, "Breathe, Ms Oehninger, breathe!"

I think I am crying from pure overload. The nurse who held my hand is dabbing at my forehead. The two doctors busy themselves at wrapping me up again, assisted by the second nurse.

I realise the placeholder is still lying next to me. Glistening, covered in semi-coagulated blood and mucus.

The realisation goes through my torso like a hot knife, releasing a new wave of silent tears. This object. This body. If it would have a pulse. If it would have a breath. They would have laid it on my breast, and I would have held my child in my arms. In that moment, I feel a loss so great, completely beyond of what I am capable of naming.

And I am utterly, utterly exhausted.

The surgeon looked at me quizzically, thoughtfully. I think she might have realised there was something going on beyond plain biological stress and body reaction. But I think I slipped into sleep even as she looked at me. The experience brought to the surface the reoccurring awareness of my deep longing for parenthood, of motherhood, and it was something I would later discuss often with Dr Chamberlain. Both Prof Aedelfrid and Dr Chamberlain were intensely curious to speak to me about this after the surgery, I think out of plain professional interest. Fortunately, for the time being in the clinic, I was able to let it go then and focus on my recovery.

The somatic, surgical, biological change liberated so many things in me, there is no other way to describe it. As much as they helped me keep a focused mind, being able to wean myself off the testosterone-blockers was like taking a deep drink of cool spring water, delicious and refreshing. The change in my body permitted me to shed so much of my unease and dysphoria. I felt as if my body was suddenly lighter, more fluid, more alive.

Even if at the time, I felt as fragile as a soap bubble.

In addition, my stay at the clinic gifted me with one of the most validating and empowering experiences. So wonderful and unlikely was the conversation, it left such a compelling memory, changing my mind-set, and affirming my sense of self beyond any compliment or supportive statement given by even my closest friends. The strange thing is, the person who gave me this gift did so completely unknowingly, entirely unaware. It is, most likely, this absolute authenticity that makes the encounter so remarkable.

Ever since I worked in clinics, I make a point to go at least one step beyond the plain "I need somebody with a particular skillset to give care and attention to this issue". I make a point to engage clinical staff in personal conversations, I always ask my doctors, how *they* are doing, and I always make a point to address nursing staff by name. It is quite incredible, what kind of responses you can get from showing them this kind of appreciation.

At the same time, I try to be mindful of other patients, or their families and significant others. There is a thing about clinics, that is removed from the real world. They are a universe apart. And contradictive as it sounds, empathy is in short supply in hospitals. In pretty much all hospital I have seen, whether as an employee, a visitor or as a patient, the staff are chronically overworked and underappreciated. Always in a hurry, never enough energy to spend time with the patients in their care. And the patients or relatives are stressed out and under constant tension, anxious to find the right treatment and be gone again. I believe it is in clinics, where the reminder of our mortality is ever prevalent, that we are brought face to face with our some of own deepest fears. It is hugely interesting and remarkable, how much complete strangers are prepared to share, when they are waiting for fate to decide over the existence of a loved one.

Day fourteen or day sixteen after the operation. I was "practicing" being upright. Walking the length of the ward still left me short of breath and dizzy as if I was running a marathon. Walking stairs was unthinkable, but a requirement if I was to be dismissed home to my apartment. As the days went by, I learnt that all the other wards were occupied almost exclusively by gentlemen, who had some kind of problems with their lower abdomen, be it prostate-cancer or something similar. Obviously, all of these lads were visited by their families and loved ones.

One lady in particular stands out in my memory. I had noticed how she had been very harrowed and deeply preoccupied to begin with. She was present at extreme hours. I think she even slept at the hospital some nights on a folding cot, and it was clear, things for her husband were grave. Gradually, over days, her demeanour became more relaxed and she became more aware of her surroundings.

It is so late, it might even be early. The clinic is asleep. The starkly lit ward corridor is empty. The monotone hum of the ventilation amplifies the sense of desolation and emptiness.

I sleep close to eighteen hours a day, so my rhythm is completely out of sync. So far, it has not been a good night for me. I am "doing my rounds," simply to work some of the tension out of my back and to bring circulation back into my feet.

The lady and I happen to meet outside the kitchenette, where she is fetching some fresh water.

My dysphoria is at its peak. I have not been able to shower for the past four days, never mind shave. I have stubble in my face. I am still just capable of shuffling along, clutching my bathrobe, my very flat chest made more flat by the hospital-gown. I feel utterly hideous.

And yet, following an intuition, I ask her how her husband is doing.

She gives me a radiant smile. Tells me how he has improved so much in the past four days. How her husband had first been admitted to another clinic and how there had been some mishaps. How she had almost lost him. Her body language speaks volumes of how very close she is to him. How close she came to losing him. She tells me how fortunate she feels, for him to have been granted a surgery slot here at this clinic, where the specialists are obviously so proficient. How grateful she is to be able to take him home in just a few days, and that they now have future years to look forward to.

I agree that, I too, have the impression, that the surgeons here are exceptionally experienced and the staff in general excellent caregivers. (*Always* be nice to the nurses and the janitors. They run the place.) I can see the thoughts turning over in her mind. Suddenly she gives me a quizzical look.

"Forgive me for intruding," she says, "I've been meaning to ask: why are you here? I thought this clinic didn't do surgery for ladies."

The realisation that I have been correctly gendered, despite my self-perceived unkempt male appearance, blossoms in my heart like a flower of warmth and hope.

Perhaps had I been feeling better? If I had felt stronger? Perhaps if I had spent more time of my life being myself, I might have disclosed that I was trans*. But I did not. All I said, truthfully I might add, was, that the clinic did in fact cater to women who had cervix-cancer or endometriosis or some such. And that I had problems with my lady-parts. Well, I did, did I not? Today, I am just a little ashamed of that.

She was deeply sympathetic and asked if I had children, clearly realising that any reasons for my requiring pelvic surgery would make future pregnancies impossible. And from there, we talked about children and families, I spoke of my nieces and nephew, how my god-child and my students were somehow substitutes for having children of my own.

What remains today, is how profoundly that question and the ensuing conversation changed so much within me. Almost as if her unquestioning perception of me, her unthinking natural acceptance that I might have borne children, and her sympathy clicked the final puzzle piece into place. Finalising a psychological process that had been set in motion decades ago, begging for completion. And thereby complementing the physiological, biological change that I had only just undergone days ago. If I pass for female in a hospital ward full of cis* males? If I am perceived as a woman even if I am un-showered, semi-dressed in a bathrobe, and have several days' worth of stubble in my face?

It was like being given permission to actually *be* the woman I feel I am. Not even getting a hot-off-the-press brand new passport with my proper name and gender in it managed to release this many endorphins.

Scream all you want about how needing validation from other people is a toxic form dependency, a reinforcement of bigot morality and an internalisation of homophobia. Fact remains. We humans, *all* of us, we *are* social creatures. We *do* rely on affirmation from others. And we *thrive* on appreciation and acknowledgement. So yes, in the corridor of that hospital ward, singularly un-magical and soberly lit with all the neon lights, I truly *felt*, that not only was I a woman, but that society was capable of giving me my rightful place. I felt accepted.

More than that, I felt welcomed.

I felt *alive*.

To this day, the memory is something I draw strength and perseverance from, when I am finding it hard to love myself.

Self image

Two more corrective surgeries to my lady downstairs followed, in intervals of six months. Mainly to improve function, particularly of biological necessities. Also, intimacy would otherwise not have been possible. And to give her a proper lady-like look.

On the other extreme, facial feminisation surgery is a thing.

I know for a fact, that self-perception remains a challenge in varying degrees a great many trans* people struggle with. Probably the vast majority. Including me. And a great many trans* women struggle with their mirror image, obsessing about how feminine they look. Or fail to look.

As I type this, in my mind's eye, I see Vanessa roll her eyes at me and say, "Honey, *EVERY* woman has issues with how she looks. Perfectly normal. *You* are perfectly normal. Stop worrying about it." And rationally, I know exactly what she means. And that she is not wrong. And more than anything else, I know that with all her heart, she means well. And she wants me to be well.

Nevertheless, two things bother me with that statement.

This is a delicate topic. While I believe that truly every woman (every human) is plagued by self-doubts and insecurities, it is not comparable to dysphoria. Or suffering from severe depressions. Self-doubts alone do not make you seek consolation in razor blades, nor do they make you *believe* yourself unworthy of appreciation. And insecurities do not make you consider stepping in front of a bus a preferable resolution to end your anxieties.

But being human is not about comparisons. And that is precisely the point. And as much as I am grateful for Vanessa's friendship, as much as I value her rational no-nonsense approach, as much as I appreciate her good intentions. Every once in a while, I feel belittled and reduced by her simplistic dismissal of my insecurities. It is important to keep in mind that each individual has their own world of perception, and each person needs to face their own sources of trepidation. And the terrors of others have no influence and no right of relativity on the challenges you face.

Before I went for my first surgery, I was ragingly dysphoric about my face. As I said before, learning to *see* myself as the woman I *feel* to be was a long learning process. And I might say, not an easy one, either. No matter how many compliments I was paid by friends, no matter how many words of encouragement Ms Steyr or Dr Chamberlain offered me, I struggled to accept myself. And I know from my counselling experience, that other trans* people struggle just like me.

Reduction of the brow-ridges, nose adjustments, refinement of the jaw. It all sounds so delicate and seductive. But there was one comment my very first chief surgeon made, that stayed with me through all the years and all the interviews with other surgeons.

"It is important to be aware, Ms Oehninger." I can tell he has recited this so often. "Cosmetically, anything is possible. I can give you the most perfect and symmetrically pleasing vulva you desire. But I want to gift you with a body that is more than just pretty. I want you to be able to live and experience your body." He pauses, to make sure I am paying attention. "Every incision, no matter how delicate, no matter how skilled and experienced the surgeon, every incision leaves a scar. And scars will always reduce sensitivity. They always lead to tensions, and always increase the risk of complications."

I like having my face touched. I enjoy being caressed. Okay, that is a complete understatement. I melt when my partner kisses my face. I would die inside, if I no longer felt that, or if my sense of feeling in my face were somehow compromised. And yes, I enjoy sexuality. It is not as defining to who I am. But I would be lying if I denied how immensely it contributes to my feeling alive and fulfilled.

I visited four cosmetic surgeons who specialised in facial feminisation. All of them studies my face closely. One of them rattled of a list of things he could do for me, and gave me a winning smile, saying, that if I took the whole package, he would be able to give me a discount (facial surgery is not covered by any health insurance). The other three surgeons were independently unanimous. Saying my face was, by standards, already quite delicate and lovely. That the risks outweighed anything they could *significantly* change in my face. In fact, one of the surgeons bluntly said, there was no ways he was going to do any work on my face. For no money in the world. That, together with the experience after my first surgery, went a long way to actually easing my dysphoria to quite a degree.

What remained, however, was the fact that I was horribly self conscious about my flat chest. I had the figure of a well developed telegraph pole, all edges and angles. And while I was *aware* that not only "ordinary" women, but sought-after models, movie stars and whatever, had figures like mine, I was severely dysphoric about my lack of curves. To such a degree, that I was loath to go swimming or wear anything that revealed too much of my true shape. Overhearing two guys laughing, "I know guys that have more than her," were far from helpful. Even going climbing turned into a gauntlet when two other girls sniggered at me, "Hey, the boys' changing room is the other door." Rational arguments like, "the right person will love you for *you*, not for your boobs," were certainly true, but they failed to soothe my heart. I wore prosthetics consequently, or padded bras, but for obvious reasons, it was a dissatisfactory solution.

Despite this, for almost three years, I denied myself a breast augmentation. Looking back, I can hardly say why. Perhaps a part of me thought I would be worth less, be less authentic if I helped myself to "artificial" breasts.

As it happened, I visited Harper and Artemisia, my Canadian best man, and his wife. Despite our very long periods of not seeing each other, of not communication at all for long spells, our conversations fell into an easy, familiar rhythm. At the time, I still wore full make-up, and I was always slightly ill at ease with public contact. Nevertheless, I was permitted to feel comfortable with my need for change, simply with how naturally they accepted me for the name I wore and the face I presented. And we got into talking about how accepting I was of my body, and what changes I desired.

As it turned out, one of their girls had gone for breast augmentation. Not because she was flat, but because she was asymmetrical to a degree that was blatantly visible during her school years. And she had suffered greatly because of it. Her parents even paid for it. And I remember distinctly, both Artemisia and Harper encouraging me, even urging me to reconsider.

Artemisia asks me, "In your normal working day. How often do you feel out of place? How often does it bother you? How often is your mind trapped in dysphoria instead of being with the people around you? How often a day does it hurt?"

And "Why punish yourself? Haven't you gone through enough? If it feels wrong, change it! Go for it! Be good to yourself. Only you can."

Harper gives me his typical piercing look. "Alice, you have more balls than most men I know."

He lets that sink in. "Other people? Who gives a f*ck what they think? *They* don't have to live your life. *You* do. And you decide what's good for you."

As I implied, this conversation happened quite early in my transition. But it stayed with me throughout. I had wanted to give it time. Because against all odds, I hoped hormones might induce my breasts to grow of their own accord. But that simply did not happen. I was probably too old for that, my growing and developing phase being long concluded. And finally, I made the decision that, yes, *I was indeed worth giving myself peace.*

I went back to see the cosmetic surgeon who had flatly declined to perform any facial changes. In all the interviews, he had engendered the greatest trust, being both empathic and sensitive, but flatly honest and authentic at the same time. He is another example of how deeply caring and mindful some surgeons can be. Doing their best to bring about a betterment of the quality of living of their patients, permitting them to be more in touch, better in balance with their bodies. And he had (has) a great sense of humour, delicate, sensitive, but on point.

I remember our interview rather fondly. He was cautious at first, but when it was clear that I was not going to request a pair of double-Ds, he was quite enthusiastic and entirely supportive. As a matter of fact, he persuaded me to go for "small" instead of "tiny", arguing that I was a tall woman, and I needed something that went with my build. From there he happily went into explaining how he could do *this* or *that* to enable me to continue climbing and pursuing other sports, but that it would still take very close inspection to register that I had implants. Furthermore, he agreed that I did have a very sharp widows peak, and that I would benefit if that were softened a bit.

What followed was another long drawn out fight with my health insurance on how much they would cover from the costs. According to German law, breast augmentation is eligible for refunding for trans* gender women. After involving a lawyer, they finally agreed to come up with at least parts of the costs, and I was finally able to schedule a date.

And so, in April 2017, I admitted myself to the clinic for what would be the last time in my transition.

It was my shortest stay in the clinic of all my surgeries so far, lasting a total of three days. But the recovery was no shorter. Breathing was difficult for a couple of days, and my lymph nodes were seriously upset. And despite that I had gone for "small", my skin was stretched taut. I remember my ribs being all shades of vivid violet through garish green for weeks. For six months, I wore a supportive corsage, much like body armour, to make sure everything grew into place and that my skin or my softer tissues underneath would not be strained.

But apart from the discomfort, my first look in the mirror without the corsage was in fact one of those psychological "click" moments.

The arrow straight fence-post silhouette is gone, instead, my body is graced with a gentle curve.

My entire self-perception shifts to where I can actually picture somebody (a man?) want-ing, desiring to touch my chest. Run their fingers down my back, trace kisses down my shoul-der…

Some six days after the surgery, I took my first shower.

Oh! My! Heavens! What a complete sensory overload! The pure sensation permit-ted me to believe someone would want to caress and kiss my breasts as something responsive and alive. Moreover, that I would not only enjoy it, but that I would actu-ally melt under that touch.

Getting fitted

In connection to top surgery, back in the days where I was still flat as a telegraph pole, I helped myself out. Either by wearing prosthetics, or by wearing padded bras.

I knew where I would get what I needed. Today, it is one of my favourite dessous places. Nevertheless, at the time, going there cost me quite the effort to overcome my anxieties, since the two shopkeepers knew me from way back, when I was still buying men's underwear and I accompanied Wiebke when she bought her undergarments. And after a particularly unpleasant episode in *another* shop, I was twice as tense.

Yes, of course I shopped a lot over the internet. But I wanted something "nice", and I wanted it to fit well. I asked Vanessa to come along for moral support, and to make it look less like I was "a guy getting off on dressing in ladies' underwear".

One of sales-ladies clocked me immediately, probably recognising my face. But just as obviously, she must have taken in the women's clothes and the hairstyle, and she seemed satisfied to just wait and see. I asked for what I needed, padded bras or bras with formed cups, and in which size range I needed them. Again, while still a bit cautious, she seemed happy to provide me. And Vanessa and I disappeared in the fitting booth, where she gave me pointers what I should look out for, the two of us giggling like teenagers.

I picked several comfy bras with formed shells in suitable colours and brought those to the counter to pay. The lady kindly and cheerfully informed me, that there were in fact matching slips available. And would I be interested? This was October 2015, before my GRS. I paused, thinking for a moment, deciding that my body was likely to change a lot, and spending too much beforehand was not sensible (these were not cheap). So I thanked her sincerely, and said, that no, not at the moment. But that I would happily take her up on her offer in six months or so.

I could actually see her mind working, reassessing the situation. But she did not miss a beat. She thanked me for my purchase and let me know that I was welcome anytime.

I go there on occasions, and I am always greeted with warm kindness.

And yet, what stands out, is a visit sometime after my top surgery. Again, both ladies were there, and again, the same lady approached me, asking what she could do for me. The fact was, I had lost a lot of muscle mass in my chest and shoulders, so I needed some new bras. She showed me some models and handed me what she thought was the right sizes, and yes, I also took the matching slips.

I was on my own this time. And my top-girth still felt new. And since nobody taught me how to properly fit a bra, I was not sure if was doing well. So when the lady asked through the curtain, did I need assistance, I gratefully said, yes, if she would please check if the size was right.

My back was turned to the curtain, but there is a full length mirror, so I saw her entering, and I saw her face when she came inside the booth. The lady's jaw dropped. I have rarely actually seen that happen on a person, but this was a showcase example.

She exclaimed, "Wow, you look good!" And then she must have realised that she had just made a very personal statement about a customer. She went red as a beet, and I could actually watch her putting the pieces of her professional sales-assistant back together.

So, yes, I got fitted, and I go there on occasions when I need something pretty and comfy. But of course the compliment made me glow like a sixteen-year-old at their first date. The spontaneous reaction of the lady in the shop, the pure, unadulterated moment of surprise in her face and the fact that she made me a compliment without ever really meaning to. It was just so authentic.

And it went a long way to reassure me, that I no longer looked like a freak or a mistake of nature. But that I was actually attractive in some people's eyes.

Realignment

Another jaw-drop moment was with my birth mother.

My mother obsessed about my requiring GRS. Well, actually, she obsessed with my entire topic of being trans* gender. From our early interactions, when I told her about my dysphoria and my decisions to get a divorce and change my life, I registered a *lot* of ambivalence on her part. She was very obviously grateful that I had made a decision to be mindful of my own needs and to pay myself better respect. I think it did preoccupy her that I was unhappy and out of sorts. But the gender thing really threw her for a loop.

I got the impression my mother had a very specific picture in her mind of who I was and how I was. Which was strange, because after all, she had never really spent that much time with me. Or perhaps not so strange after all? Regardless, she seemed to believe that I was an overall successful alpha type male who drew on all the advantages of having privileges in a system that was patriarchal from the top down. Perhaps because I was clear and concise in drawing the lines between my mother and myself?

My Mum readily acknowledged (acknowledges) that there are fluid borders between genders and that people had both attributes to their soul, but as is often the case when people are truly confronted as actual individuals in their daily lives, my mother floundered with readjusting. I think, most difficult for her was letting go of this alpha male image. Which I believe meant, she had to let go of a personal concept of antagonism. A reoccurring topic of debate between her and me was, how women presented themselves in modern societies. Getting her to permit me to actually take part in a discussion, of where I saw women's identities and women's rights in the world, took serious work. Permission in this case meaning, that she would discuss this with me as a woman, and not as a patriarch. Where women and their roles were developing themselves to, and what women wanted to achieve for themselves. And how all of this implicated changes in the roles for men and male role models. I think it challenged her to acknowledge, that I had valid stakes in this discussion at all, or that my stakes were the same (or at least similar) as hers.

Come to think of it, this was also a heated topic I repeatedly discuss with my friend Bernadine, who is also a sex therapist and quite the heated old-school feminist.

I believe what finally convinced my Mum, was the plain fact that I *demanded* to be in on the discussion. Reminding her that I had given up of all my "privileges". And that I needed to watch my back in particular settings or in specific locations as much as any other woman. And that travelling to certain countries on my own now entailed a severe safety hazard. This was something she could relate to: needing to fight for recognition and the fact that physical and emotional inviolability was not something to be taken for granted.

Incidentally, I never told my Mum about Andrin. I do not want her blaming herself, or Francesco. And I do not want to give her cause to believe I might be blaming either of them. I told her about the scene in Kindergarten, and I implied that I had indeed experienced tensions brewing when out and about. But that was as far as I went. I saw (see) no point in confronting her with my experienced violence. And Nancy whispers in a very quiet voice in the back of my mind, *"never mind the fact that you're afraid she won't believe you."*

Another issue my mother struggled hugely with, was the concept of surgery, in this case GRS, as a healing process. More than for most people, for my Mum, the integrity of the body is something that certainly extends far into the spiritual. She was reluctant in the extreme, to accept that I needed GRS to find some kind of balance and peace with my body. That it was a necessary step to live a life (including an intimate life) that would fulfil me. Her refusal to accept swung between extremes of suggesting various ways of taking a "gentle" or a shamanistic approach by way of permitting the soul to find peace. Possibly with the aid of phytotherapeutics (plant derived medicines) or homeopathies. To outright refusal to discuss any kind of standard clinical approach. I think in her mind, academic medicine was dominated by male doctors, gods in white, and therefore by extrapolation, the entire field of surgery was a violation of the female by the male. And that may to some extent even be true. There are certainly a great many aspects of academia (and for the world in general) for which that holds true. But all of this contributed nothing to the solution of my problem: that I was no longer capable of living with this penis and that *it had to go!*

And so, I simply stopped discussing it with her. I never told her that I had a surgery date.

Much, much later, the topic came up again. I no longer remember why we were even discussing it.

We are sitting on cushions in my Mum's living room.

I love my Mum's living room. Part Buddhist shrine, part Hildegarld von Bingen herbarium, part ultrafeminist library. A portrayal of my Mum's biography and testimony to the various stages of her life. Tucked away in nooks are things I crafted through the years, candles of beeswax, candelabras of forged iron, vases of glazed clay.

I recognised the signs, my Mum is about to plunge into one of her rants about why I should **not** *mutilate myself like that. Why surgery is plain wrong and how could I possibly do that to myself.*

I interrupt her before she can get going, and tell her,

"Mum, it's done. It's over."

She shakes her head. I know the movement. It's as if she could shake off the words she had just heard and then she will pick up the thread of her own train of thoughts, overriding any other truth. And it comes to me that I know how we can solve this.

Naturally.

Seconds later, I am nude.

I think it was one of those "click" moments.

I have to smile to myself a little, as I see conflicting emotions flicker across her face. All she really says, is one word, "gentle". Her face tells me, it is a statement of peace and acceptance. Tentatively, she reaches out a hand to touch, and then stops herself. As if I would break, or pop like a soap bubble.

I believe, my mother expected me to have a body laced with scars. Disfigured and maimed, broken and crippled. Instead, I think she saw a reflection of her younger self.

Since then, the tension between us is gone.

Instead, we are nurturing a very tender blossom of affection and mutual respect. I register in her, a great deal of worry, anxiety even. But it seems to be the anxiety a mother has for a daughter growing up in a world full of societies that are not always good to women. That are sometimes atrociously horrifying, the way they treat women.

We still look at each other from different sides of a narrow gorge. However, I like to think it is the age gap, and no longer the gender gap. Sometimes the wind carries away the words that are spoken and we misunderstand one another. But there is a trust there now, that we both have the best intentions at heart.

And I register a considerable amount of pride in my mother. Acknowledgement that I am more than a male-born concept of what a woman should be. That in heels or in hiking boots, I own the ground I walk on. I carry myself with dignity. And that I am ready and willing to fight for my place in the world.

Loose ends

Something that retreated almost into the background, was, that I filed for divorce.

I think, if the court had not set precise dates and issued official summons, and if lawyers did not expect expenses to be paid, Wiebke might have ignored all my requests, just as she ignored so many other things. I rather think Wiebke got the better of me on several accounts, because I simply did not want to put myself through the process of sorting out what belonged to whom in a courtroom. But I really did not care at the time. And, yes, I was afraid of the confrontation.

It was a sad thing to do, and I cost me many tears, because obviously, it sealed the fact that Wiebke and I were done with each other. Nevertheless, it *was* another significant step into independence and self-determination. And I was glad and grateful for it to be over.

For several years, she still texted me two-liners for my birthday. Texts avoiding mention of *any* name. Making offers and plans that never come to realisation. And for several years, I felt I needed to find some sort of closure with her. Together. Until something in me clicked. And I texted her, that if she was not capable of using my name, not capable of committing to a meeting, then perhaps that was something to look at. And call it quits. I have not heard from her since.

Completely unrelated, but significant to the timeline, Ms Steyr went into retirement at the end of the year I had my first GRS. Every once in a while, we have dinner together and catch up on each other's lives, talking as friends rather than former client and therapist. To this day, she remains a person very dear to my heart.

Overall, I can say, one of the biggest challenges is, that you do not actually know, how much your healing body can take. About straining or distending healing sutures. For the first four months after my GRS, I was not about to ride a bicycle. Just as directly after my top surgery, pulling a t-shirt over my head was a no-go. Perhaps I was just simply overly careful, but I do not truly believe that.

But as Vanessa says, I am good at maintenance and hygiene. I am obsessively careful about keeping things clean, be it my body or my apartment, and prevention of infections. Chalk it up to being a medical laboratory technician who teaches sterile work and clinical DNA analysis. Tendencies to OCD is a clear advantage, if not a job prerequisite. It is a standing joke in Vanessa's family. I come in, I greet the family, I greet the dogs, I wash my hands, Bart hands me a fresh towel.

I am grateful beyond words for the gift of orientation and comfort Vanessa bestowed me with, when she was there when I woke from my narcosis. My heart breaks a little bit for all those other trans* people who wake alone, without a trusted or loved one to hold their hand. And I am grateful that I was able to reciprocate the gift some fourteen months later when Vanessa required surgery herself, concerning ripped ligaments in her foot. In addition, I was able to put my acquired proficiency in lymphatic drainage massage to use.

The aftercare of a MTF GRS (male to female gender realignment surgery) is intense. The biology of the newly constructed genital aperture is unfamiliar to begin with and the body is still finding its new point of balance, so to speak. And the neovagina, called so in medical circles, does not come with the same self-lubricating, self-cleaning properties as that of a cis woman. At least not immediately. As I indicated, to begin with, the biological body does not immediately recognize the vagina as being a part of it. And if not properly cared for within the first twelve months, it will actually re-shut itself. As some of my more inattentive sisters learnt the hard way. Consequently, the anatomy needs to be maintained, both in terms of hygiene, and in shape. For eighteen months, I spent close to two hours a day, simply taking care of my body. This was probably excessive, but it did permit me to avoid any infections and complications. And I dare say, I am profiting from that today.

I am not downplaying the FTM surgery. On the contrary, I have spoken to plenty of trans* males, particularly Franco from our support group, to learn that the "downstairs" steps are complex and the process tedious. And that this is a complete understatement. Nevertheless, I am not an expert, and I do not want to miscommunicate.

I suppose my flower will never be a perfectly symmetric porn star. But since I never had ambitions in that direction, I am not bothered. My specialists are very sweet, offering moral support and affirmation about how well I am doing. I have a renal specialist who looks after my kidneys, and performs the exams necessary to look after the remnants of my biologically male anatomy. It is rare, but cis* women get prostate cancer too. He tells me, it takes a very precise inspection to tell I am trans*. Considering that other specialists have performed ultrasonic exams, looking for my ovaries and womb, and being nonplussed by their absence, I am confident he is not just humouring me.

Another thing not to underestimate, is the aftereffects of the anaesthesia. It took me three months to be able to read and *remember and comprehend* a standard DinA4 page. It took me six months to train my cognitive faculties back to their original acuity. I checked out several brain trainer apps for my smart device, and I trained daily with those.

I am good with my hormones. Most of the time. Yes, they cause mood swings. Do they ever. So, no, nothing is ever easy. Some days are so bad, I do not really want to leave the sanctuary of my apartment, because everything is stressful and facing my job, facing my students, even facing my friends, is a severe challenge. I try to be mindful of what are ripples caused by hormones and what are the real difficulties, worthy of distress. I try to take my hormones as regularly as possible, so as not to provoke further amplitudes.

I am even more temperature sensitive than I used to be. I did not think that were possible. Still, I am ill significantly less frequently than I used to be, so that is good. I still go climbing with Darren, even if climbing has become just so much harder. Some things I am simply no longer capable of. Likewise for heavy lifting, carrying shopping bags, moving furniture. My muscle structure has changed entirely. As I write this, four and a half years after my first surgery, I feel confident, comfortable, and actually pleased about what I see in the mirror. On most days. The bottom line: I am at peace. I am happy. And yes. I would totally do it all again.

I gave myself another half year to heal completely.

And then I took a look at the dating scene.

To put it bluntly, after seven years of abstinence, I was feeling the longing for a human touch rather strongly.

(10) Being Good Enough

Reflections…

Peeling away the layers.

…looking past the decoys and the self-defences.

Looking at what you truly are.

Can be one of the most frightening experiences,

you will ever make.

And it can equip you

with so much raw energy…

…that you wonder how you ever drew breath at all

before.

This chapter deals with insights. Looking at ingrained patterns and conditioned responses, transgressions and coping mechanisms. Mine. And those of others. Tread with care.

We humans excel at deluding ourselves.

We are experts at ignoring the obvious. We are fully capable of living in conditions that are *so* hostile and depraved, when viewed from the outside, it boggles the mind.

It is a survival tactic. Our instincts permit us to blend out long-term threats and concentrate on the immediate problem of continuing to live. Even if it means existing from day to day. Or even from breath to breath. We blend out the fact that, if we fail to do something to change the situation, then tomorrow will be so much worse. And so, humans are capable of existing in environments that slowly spiral into an abyss. Be it physical or emotional. And if you were to put another person into that same situation, they would probably go into shock and possibly even die in very short order. Simply because they have not learnt to shield themselves appropriately, and cope with the adversities.

At the same time, our mind shields us from the insecurity of change. Controversial as it might be, the triune brain theory is a great model here. Our protoreptilian complex interprets any change as a possible threat. After all, any change from the present situation confronts us with the unknown. And perhaps we are not equipped to deal with the unknown, and so we feel safer in the present. And our paleomammalian complex is little better. Particularly if experience has taught us, that any change will likely be for the worse. And so, we delude ourselves into thinking that we are better off dealing with the misery we know, rather than change anything and risk things getting worse.

It is this ability to dissociate, that permits people to survive extreme situations of duress and existential crisis. Or to exist in slums, ridden with abject poverty, disease, and crime. And I would assume a connection to patterns of dependency, leading up to Stockholm syndrome.

This can continue indefinitely.

Until you come to the point where your neomammalian complex finally realises, that any further deterioration of the situation *will* kill you. And maybe, just maybe, your neomammalian complex will be able to override its two older cousins.

On another note, I think it worth mentioning that my own experience with counselling confirms the experiences counsellors make all over the world. When you are in your role as a partner, then you are emotionally involved. And you cannot take on both roles at once. You cannot be partner and loved one, and counsel your own relationship. Of course you can try to look at your constellations of feelings and perceptions as rationally as you can, but you cannot ignore your own feelings in which you are *immersed*. And your own perception remains coloured by your own feelings of any situation. As a matter of fact, my friend Bernadine, who is also a sex therapist and a relationships' counsellor, was married to another counsellor and coach. And the crash of their marriage was *epic*. The emotional fall-out, the repercussions, and recriminations, lasted longer than the actual marriage had.

The next thing is, how a person deals with their emotions and perception, and what happens when one of the two people involved has a rational approach, and the other an emotional approach. That too may go south rather quickly, and the good intentions of rational analysis may not be appreciated. Quite to the contrary, many counsellor's partners view it as a depreciation, even a betrayal, to have their loved ones take on a meta perspective and try and work through a quarrel rationally. Wiebke became entirely vitriolic if I analysed a situation and applied nonviolent communication (something I rely on, on a daily basis with my students), and I know of other couples, who shared similar limits.

Which is why friend-sight is one hundred and ten percent.

Choices

There is nothing pretty about suicide.

It is a hard and very lonely act. So cold and bleak as to freeze the soul to ashes. And despite of how it is sometimes portrayed in literature and song, there is no glory. There is nothing beautiful or poetic about it.

There is no redemption in suicide.

Suicide is a capitulation before the feeling of the utter inability to cope and an overwhelming self-perception of inadequacy. It is the complete breakdown of any hope that things will ever get better.

All there is, is despair.

And of course, it is a swan song. A last final scream of impotent rage. Possibly even a scream of accusation. An indiscriminative accusation, at all those left behind. Who now must deal with the shards and the ashes. The ambiguity and the unrelenting insecurity, of never truly knowing the why and the wherefore. And who have no chance at ever understanding.

And it robs them, too, of any chance at contributing to making anything better.

It was this realisation, that kept me from suicide. That I did not want others to be hurt by my decision.

Only later. Much, much later, did I decide to *live*.

What *is* interesting, is how it condensed my life to relationships *to people to whom I veritably, truly felt connected*. My Dad. Eirian and Seraphina, my two sisters. Evangeline, my chosen Mom. Nimue and Roman, Linda and Melanie, my nieces and nephew. Names that also came up were Rafet, my friend in Zürich. Darren and Suzy. (Vanessa and her family, my friend Ianto were not yet around then).

And, no. The fact that Wiebke's name does not show up on that list is not an oversight.

Despite my affection for her, Wiebke was no longer among the people who gave me reason to live. Nevertheless, I wanted to avoid making her feel pressured or coerced into something that did not come naturally. So, I never told Wiebke that I was suicidal. And I am extremely grateful that I did not go through with my intentions, because the symbolism of sitting on a bench under a tree was something that I knew Wiebke was familiar with. And that would quite simply have been pointlessly cruel on her.

Still. I remain perplexed by how unsurprised she was, by my seeking counselling, and how she stated therapy would be good for me. She never did say, what she hoped would come of it.

Incidentally, should you really have someone on your hands who displays distinct tendencies or has expressed the intent, for goodness' sake do not leave them alone. Not even to go pee. By all means, talk to them. In fact, keep them talking. Listen. And do not be afraid of offering opinions. If they are truly thinking of killing themselves, remember, the situation is already at its worst. Short of handing them a means, there is probably not much you could do to make the situation deteriorate.

But your being there, your sharing this moment of your life with this person, your offering a moment of warmth and care, could make the difference between life and death.

Being Selfish

The curiously funny thing about fortune cookie wisdom is, reading it is close to useless. Advice is close to useless. Regardless of how wise. Or how fitting. Or how well intended. I am convinced, the only thing we truly integrate, the only thing useful to our minds and our self-care, are the insights we discover for ourselves.

Which is possible the reason why humanity is so *dismally* bad at learning lessons from history.

Being generous with your time is all very well. Being selfless with your energies is all very noble. Being unsparingly attentive and helpful, is sweet and kind-hearted. It will probably contribute to your being liked. And hopefully, appreciated. And in a healthy relationship, what you give, balances out with what you get out of your contribution. But if you are giving away more than you are getting back, it is going to make you unhappy. It will drain you of energy, drain your life of joy, and drain your self-esteem. And if you keep this up, *it will make you ill*.

From so many of my experiences with people, I have come to believe, our bodies reflect our souls, our inner peace. And while I would never imply that a person is to blame for their sickness or debility, I believe being constantly out of balance, being troubled for long periods of time, being depressed, *does* have a significant and measurable impact on our health. And I have witnessed this manifesting itself as eating disorders, migraines, autoimmune disorders, ulcers, allergies (also immune disorders), cardiac conditions, and cancer. And I believe with all my being, that even if I had not considered suicide, had I continued living the way I did, I would have died possibly years, possibly months later. I am convinced, my body would quite simply have done its best, to put me out of my misery. To give my soul peace.

And to the people who love you, it does not matter if you opt for suicide, which leaves them troubled and emotionally maimed. Or if you die of stroke or heart attack, which leaves them bereft. Or if they watch you waste away over the space of months under chemotherapy.

What evolved alongside of all of this was, that I grew aware of just how closely my self-esteem was dependent on the opinions and assertions of others. Most particularly that of Wiebke, of course. How strongly my past had conditioned me to question myself. To see myself as *invalid*. Worthless.

The perfidious thing about being trans* gender is, that:

*You *know* there is something wrong with you.*

*Because there *is*.*

You are in the wrong body. So. If others tell you, that you are an accident of nature, then they are in fact reinforcing *something that you already believe*. And if they tell you, you are wrong, your ideas are wrong, your thoughts and your opinions are wrong, your perspectives and your memories are wrong, then that, too, is something you are far more likely to believe than any cis* person with a healthy self-esteem.

In these months, I grew aware, of how I was conditioned to subordinated my choices to those of others. And. How easily I assumed responsibility, even for things I was not to blame for. And just how far out of my way I went, to please others. Ms Steyr permitted me to analyse my behaviour patterns, particularly those which contributed to my doing things for others, which actually drew far more of my strength than I got in return. Behaviour modelled to soften the blows and ease the discrimination, dating back to my primary school years. To my kindergarten days even.

And with that, I came to realise, just how closely my self-perception, this role of this perfect gentleman I was living, was tied up in my need to somehow validate my identity and justify my existence. I became fully aware, that I had banished even the minute aspects of my female identity that had shone through. I dressed as others expected of me, and how Wiebke asked of me. And I behaved according to the role I played.

I realised that in my current state, I hardly recognised this man anymore, whose life I was living. I realised I no longer got any meaning in return for playing this role. I realised that I had neither the strength, nor the will to continue doing this. I realised, that I had reached a point, where going on would kill me. By aneurism, by cardiac issue, by cancer. Or by suicide.

I was broken.

The thing about the breaking point is, that it confronts you with the finite truth. That regardless of whether you suicide, or whether you continue as before, there will come a point at which you will die. That you can no longer be there for others. Thereby, it removes the excuse, that what you have been doing all along, is sacrificing yourself to be good for others.

And it makes you face, that you can only be good for others, if you are good to yourself first.

I had to *learn* that self-care is not a matter of being selfish. It is a matter of survival. Because sacrificing yourself to the point of where you have nothing left to give, will sooner or later end you. Even quicker so, if you receive neither appreciation nor recognition for the heart blood you invest. You are only capable giving care, if you actually have something to give. You can only be there for others, if you are there for yourself as well.

I had to learn to say "no". I had to learn stand up for myself and my points of view. I had to learn to care less for what other people thought, most particularly, what they thought of me. And I had to learn to watch my strength and to look after myself. It was one of the hardest lessons to learn, and even today, it remains hard work.

And finally, I had to learn, to give myself permission, to ask for help. And that it was okay to do so.

It became clear, that it would take three things to somehow continue living. To begin with, I needed to take better care of myself. I needed to rebuild a sense of self, and self-esteem. I needed to stop feeling condemned. I needed to rebuild a healthy identity. In whichever way. And. I needed to sort out my relationship to Wiebke. And. I somehow needed to consolidate the two.

Who am I? And if so...

I went back in my mind, to see where this person that I was, had last been happy. Or even content. I tried to find a place in time where I last was at peace with myself. At peace with the people around me. At peace with who I was to the world.

Who was I, when I still trusted myself?

I tried to recall what it took to be happy. I tried to recall what I needed to feel fulfilled. Valid.

This man, whose face I wore, whose time I measured, felt completely absent. In fact, it was as if he barely existed. This did in fact mean, going into dialogue with Nancy. Which turned out to be not quite so easy either. She was equally elusive, insubstantial, and reluctant to communicate at all. For stretches, she just wept. Or, thankfully less frequently, she would work herself into a fury, like a phoenix of rage and self-hate.

I can no longer tell if this is the memory of a dream or a construct from my sessions with Ms Steyr, or with my later therapist, Dr Chamberlain.

I am standing in a dark hallway or a wide corridor. The walls, floor and ceiling are featureless grey concrete. One direction of the corridor is in utter darkness. And I intuitively know, that the darkness becomes so complete, the walls, the floor, any kind of physics simply stops existing. A darkness so deep, it consumes light, just as it consumes hope.

The other end of the corridor opens into an exit, in contrast so bright, that it too is almost featureless. There are hints of sand and rock, grass and trees. Hints of living green and a sky so blazing as to be almost white.

I am outside myself, looking at this person that is me. I too am featureless in this world, a dark silhouette, unremarkable and without gender. A shade of a person, stripped of all personality, any defining identity etched away. Standing motionless. Just standing. Unable to go back the way they came. Intuitively knowing that going back would be cataclysmic. Just as unable to go forward.

Strengthless. Frozen.

Fading…

A girl walks out of the darkness of the corridor.

Or does she walk through the wall…?

Unlike this person that is me, she is not featureless. She is of undeterminable age, sometimes seven, sometimes seventeen. Sometimes she wears a bright orange skirt and a red t-shirt with dark red flowers. Sometimes she wears knee high laced combat boots, a black skirt, and a matching frock coat. She always has long hair to her shoulders, dark blonde as mine used to be as a child. She has been crying. Bitterly. Her eyes puffy and red.

Very gently, she takes my hand.

The hand of this person that is me. This shade. And patiently leads me to the edge of the brightness. Step by step. Right to where the light begins. She lets go of my hand, wipes a sleeve over her face. Gives me an encouraging look.

My vision begins to shift. I am sometimes looking from the outside at the two figures, sometimes I am the figure, looking down at the girl. She motions, wordlessly, that I should go on. But it is clear, that she will not follow.

I remember going through that vision so often, and every time, I tried to see the face of this person that was me. I tried to see who this really was. And I could not. I failed. Or there is no face.

It was over the course of several sessions with Ms Steyr, that I came to realise, that the identity of this man was gone. I could no longer be him. I could no longer call him back. This man whose life I had been leading. He was too tired, too sad, too much in despair. Too worn out by the constant load of shame that he carried around. There was still a love there for Wiebke. And there was still a deep tenderness and hope there for Nancy. But he simply did not want to continue. Not this life. Not like this.

I had never been so cold in my life, a deep and marrow-aching frost. Even in high summer, I wore long sleeved shirts and I had regular shivering chills that had me shaking so severely, I could barely hold a mug of tea.

Of course, I realised that I could hardly turn back time and become eleven years old again. Any more than I could just up and change my past. Aside which, I was grateful to realise, that there were memories I was that fond of. Memories I did not want to sacrifice.

Nevertheless, the man whose life I had lived, remained gone. Nancy had, if you will, stepped in to fill his role. But she did not live it. She just went through the motions, existing by proxy and barely maintaining a facade. She too, was just as fatigued. And haunted by too much pain.

And Nancy was haunted by her own incandescent anger. Looking back, I was deeply, deeply afraid of this fury and its seemingly limitless power of destruction. All the more reason to keep it firmly under lock and key. It was this fear that played a significant part in why I had such difficulty showing my true self to anyone, including myself.

And yet, the longer this in-between state lasted, the longer I lived and breathed like the woman that *I was*, the more acutely aware I became, that this felt *right*. Very reluctantly, and over the course of several more sessions, I permitted myself to actually accept, that the declaration I had first made in Ms Steyr's office was more than just a statement. More than just a description of whom I had been in the past. *That I* was (am) *in fact a woman*. Today. And that this needed to be addressed, in whatever manner.

And. That even the most sincere promises are tied to certain conditions. And if those are no longer fulfilled, if the basis to those promises has disappeared, then it is necessary to examine current state of things very closely.

The realisation slid into place, that this would have far-reaching consequences.

And that it was time to start making changes.

Never too late

Aside from the explicit need for self-care, another revelation was, how it is never too late to be good to yourself.

Any improvement to your overall situation, any gain in joie-de-vivre, is worth its while. Every investment of time, effort and energy that makes you feel better about yourself, about your life, about a particular predicament, is well invested, and absolutely worth it. Any stability and strength you gain to live with life's ambivalences.

And I cannot say this often enough, there is no such thing as too late. Every decision to taste joy, to breathe life. Every decision to permit yourself, *to be kind to yourself*, is a good one.

I have watched Wiebke beat cancer. Free of relapses and metastasis for ten years. But I think she died, somewhere along the way. She still goes through the motions, she still goes to work, still looks after her father, still interacts with her relations. But from what I see, from what people tell me, the life and any joy is gone. And I weep for this human. I loved (love) her very much.

I have watched a two people die from cancer. And both of them *celebrated* each moment with loved ones, each bite of food they were able to relish, each gift they were able to bestow on others, each kiss they were able to give. They drew every possible joy from the days and heartbeats that remained.

It is a choice you make, to acknowledge that you are facing a challenge.

A darkness.

And, yes. The darkness can be so utterly draining. Asphyxiating, and paralysing. Like an insidious venom, like plutonium creeping through your lymphatic system. A darkness in which words like joy and hope lose their meaning, and the letters no longer make any sense.

And yet, my life shows. And I dare say, the lives of other people who I have met, show. There comes a point where you make a choice. There comes a critical moment of truth, where you decide.

To take that next breath. To make that next step.

To step out of the darkness.

And. The choice you make is, whether or not to look at what led into a state of depression. *And what keeps you there*. Which choices, which interactions. And whether you look for behaviour patterns which weaken the spirit and self-esteem. And the choice is whether to *work* with the issues that lie at the root of all this.

Your problems, your challenges will not magically disappear. The darkness does not up and miraculously lift. In fact, facing what lies ahead, will possibly cost you so much in tears, in pain, in blood. That you will sometimes *doubt your decision*.

But you will have two things you did not have before.

And those are

Hope.

Purpose.

It is never too late.

Being a survivor

The first step of my therapy with Dr Chamberlain, was to go over my biography. I expected this. Technically, my primary hope for my therapy with Dr Chamberlain was that he would indeed confirm my gender dysphoria and thereby enable me to transition. Meaning, that with his help, I would gain access to HRT and GRS, and get my name and gender legally changed.

And superficially, everything was fine. Whatever it was about my person, he never seemed to doubt that I was (am) trans* gender. We went over my insights concerning my lack of self-assertion and security. I believe my telling him of my therapy with Ms

Steyr, and the recognition concerning the necessity of self-care went a long way reassuring him that I was reflected and dedicated to empowering myself. But he did invite me to look more closely at what had led me to the brink of suicide.

And away again.

Piece by piece, he discovered (I discovered) how deeply insecure I was in my interactions with other people. How I struggled with self-esteem and how I barely felt myself worthy of attention. Never mind love. How I felt invalid. He would often say, slightly bemused, slightly sad, I excelled at cutting myself down.

He picked up how I repeatedly failed to defend myself or stand up for myself. How I subordinated my choices or preferences for the sake of avoiding a confrontation. How I went out of my way to please others, how *far* I went out of my way. He expertly and gently pointed out how I was fabulously proficient at obsessing about other people might have thought. Or about what they might have wanted. And what I needed to do, to put me on favourable terms with them. And how much this ruled my behaviour.

And with infinite patience and kindness, he brought me face to face with the fact, that if other people treated me in ways that were outright hurtful or transgressive, how I would always find ways to rationalise, trivialise and excuse their behaviour. Most particularly if loved ones misused my affection for them. How I always ended up blaming myself.

And Dr Chamberlain neatly and empathically summed up how all this tied into my being abandoned by the people on whom I was dependent, physically and emotionally. And how I did everything in my power, to prevent myself from being abandoned. Or abused. And how all this reinforced the patterns of self-effacement.

My mother who was never really present when I was an infant, my not being worthy of her love. My Dad who was not truly able to protect me from my mother's fury. Losing my entire world at the age of six, and thereby losing Evangeline (As a child, you do not differentiate between losing a person and being abandoned by that person). Being thrown into an environment where I did not speak the language and where I almost lost my father. Being made to return to Zürich with my mother (*Whom I believe hates me. Being abandoned by my Dad. Perhaps he hates me too?*) Finding that the Zürich I knew was gone. And with it, Evangeline gone. Peers who teased endlessly. And those were the good days. Friends who turned on me. Growing up with a stepmother who hated me…

Not good enough. Not ever good enough.

And so he guided me further and deeper into my psyche and into my past. I told Dr Chamberlain of Nancy. How I had gotten the name, and how thirty-odd years later, it no longer... ...felt right. I think, for one thing, his curiosity was piqued by this. Beyond that, I have gotten to know him to be uncannily accurate in his intuitions. He was (is) always very... ...I am inclined to say, respectful. Mindful. He rarely makes opinionated statements. Most often, all he does is ask questions. How I feel about things, permitting me ample time and volume to explore my own feelings and experiences. But he did (does) give excellent pointers about connections, and how things fall into patterns. And he leaves it up to you to decide whether the patterns feel congruent or not.

Dissociation

Superficially, I was stable. I was able to keep a job, I paid my bills on time, I was able to keep myself fed and I had a hygiene routine. I had friends with whom I cultivated a deep and meaningful relationship, not a great many, but I made the ones I had, count.

Nevertheless, one of the questions that really preoccupied Dr Chamberlain was, where my panic attacks came from. I had times where lost my breakfast right after I had spent an hour doing my makeup with the intention doing some light shopping. Or simply feel myself free to move in clothes that suited me. But obviously, I was far from free at heart. Dr Chamberlain said he had met few, who carried so much fear of aggression and depreciation. Our discussions always came back this: despite that I felt very much in touch with my feminine side, despite that I very clearly knew I was a woman, I found it extremely hard to overcome something that I perceived as an inner barrier.

It had nothing to do with propriety or moral "well-bred people do not do this". But I suffered extreme anxiety when showing myself to society. Even more so, when I lay open the facts to someone I cared for. Someone I trusted. The memories of the other kids in kindergarten and the memory of Jeremy were easily available. But it was through the sessions with my therapist that I realised, just how deeply all these experiences had contributed to my view of the world. And how I came to expect to be treated by the world. The *years* of continuous teasing, bullying, and abuse from my school peers had certainly thoroughly abraded my self-esteem. And it went a long way to explaining why I subordinated so many of my choices. Why being accepted by others was so paramount.

And how I associated disclosing myself as a girl or a woman with abandonment, ridicule, depreciation, violence. Particularly from people to whom I felt close to. Dependent on.

Ironically, the men in combat-boots in Zürich were more of an afterthought. I think what made them less frightening, was that this kind of behaviour is naturally associated with the skinheads' kind of mind-set. Whereas with Jeremy, it was a breach of trust. After all, I had been friends with Jeremy for three years, sharing adventures and bonding through interests. In terms of children, that is almost half of your consciously aware lifetime. And my relationship to Dave Mackay was highly ambiguous. Much as I crushed on him, I was well aware, that any disclosure of my feminine side might well have had serious consequences.

Going over my past step by step, stumbling across the locked vault that was the memory of Andrin was only a matter of time. I had hidden away that recollection so well from myself, that its recovery turned into an all-out flashback. I relived the experience with all my senses right there in Dr Chamberlain's office. Opportunity enough for him to prove how experienced and mindful he was at intervention with episodes triggered by trauma.

The first flashback was followed by many others. Along with vivid nightmares and more panic attacks. Dr Chamberlain's first priority was to stabilise me and permit me to deal with the anxiety, so it no longer crippled me quite so badly in my daily life. One of the things he taught me was the 54321 self-centering technique refined by Yvonne Dolan.

Here and now

I walk through it.

I stand in that room. Walls grey as dust, the single light bulb casting a yellowish cone. The scent of imprisoned time rising off the floorboards, off the blue-and-grey bedcover.

The ambivalence.

The guilt. Of being in his *room. Of being sexually curious.*

Versus the blinding, asphyxiating, TEARING of my being. Andrin's voice, pathetic, pleading. So completely at odds with his brutality. So often, I taste that stifled scream at the back of my throat. The duvet growing wet in my mouth. Feeling his iron grip in my hair, his weight locking me in place.

And yet, all I have are fragments. Glimpses. Flashes of memory. Like touching a glowing hot-plate, my mind completely refuses to linger.

Bringing this to the surface. As distressing and horrible as it was, being able to look at the experience and talk about it for what it was, a violation of my being. It freed so many energies that had so far been trapped or bound. I would assume, all the resources that my subconscious required in maintaining this shield, this protection from such an overwhelming and threatening memory, were now available to be put to other use.

Yes, 17-year-old-me was inquisitive. Yes, the days spent with Andrin had the thrill of novelty and sexual exploration. Yes, I followed him to his room. Yes, I had been thinking of making out. With Dharinee. Or Guang. Dave.

And yet I had issued no invitation. Offered no consent to what followed. It was *his* doing, his transgression. Andrin had a choice. And how he chose was *his* responsibility. He took from me any choice. He took from me what was *not his to take*. I needed to see myself struggling. I needed to see myself fighting. And thereby realise, that *I made it clear, that this was *against* my will*. And I needed to realise, there was no way I could have fought *more*. He was older. He was heavier. He was stronger. And, he was more ruthless.

It was only by looking at my past, and working through the process, that permitted me to begin to heal. And to gain a perspective, begin replacing things in their correct relation to each other. Being able to see that, at the time, under the circumstances, nothing I could have done would have changed the outcome.

And by doing so, I actually felt cleansed to some degree.

I needed to *learn*. That the easiest, the most commonly applied method of exerting control, even beyond the immediate actual transgression, *is to blame the victim*. To make them feel they are at fault. To make them feel ashamed. For something for which they bear no responsibility.

And finally, I realised, she needed me. Nancy needed my help.

I was able to reach out and help this seventeen-year-old girl. Tell her, that she would survive. That everything was horrible now, but that she was not alone. Tell her that it was going to be okay. That it was not her fault. Take her in my arms and give her a place of security, where she could cry herself out. Safe from Andrin. And safe from the flames of her self-loathing fury. Give her someone she could talk to. Or scream at. And reassure her, *show her*, that at some point in her life, it would all be okay. And she would be free.

And be a part of me again.

Around the same time, Vanessa and I spent a lot of time together, so it was bound to happen. She witnessed one of my flashbacks, and due to her being active as a first-responder, she actually read my behaviour right. So I told Vanessa about Andrin. The first time ever that I spoke to anyone, other than a therapist, about what happened. She was deeply touched and sympathetic. And for the first time, I understood how important it is to entrust people outside the professional circle. How cleansing it can be, to have your traumata and your fears validated by a sympathetic friend. How important it is to be *real* to your friends, even in the things that are deeply troubling.

To make all of this perfect, Vanessa lent me her baseball bat to put next to my bed.

In the moment Vanessa says that word,

"Baseball bat."

Children's voices, many. Shouting, cheering, gleeful, excited.

The yellowish grass is stunted, short, coarse. The ground is a dusty, with patches of reddish sand. The glaring sun casts shadows, sharp as if cut with scissors. The sky is a blue so deep, you could swim in it, towering white cumulus are floating above.

White as the school uniform I am wearing. I am seven years old.

I am playing softball at the International School in Dar es Salaam.

*I can feel the texture of the bat. I can feel the weight and momentum as I swing it in a full arc. The sharp impact transmitted along the shaft as I hit the ball, the hard, metallic *smack* sound.*

And in my mind, something *changed*.

Nancy was still terrified and hurt. She still flinched at looming movement or threatening gestures. Or at harsh and aggressive voices. But with the baseball bat she had a defence that would not turn against her quite so easily. The nightmares did not grow fewer. Not yet.

But going back to sleep became easier.

It was also *then*, that I truly realised, Nancy was everything I dissociated and compartmentalised about my life. When I withdrew from cruelty. She had un-learned to love herself. Of course she had.

And it gave me the understanding, that it was *her* strength that I drew on, when I survived.

It was time to show her some appreciation for standing between me and my memories all those years, and letting me sleep more or less untroubled. I like to think in turn, that being re-integrated permitted Nancy to heal. Being welcomed back, being shown love and appreciation, I can only describe it as a feeling of being healed. This contributed so immensely to my feeling *whole*.

And I felt able to place the blame with the person who committed the crime, instead of blaming myself. I no longer felt ashamed or filthy. As if to strengthen this, it was one of the rare times that Dr Chamberlain actually volunteered a personal statement, saying that it is *not* the victim who is tainted or dishonoured by the transgression, rather that it is the rapist who defiles themself.

Realising this and speaking out loud, that I had survived. That I had survived because I was strong. And that I could draw on my resources if I needed them. The awareness that I could centre myself if I was faced with extreme situations. Focus entirely on what was needed to get through. And reduce everything to that. To survive. All that went a long way to permit me to feel more confident about myself. And it permitted me to look at my anxieties and see them for what they are: ghosts of the past. And all of that gave me sufficient strength to overcome the anxieties and put the ghosts to rest. More or less.

I became aware that I could rely on my patience, my resilience, and my ability to dissociate if needed, if I felt a wave of anxiety. To keep myself safe in the here and now. Today. And to able to look at transgressions without losing myself in the pain or in the violence. And with it came the secure realisation that nobody like Andrin can break me again.

And going one step further, through my experience, I can empathise better with others who have gone through similar things. And hopefully, help them properly identify, and face, their monsters.

Solace

It was around this time, that I went for a skill enhancement training in systemic coaching, to support people going through difficult change processes or who needed support and a fresh perspective in resolving a crisis. It was in fact *the* training I had cancelled, in order to take care of Wiebke while she was undergoing her chemotherapy.

Looking back, this seems to be one of those truly fortuitous coincidences. The group of participants, mostly women, were a cheerful and enthusiastic bunch. All of them deeply sensitive and caring people. Borne by, to the point of being driven by, the ambition to bring about a betterment for other people, and in a broader sense to engender a change in society towards a more mindful and sustainable way of living with each other.

Rhonda and Janis stand out in particular, the two of them becoming close and trusted friends. Rhonda is a wiry, tough-ass lawyer. Hard and analytical on the surface, and ruthlessly fair. The only person she is not fair to, is herself. Tender and vulnerable once you get to know her. Deeply empathic and compassionate, she and I shared a great many insights and complemented each other's perspectives. How we want to incite more awareness in the people around us. Janis, like Rhonda a single Mom, but with both her girls still preschool, Janice is a sweet natured physiotherapist, a dedicated caregiver to the core of her soul. So much so, that she, too, risks losing herself in her generosity. It was Janice's enormous capacity for finding common ground that resolved many tensions. Along with her guitar and her lovely singing voice.

This skill enhancement course involved a great deal of self-reflection on our personal histories and how our personalities developed. And of course, all of this was a part of what we discussed and worked with in our group. These people, these friends, these siblings in spirit. They do not feature prominently in this book, but they are a key puzzle piece in my development and my healing. The fact is, that the people in this community, and our insights induced by processes and learnings from this course, all of this contributed a great deal, to enabling me to entrust people with myself and with my biography.

Gradually, I opened up to people other than my therapist, other than Vanessa, and this reinforced this valuable lesson. Experiencing the reactions of friends, and later David, my partner. Seeing them shocked and saddened that I had to go through this. There are few things as strengthening and affirming as solace, sympathy, and warmth found in friends' arms, or on friends' shoulders. Or in a partner's arms, letting him wipe away tears and just letting me *be*.

I found opening up, about my being raped, extremely difficult. For all the obvious reasons, I felt filthy, I felt worthless, I felt ashamed. I felt I had brought this on myself.

And to a very significant degree, *I failed to believe I had a right to call myself a rape survivor because I was trans*. I had this inner movie that since my past had a male exterior, and since I had lived extensive parts of my life in a male role, I did not "qualify" to be raped. Completely absurd, and yet, it was the belief I had internalised.

To be honest, my mother contributed to this to some extent. From statements she made, or questions she asked, I felt that she was struggling with the concept of her forty-something year old "son" actually being a woman. After all, I had hitherto enjoyed "all the privileges" of being male. And in her view, I had contributed my part to the discrimination and debasement of women. But then my mother is also of the opinion that I had an unblemished childhood, and that I was the (masculine) life of the party. The fact that I earned my salary in a typical women's job and that I went out of my way to empower and support the woman I was married to, in the pursuit of *her* power career, seemed of no import to my mother.

But that too, was something I learnt to look past.

I never was a showcase male. So much so, that I was regularly clocked as queer, or gay. As a matter of fact, in our early days in Zürich, it was a game Wiebke enjoyed playing. To walk past gay bars with me, and see how many heads turned. I mean, most of my friends outright thought, and openly stated, that I was "delicate and effeminate". That I was a very sensual person.

So, I learnt to permit myself to *feel*. I learnt to *not* relativise my feelings, my intuition, or to question their legitimacy. I learnt to mourn the fact that I was a victim of sexual assault. To mourn the loss of innocence and inviolacy. To feel valid and unshaken in my identity.

And to feel my backbone of forged steel, and the indomitable will it had unknowingly gifted me with.

Violence

Retaliation was something I was never physically capable of. I was always the weaker one, or outnumbered. As a consequence, retaliation never established itself a solution in my reality. Unfortunately, it also made me an ideal victim, and this is something I internalised entirely.

Nevertheless, I am fully capable of obsessing about violence.

That girl who can turn into a dragon is still very much a part of me. Or *again* very much a part of me. And she is still capable of drawing on that raving, incandescent fury. And most likely, this contributes towards my love for role playing games, in fantasy or sci-fi environments, where I can be subtle, but powerful.

So, do I have fantasies of retribution? Hell, yes, I do! They involve a can of high-octane kerosene and a box of matches. There is something very satisfying about the "scritch" sound of striking a light. Or maybe go for the welding torch after all? Make no mistake, these fantasies are reserved for Andrin. Or those skinheads. Or for warlords, rapists, predators…

So, when I stopped shivering and cowering, and started seething instead, Dr Chamberlain was rather pleased.

Apparently, it is entirely healthy to get angry about being violated.

He was clear on how he saw this as a healthy step out of being the victim, to where I was actually taking action. It did not matter what kind of action, not at this point, but it was important that I feel at all empowered to *do* something to protect myself. As a matter of fact, he actually suggested I place a kitchen knife next to my bed, so when I would meet Andrin in my dreams, I would be prepared. I forewent the knife though. Too messy. And way too much danger of self-injury.

And yet the fact remained (remains), I was (am) deeply afraid of my own fury, and the potential for destruction contained therein. Learning to *permit* myself anger was an excruciatingly hard lesson.

There are a few examples in my childhood, where sometimes by accident, very rarely by design, I hurt one of my friends. Friends falling off bicycles due to my inattention, or me causing bloody knuckles in wild fencing matches. And despite my playing softball, I am atrociously unskilled at throwing. There are several instances throughout my life where I severely regret ever having tossed a ball, because by freak luck, they caused maximum possible damage. Nevertheless, I was able to sort those as accidents.

But hurting other people on purpose remains out of the question.

I have nightmares on occasions, even today. Vivid, lucid dreams of transgression, of being violated. And every once in a while, I dream, I manage to get the upper hand.

I manage to break free. I manage to get my hands on a rock, a stick, a knife, a gun. *Anything* that can be used as a weapon. But they keep coming. They just do not let me go. I cannot break completely free. They keep hurting me.

And so, I bludgeon. I hack. I slash. I burn. I shoot. I throttle.

Feeling my aggressors' hatred, their complete lack of regard, is destroying. But I do not feel filthy on waking, not anymore, not for being violated. Because they are responsible, and they are guilty. But dreaming of my hands slick with blood, is almost worse than dreaming of being raped. Perhaps it is worse. Because I never seem to be able to "get the job done properly". None of my assailants dies easily. Some do not die at all. My struggle to free myself always deteriorates into a brutally cruel grind, distorted and surreal, my assailants' rictus mocking my inability, my disempowerment, to neither set an end, nor free myself. Waking up from those dreams always leaves me feeling very desolate and… …drained. Empty. Dehumanised. And those kind of dreams truly do make me feel filthy, of the kind, that does not wash away. There is no other way to describe it.

Despite my capacity for imagination, all my fantasies of fiery rage end in forlorn depletion and an empty world, tasting of bitterness and ashes. Any satisfaction in retribution is burnt to cinders along with everything else. When it really comes down to it, I do not have the heart for violence. Not even in role playing games (I still cannot bring myself to perform a renegade run). Particularly when I *know* that no vengeance will ever un-break me.

I think because I had so much experience of what it was like to be on the receiving end of violence, both physical and psychological, that I grew to be very mindful and very much aware of what it does to people. Obviously, if threatened with that kind of violation, I will defend myself. But given any range of choices, I will always choose the least violent. Attribute it to my role models, like my Dad, and Evangeline, who thoughtfully resolved conflicts with gentleness.

All my life's experiences come to one unanimous conclusion.

That the only thing violence is capable of creating, is more violence. The only way to deal with bullies and cowards is to empower them and to teach them. But teach them with love, not with hate. To offer them a way out of the violence. To give them a role model worth looking up to.

To lead by example.

I have not forgiven Andrin, or those men in Zürich. But I have forgiven myself. And with that, it no longer controls me. And it allows me to step back and see who is truly weak.

Transgression

Since we are on the topic of violence and transgression.

Isaac Asimov wrote, "Violence is the last resort of the incompetent". I believe that there are so many levels of truth to that statement. Violence is often the easiest and most immediate solution. And being economic creatures, we humans *do* tend to lash out before we have actually thought the consequences through.

I believe people who resort to violence are in fact weak. That is not to say, that they are inherently evil. When I say, bullies need to be empowered, I mean to say, that I believe such people have become bullies because they feel they are without options. They lack the resources. And this makes them insecure, scared. They are, at a very deep and basic level, afraid of being deficient. They are afraid of being inadequately equipped to survive in this world. We, all of us, are to some extent, hurt children. And we all want the hurt to stop.

Nobody taught them to use their abilities to strive for a win-win solution. And in a world where admitting to vulnerability and requiring outside support is considered a weakness. In a world where saving face is paramount. In a world where violence as a method of raising children is largely unquestioned. In a world where the lone wolf always saves the day by means of massive firepower or martial skill. It is not surprising that so many people resort to violence. So many of our societies cultivate the image of the hard und unbreakable human. Because we are afraid. Afraid of being singled out and targeted, afraid of being hurt, afraid of death. It is a self-perpetuating cycle.

So, yes, I think violent people are weak. And lazy.

Because facing your fears, and looking at them for what they really are, is hard, hard work. Going into confrontation with yourself, instead of with others, is taking the longer and more arduous road. Winning respect, instead of inciting fear, requires you to drop your own guard. And it requires you to put in genuine, authentic effort. To be your best possible self. But I believe, the rewards are greater by magnitudes. We win. All of us.

Actually showing yourself vulnerable in a situation of conflict takes trust. Trust in yourself. That you *know* who you are and that you are confident that you cannot be broken simply because someone has a different opinion. Trust that ultimately, we are *all* of us driven by what we think we need. By our desires and wishes for fulfilment. We are all human. And we need to trust in that we, *all* of us are capable of empathy. And trust needs to be earned. Again, that takes work.

And yes, I do believe that "wild-west-justice" has nothing whatsoever to do with justice and that nothing is gained by retribution. On the contrary. It feeds off a reptilian sense of insecurity, ensuring that the enforcers rest assured in their sense of being indestructible (deathless). And all this will only contribute to the cycle of violence and counter-violence continuing to turn. It is a system ruled by fear. Instead of compassion and respect. It is emotionally immature.

Ironic, how all those transgressions contributed to my sense of fairness and compassion. I am grateful that they did not poison me.

Of course, I have no easy answer for people who outright gain gratification from depravity and cruelty. Other than, that I will not tolerate it. And I am acutely aware, how such people trigger my most incandescent fantasies. Perhaps I will hang on to that welding torch after all…

I continue to hear statements like, "but it made you stronger".

Um, **NO!**

Being violated does not make you strong.

It makes you broken.

And people excusing their transgressive behaviour by claiming that it made you stronger is just so much bovine faeces. Because they had no intention to make you strong. Because gratifying their urges and masturbating their egos was all it was ever about. And perhaps they even needed to see you breaking to "reach their peak". So, no, do not tell me that they had any interest in seeing you grow stronger. Why would they?

What made you strong was reaching out to your own inner resources and surviving. What made you strong were all the people, real or subconscious, who had your back. Who helped you up. Who were there for you as you recovered your sanctity, your dignity, your emotional and biological integrity. People who cared.

But ultimately, *you made yourself strong.*

Nobody is only good. Nobody is exclusively evil. Ultimately, I am convinced, neither had Andrin any homosexual tendencies, nor did he view me as a girl. Rather, I think my declaration that I was a girl, contrary to biological evidence, unsettled the self-assurance of his masculinity completely and threatened his worldview, ergo his existence. Bearing in mind that he had shown himself vulnerable and weak by admitting he was sexually aroused. I believe that he felt required to (1) provide immediate and undeniable proof of how much of a (potent) man he was, and (2) obliterate this threat to his masculinity and re-establish the sanctity of his universe. And the easiest way to achieve both of those was to rape me. As in so many cases, it had little to do with sex and so much more to do with control and dominance. As for the skinheads, I suppose the same applies to them. Even Jeremy needed to reassert his control over his own immediate universe.

None of this excuses their behaviour.

However, it explains it.

Moreover, in understanding how these patterns arise, enables us in ways to approach such people. And show them ways to acknowledge their insecurities without them losing face. Teaching them to fight their fears and aggressions instead of taking it out on other people.

We do not need more hard people in this world. We need more people who are capable of remaining mindful of the hurt child in all of us, even in a heated situation. Especially in a heated situation. People willing and capable of taking a step back in a conflict. And coming up with win-win resolutions.

And that takes empathy. Compassion. It takes maturity.

Hindsight

For a long while after I moved out, for a long while after I reclaimed my independence, I still felt horribly, horribly guilty.

For having failed as a husband and as a partner, for having abandoned Wiebke (yes, I had internalised that accusation quite successfully). For the first five years after leaving Wiebke, I would have vivid nightmares. Of fruitless discussions turning in endless circles, of facing hypocritical accusations and scathing depreciation. Wiebke's last look of ridicule and disgust.

And for a while I thought, only some word of forgiveness from Wiebke would bring closure.

However, Wiebke did (does) what she did best: she ignored me for the better part of the year. Only to send me text messages out of the blue, saying something along the lines of, "Hey, how are you holding up, we should totally get coffee some time, just not right now, I have tremendous stress in my job, I'll call you when I have time." I have no idea whether she did this with conscious intent, because she truly might enjoy playing mind games. Or because she was authentically at her limits and simply did her best to cope with what life threw at her. I like to believe the latter.

Being deficient

I had indeed internalised that I was an undesired accident of nature. Through the prolonged experience of neglect and abuse, throughout my infancy and childhood by my mother. The years of teasing, bullying, and betrayal by people I perceived as friends. It took my growing up, being emotionally and rationally capable of analysing the repercussions of feeling abandoned by my playmates and ostracised in school. The woman who gave me life, rejecting me. Friends withdrawing or simply fading away over time. Jeremy turning on me, the Mackay family turning away. On top of that, Andrin's violation of me exponentiated my lack of self-esteem by so many degrees. He broke whatever remained of any confidence I had in people. Or in myself. Effectively preventing me from ever truly trusting *any* bond to a person, regardless of how much I loved them.

And. Thereby also preventing me from ever truly going into confrontation. Even if I felt I had been treated unfairly by people I cared for. Or standing up to people I depended on. I never really believed anyone would stay with me and love me for my sake. I believed that if I spoke up or defended myself or my perspectives of a situation, I would be abandoned. Or worse.

And in a very detached part of my mind, I was speechless at what my mind was capable of. That I had locked away the memory for so many years, completely obscuring any thought or association. And thereby permitting me to live seemingly unfractured, seemingly at peace. I remember being staggered with disdain and consternation at this insight, how much I had betrayed myself.

For a long while, therapy consisted of reflecting on my relationship to Wiebke, and the repeating patterns of my behaviour. And hers.

She was far more experienced in the ways and the workings of the administrative side of life, setting up insurances, keeping tabs on taxes, looking after health insurance. I simply had nobody to show me these things, and therefore relied on what she was prepared to show me. And there was Wiebke's extraordinary memory of dates and birthdays. Particularly when we argued or fought, she would come up with pinpoint memories of who said what. In the early years of your relationship, I was better at keeping an overview of how puzzle-pieces and lives fit together. Such detail had so far been insignificant to me. So when we fought, I did in fact doubt my memories. More importantly, I was unable to articulate why I intuitively felt her arguments to be off, to be unfair.

And finally, there was the Epstein-Barr infection, the Mononucleosis infectiosa. That alone shifted the dynamic between us, where Wiebke was seemingly dependent on my support. But I rather think it was the stone over which we both tripped, from which our imbalance and our co-dependency grew.

Contradictions and control

One of the things that impressed me about Wiebke, was that she seemed to know exactly what she wanted. She had very precise ideas about the kind of environment she wanted to work in, what she wanted to do and what her work was worth. She has a taste for interior, living space design and art that was rather expensive, but then so do I, we complemented each other perfectly in that respect. She was extremely supportive in my going to art classes and showed great interest in what I was doing.

The contradiction lay in how she paid me compliments for things she liked, but how she could be extremely condescending or withdrawn if our ideas or opinions deviated.

Talking about feelings was fine, if it was about other people's feelings. Talking about her own… …not so much. I was constantly kept second guessing myself. Did I offend her? I think I offended her. I did not mean to do that; I am so sorry. The number of times I found myself spiralling into an apology loop makes me so ashamed today.

Another aspect was, how clearly she claimed her independence, reminding me time and again, that romance had not been on her agenda when she moved to Zürich. This contributed to some extent to my hesitating before giving up my existence in Zürich and moving to Ulm. But move I did. What that said about *my* commitment did not seem to register. Even in later years, she remarked, how she would easily give up our relationship if a career opportunity presented itself. She always emphasised how easily she was prepared to cut loose and do her own thing. She told me verbatim, if I stuck around and got my heart broken, then it was nobody's fault but my own, after all, she had warned me. Today, I realise how severely this triggered my fear of being abandoned, and how I did everything to prevent that.

It was a slow, slow development, barely perceptible. As open minded as she was to begin with, about where I shopped for clothes, and how I dressed, I was given to feel very clearly, that if I was going to be a son in law to an esteemed physics professor, or the spouse of a project manager, then I would need to present myself in befitting manner. And that my unobtrusive-androgynous wear or my low-key goth was immature and out-of-place. On good days, it was, "Yes, I know you prefer something else. But. You would look so *good* in a suit. And that shirt looks so good on you, look, I will even buy it for you". On not so good days, it turned into, "What? You really want to walk around in that? There is now way you are coming along like that. You want my parents to feel ashamed?"

Little else triggered me, like the topic of punctuality. And it remains a sensitive nerve today.

Wiebke always prioritised her work over *everything* else. This was a reoccurring theme through all her employments. And of course to a significant degree, I empathise, since work is defining and existentially necessary. Nevertheless, the pure number of hours that I spent waiting for her (we worked at the same sites, we commuted together) to finish up her work, end a meeting, finalise her minutes, complete her shift, come out of a call, all these hours amount into months. It was something I learnt to overlook and deal with humorously, because pointing it out brought about fall-out, the kind of which I was not equipped to deal with.

I like being a little early. Not an hour, but at least some minutes. So I can be not only bodily present for my students, but also have some time to check everything is in order, and make final preparations. Instead, I was regularly late. Not because I did not get out of bed, or out of the shower on time. But because regardless of how early I set my (our) alarm, regardless of how much or how little buffer I planned for, Wiebke would always delay us. The fact that I needed to be on time, seemed to be entirely out of her scope of awareness. The fact that I was setting an example to generations of students and trainees, the fact that my efficacy and therefore my reputation hinged on this, appeared to be utterly of no import to her.

Of course, I addressed this a number of times, and I tried my best to do so in a way that was solution orientated. Instead of bluntly accusing her of being unreliable, untimely, and irresponsibly disregardful of my schedule. But regardless of how diplomatic or directly I asked her to please keep the requirements of my job in mind, as well as hers, it remained a topic on which Wiebke tolerated no kind of criticism.

I could say the same about household chores and tidying up. The number of mugs of Wiebke's coffee, several days old, and often with the faint fuzz of mould, that I picked up and washed, completely defies credibility. And even as I write this, I feel petulant and ridiculous. And yet. It was the attitude and the *regularity* of it that got to me. That made me feel depreciated. It was as if we were in an unspoken competition with each other. Whose thread of patience, whose sense of feng-shui or just basic cleanliness snapped first. I lost those as a matter of course…

I am sure I was far more balanced and resting in myself, when Wiebke and I first met. I was rather better at challenging her statements and opinions. Better at confronting her and pushing topics that mattered to me. And of course I *wanted* to please her. I *wanted* to be supportive and reliable. But so many things happened that changed that, in the months following our becoming a couple. And continued to change, in the years that followed.

I trusted her in a great many things, for example art and furniture. We had a large degree of overlap. So, when she asked me my opinion, often I went along with what she had suggested in the first place.

Mature and rational as Wiebke could be about choices of material things, whom to consult about tax refunds, dealing with rude waiters, she was entirely more volatile and easily unbalanced when she felt vulnerable, when she felt threatened, or abandoned. She was readily prepared to admit that she had ordered the wrong reagents in the laboratory, or put a dent in another car.

However. Clearly stating her expectations was extremely hard for Wiebke. Naming and addressing actual wishes and desires, was nigh impossible. The perfidy about this was, that she appeared to let me make a free choice. But if my choice turned out *not* to be what she had wanted me to choose, then she let me feel *very* clearly that she was disappointed, withholding affection or even breaking off communication altogether, giving me the cold shoulder. Admitting that her expectations were unfulfillable, that her loyalties were not transparent, was not her strong point. Admitting that she needed, *wanted* another person's support in her life, was not possible. Nor the admission, that she, too, had contributed to a misunderstanding that led up to a fight. That her reactions had been out of proportion. Backing down, or admitting she needed help, was something she viewed as a weakness and a loss of face.

I think she was aware to some degree, that she coerced rather than convinced me on some very central choices. Like how much time to spend with whose family. Or when I called her out on her chronic lack of punctuality. I assume, she felt left alone with the responsibility. It has taken me a lot of time and distance to see this clearly, how we were caught in a positive feedback loop of self-protective behaviour. Her defensive attitude effected that *I did not permit myself vulnerability either*. As a consequence, we both stopped communicating honestly about our needs and our vulnerabilities.

There are few things I control as well as my temper.

And even if I was angry and hurt by Wiebke's contradictive behaviour, when I realised, she was being unfair, or when I felt coerced and blackmailed, I never lost my temper. As a rule, my first approach was always gentleness and patience, trying to get my point of view across with logic and reason. When that did not make any impression, I repeated what I had said content wise, but in a much tighter and controlled tone of voice. I never raised my voice though. And if making my point more with more tension did not bring about a change, I withdrew from the argument, believing any further argument fruitless.

I sometimes even got the impression, my keeping my temper in check, riled up Wiebke even more. When I would cease to argue, she would accuse me of not caring, and lost her temper completely. Possibly, because it brought her face to face with the fact that she could not control *my* temper.

If she was in a sour mood, she could be viciously aggressive in an entirely passive way. Wiebke was an accomplished fencer of unspoken accusations and implied recrimination. She wielded guilt with unerring precision, capable of cutting me to the bone. I do not know that she was aware of this herself. I hope not.

Just as I am sure that she was unaware, that every fight or argument we had, it took her slightly longer to recover her temper and find her way back to communicating at eye-level. The first time she felt wronged, she was mad for an hour or so. That escalated to her being withdrawn and silent for days, then weeks, then finally for months (we were together for eighteen years). If I actually addressed this, or called her out on being coercive, it only turned so much worse. I remember early on in our relationship, doing the mental maths and extrapolating, that at some point, Wiebke would be in a state of passive aggression for half a year. In the end, she topped that by more than double. Today, I recognise that as a sign of how deeply injured she was.

As supportive as she had been about my art classes in Zürich, or about my going dancing classes with one of my lab colleagues, once we had moved to Germany, Wiebke became tight-lipped and distant if I spent too much time on my own. Which was strange. After all, she regularly spent whole weeks away on business trips. I do not think she realised how inconsistent that was. Instead, she repeatedly said that I abandoned her, accusing me of being an egoist, that I was not worthy of her loyalty.

This pattern repeated itself in different ways.

Wiebke accused *my* father of being withdrawn and giving her the cold shoulder, something that puzzled me genuinely, because I knew, my Dad was quite fond of her. But my Dad being who he is, he was not particularly articulate about this. My Dad is good at many things, but if it requires words to express emotions, then he is awkward and hesitant.

Every few years, my Dad took it upon himself to visit Europe, to catch up with long term friends and family. Wiebke suggested I take a holiday for him and that we permit ourselves some quality time just the two of us. Even then, I had the impression that she was not altogether at ease with my being away without her. So instead, I arranged for a trip for the three of us, hoping that they would grow a little closer. But when we actually came around to going on the trip, she withdrew at the last minute. Insisting that we go, just my Dad and I. And when I returned, she seemed to have completely forgotten that *she* had refused to come along. That she had stayed behind by her own decision. Accusing me of going off on my own.

And of course this repeated itself again, in my Trip to Scotland with Rafet. Wiebke insisting that we go. To the point of becoming irate, implying that I was an unreliable and disloyal friend if I did not make room for Rafet. But accusing me of having abandoned her upon my return. I understand that in her world, in her reality, this holds true. *She feels betrayed by me*, and short of time travel, there is nothing I can do to change that. That too, was something I needed to learn. That our world could touch, even intersect, but they were not the same. And I needed to learn, *that my world, my truth, was as valid as hers.*

Again, in retrospect, I did not contribute to breaking these patterns. Because, to put it blankly, with me, she had a partner that accepted her behaviour. As I said, I am sure that part of what drew her to me, was that I was empathic, sensitive to her needs. It is deeply ironic that this precise state of being turned on us. The only thing I can say in my own defence today, is that I was aware something was wrong. Acutely so. But I was not able to put the pieces together. And I was, in fact, afraid of confronting Wiebke. I was far too sensitive to her moods, too frightened of being rejected by this person *who had seemingly accepted what I was*. And I know, I enabled her in this toxic behaviour, more than I supported her.

I was, at the time, not capable of reflecting that. Just as I was not capable of reflecting, that in accepting the blame, in accepting that it was my fault, in accepting the accusations as justified, I placed myself firmly in the role of the victim. *That I resigned myself to being disempowered.* And that, too, permitted a part of me to absolve myself of the responsibility. It took distance. And it took outside help, to look at that network of causalities, and realise the connections and repercussions for what they were.

Isolation

Solveig, Wiebke's mother, was *the* archetype of the maternal figure. Solveig had started studying pharmacy when she and Torben got to know each other. When the two of them left East-Germany (yes, back in the cold war, when crossing a border got you shot for treason), Solveig kept a paying job *and* raised a family, devoting all and any spare time to her three daughters. And maintaining the perfect household.

All the while, Torben finished his studies. Following which, he devoted all his time, and then some, to his physics department. As much as Solveig was the mother of the family, Torben was very much the archetypal distracted professor. And the patriarch. Make no mistake, he cannot be blamed for growing into that role. The only thing he could be blamed for, was not learning otherwise, while his wife still lived. Wiebke described him time and again, how he was absent for much of her life, how he seemed content to know his family was there, but to remain apart from them. And if the opportunity arose, he would invite the cream of the physics world into his home, and present his perfect family.

So, it is not at all surprising, that to Wiebke, her mother was the central figure of trust and the focus of affection. Even more so, and I witnessed this repeatedly, when Torben spoke so depreciatingly of women. And of the medical profession. And took his family quite simply for granted, as if it were another law of physics, that he should have these people in his life who doted on him.

I understood that Wiebke was deeply, deeply hurt by her father's depreciation and what she most likely perceived as rejection. I suppose it is logical, that she was clearly unsettled by the deep loyalty I have to my father.

What I had a very hard time with, was how she projected the faults and shortcomings she experienced in her father's behaviour onto *my* Dad. Wiebke accused my Dad of ignoring her, of speaking ill of her, of neglecting Amahle and discriminating women in general. I did in fact call her out on that and pointed out to her, that she was describing her father's behaviour. *That did *not* go well*, despite of how diplomatic

I was about stating my case. Without meaning to, she made her loyalties very clear in that respect, and they obviously did *not* lie with me.

I believe Wiebke was outright aghast at how little trust and affection there was between my mother and me, relative to the bond between Solveig and Wiebke. The fact that I would even hesitate to drop everything I was doing on the spot, in order to attend to my mother, was probably something Wiebke could not even comprehend. Instead, there was Evangeline. And my deep emotional rapport and the unthinking trust I had in Evangeline simply stumped Wiebke. Every so often, she would implicate, that my bond to Evangeline was unhealthy and that I was better off strengthening the bond with my mother.

I think it is safe to say, that Wiebke was jealous. That I did not love my mother unconditionally. That I took the liberty to keep my distance. Just as I am sure she was jealous that I had a father who not only took time and interest in the things I did, but openly showed love and appreciation at my efforts to see him. But admitting to jealousy would mean she would need to admit, that her family was not quite as perfect as she painted them. And admitting emotional faults or weaknesses is not in character for Wiebke.

All of this contributed to another contradiction. Wiebke often urged me to reach out to my family, spend more time connecting to them or go visit them. When I phoned them, Wiebke would find things to do nearby or sit herself next to me. And fidget. At some point, I opted to put the phone on speaker, so Wiebke could listen in, and that would eventually turn into a conversation between Wiebke and whomever I called. And I would sit on the side and just listen.

At the same time, there were so many episodes where she vented to me, speaking depreciatingly of my family. Aside from what she accused my Dad of, she questioned his motives and his achievements in providing so many clinics in Lesotho with clean running water and reliable power. She was recriminating of my mother, downgrading her lifestyle and her ridiculing engagement in women's rights. And while I do question some of my mother's choices and while I regret my mother's priorities in my infancy, there is no question of how much impact my mother's engagement has had. Wiebke belittled Evangeline and her dedication to the inclusion of refugees and her work in counselling abused children. She basically accused Evangeline of living an illusion, saying there was no ways a single person could make a difference in society anyways.

Wiebke was often tense or appeared pressured when we were actually visiting, regardless of whether we were with my Dad in Johannesburg or my Mum in Zürich. She certainly did not seem comfortable. Perhaps she felt she needed to prove her value or her worthiness. Visiting Evangeline in Bern was particularly bad, and the competitive friction between her and René defied belief. She ridiculed René and his work as an artist, something I quite simply did not understand. But then René's insecurity *is* his mayor weak point, and Wiebke is very good at finding those.

And time spent with my family was time we did not spend with her family. She never said as much. But Wiebke's implications were clear as they were various. We never spent enough time with her family, no matter how many weekends we drove to her sisters' or her parents' places.

In retrospect, I can actually pinpoint when and where I withdrew myself or where I restricted contact to my family. Either to protect them from grief, or to protect myself from abrasion. When Wiebke questioned me, why I did not phone more often, it only contributed to me feeling even more guilty about neglecting my family. But I did not want to burden them with my confusion and turmoil. I realise today, that I had grown to be ashamed and uncomfortable. For Wiebke to interact with the people I loved. And I was so horribly ashamed for that, being disloyal to them, being disloyal to my partner.

Another problem with my role of this perfect gentleman, was, of course, that I was never capable of upholding this permanently. I had gratefully taken the breaks Wiebke's frequent business trips allowed, or the rare occasion that I went on a training course myself. I took these brief periods of respite, to retreat entirely into myself, barely touch anything in the real world around me. I submersed myself in books, movies, or in RPGs. Anything under four days, I would break off all contact, and let the girl in me breathe, not phoning, not texting.

This made Wiebke immensely insecure. She would be tight lipped and cold for prolonged periods of time if I did not call in every twelve hours. I was aware of this. And unfair as it was towards Wiebke, I literally saw myself almost incapable of breaking the pattern. I believe it was simply the outlet Nancy needed. But I was not aware enough of that at the time.

Wiebke said, she was anxious for my safety. But considering how extreme she reacted, I wonder today if she was not worried about my loyalty and my fidelity, something which simply never crossed my mind. For starters, I never saw myself capable of betraying her. But if that was the root of her distrust, then it does cause me disquiet, as to what she had experienced in her past before she met me, and why she would think I was cheating on her. And where *her* fear of being abandoned came from. After all, she had told me she had never previously had an intimate relationship.

We are basking in the afterglow, talking quietly. Both of us relishing the warmth of the sun of early summer on our skin.

Wiebke looks at me, lost in thought. "What went through your mind?" I look at her queryingly, waiting for her to explain her question. "What did you think, when I told you, you were my first?"

For a brief moment, I think of Nat, and how she seduced me when I was twenty-two. Now I am twenty-six, Wiebke is thirty. I think of my early years in Zürich, and how I sometimes felt lost. I voice the first complete thought that presents itself.

"What happened to you?" I ask, "What happened, that you should not trust anyone for so long?"

Wiebke looks at me as if she had seen a ghost. "That is NOT what you thought!" Then her face turns sad, "Is it?" She pauses. "Don't think that. Don't ever say that again."

She deflected the conversation. I have no recollection what we spoke after that. The vehemence of her first reaction stayed with me though. And looking at the possibilities with what I know today, it paints a very disquieting picture. But it was obviously not something she wanted to talk about, so I left the topic alone.

Or perhaps, it was not something she experienced, but something she observed in her parents?

Regardless. It remains another mystery that I failed to explore. The more I look back, the more things I stumble across that make little sense. Perceptions that every so often, things in our time together were not as they seemed. With my independence, some implications cropped up, that Wiebke was not always as straight as she made herself to appear. My financial advisor stated that there were several gaps in our history, that simply cannot be explained in any way. But while that stings a bit, I can afford (literally) to let it go and just move on. What truly troubles me today, are the three episodes where I thought Wiebke might be pregnant.

How much iron in Irony?

Our wedding was quite the source of conflict. It brought to the surface how different our ideas and our emotional centres of focus lay. For Wiebke, the wedding was a display of social connectivity and status. Success and gravitas. The reaffirmation of being embedded in a very wide clan, and emphasising the significance of her own family within this clan. Possibly even the paying or equalising of ancient debts between these very old, very established arms of this clan. Personally, I got the impression, it was one of those covert duties which would be denied, were it ever addressed directly.

To me, the wedding was the affirmation of a very intimate promise made to the person I loved. Something I was only prepared to share with very few, and I required that the people present should be… …meaningful. Which meant, on my side, there were fewer blood relatives than people to whom I had an emotional rapport.

All of which would have been perfectly okay, had there not been so many unspoken wishes and desires, so many conditions Wiebke saw unfulfilled, but never actually vocalised. Until it was way too late, and all she was left with, was recrimination.

I know for a fact that, for a great many people, we were one of those perfect couples. I think for some of our friends, including Suzy and Darren, Krista and Adrian, were even something like role models. For a while. Athene once confided in me, she found us almost sickeningly sweet. Astra, Wiebke's own sister, sometimes looked a little wistful when she watched us. My Dad commented on how well we complemented each other.

We unconsciously seek that which is familiar.

The true ironic tragedy of our failed relationship is, how in so many ways, *we were perfect for each other*. I think Wiebke and I could have learnt immensely from each other, could have grown to be really close, supporting and enriching each other in so many ways. With or without my being trans* gender.

I really could have learnt to stand up for myself, in the face of someone, on whose judgement and benevolence I was emotionally dependent. I could have learnt to fight in a healthy way. And I might have learnt that I am entitled being my own person. And I dare say, Wiebke could have learnt to permit herself to be vulnerable. To relinquish control. And to be able to compromise without viewing it as a loss of face and loss of status. And to permit both a partner and herself, to be imperfect, but still lovable.

Torben rejected (rejects) any kind of medical assistance. I personally believe he did so, because accepting help would have confronted him with his own vulnerability. And weakness was something his Saxonian upbringing, where *everything* is about maintaining an immaculate and impenetrable facade, would not tolerate. Not really his fault either. I believe Torben was overwhelmed by the multitude of things that can go wrong with the human body. And by the ambivalence of medical science, so far from the linear reliability and precision of physics. And the easiest way to dismiss his insecurity, was to discredit the medical professions. I believe one of the most fatal things Wiebke internalised from her father, was that she was worthless if she was weak. And of all things, she chose to study medicine. It makes me wonder if she did it to prove how strong she was? Just as I believe she internalised from her mother, that she was only of value, if she sacrificed herself, her own goals, and her needs to the convenience of others, and the outward projection of a socially accepted image.

But then of course, we all want to please the people on whom we are so closely dependent. The people which we are expected to love unconditionally. And we *do* internalise what we are confronted with. Because as children, it is the only mechanism we are given to survive the ambivalence and insecurity around us. Just how I internalised my Dad's preferred defence of enduring a storm to come out stronger on the other side.

I know both of us, Wiebke and I, had suffered grievous injuries in our pasts. I know that the parallels between Wiebke's relationship to her father and my relationship to my mother were (are) almost spooky. There were occasions, where Wiebke almost wept from sheer anger and frustration on her father's account. Where she told me of his dismissive comments, his depreciation, and his lack of regard. I knew how she struggled to be worthy of his attention, his love, his *loyalty*. And I know that she too felt abandoned by him, and betrayed. So, it is not surprising that Wiebke had similar issues to mine, feeling insecure and unworthy. And she had certainly learnt to keep up appearances of seeming invulnerable and hard.

At the same time, she forbade herself feeling, never mind showing this anger, this frustration. I am sure she felt she was betraying her father, her family. I am sure she felt she was being ungrateful and plain unworthy. In her darkest moments of self-doubt, Wiebke would call herself a monster.

And not all my love, or care, was able to heal her.

Guilt is truly a weapon of mass destruction.

I also know she struggled with the role model her mother offered. The devoted mother who had given up everything, earning enough to give their family a start in the early years. Who had kept nothing for herself to enable herself to singlehandedly provide for the perfect home and raise three perfect daughters. I suppose Wiebke hesitated, as so many well-educated women do, to sacrifice her self-actualisation and her self-determination simply to "stand at the stove" as she put it. And Wiebke raged against the patriarchal glass ceiling as much as any other woman with ambitions to show she is at least as good at generating added value.

Perhaps there was a connection in her refusal to seek any kind of help or support from a neutral third person? Or to see any kind of therapist. The fact of how viciously defensive she became if I criticised her father brought up that thought. Maybe she knew deep down, that looking at her own patterns would require her to look beyond the gloss and the apparent perfection of her own family. And her place in it.

It remains a most bitter insight. The most fatal thing you can do, *is to devote your life to pleasing a person, who deep down does not believe they deserve to be pleased*. Because regardless of what you do, you are destined to fail.

Another deep irony of our relationship was, how both of us were so far from classical stereotypes. Wiebke had so many defining attributes that might generally be associated more with stereotype male behaviour, rather than female.

And please bear in mind, I say stereotype. I am not implying she was gender dysphoric, she showed no signs of that. But I do rather think that she would not have minded being born as a man, and some of her behaviour patterns distinctly reflected that. And considering her family constellation, it would certainly have pleased her father.

But perhaps, instead of using the term "stereotype male", I should say, Wiebke showed behaviour that was distinctly alpha. And that is something I was certainly not.

She was (is) ambitious to the point of being driven. She was really consumed by the need to prove herself; her self-esteem depended heavily on her performance, and on the reflection of her performance by others. I am certain, this contributed to her avoiding any commitment to any romantic relationship before she met me.

In later years, conversation revolved entirely around her job and her career. To the point where the emotional side of relationships to long-term friends were beginning to deteriorate. Long term friends spoke to me, of how Wiebke's interest in them seemed not so much that she listened to what they told of their lives, but that she was able to place her opinion and give her advice. Make her presence felt and have influence. Conversation was not so much about exchanging experiences or showing appreciation, as much as placing her achievements and proving her success. I would be doubtful of my perceptions, if it were mine alone, but many friends approached me with concern and puzzlement about Wiebke's behaviour. Ironically, this enabled me to trust my intuition as reliable and congruent.

As I said, she regarded showing vulnerability as a weakness. Failure was a loss of face. Talking about her feelings or wishes was nigh impossible for her. Admitting that she had hopes and needs at all that she could not fulfil herself, being required to admit she needed support, was a paramount disgrace. She demanded of herself to stand her own woman and be dependent on nobody. Not even her partner. There was always a point, after which Wiebke would not back down from a decision. *Even if it was clear that the consequences would be disastrous.* Her pride (her own words) would never permit her to let down her guard, never-mind be weak. Doing so would be admitting defeat and losing face.

We spoke about pride once, and I offered her my opinion, that my dignity was not founded in pride. That I view pride as a weakness, rather than a strength. The discussion went very badly indeed, and Wiebke made sure I knew, that without pride, I was worthless and useless. I think she was unaware of with how much loyalty I had her back, when speaking about her to other people, even if I felt she was wrong.

I believe Wiebke even viewed her becoming sick with cancer as a failure and a betrayal of her own body. A loss of control. And she went to extremes, to avoid looking at, or talking about, how her self-perception had suffered from losing her breast. Which of course also meant, we never approached the subject of how she might have viewed my being trans* as an encroachment of her territory. As a threat. The strange thing is, she could deal measurably better with having brain cancer. That seemed "honourable". But having breast cancer was somehow "impure" and she forbade me to ever speak of it, never mind talk it through with our friends. Being seen in a debilitated state, having friends witness her "weakness" was something she simply would not tolerate.

A gentleman obliges

So, what surfaced alongside my co-dependency, was how I had built this persona of the perfect gentleman. I catered to Wiebke's wishes, I led a life that served her family. And I had more or less neglected to lead a life of my own.

And that worked beautifully. It worked while things were good. While *we* were good. For as long as I got some form of recognition or appreciation for what I was doing, for being a husband and a partner. Ideally, I would get love and proximity, even intimacy.

I would feel whole. I would feel worthy.

And it worked for as long as Wiebke was able to overcome her hurt-phase and permit herself to be approached. It worked, because I intrinsically felt I was invalid. I felt unable to point out the injustice and the unfairness. After all, I *knew* at the bottom of my heart, there was something fundamentally wrong with me. So I always looked for the blame in myself. And it never crossed my mind to point our Wiebke's behaviour was on occasions intolerably disrespectful and not contributing to sustaining our relationship. But I failed to set limits. I had never learnt how. And I failed to learn in time. And she failed to recognise when she crossed boundaries. Or when she dismantled me so utterly, that I failed to be honest about my feelings. I failed to learn in time how to observe the complete constellation rationally and from an outside perspective.

So, when that broke away, when I no longer got any kind of appreciation or affirmation, I broke apart. This perfect gentleman broke apart. And I was forced to look at the pattern. And I was made to realise, that I was doing everything to uphold an illusion. I realised I would have to start actually looking at my own needs and desires, and stop living a life by proxy.

And it took a person apart, someone neutral and without judgement, who would walk me through my experiences and permit me to reflect upon how it all connected together. Someone who reassured me, I was safe. Safe from the accusation that if I came to the conclusion, I was being treated unfairly, that I was not being disloyal and therefore unworthy of love.

I may be projecting, but I believe Wiebke always had trouble loving herself. Being kind to herself. The impression I had, was that by the end of the cancer therapy, she truly hated herself. She certainly seemed to hate me. There was probably love there too, but that was buried under far too much pain and fear, she could no longer show it. I know she made two or three efforts to remedy the situation from her side, once she realised that I was serious about moving out. Unfortunately, those did not include accepting help. And to be bluntly honest, by that time, I no longer trusted her tokens of peace.

Looking back, it breaks my heart to know she was simply just as overwhelmed and helpless in these situations as I was. So, yes. There was certainly plenty we could have taught each other and learnt together. We complemented each other in ways that were almost uncanny. And yes, she certainly deserved better than to have a partner who failed to call her out on her weaknesses and enable her to grow. Gently. A partner, with whom she felt safe to be imperfect. And yes, it is surprising, even alarming, how much we intuitively seek what is familiar. How much we are guided by our own internalised patterns and our unconscious expectations of how people react and behave.

To a significant degree, I am disappointed. Angry even. Fair of me or not, considering what a bright and well educated woman Wiebke is, I expected better of her. I expected her to approach the chance of looking at our injuries, hers and mine, looking at what it would take to heal them, with an open mind. And even more so, I would expect her to be able to communicate her needs and desires without being depreciative about it. And some of her behaviour patterns implied long-term psychological scars running similar to mine, making me wonder if and *what* she had made herself forget. And of course I knew (know) the self-defence mechanisms all too well, that ward against looking at our painful past.

There I go again, rationalising her behaviour. But I *want* to believe, that this woman I fell in love with, has good reasons for being who she is. And I *want* to believe that we were more than just two people projecting our needs onto someone convenient.

Today, I remain comforted in the knowledge that I gave us both ample time. And I believe I took into consideration, that Wiebke had gone through a lot. And that the breast cancer had to some degree eroded her self-sense and of womanhood.

I made so many offers of finding common ground. And finding somebody neutral, whom we could both trust to see the bigger picture and the interconnectivity. Someone who would help us get through this together. And I remain assured, that in all the years, the only dishonesty on my part was that I failed to inform her of my HRT.

And ultimately, it always takes two to work at making a relationship work.

So, yes, I am sad.

I am sad that I failed to realise and learn, what I needed, whom I needed to be, while there was still time. And I am sad for having discovered strengths and resources, insights and attributes, that were dormant or buried, only after I left her. I am sad that it took a divorce to permit myself to truly uncover the person that I am. I am perplexed and shocked at the fact that Wiebke did not take the chance of help when it was offered. I mourn, that she does not acknowledge Alice.

Wiebke has recovered health wise. She is free of relapses, she is free of any malaises or infringements. But as far as I know from various sources, nine years later, she has not picked up any aspect of her life, other than her consequent immersion in her work. And taking care of her father. Focusing on the two things that repeatedly lead to disappointments and depreciations. I would wish her, that, like me, she should feel the refreshment of having survived. The joy of being alive. I would really like her to take this second chance and live her best possible life. To the fullest.

And I miss our conversations. I miss our enriching exchanges about art, looking at galleries and marvelling at exhibitions together. We both *grew* through how we complemented each other in our travels. There were times, when we understood one another without words, and we gave each other peace and security. I valued our perspectives on science and society. I loved the fun we would poke at people and each other. I loved how she laughed.

I loved how she looked at me, when things were good.

I am sad for her Heartache. And for mine. I am sad for missed opportunities and for things where we both could have done better, deserved better.

But overall, I find comfort in the fact that I have done the best I was able. And nobody has a right to demand more of me than that.

Not even myself.

Being forgiven

There came the point where I realised, I had analysed and worked through all the grief and anguish that other people bestowed me with. That I had tracked down all the sources of feeling insufficient and invalid. I had worked through the patterns of accusations and of dependency that ruled my past relationship and the conditioned reactions I fell into in my interactions with other people.

And yet, I was still caught in needing some form of absolution from Wiebke. I still obsessing about my guilt. And I still felt worthless.

I can still see Dr Chamberlain sitting across me, his brow furrowed, his eyes shut in deep contemplation.

"Why do you feel responsible to this *degree? Why should you spend so much time trying to solve her problems instead of looking to solve your own? And more than anything else, why do you feel* so very *guilty?"*

The answer is as simple as it is obvious. Because, as so many fortune cookies and self-help books will tell you, I did not need anyone else's forgiveness.

I needed to forgive myself.

Compassion

But for what? I went over the last years again with Dr Chamberlain's help, looking more closely at where the pain was most severe. I had made the decision to lead a life in the role of a cis* male, because I wanted children of my own. I wanted a family. It was the reason why I committed myself to a het*norm relationship with a cis* woman in the first place. I felt Wiebke and I had enough common ground, and I was attracted to her. And of course, there was the fact that she did not douse me with boiling water or run screaming upon learning that I was trans* gender. And she did not seem to mind that I was not altogether stereotypical male. As I said to My Steyr, many years ago. I expected neither my life nor my relationship to be perfect. But I expected our relationship to work. And I had in fact hoped for children.

Dr Chamberlain and I came back to the query he had asked me right at the beginning, when he introduced the possibility of HRT. Whether or not my wish to be a parent had changed. Which of course it still had not. However, being in my mid-forties, I saw no viable or realistic way I was going to become a parent, never mind a Mom. Making my fulfilment dependent on that would be downright ill-advised, setting me up for disappointment.

And yet, he recognised how obviously painful the topic was for me. And perhaps he was following an intuition when he led our exploration of my marriage to where and when decisions were made for or against children.

He muses, summarises, "Were you as open, as straightforward as you are now, about your desire for children to Wiebke? Did she know this?"

"Yes. Yes I was. As a matter of fact, it was one of our earliest serious conversations about where we were going to go with each other. I said I was trans. I said I wanted children. I said this was why I had decided on a life as a man."*

"So, you made it clear. That children were among the primary things you wanted from this relationship. What about her? How was her position on that?"

It hits me like a wave. No, Wiebke seemed fond of children, but having them? No, she wanted to be successful. Build a career and a reputation. Which was why we had agreed that, should we have children, I would be the one to take care of them primarily.

He asks me very gently, "Did Wiebke ever actually tell you that she wanted children?"

No. As a matter of fact, she did not.

And with these reflections comes a deluge of insight and memory. Flooding the library of my subconscious as if my brain were a mirror, un-shattering in reverse.

And with the insight comes pain. And shame.

There *were* arguments where I stood my ground and I rationally deconstructed her accusations, telling her she was being unfair. This never went well. Having her arguments disempowered never sat well with Wiebke, and she retaliated with everything she had at her disposal. Few of Wiebke's remarks ever shut me down as solidly, as when she said, "Thank God I never had children with you."

For the remainder of the session, I struggle with tears. And Dr Chamberlain struggles to piece together how I got from "she didn't say" to "she is relieved" and exactly why this statement results in my breaking down completely. Even after five years of therapy, it still tests the limits of my trust to disclose this excruciating chapter of my history.

I told him how the remark was an implication that I was not worthy of her affection, not worthy of her loyalty. And. Not worthy of bestowing my care on another human being. Not good enough. Not worthy of being a parent.

Okay, so that much was obvious.

To permit him to make any kind of sense of the whole mess, I told him about Wiebke's Mononucleosis. And the pregnancy. About complications due to the enlarged spleen, that could potentially have become life threatening. How we were both utterly at the end of our strengths and resources from the long fatigue syndrome. How there was a real chance, if we were to keep that baby, she might die, and I would lose them both. I told him, how she had forbidden me to ever speak of it. How we had never grieved together.

I told him of the guilt over that decision. Obsessing over what I had maybe missed. Or failed to contribute towards preventing Wiebke getting pregnant in the first place. And the guilt over being even slightly relieved over not needing to cope with the added responsibility of caring for another life, after having taken care of Wiebke in her fatigue for the better part of a year.

And I told Dr Chamberlain of the three pregnancies that had somehow registered on my awareness, how they stayed with me, regardless of the fact that Wiebke denied anything ever having taken hold.

And of course, her accusation, Wiebke's stating relief at not being connected to me through a child, struck me to the core. I think what hurt even more than the actual implication, was, that the person I loved would use that to hurt me. I realise today, just how much of my trust in our relationship that cost me.

A part of me fully expected Dr Chamberlain to be disgusted by my crime. To my relief, he did his very best to comfort and stabilise me. He took great care to go over and reflect, that for starters, none of this was my choice to make alone. That we had taken precautions. And that under the given circumstances, with the given information, with what I had at my disposal at the time, it was a rational and sensible choice to make. I deeply appreciate him for his care and for his efforts. And looking back at all the facts I had to draw on, yes, most likely, I would make the same choice again.

Nevertheless. I feel *so* deeply wretched about this abortion.

After all, having children was *the* reason I had opted for a life as a man in the first place.

Most particularly, since this is the part of my life that I had wanted to "get right". Do better than my mother, who confronted both her daughters with the vision of having been "not had". (Yes, Mum, I know, glass houses. Just look how that turned out).

There is no kind or gentle way to say this. Wiebke *ensured*, that I wholeheartedly believed, that I am not good enough to be anyone's parent. That I am not good enough to have children. That I am not good enough to be loved.

Dr Chamberlain reminds me, that instead of locking the memory away, I could instead bring it to the light. Let it breathe. And perhaps even share my experiences and my joys with this unborn soul.

And I feel something inside myself change.

I realise that denying this memory would feel like burying this baby all over again (in my mind she is a girl. And yes, she has a name). And I feel within me, that instead, I could share my memories. Let her see the world through my eyes. Let her be a part of my life in this way. If failed to love her in all the past years, then all the more reason to love her now.

And perhaps we both could find peace.

And by his implication, Dr Chamberlain reminds me, that nobody has a right to tell me I am not worthy. That anyone else's judgement is quite simply not *valid. That I alone decide. And that I have a right, and an obligation, to be kind to myself, as well as others.*

Our session draws to a close. I am still sobbing, struggling for countenance. Today, I will be more grateful than aver to seek refuge and solace in my partner's arms. A thought flashes across my mind.

"Do I have to tell my boyfriend?"

Dr Chamberlain gives me a thoughtful look. "No. you don't have to."

He smiles his secret therapist's smile. "But you may."

And just like that, I feel free. With his simple permission, Dr Chamberlain has reminded me, that I am empowered to make my own choices. And nobody can make them for me. And that I alone must answer to myself. And that with truth, comes freedom. The freedom to be completely open and honest. To be myself.

David, my partner, picks me up from therapy. Being who he is, he picks up on my mood of course. Asking me if I am okay.

But it is too fresh, too raw. I cannot deal with this now. Right now, I just want to feel the comfort and the security of being able to lose myself in his hug and soak up his warmth.

Later the same evening, he and I are in the kitchen. We are busying ourselves cutting vegetables, sharing the homely comfort of preparing food together. But my mind is not on the carrots or the fennel.

Hesitantly, I ask David, if he has the mind for a serious talk.

I turn away. I cannot face him, I cannot bear to see his face, I am so afraid of seeing disgust and loathing there. I tell him, in halting steps, of what I have done in Zürich half a lifetime ago.

I am supporting myself against the kitchen counter, shaken by sobs. He says nothing. I hear footsteps. Somewhere, in another part of my mind, I hear a door slam as David leaves my life, and I remain unlovable.

Instead, I feel David's arms reach in underneath mine, and he gently turns me around to face him. But I am not ready to do that. I bury my face in his chest, letting him hold me close. He rocks me gently, while I sob into his hoodie. I feel the warmth of his breath in my hair as he kisses the top of my head.

"What a hard, hard choice you had to make. I am so sorry that you had to go through that."

He does not belittle me. He does not relativise my pain. He does not accuse me or berate me for the atrocity I committed. All he does, is permit me to be sad. And he offers me what comfort he is able. And to him, I am still beautiful, still worthy of his love. He presses me tight against his beating heart.

And together we mourned an unborn child.

Being self-conscious

As is so often the case, our sessions go through my mind for several days to come. And I spend time, turning thoughts and insights this way and that, analysing and re-evaluating. Checking if the conclusions I have come to in Dr Chamberlain's study still hold up in everyday life. Readjusting if necessary and making notes to share with him during our next session.

It goes through my mind, that I have betrayed my child twice. Once in denying her life. And a second time in permitting any memory or mention to be buried and sealed in a mute void.

It was several days later, that I finally made the connection.

I have spent most of my own life in a state of dissociation.

I had stopped looking after myself at the junction that was the abortion. That was the point where I had more or less given up on setting goals beyond making a living and being this perfect husband who pleased everyone.

I stopped painting. I let myself be deterred from buying clothes in the ladies' department. I stopped standing up for myself. I had stopped believing in myself and I had stopped believing that I was worthy of determining what happened to me and where my life went. If I deny my own child, how can I possible deserve a life of my own? After all, I *know* I am broken. I *know* I am a freak and a mistake of nature. And I do not deserve to be happy.

I have accompanied three people through chemotherapy. I say accompanied, but perhaps closer to the truth is watched? I have dabbed away the blood oozing from the puncture-marks left by the immobilisers around the circumference of the skull. The hair had not yet been singed away by chemotherapy at this point.

You keep giving pieces of yourself. Pieces of your heart. Pieces of your soul. To try to appease and please those on whom you depend. Or you think you depend. Those who determine your worth and your value by the way they treat you.

At what point does doing something out of love turn into self-deprivation and self-neglect? No matter how much I endured. No matter how much I cared. It was never enough. I was not able to fill the holes in others. I was not able to fulfil their longings or their hungers. I was not able to make others whole. You cannot help what does not want to be helped. You cannot heal a human who believes they do not deserve to be healed.

Unaware, that the person I loved, hated herself with the same intensity I hated myself. And I wondered why I felt so incomplete. So weak. So empty. So worthless.

I feel guilty. For abandoning my baby. For abandoning Wiebke. For abandoning her family. For neglecting my own family. For abandoning the man whose life I destroyed. For abandoning Nancy. For neglecting myself and not making more of my life.

Again, my thoughts returned to the point of what to do with my remaining life. And again, I came to the conclusion, that the only way to make anything good come of all of this, is to follow the ideals and the core principles that I hold dear. And perhaps that can be an example for others, from which they can learn. Not just the vocational training that I offer. But also what I offer in counselling and in the sum of my own insights and learnings from my experience so far. From being a survivor, from being gender dysphoric, from being experienced in clashes between cultures and genders. From being made to face choices between lives.

And that I can offer friendship, love, compassion to the people close to me.

And I again, I came to the conclusion, that I cannot please everyone. Forgiveness is not something you earn. And. I cannot make myself dependent on other people's approval. The only way to be able to be strong for others is to be strong from my core. To consider well what I give away. I can only be at my peak, I am only capable of contributing my possible best to the people I love and to society, if I am at my best. If I am whole. If I am resting within myself.

And the only way to achieve that is to be kind to myself, as well as others. By way of practicing mindfulness, and gentleness with myself.

So. Have I forgiven myself?

No. Not really. It remains one of the very few decisions that I truly regret, with every fibre of my being.

In the full awareness, that I might right now be obsessing and feeling guilty for having made a decision that cost both their lives, Wiebke and our child.

So, no. I have not forgiven myself. But I no longer punish myself either. Not by sharing my life with someone who makes it clear that I am not good enough. Not by making myself pretend to be someone I am not. And not by obsessing over my guilt. I do my best to be aware and mindful, to no longer make myself dependent on anyone else's forgiveness or approval. I no longer place my fate in other people's hands out of fear of being confronted with hard choices.

And above all, I will not make the mistake again of burying memories. I do my best to be *aware* and *in* my emotions instead of in denial.

And in the same breath. Instead of locking away the man whose breath I drew all those years, embrace him as part of who I am, as a whole. And offer him sanctuary in my soul. He, too, deserves peace and warmth.

We are human. We are subject to change. Security and continuity are illusions. And every once in a while, we are confronted with choices that bring us one, or even several steps, beyond what we are capable of bearing. These choices have the potential to break us. But that, too, is a part of being human. And every person has their own limits and thresholds how much they can take and how far they can go.

I am human. Every day, I strive to be the best that I can.

I will do my best, to do more than simply be content with what I have. I will be mindful to measure myself against the woman I was yesterday.

I know that I have more strength than I have permitted myself to believe in the past. I have proven, that I am capable of keeping my wits and my capacity together in times of extreme stress. I will stop being a victim. I will empower myself.

I have a right to feel anger and betrayal.

And.

I deserve love. I deserve compassion. I deserve dignity.

I accept responsibility. To be self-determining and self-responsible. That is freedom. To be accountable, to stand up to my weaknesses and own my mistakes. To face the truth of what I am. To be self-aware. To be free of the need to pretend or hide.

That is freedom.

Reflection

Of my many discussions first with Ms Steyr, and later with Dr Chamberlain, some stand out in their uniquity, leading to key insights and epiphanies.

Several times, Dr Chamberlain and I explored the possibility, that supposing I did in fact continue my life in the shoes of a man. Supposing my marriage had not run aground. And supposing I did have children of my own. Supposing I had truly found contentment in being a parent and living the role of a father. Would I have been able to live as a man?

I think not.

At some point, the role of parenting steps into the background, and the children take flight. And the parents are left to look after their own dreams and devices. Live their own lives. I believe, eventually my need to express my female side would have pushed through and would have demanded more and more room and attention on my life. I believe, sooner or later, I would have wanted to transition. Needed to transition.

It took the realisation that I could fulfil *no-ones* needs, if I was not myself.

The biography of many of my friends and acquaintances support this. Some of them trans* people who made a choice as late in life as after their retirement and after their children had graduated from university or vocational training.

I remember one distinct, altogether enlightening discussion with Dr Chamberlain. It was one of those few times, that he volunteered a concise statement, mentioning, that perhaps in a male role, my feminine soul might have expressed itself less benignly (my wording, not his. He was far more kind). That I might have, as so many parents do, expected my children to fulfil *my* needs and requirements by proxy. That I might have expected any daughter of mine to be extra effeminate, or that I might have failed to build a healthy rapport with a son. Mirroring my own mother's behaviour.

I remember *blanching* at the realisation. Of how much truth I felt there to be in that hypothesis. That I might have truly taken an unhealthy degree of influence in their lives and that I might have made them unhappy, inhibited their own free development. And. Looking at my history of toxic dependencies and imbalanced relationships, I do not enjoy thinking about what kind of a role model I would have been for my children. What kind of patterns would I have passed on to them?

None of all this cured me of my Baby-Fever. Curious, isn't it? I read the idiom. And I immediately knew, *"Yup. *that's* the name for what you're feeling"*. Watching all those happy parents at the playground, pushing prams, and yelling after fleeing tod-dlers.

Perhaps it is good that I never became a parent? Perhaps it good that I spared a child the torment and insecurity of having to watch a parent struggle with themselves in such a way?

I did not want to have children to *get* something.

I wanted children, *so I could give...*

All of which reminds me, that that is what I do, when I am there for my students. And again, this reconfirmed, it is so much easier to permit other humans to be them-selves and be self-determining, if you are resting in yourself. At peace. One more rea-son, if more were needed, to encourage people to be honest with themselves, and live their own truths.

Another thing we spoke of, Dr Chamberlain and I, was adoption.

As a matter of fact, it was a topic Wiebke and I spoke of a number of times. At first, she deflected the topic by saying, there was still time and opportunity for us to have children of our own. At some point, she switched to the argument that we were too old to adopt a baby. And later still, she categorically refused to discuss, saying, there was no ways any adoption agency would give a child into care of a "sick" parent.

Later, when I was on my own, Dr Chamberlain asked me, did I not want to push for adopting a child on my own? After all, the wish and the desire to raise a child or children was (is) still there. But firstly, there was the case of my being a single woman of fifty. Adoption is hard enough in many countries, and Germany is no exception.

And secondly, being trans* is a stigma that few adoption agencies are willing to overlook. Perhaps I simply ran into the wrong people. But that still raises the question, who these people are, that are bestowed with the right to decide over the fate of an-other human being. Yes, in Germany there is a law in place that demands that I be treated like any other person would be. But the people that enforce those decisions are humans with cultural and personal biases. The assumptions and prejudices go entirely off the chart. The plain fact that a person questions their own gender identity, is so far from the "normal", that most people seem unwilling to envision trans* people as caring and mindful parents.

Which stings more than just a little. Considering how low-income parents, single or otherwise, are often forced to entrust their children to the television and smart de-vices for the upbringing. Considering how anyone can become a parent, regardless of how emotionally immature or unstable, as long as the biology is functional. Nobody seems to want to question that.

To some degree, I berate myself that I did not transition sooner. To some degree, I envy younger trans* women. For them, there is still some hope of being able to adopt a child. But then, that is a completely futile line of self-reproach and condemnation. All it leads to is more sorrow.

It gives me peace to some degree, that I have a great many students and trainees, for whom I am an example in exacting and reliable working ethics. And to whom I can serve as a living example of overcoming boundaries between cultures and evolving beyond traditional gender roles. I experience myself as efficacious and empowering. My views and experiences are respected and valued. Even more so, some of these youths and young adults entrust me with things they do not even confide to their parents, because they need the perspective of someone who has broken the mould.

And in the meantime, I have a loving partner, who entrusts me with his growing son.

Happily ever after…

…because obviously, there is no such thing.

There are plenty of articles, blogs, posts, narratives, book and even comics on and by trans* gender. All of which speak volumes of the paths trod, as well as books of advice and reference for both the trans* people as well as their families and friends.

They tell of the tedious and humiliating legal hurdles, the diminishing and depreciating prejudices of society. They tally the uncountable obstacles and challenges that devour all joy of life and make days stretch into an infinite corridor of self-doubt and depression. They illuminate the abject terror and despair of being rejected by your family, the parents that gave you life and the siblings you grew up with. Documents of families torn apart, and people being ostracised beyond reconciliation.

Or. Witnesses of family ties strengthened. Heart-warming examples of support and love that moved mountains and transformed borders. Pun intended. People, humans, capable of imagination and willing to overcome insecurity. Empowering each other to grow closer and better connected, laying foundations to unshakable love that enabled borders to be crossed and limits overcome. All these lives, all these fates, so deeply touching.

No fate but what we make

For about six years, I put a great deal of effort and attention into our support groups, the youth group and the adult peer-group.

At some point, Marie accomplished her goal. She got her certificate as a non-medical counsellor and set up a practice explicitly for trans* people. Marie knew Franco from her networking activity to raise awareness about trans*. Both are politically active and engage themselves for the improvement of conditions which trans* peoples are required to fulfil, to have access to medical care and get their legal status recognised. Franco is a trans* guy, with the looks and the demeanour of an exuberant young bulldog. Cheerful to the point of being alarming. Helpful and engaging, he is exactly what our youths need if they are down and out with dysphoria.

Franco and I supported Marie in our monthly meetings for grownups, where we mostly talked and exchanged experiences in the traditional sense of support groups. Marie asked me to join in the supervision team, because she knew I had many years' experience in dealing with youths and young adults. We set up a second group twice a month for youths, where there was more focus on providing a safe and accepting environment for "our kids", with games, arts and crafts, warm meals and generally providing unobtrusive guidance. Most of the people had a long history of self-harm, dissociative patterns, making harmonic and productive social interactions a challenge on occasions. Nevertheless, taken individually, all of them were (are) graced with amiable and charming qualities. Some of those kids grew to be very close to my heart, and some of the adults became closely appreciated friends.

To begin with, our support groups were a source of solace and purpose. For the first two years, I spent increasing amounts of energy in attending the people there.

I felt comforted by the fact that I was far from alone in my situation. Although to be honest, that wore off rather quickly. Being who I am, the others in the groups quickly realised that I do not ask "how are you?" as an empty turn of phrase. So, with regularity, I ended up doing what I have been doing since high school, namely, offering common sense reflections on other people's challenges and quandaries. I became rather popular, but it also placed quite a demand on the availability of my attention. My strength was in very short supply. And saying "no" was still a learning process.

Another thing I came to learn, was how all support groups were pervaded in varying degrees by a hierarchy. All of it subliminal, but no less powerful and important. And heaven forbid you broke the rules. There were different rankings. Who was furthest in transitioning? Who had the best passing? Who was the prettiest (How stereotype is that?). As irritated as I was by this behaviour, it took me a while to realise what was happening.

But what disquieted me most of all, was how there was a constant competition of *who had it hardest*. Who had suffered the most. That instead of supporting each other, and contributing to positive outlooks, instead of looking for solutions, we commiserated and fortified each other in our self-perception as victims. Again, it took me a while to figure that out. When I did, and it was quite the epiphany. I tried to gently steer conversations away from lamenting how cruel the world was, how powerless we were. When "gently" failed, I tried to, more directly, ask questions about what it would take to feel empowered. I told people how every step I took made me feel slightly more secure and self-assured. To make myself aware of my successes, even the small ones. How it contributed to my being able to face society. That caused quite some friction.

And finally, grateful as I was (am) to Marie, and how she played a very central role in my finding the right people to turn to, she is very much a micromanager. Born, I am sure, out of her genuine dedication and desire to enable and empower people to live their best possible lives. But at some point, we no longer worked well together. She gave me the impression, I was welcome to "babysit" either groups, playing board games or cooking for them. But she tensed up immensely if I talked to people about things that went beyond the superficial. Even though she had specifically asked me to support both groups *because* she knew I had experience with guiding people. Particularly youths. She regularly inserted herself into any conversation I was having, even if it was clear that it was personal and confidential. To the point where she derailed discussions, distracting from the topics, changing the subject. Or she would openly belittle my opinions. If it had been just my perception, then I would have questioned my judgement. But since other people spoke about these kind of patterns on Marie's part, I have been able to trust my sensibilities more easily.

These things, together with the demands and working hours of my paying job, would later to lead to my gradually dropping out of the circle. But that was almost four years later.

What remains, is, that I continue to offer counselling and support for trans* peoples and their families. I do not advertise, but that does not seem to be necessary. Every so often, I get asked for my insight or perspective. And what remains, is a connection to some few very dear friends, all with a unique and worthwhile biography.

Vivienne stands out in particular, in a lot of ways. Vivienne is a wiry and highly energetic lady, sometimes medieval goth, sometimes butch, sometimes femme, always assertive, always lesbian. She sometimes hints at the atrocities she experienced in her early days of being trans*, in her home city of Bengaluru. Today, she is a crack web programmer and a games enthusiast, and I like to think she is one of the most successful trans* women I know. Successful in the sense that she has achieved a level of "normality" in which her dysphoria has become largely insignificant.

Today, she is happily married to Alexandra, and the two of them are hoping to raise a family. So far, the family consist of the two of them plus Isis, a beautiful kitten somebody had abandoned, but I know they are still hopeful. We do not meet often, but I always enjoy seeing Vivienne and Alexandra, and our cookouts often end up turning into long nights of old-school role playing board games and high adventure.

Naomi is one of my favourite and trusted shopping partners. She is a fragile flower, heart-breakingly beautiful in that perfect androgenic high-end-trans*-fashion-model way, and I am permanently worried about her weight. Or more precisely, the lack of it. I believe her dysphoria partially manifests itself in unsteady eating habits, despite the fact that she shows a healthy appetite when we go out together. Despite her fragility and caution, Naomi is a strong and clear-headed, clear-hearted young woman and she remains unerring in her striving to fulfil her dreams.

I feel very happy and very privileged to have been there some years after we met, when she had her hearing before court. Together with her (identical twin!) brother, I witnessed her getting her name and gender legally corrected (Same judge. He even recognised me, greeting me very cordially). Moreover, I am grateful beyond measure to be able to "balance out" the gift of comfort and sense of belonging that Vanessa bestowed me with, when I was able to be there for Naomi, when she woke from her first GRS.

I am immensely relieved, how Naomi is exceptionally mindful and cautious is. About what steps to take, which surgeries to undergo. Naomi is obsessively dysphoric about her face, like so many trans* women. And some of us choose to start out with the high-risk-low-yield facial feminisation surgery (FFS), thinking that is what is requires, for them to be accepted by society. Instead, Naomi realised that the only battle was with herself, and that the central issue of her dysphoria was with her anatomy.

Ianto is a very precious friend to me. They identify as gender fluid, predominantly male, ergo I use sometimes they/them/theirs, sometimes he/him/his pronouns. They are currently completing their master thesis in art therapy, supporting Marie in her political engagement, while investing enormous energies and time in raising public awareness, as well as juggling a supportive job to keep themselves fed. In connection to the study course, they spent a very formative year in Wales, and I dare say they internalised a great deal of the culture there. Contributing to that, was how the whole university environment was so naturally inclusive, in stark contrast to the experiences they had made in Germany so far.

A natural platinum blonde, Ianto is an energetic bundle of muscle and enthusiasm, with a passion for mountaineering, soccer and Dr Who. Complete with barely contained dysphoria and all the insecurities that this comprises, they often struggle with seeing the beautiful boy that they are. Ianto, too, has a past where they gave up their own identity for the sake of living a life of being the perfect girlfriend, bringing themselves to the brink of extinction for the sake of fitting in and pleasing someone else. So we share a great many similar experiences. In addition to that, we share our love for art, as a form of self-expression, and as a form of communication.

With Ianto, better than with anyone else, I am able to talk about emotions and emotional scars, expressions of dysphoria and behaviour patterns. And how to deal with all of those. We understand each other intuitively, sharing insights both on counselling as well as reflecting art concepts. As often as we can, we work side by side on our respective projects. Which, as we often say, is not nearly often enough.

Malva shares one thing in common with many gender dysphoric women, who make the decision to transition in their adult life. In her past, she excelled at performing an alpha male role, simply to evade the fact that there was a deeply troubled female soul, agonising to come to terms with this body she was born with. Another irony she shares with so many: it does not matter who tells her how beautiful she is. Malva has legs up to her chin and a lovely athletic figure many women would be jealous of. She has a face of delicate classical beauty, framed by naturally luxurious hazel curls.

Today, she is mostly harrowed by the discrepancy of the perfect woman that Malva *is*, and the reflection she sees in the mirror. I get the impression, the past now cruelly haunts her, because today, she often struggles to see past the imprinted male image of both her reflection in the mirror and in her behaviour patterns. She is deathly afraid of being imperfect. And so, she pursues high-risk-low-yield facial feminisation surgery, instead of going for the root (horrible metaphor) of the problem. And, rather than face the result of a less-than-best GRS, she goes bungee jumping, hiking gruelling trails and sky diving.

But one day that girl is going to make her own rules. And she is going to laugh about all the fuss she kicked up.

I have met trans* women who had even more extreme histories, who told of inhuman, self-effacing risks they had taken in active military service on the front line, where the borders between death-wish and proving-themselves blurred. Or, people who had punished and demeaned themselves by proxy, as subs in an SM environment, only to become majestic, self-assured women.

We are what we are:

Self-made people.

There is limitless freedom in that. And abject terror.

Stories

I shy away from the word "stories".

Story implies something derived. A fantasy, a tale spun to amuse. However, we do not talk of our paths to entertain, or to satisfy whims. We write for ourselves, just as much as we write for others.

We write to give a fellow trans* humans a lead. Having different options presented is invaluable when you are confronted with a hard decision. *Knowledge is key to empowering people.* By writing, we give them the means to make informed choices. It is comforting to some degree, to know what decisions you will be faced with. And of course the simple knowledge, that you are *not* alone. The same thing goes for the friends, families, and loved ones of trans*people. It is so important remember that they too need to go through their own process of change.

We write to be heard. Of late, gender dysphoria has become almost something of a distraction from the daily hamster wheel. Exotic (erotic?) and delightfully transgressive. Despite this, in a great many societies, being trans* still bears a very real risk of being ostracised, discriminated, abused, or even murdered.

We write to share. Because *one* version of the truth is often incomplete. Never enough to portray the complexity of what a person is, or how our world develops. And yes. Of course ego plays a role. To say otherwise would be a lie.

But I think most of all, we write to heal.

I write to analyse. Writing helps me think. Putting things in order. Getting an overview. Finding connections, discovering patterns. Realising and comprehending the interconnectivity of actions and interactions. Bringing into focus. Refine an idea, until it feels "right", balanced.

Demons of the outside may be defeated. Or not. Either way, they can be avoided. But demons of the inside? They survive. And evolve. Just like you do. Healing has everything to do with getting to know those demons. And perhaps make peace with them. And realise, they are just another aspect of who you are. To write is to make them *real*. Give them a name, a weight. It brings out the demons from where they are hidden and obscure. Insecurities. Fears. Traumas. Writing places them *outside* of us, tangible, real. Makes them manageable. It puts them there in front of us. Once the challenge is recognisable, we can get a leverage and a handle, allowing us to plan a proper approach and strategy.

Writing about fears makes them known. It burns away the secrecy. And in doing so, it takes away the viciousness and the power these fears have over us. Because nothing is as terrifying as the unknown. Writing about fears takes a decision. And in deciding, we take action. We are empowered. And once a problem is no longer secret, there is no shame anymore either. To place it outside of ourselves. It is a healing process, a cleansing.

And it gives us another perspective. It permits other people to contribute if we feel to be out of options. And of course, sympathy and support are always welcome.

Speaking of secrets. Another dilemma was, do I publish under my name, or do I adopt a pseudonym? Vanessa cautioned me, about how vulnerable I am making myself. I am well aware of how some of the things I have written about here, have led to other people losing face, losing jobs, losing families. Losing limbs, losing lives. Which, incidentally, is why I wrote about them in the first place.

And yet. I do not feel vulnerable.

I have so few secrets now.

It is entirely liberating. I do not waste energy on keeping secrets. Or maintaining masks. Or upholding shields. I have so much energy to focus on what is important. Hiding behind a pseudonym would have felt like betraying myself all over again. And what of credibility? How can I write a book, advocating the need and the right *to be your true self*, if I write it under a false name?

True. Were this another country, with another state of law, then I might not be so confident (As I write this, the USA has toppled the rights of women to determine over their bodies). But here in Germany, I trust the legislative and the judicative to ensure my inviolability.

As for my safety? I am a woman.

I watch my back. I watch my environment. And I watch my drink. I watch where I am going. And I watch out for other women. I tell people where I am. I have a friend on speed dial. Nothing can be taken for granted.

And yet, in cargo pants, or in a cocktail dress, *I own the ground I walk on.*

Fairy Tales

Being trans* gender has always had something of a surreal quality for me. The simple fact that I can give up living one life under one name and identity, and start a new one with an identity, truer to who I am, has something entirely magical.

Nevertheless, in some books I have read, I felt something missing. Even more so in newspaper articles, interviews, and blogs. The shorter the prettier. The general focus is very much on coming out to your friends and family, and how *incredibly* hard that can be. So much fear. So much sorrow. Many of them lead up to the point where the name and gender is legally changed. And possibly, surgery is approved.

And then they lived happily ever after.

End of story.

In these sanitized versions, there is no room for error. No room for ambivalence. And thus, no room for learning or growing. No room for a living, feeling human.

I understand. Facing the ambivalence. Facing the fact that that the entire situation might in fact have gone south, is a thing so frightening, that we want very much to blend it out. We like to pretend that there was never any kind of doubt and that we were always sure of what we were doing, and where we were going. But that is an illusion. A fairy tale. The truth is: we doubt. We avoid. We distract. We procrastinate. But precisely *that* is the work that we are required to do. The lesson we are required to learn. To overcome.

Going through a hard phase. A depression. A mayor life-shaking crisis. Coming out as a homosexual person. Transitioning as a trans* gender person. The process of determining your own path. The process of standing up for yourself.

It is never done.

Life continues to be a process of evolution.

A significant number of people I counselled, appeared to be blissfully unaware of this. Or blatantly deny it. They empowered themselves, they overcame all the hurdles.

Life was filled with the shine of novelty and renewal, the thrill and the adrenaline were intoxicating. But once that wore off, they found themselves still facing their demons. Still facing the monumental task of surviving day to day.

It is tempting to think we can start over, ignoring our past. But the person we are, still has to live with the patterns and conditioning, with the memories and prejudices of our past. Not everyone has nightmares or flashbacks. But not looking in the mirror, not getting to know yourself, is like leaving the process incomplete. The identity is incomplete. We need to be aware of the patterns that we in assumed as our own in our childhoods, the people that shaped us. We need to be aware of the core beliefs which model our behaviour and our responses.

We have saved ourselves, *and now we need to make it worth it*. We need to *live*. And to do so, we need to live in the present and be *aware*, of what the past has shaped us into.

And. Your life, your decisions have repercussions. All the people confronted by the changes you effect, are reflected back at you through your social circle. I understand that cis* people are surprised. They have a right to be. It was this exact stumbling block, that threw Stephan, my supervisor, for a loop. He was of the opinion, "great! He has had surgery, he is now a she, and we can get back to business". It took him over a year to come to terms with the fact that my psychological process was far from over.

Coming to terms with yourself is just the beginning. Who you are, who you want to be in society, at the workplace, in your family. You need to figure that out. The steps to achieve a life that reflects and resonates the *person* that you are. Entrusting to others who you are. In society. That is essential to living a fulfilling and happy life.

I am grateful beyond description, for all the things that turned out to be possible. And I am grateful that today, I am aware of the innate strengths I was given. The insights I learned along the way. The resources I trained and acquired that I have, upon which I can draw. They have brought me this far, and I have the trust and the confidence, that they will continue to serve me well. I am filled with joy and hope at the realisation that, yes: This is good. This is worth living for.

I promised myself that I would not permit memories of terror and anguish to keep me prisoner. I will not be a victim. I promised myself I would not be somebody people pitied.

So, yes. I dare say, I am good enough. I am good enough for me. And everyone else? Is neither qualified, nor entitled to judge.

I am capable of determining my own way. And then some.

I am powerful. I am empowered.

I have purpose.

I have hope.

It is never too late.

(11) Being Loved

Vulnerability…

…there is something so intoxicating about it…

Being aware.

Living in the moment.

Terrified. Trusting. Alive.

Time slows…

…and the music fills you with pounding, pulsing life.

To be truly yourself.

To be seen by your loved ones. As yourself.

To be loved by another. As yourself.

There is nothing more empowering than being true to yourself.

After my last surgery, I gave myself another half year to heal completely.

To integrate my body awareness.

I consider myself lucky. My "new" anatomy felt natural, and I felt at home with myself and in myself almost immediately. Going climbing, going dancing contributed worlds to enabling me to feel good about myself. Rhonda, my lawyer friend from the coaching community, unknowingly pushed my boundaries by invited me to join her in the sauna. What a breakthrough that was!

Friends like Darren and Suzy, Athene and Eddie, Vanessa and Bart, each contributing in their own special way to my wellbeing and balance. Micha and Gerlind, Roddy and Stephan, my Friends at work. All of them welcoming Alice into their lives and into their hearts, with their easy, matter of fact way of taking life as it comes and emphasising the good things. All this helped me just *be* and not second-guess myself constantly.

And life in general just got so much better.

Body language

I do not believe that people are born with a sense of fashion. I believe that is something we acquire. Nevertheless, I am extremely lucky that, in Wiebke, I had a partner who appreciated my company whilst shopping. We actually made an excellent team. So, readjusting my style or clothing did not take that much experimenting. I felt quite confident in my choices of what to wear and which colours would suit me.

I know my body language changed by volumes in the months following my decisions to be good to myself. I like to think, I stopped censoring myself. Stopped trying to be mindful of not permanently broadcasting my more sensitive self. Stopped doing my best to speak in my deepest possible baritone and in an expressed "masculine" way. I just stopped trying to hide.

That took some work. After all, there was decades of conditioning to overcome. What helped, was the elation I often felt at being free. Free to express myself, free to pull out all the stops, free to bask in this new-found joy of life!

Roddy, my colleague from work, said, since I changed my life, I veritably *glowed*.

And of course, *that drew attention.*

It was one of the things, that took the most getting used to. In my life as a man, I was not very outgoing. I was shy. I still am. But in the past, I was usually happily oblivious to how people reacted to my body language. As a matter of fact, Wiebke often laughed at this, and made good natured fun about how I had been checked out by both girls and boys. I believe I simply failed to register this half the time, because I was so busy censoring myself. And now that I was no longer busy watching my own every move, I was free to observe my environment. And since I felt so much more vulnerable, I was busy watching other people, how they reacted to me.

And I realised: boys, men, *they are always looking*. Okay, so that was not really news, I knew men checked out women. But to constantly feel myself under scrutiny. And to feel *supremely* insecure about my appearance, and what kind of image I presented, that took immense work to overcome. And what was new, or at least, what I had never really noticed was, that girls, women, look too. At other women. I like to think I had previously been aware of the pressure and demands that society places on people, particularly on women. Always being measured, always being judged. But this was an entirely new level. To the point of where I sometimes felt raw.

And one thing I needed to learn in a hurry, was, that a lot of people (yes, mainly men) freely interpret your body language as an invitation, to take all sorts of liberties. I needed to learn how to defuse situations, delicately but decidedly, where obvious expectations were involved. Needing to decline unsolicited attention politely, but firmly, was something entirely new.

Part of what made it significantly harder, was, that I was still going through a finding phase. Where part of my mind was still all overwhelmed with, "Ohmigosh! I can be alluring! I can be sexy! I am desirable to others! Is this cool or what?!?" The ambivalence of feeling *good* about being attractive, whilst still maintaining my own boundaries, my self-determination, was confusing at first. And there were situations, where in retrospect, I could have smacked myself, because I had been blatantly stupid. Unlike the pubescent girls from my school days, I rarely had the security of a friend, who had my back. I was of an age, where people expect me to *know* what I was doing. And finally, I was *acutely* aware, how I did *not* want to feed the misconception, that any woman wearing a smile, or a short skirt, is asking to be felt up. Or raped.

Going out with Vanessa on occasion, my modern cowgirl friend, was a huge lot of fun. The two of us (are) were entirely capable of flirting without intent, and giggling like teenagers at the reactions. But there were incidences, where I came up short, realising that I no longer felt at ease. Situations where obviously someone had read way more into our banter than we intended.

In one instance, this led to a salesman stalking me for over eight months. I was shopping for a bed (of all things), and somehow, he got the *entirely* wrong impression. Even though I had made it *unmistakeably clear* that I was interested in furniture, and nothing else. Explicitly saying so changed nothing. He was still texting me half a year *after* the bed had been delivered, *sincerely expecting me to drop my knickers for him*. Those were days when I checked my door twice. After all, he knew precisely where I lived. It was an excellent lesson of watching what I was doing, and keeping a cool subroutine running, thinking ahead. Even if being with my bestie happened to have us drunk on fun.

Going out with Naomi is always divine. We usually make a day trip of our outings, treating ourselves to a sumptuous brunch, just right to give us an adequate foundation for a day of shopping. Not that we buy a lot. But the sifting and the browsing leads to all kinds of metaphors and insight to our lives, and we share conversations of all the hopes and challenges we carry. To some degree, she is almost like a sister. And we too, giggle and squeal, as we share juicy stories of passing strangers in the night. Occasionally, I catch boys "looking" in our direction, but so far, our bubble of sanctity has not been breached.

Often enough I was alone, where encounters developed randomly from any given situation. Going out in the evening, walking to a friend's place, or even simply shopping for groceries. Travelling. Situations where *no* flirting had been involved. Where it became necessary to clearly draw boundaries, that I was not interested. Situations where it was sufficient to just be walking past, *where all it took, was to be present and be female.*

I was given a most impressing example, of what women sometimes have to deal with, on my way back home from a seminar. I was taking the motorway from Hamburg south in the direction of Ulm. I had been on the road for the better part of five hours, so I decided to take a break, stretch my legs a bit. And go to the restroom. And treat myself to a fresh coffee. Pretty much in that order.

It's a Sunday, late afternoon. The air is brisk, refreshing. I meander aimlessly along the abandoned picnic tables, blending out the highway traffic, watching the sun set through the naked trees. At some point, I feel the chill, and I head for the rest-stop café.

Business is slow. There are three guests in the entire café. I find an empty table next two men. Flannel shirts, faded jeans, cowboy boots, base-caps. Truckers? They are in good humour, obviously sharing a highly amusing anecdote. The waitress comes over and takes my order. She too seems in excellent spirits, possibly looking forward to the end of her shift. She banters with the two men.

The waitress brings my cappuccino, asks if I would like anything else. The men at the next table chat and laugh quietly to themselves. Crockery rattles somewhere in the distance. My mind is still on the seminar, going through conversations, going over insights. Peripherally, I am aware that outside, twilight is changing into dusk.

The waitress comes to check. The two men at the table next to me wave her over and pay, making cheerful small-talk. She wishes them a safe drive, and makes off with their cups and plates. They pull on their coats. One of the men tips his cap and gracefully bids me a pleasant evening. I smile at him, and nod, over the brim of my cup.

I am alone with my cappuccino and my thoughts.

Or so I thought.

*I am pulled into the here and now by an *unmistakable* soundscape.*

I had completely forgotten about the third man. He is sitting alone at a table diagonally across from me. And he is obviously, *audibly*, watching a porn flick on his smart device. Except he is not watching the screen. He is staring straight at me. His hands under the table.

I am so surprised, I have no idea how to deal with this.

Two things go through my mind.

I could put on my best ice-queen face, go over, and offer him a paper hanky.

Or. I could pour the remains of my cappuccino in his lap.

It dawns on me, that, were I to stand up, the man could almost look me level in the eye. Even if he remained seated. In fact, he is built like a prize bull. He could probably break me like a toothpick. Or hold me down *without breaking a sweat. And. My coffee no longer fulfils temperature requirements sufficient for self-defence.*

Not that he has given me actual cause. *So far.*

I really want, more than anything in the world, to be *gone*. Where is that waitress when you need some backup? I grab my coat and handbag, and make for the hallway. I manage to find the waitress. Did she hear any of that? Is this a regular occurrence? I pay for my coffee. She is still her bubbly, cheerful, seemingly carefree self.

Okay, Alice, you've got this.

I step out into the now dark parking lot, and check my surroundings, before heading to my car. Even as I drive back onto the motorway, I check my rear-view mirror, looking for anyone following. And I make a mental note not to stop by this motorway rest-stop again.

Point of fact, nothing happened. And Vanessa did giggle about how I had probably missed a great opportunity. Yeah... ...nope, thanks.

The encounter left me shaken. And it contributed enormously to my awareness of what women are faced with as a matter of course, and how I was now irrefutably on the receiving end of this kind of attention. Solicited or not.

Nevertheless, this case, and others like it, are the obvious ones. Where my need to set boundaries is clear. And making a decision is easy. Less clear are friendships, where I felt a change happening. A surreptitious undercurrent, a tension previously not present. Those are far more obtrusive and confusing; causing unease and distress every time I meet the person in question. Again, I felt an acute ambivalence. Of being charmed by the attention, because these were men that had known me for years. So obviously my change of exterior was convincing. And yet, being thrown off balance, because sexual tension *with intent* is intrusive in a friendship. Sharing jokes, exchanging quips, duelling wits? Yes! Count me in! Sharing the linen? On the job? Oh, hells, No!

But the one proposition that really takes the cake, was an invitation from someone to whom I am related biologically. Even if the relation is peripheral, how do you ever face someone like that again? Strange creatures, men. A stereotyping and discriminative statement. Based on experience, lads, based on experience. Own it.

So, yes. Learning to draw boundaries and set limits was an absolute necessity.

I still believe most cis* men never even think about this.

Conflicting desires

It is so strange, even amusing, how I did many things as a woman, that I would never have dreamed of doing in my role as a man. Some will view this as the epitome of female sexual autonomy, emancipation, and self-determination. Others will scream hetero-patriarchal preconditioning. Others yet again will rant about fall-from-grace, deterioration-of-moral-values, and how we are all going to go to hell in a handbasket…

Love it or leave it, peoples, *this is part and parcel of being human.*

I cannot deny it. *I do not **want** to deny it*; I am a passionate and sensual person. This is the bare, unmitigated truth. And after seven years of abstinence, my libido was growing cheeky and progressively more demanding in "getting some". Add to the fact, that I was still undergoing a second puberty. There is no polite was to say this, but I was probably more desperate for a lay, than a solitary apartment cat in heat.

It was time to take a look at the dating scene.

Admitting to myself, that I was drawn to men as well as to women, was laughably easy. The only thing I analysed closely, was the possibility of this attraction being just an expression of my need to feel validated, by having a cis* guy's attention. But then I have always been drawn to both ladies and gents. In our good times, Wiebke and I frequently sat in cafés and pointed out attractive or seemingly interesting people to each other. Not with any intention, simply as an amusing way to pass time.

So, yes, I am bisexual. Or more accurately, the shape of my partner, their biological state, does not really matter. I feel drawn to authentic people. People who radiate being at peace with themselves, with their libido. And who experience sexuality as something beautiful, releasing and fulfilling. My passion will readily resonate to sexual tension. I find a body, any body, writhing and dancing with eroticism to be intensely arousing.

So, the change from being perceived as a male partner, to being a female partner, was not even worthy of mention.

Except perhaps for the fact that, no longer having a penis meant, I could actually permit myself to experience my own body, focus on what was happening in me. I no longer needed to put effort into retouching reality in my mind while being intimate. There is something ultimately freeing in relinquishing that kind of control, and just existing in the moment.

What *did* however take some recalibration, was, whether I required sexual fulfilment with or without emotional intimacy. Oddly enough, in my life as a man, sex without emotional commitment never even occurred to me. Always in the hopes of raising a family, *I was trying to be a man I myself would want to spend a life with*.

But with the loss of any possibility of giving life to children of my own, that could no longer serve as a guiding beacon. Besides which, stepping across the limitations of gender roles, being required to bare my soul (and body) to so many people, I suddenly felt freed from so many constraints, I seriously needed to reconsider what I wanted from life. All of a sudden, I questioned whether or not I truly wanted a steady relationship. Did I really wish to have someone in my life? Did I really want to limit that newfound freedom of self-expression by binding myself to another person?

One-night-stands most certainly held an enormously strong appeal to me. The simple fulfilment of my carnal needs (combined with the need for validation? Still a question mark there). I could easily have done that and never even hinted at my past. And thereby circumvented the entire issue of ever being required to out myself to any partner, cis-het* male or lesbian.

Working boy

How do I describe *how scared* I was? Of my first encounter with *any* partner, male or female.

I *obsessed* about what might happen, should I fall into the wrong hands. My past experiences of what happened with Andrin preyed heavily on my mind. The skinheads putting me in hospital did not improve matters. True, the violence had come entirely from males. But at the time, I felt myself drawn to males significantly more strongly. I spent ages agonising over that.

At first, I thought I might go for a one night stand, and simply go stealth. Not reveal myself to be trans*. But that conflicted heavily with my need for any partner to go slow and generally be mindful, be gentle. I really needed to feel *safe*. And apart from the obvious "no" or "stop", I needed to be able to say, "well, maybe not this, but that" without a partner taking offence. Or losing interest. Or getting creeped out. I realised, I *needed* to be able to concentrate entirely on myself, and focus on what was happening in me and my body. *Without* being required to be considerate of any emotional insecurities of a partner. Egoistic of me? Possibly. But I truly did not want to burden any partner with needing to ensure my emotional safety in such an intricate and complex situation.

Yes, of course I was overthinking it. But that is part of who I am.

The longer I obsessed, the more I favoured the idea of getting professional help. After all, there are such people as male escorts. And there are specialised male escorts, who offer services for women with impairments. Or scarring, from a birth. Or recovering from intimate surgery.

I am entirely aware, that paid sexual services are a taboo in pretty much *any* society on this globe, a topic hotter than tradition-driven-sexual-mutilation. Possibly even hotter than abortion, or sexual self-determination of women. And there are few other topics that are so entirely *RANK* with double standards and hypocrisy. There are two things that I will say here on that account: (1) That there is something *utterly grounding* in being dependent on *so* many other peoples' proficiency and talents, simply in order to acquire genitals that harmonise with your soul. And (2) if I have the assurance that the person selling their skillset does so with informed consent, where is the problem? That there is a transaction involved? *We all sell a skillset.* Each and every one of us. And if you are still feeling the urge to act superior and sanctimonious, ask yourself, exactly *why* do you feel so threatened?

I no longer feel guilty for being human.

I think what cinched the idea, was that Vanessa came up with the exact same suggestion, without me ever having hinted at my intentions. Just goes to show how alike our minds sometimes work. And. In western Europe, there are probably not many mature male escorts, that have been coerced into sexual services, unlike women or minors. Turns out, getting a date with an escort is ridiculously easy. And so it was, that I used a business trip as an opportunity for a fine dinner and date with a very charming gentleman.

And a gentleman he was. A little older than me, he was an expert conversationist, observant and accommodating. He had me blushing like a schoolgirl. He permitted me to feel safe and at ease. And he permitted me to tell him how I was trans*. And how I needed his help in overcoming my own fear of intimate contact. How I needed a safe opportunity to get to know my own body. Informed consent, remember?

I remember, he was quite nonplussed. And perhaps it was his turn to be nervous? He certainly had a great many questions, and we spent quite a while talking. And yet, it was *his* gentle insistence, that actually got us up from the safety of that restaurant table and into my hotel room, by reminding me, that if he was to help me work through anything, then perhaps it was best we not procrastinate any longer?

My heart is in my throat as we make our way back to my hotel. He keeps up a steady stream of irrelevant small talk, pointing out the sights of Frankfurt, doing his best to keep me distracted. It is good that he has his hand at my elbow, or I might wander straight into traffic.

He waits to be invited inside, closing the door behind him. And it occurs to me, consent is given in so many ways. In so many steps.

A semi light from a lamp by the bed illuminates his frame. After spending an entire evening in conversation with this man, it finally dawns on me that he is probably twice my weight. I feel my hands grow damp. I can feel my own heartbeat, hammering in my throat.

But he doesn't give me time to become any more nervous or get caught up in doubt.

Gently, but without hesitation, he pulls me into a full body hug. His one hand glides up the back of my neck, cradling my head. To my utter surprise, he kisses me deeply, exploring my lips and toying with my tongue. His other hand is wandering…

…the world falls away…

Wow… …WOW!

And is that? O! M! G!

So that is how I found out that I am quite capable of causing an erection. And that *other* people's erections are completely and utterly *desirable*.

*An undeterminable time later, he pulls back from his kiss. We are both on the bed, both topless. Another opportunity to learn just *how* sensitive my topside can become.*

He looks at me with a mixture of confusion and regret. "I can't go on. I am truly sorry, but I cannot."

I must look stricken, because he keeps apologising. He makes an attempt at explanation, but breaks off as he realises, he doesn't even understand what he is experiencing. Or perhaps he is simply doing his best to protect my feelings?

My own passion has gone up in ashes in a heartbeat. I can taste the bitterness in my throat. In fact, I am close to losing my supper. I am aware of a storm of emotions. Realisation, that I had been acutely aware that this was the risk of being up-front with a cis-het* man. And that exactly this had come to pass. Deep, heartrending pain of rejection.

Tempered by the realisation, elation even, that regardless of how this encounter ends, I have conquered my fear.

On the surface, I am utterly calm. I permit myself a slight sadness. And stop his stream of apologies with a last kiss.

Even as I watched him walk down the hotel corridor, I realised that rejection is a part of life. But in this moment, it was hard, almost impossible to distinguish between *his* confusion over what I am. And me as a person being *reduced* to being trans*. And, by implication, unworthy.

I text Vanessa to let her know I am safe. And ignore her elated requests for juicy details.

And I did something I had not done in many years. I concentrated on my breathing. I put everything in my head *outside* myself. I concentrated on feeling *nothing*. I concentrated on minding just my own body rhythms and the flow of breath.

And I slept like the dead.

Rejection or not, obsessing over reasons he was unable or unwilling to provide, was not going to help me. What remains, is the realisation that only I can give myself permission to let go. And regardless of what did not come to pass, he had helped me find my way.

Matters of the heart

What followed was a truly wild time. By my standards. For a brief interlude, I had my adventures and then some.

Following the advice of a well-meaning friend, I made the mistake of trying out Tinder. That did not go well. Simply none of the people I met resonated in *any* way. After that, I gave things like Tinder a wide berth.

I am not a bar girl either. Sitting, nursing a drink, waiting to get chatted up simply does not suit me. I am very fond of music places, clubs and discos, but then I go there to dance, not to date. Instead, I find dating sites to be of a clarity of intent and the honesty of purpose that convinces. While still allowing for enough fine tuning. Pretty much all the dating sites have evolved so far as to allow you to search on both sides of the meadow (sorry, very binary of me). And some are really cool in the way that they allow for refinement. At the same time, I like to ponder my options and reflect my choices, so I prefer Internet via a laptop or a tablet, rather than a swipe-left-swipe-right smartphone app.

I started out with something that was plainly and blatantly a one-night-stand. It was a calculated affair. I might even say, it was dispassionate. I made absolutely sure we both knew that there would be no strings attached. *And no collateral.* Made so much easier, that this was abroad. From it I learnt, the bare mechanics of being sexual as a woman. And it confirmed, that yes! I did indeed like boys. Men. And yes, sex could be enjoyable.

That all my surgeries had in fact more than paid off.

What an epic *HIGH*! What a flood of sheer relief and delight. How immensely liberating and gratifying to feel that all my choices added up. And that it was good. That I felt whole. My partner seemed satisfied, so it cannot have been all that bad.

For seven or eight months, I simply followed my curiosity. Trying out, picking and choosing from the opportunities that offered themselves. While still doing my best to remain safe, and not risk anything irreparable on either side. I like to think I was careful. Whether for adventure or for commitment, I am extremely choosy. And I was rigorous not to date anyone who was in a relationship, married or otherwise. I was not going to be a reason for someone getting their heart broken. Because it turned out, pretty much anything *will* offer itself, if you are a lady with legs and a little something of a top girth. And, no, I never mentioned I was missing ovaries, not at this point. And it brought into focus how differently, almost stereotypically, women and men differ, in how they share their passion. I came to find that difference in expression to have its very own, entirely stimulating appeal.

The question was, was it permitting me to unwind? Or making me unravel?

At some point, I dated Holger, a man who labelled himself as polyamorous. He introduced me to Jessica, his "prime". She was very pretty in a girly-hippy kind of way, possibly fifteen years younger than me. I had the impression, she was more or less permitting herself to just drift along, and I would have been curious to witness what would happen, should she discover her purpose in life. Beyond sexual gratification, that is. Considering Holger's attempt to reconnect with me, three years later, she might just have made up her mind, to put that head of hers to other work…

He also introduced me to his circle of his friends, who called themselves a tantric society. Truth be told, I have no idea how they distinguish themselves from any other swingers' club. But the fact that this was a closed circle offered something akin to safety. They were good natured people, a little shallow perhaps, but overall mellow. A fair number of them were quite spiritual, dabbling Buddhists. Aging flower children, reminding me of my parents back before we left for Dar es Salaam. That was a very strange déjà vu.

I will freely admit, I learnt a lot from them. I learnt that enjoying sex is nothing to be afraid of, or feel guilty about. And if I remained true to myself, that I had nothing to be ashamed of, or regret. Okay, so I had already worked that one out by myself. But watching these people share, did in fact remind me, that I am far from the only one. And it was a clear reminder, that as long as consent is freely given, as long as everyone involved is mature and honest about their motives and desires, anything can be, and is, possible.

And that carefree is not the same as careless.

Among the most important insights the experiences gave me, was to be very mindful of my own limits. That there is no weakness or shame in setting them. For example, while more than one partner at any one time sounds very juicy and enticing in a porn novel, I found it confusing in practice. Disturbing even. That instead of being able to lose myself in passion, I found myself fighting anxiety. Images of multiple hands and limbs from other experiences creeping into my consciousness. Not even concentrating on other people's passion could prevent me from breaking away, hyperventilating and panicking.

Of course, they asked me where these flashbacks were coming from. But they did not seem genuinely interested in listening. Instead, I rather got the impression they wanted to offer quick fixes, because my anxiety got in the way of chasing orgasms. As for Holger and Jessica, despite my shielding them as well as I could, I think they were outright overwhelmed by the intensity of emotional fall-out I confronted them with. I am quite sure they, along with most of the group, were out of their depth. And Buddhist serenity along the lines of "well, you just need to let it go" did not help me. Friendly as these people were, I felt the circle to be superficial. I did not feel free to disclose my past, neither why I had flashbacks, nor anything else about me.

Finally, and this is the most important conclusion that I drew: I found that some-one wanting me, someone desiring me is fun, and feels immensely empowering. But in itself, by itself, is not enough. What all these encounters completely *failed* to do, was touch me in any way that *stayed*. I found that tearing down all limits, also took any existing *intimacy* with it. And while there was unity, in some cases, there was even affection, there was no love. Not the depth of trust, that enables true intimacy. And commitment. And even the most sparkling firework felt cold in the afterglow, if the person you shared it with, felt unconnected. If it was about the fireworks, and not about sharing.

In my previous life, I never questioned this, but as Alice, I felt the necessity to test this limit. All these experiences confirmed, that, yes: I need someone who wants to hold me. As in, committed to sharing my time, sharing my experience of this life. *Someone who is going to share *their* life beyond the bedroom*, share the rational and the emotional, thus contribute to making both our lives richer, more colourful. I need someone whom I can entrust with my exuberant joy, without them being over-whelmed. And. I need someone for when times are hard, who sticks with me in my bad days. Someone unafraid to share my emotions. I need a partner who is unafraid of what I am and is ready to love all of me.

I do indeed need someone, whom I permit to touch my soul, as well as my body. And being desired is not enough. I need to be loved.

Keeping it real

This is a good an opportunity as any, to say this.

Regardless of who you are, and whom you desire. Talk to your partner(s).

Tell them your deepest, most intimate desire.

Because unless they are superhuman, *they haven't a frikkin' clue as to what is going on inside your mind.*

Of course, you could keep them guessing. And hoping. And searching. And likely get frustrated. And become frustrated yourself. And go searching for another, more perfect partner...

Or. You could trust. And drop your guard. And show yourself vulnerable. And tell them straight up. What you want. What you need.

Could be, it might change your life.

Now on platform one...

So, when I decided to tackle the issue concerning the long term, I burned all my previous accounts, and registered with one standard and one non-standard dating sites. I never spent much time texting back and forth. Which does not mean I wrote little. One-line replies were an immediate knock-out criterion, anyone unwilling to commit effort into communication, in putting thoughts into writing, I considered a waste of my time. I insisted on meeting face to face as soon as I felt confident that there was common ground. Body language speaks volumes. Facial expressions convey things that words never will.

Since I was no longer dating "for fun", any kind of intimacy was out of the question. On a first date, I restricted physical contact to handshakes. A very light hug at best, if I had the impression the person was serious, and I liked them.

I never disclosed myself as trans* on a first date either. As a rule, if I really liked the person, and if I was confident that there was potential and they were capable of commitment, I told them about myself as soon as possible. I felt (feel) anything else to be unfair. Three boys assured me that, no, there was no problem, but I never heard from them again, not even to say, "Do not call or text me". It is truly sad how deeply afraid cis* men are of being thought of as homosexuals. I think my learning curve was quite steep. I grasped quickly enough to tell what kind of men were self-assured and solid enough in their own identity, not to get shaken up by the idea of my past.

I think the ladies I went on dates with, were overall less shocked by my exposition. But also, more cautious. And instead of homophobia being the problem, I think they rather were not able to look past the fact, that I had been born with a penis. Perhaps they felt, that my past of being socialised as a male would... ...I have no idea *what* they thought. I got the impression, they were looking for the proverbial a fly in the ointment. Whatever it was, it was clear, that they were far out of their comfort zone.

At least body language does not lie.

On the upside, dating people on the high end of forty, none of them expected me to bear them children. These lads and lasses all had their family founding days behind them. On the downside…

…what is creepy, what I found downright disturbing, is how this turned out to be so much more dangerous than simply dating for fun, where it was clear, that fun was all it was. At least the handful peoples I had casual sex with, were honest about it. But I met an alarming number of men (yeah, sorry boys) who seemed completely without conscience or scruples about betraying their wives or girlfriends. Even on emphasis that I was looking for a committed, long-term relationship. As in years, not days. And I learnt the hard way, that they *do* exist: grown men with the moral maturity of a three-year old who has only just discovered that telling the truth is optional. Who will blatantly lie to you. And who are SO GOOD AT IT, that you hardly notice. And apparently, they see nothing wrong with their behaviour either.

Aside from the guys who betray their partners, there is another specific type of male that really raises my hackles. Newly divorced, kids out of the house and eager to spread their oats. Luckily, I proved to be a fast learner in that respect as well.

I did make one mistake. I suppose it confirms, that making mistakes is part of the learning process. I was dating this alpinist, and we went climbing together a number of times. I have to admit, he was persistent. Which I mistook for commitment. He was reliable in securing me at the rock. So ultimately, I thought he might be reliable in having my back otherwise too. At some point, we became intimate. I was cautious, but not as much as I might have been, were this a random encounter. Until I had to see my specialist about what I thought might be a serious UTI. All things considered, I got off lightly. It turned out to be nothing truly nasty, easily taken care of with antibiotics. But my gynaecologist confirmed it to be a specific microbe, that you only get from anal sex. And since that is a hard limit for me, for all the obvious reasons, it *was* undeniable proof that I could not trust him to be honest with me, never mind keep me safe.

Me being me, I wanted to know what else I had been exposed to. And I wanted to ensure that any future partner of mine would be safe. So that is how I learnt, that waiting six months for a second HIV test to confirm that you are truly negative, is as close to living hell as being dysphoric on a really bad day. Your entire life goes on hiatus, and you constantly have this abyss looming under your feet. Not fun. Not recommendable.

But apart from that brush with disaster, I met several very interesting people, both ladies and gentlemen, and I really enjoyed getting to know them. Looking back, I learnt enormously much about myself and my emotional needs from all those walks, encounters in cafés and restaurants, from all those discussions and explorations. I got to know quite a number of interesting and unique biographies. I never regretted going for online dating. There is a clarity and an honesty that I find very relaxing, when you know that both of you are there to find out if there is sufficient common ground to support a lasting relationship.

And with every date, my needs became a little more clearly defined. Turns out, those are quite specialised. Interest in travel, learning lots about different peoples, curiosity for cultures is a core requirement. Or, I lose my talent for German when I get emotional, much to the amusement or confusion of some people. Hence, I *require* that any partner be intuitively fluent in English, quite the challenge in southern Germany. And the person must be receptive for new ideas. Dedicated but not driven. Fun, but not superficial. Self-aware, self-reflected and mindful, honest with me and with themselves. A person with clear ideas about what they expect of, and are prepared to commit to, a relationship.

Bruno was one of the truly decent boys, mature, quietly self-assured, and full of good-natured humour. Quite the looker too, well built, with shoulders you could have a solid lean on. Heavens, did I fall hard for him. But decent also meant, that he straight up told me that (1) he felt intimidated and unsure of whether or not he could really deal with everything that I was, and that he would rather not risk hurting my feelings any more than was already the case, and (2) that a friend in his neighbourhood had plucked up the courage to date him, and that would make his life, particularly his life as a dad so much easier.

I like to tell myself, that he told this friend about the totally rad-ass lady he was dating. And that she had panicked at seeing her long-time secret crush slipping through her fingers and had simply seduced the man. Or, he had simply fabricated a plausible excuse to save himself the bare-naked truth and to prevent me from getting seriously hurt. Ah well…

I have to admit, I think I, too, broke at least five hearts on the way. Men, and one lady, whom I told, that, yes, our conversations were pleasant, and our walks were delightful, That I thoroughly enjoyed our strolls or our dinners together, that I appreciated their manners and their physique. But that, no, I simply *failed* to feel butterflies. I like to think I was gentle. Respectful. But I was ruthlessly honest, and in those cases, completely unwilling to compromise.

Until I met David.

A dream unthreatened

This is a shout-out to all those I say deserve the designation "Real Men".

David is living proof that there *are* cis-het* males who are entirely cool with trans* women. And by entirely cool, I mean free of expectations and prejudices about trans* people, unencumbered by ideas and stereotype ideals they feel I should live up to. Unthreatened in their own masculine identity, unshaken in their self-perception of social status, unworried about what others might think. And uninhibited in their libido. To David, I am simply a woman with a very colourful and multifaceted past, some special needs, and this makes me interesting.

…and self-aware, analytical, sensitive, mindful, patient…

And without ovaries. In my mind, I can see his boyish grin, as I type this. It has its upsides too.

That is not to say he is an expert at things Queer* or that he is without stereotype cis-het* notions that are plainly off the mark. He is not. But he is largely without prejudice, and he is willing and exceptionally capable of taking people and situations at face value. He is largely free of any toxic masculinity. He is capable of being part of a group of friends, without any kind of alpha superiority drama. And he is fully capable of recognising his own misconceptions, capable of laughing at himself. I always found that so attractive…

Mutual attraction

What immediately struck me about David's online profile, was how well articulated it was. I could tell (I thought I could, anyways) that this was a human, who had thought long and hard about his own emotions and internal processes. Who had analysed his needs and requirements, and was able to distinguish between the essential, and things he would be willing to take as they come. It was obvious, he had spent considerable time and effort into putting this into words.

…and good looking to boot…

I could tell the photos were professional quality, no shopped selfies or holiday snaps from a decade ago.

We texted back and forth for about two weeks, exchanging all kinds of background, and speaking of casual things, preferences for food, what we did for a living. Superficially, what we expected from a partner. Again, David sent no one-liners, but long, detailed letters that had obviously been spell-checked. And I was pleased to see, he was as eager as I, to get real and meet in person.

He immediately made the suggestion to meet in Ulm. From Munich. That it meant a solid ninety-something-minute train ride, simply to have a walk and a coffee with a girl, seemed to him not even worth hesitating over. I admit, I was impressed. We agreed to meet at one of my favourite spots, the main gate to the Ulm Minster. I experienced a slight ripple of irritation, thinking of my wedding in the Minster, many years prior. But I decided that perhaps this could be a good thing. Turning a full circle. Call it precognition, call it rose-tinted denial, I had a feeling this meeting had a lot of potential.

David turned out to be lanky giraffe of a man, moving with the same deliberate, slow-motion elegance. With kind eyes that twinkle with delight at the colours of the world, that shine at the prospect of an exquisite meal, that crinkle with quiet and subtle humour.

We discovered, we have so much in common.

We started off in a café, and David told me that he originally hailed from Berlin, but that work had taken him Via Hamburg to Munich. He told about his solitary trips, business and otherwise, to every kind of city. How he likes to discover on foot and take photos. How he loves aquariums and botanical gardens. We got to talking about Ulm and how we were both connected to the city. David has a long-term buddy living in Ulm. Someone who offered David refuge and solace during his divorce. So, yes, we are both divorced.

At this time, I still made every effort to never actually gender my ex. Always telling the truth, always one step from omitting the lie. And feeling guilty for it. Thankfully, we kept talk of our former partners brief.

Nevertheless, talking about our past relationships did bring into focus what we hoped for the future. This took us on a very long walk down one side of the Danube and up the other side again. We explored and elaborated on our needs for emotional warmth, and what we needed to feel appreciated. We talked of how security does not mean repetition, or avoidance of challenges, but commitment and trust. How responsibility of contribution is not trying to fix things for other people, but to permit them to be aware of what needs fixing. Gently. Mindfully. And remind people of their strengths. How harmony and happiness is not a permanent state of bliss, but a conscious state of mind, of awareness, of all the minor and mayor miracles and blessings. Every day.

And it came to me, how here was a man who, too, had felt powerless as he had watched his former relationship lose its fire. And he had analysed all avenues open to him. And drawn his conclusions of how finally, he could only change himself. Our exchange gave me the foundation on which I saw myself capable of building my trust, that he would be willing to commit to doing his best in a future relationship.

At some point, we both realised how hungry we were, and since David likes Asian food as much as I do, I took him to a Thai place I had known for years. It had long been one of my favourites, but this would be the first time in five years that I would go there. Alone, I would have felt anxious, but in David's presence, I felt confident, at ease. So much in fact, that it felt good to push this boundary. We spoke of Asia and our respective trips there. We had both been to China, but David had already been to Japan and Malaysia, and told me of his trips there. He was (is) a lively and enthusiastic conversationist. I think I must have looked like a moon-eyed teenager, immersed in his recollections.

It was a mellow and clear evening, the scent of blooming chestnuts in the air. There was a warmth in my lower abdomen, radiating up to my heart, that might have been the Thai curry, or it might have been butterflies. Leisurely picking our way to the rail station, where I would see David off on the train, we crossed the Minster square, where we had met several hours previously. There was, of all things, a grand piano in the middle of the square. With a pianist playing the theme of "Amelie", one of my favourite movies by the French director, Jean-Pierre Jeunet.

We listened in enchanted silence for something over half an hour, standing side by side. We stayed as long as we dared, drinking in this perfect evening, with the sky melting from rose into lavender. Until we finally had to tear ourselves away for fear of David missing his train.

We are standing on the platform.

People bustling, luggage trundling, trains grinding, loudspeakers blaring announcements, families screaming at each other over the announcements. The smell of axel-grease and hot metal, dust fused with deep-frying oil, acrid tobacco smoke from somewhere.

We are an eye of silence in a storm of haste, urgency, and impatience.

David looks at me. I can see contradicting emotions, desires flickering over his face. He plucks up his courage and leans down to hug me. Light. Careful. Chaste. I give him a brief squeeze and breathe a kiss on his cheek, complete breach of any self-imposed protocol.

"Goodbye David. Safe trip. Hope to see you again soon".

I step back. Out of reach. Back to safety. Let him board the train. A world of meaning hanging in that one short statement. He looks slightly shell-shocked, but recovers and gives me a timid smile. "I'll text you." Then he turns and climbs into the carriage.

I wait, waving, until the train disappears around the bend. For a while, I stand on the platform, looking at the empty rails. Letting the day pass through my mind. I am in turmoil.

Forget the Thai curry, this is definitely butterflies.

I have rarely been so full of hope. And so vastly frightened.

I decided to walk back to the minster square. To my delight, the pianist was still there, still playing. I stood there basking in the afterglow, taking in the fading light, watching the other people. At some point, I recorded a video to later send to David, thanking him for a wonderful date.

Informed Consent

Several weeks, many coffees, numerous walks, in multiple parks later…

Come to think of it, we had not been dating for all that long by my standards. Had you asked me beforehand, I would have said, I had absolutely no intention of ending up in his bed. Not yet. But it was clear, that this was serious, and that we both wanted this. Wanted this budding relationship to work.

And that meant, I had to find a way of introducing *the* topic. Before anything irretrievable happened.

We had finished a supper that we had prepared together. Preparing food together would become something of a ritual for us. He was sitting at the kitchen table, high like a bar. Everything in David's kitchen is tall. Just right for working. I had just finished drying my hands. He was setting up pieces for a board game.

I walk around him, my hand automatically gliding over his shoulders, up the back of his fade cut. I relish the feel of his short, bristly hair under my fingertips. I can see the surprise in his eyes. He is still unaccustomed to my easy, matter of course gestures of affection.

Something in his smile makes my hand linger. He reaches over, arm around my waist, and pulls me closer. His lips hover over mine, slightly parted. There are emotions moving in the depth of his eyes.

I can feel the heat rising in my cheeks. Giggling, I remark, "We are not going to even start our game if we continue like this."

He shrugs slightly, pulls me closer and whispers, "We have all the time in the world".

I melt into his kiss.

Much, much later. David is still sitting on his barstool. I realise, at some point I must have straddled him, sitting snugly in his lap. I am *acutely* aware of the heat of his erection, radiating through his jeans. His hands have gotten progressively more adventurous, explorative. If I am going to entrust David with my past, it must be now...

I take a very deep breath, shivering slightly with building tension, endorphins giving way to adrenaline. Freeing myself of any expectations as best I can, freeing my mind of fear. Freeing myself of the memory of rejection. Withdrawing slightly from his tight embrace. Trying to ignore the metallic taste of fear, rising at the back of my throat.

"At the risk of killing the mood, do you think we can have a serious talk?"

I watch him gathering himself, collecting his wits. I know the signs. He nods, "Of course".

I take three more shuddering breaths. Climb off his lap. My legs shaky, for so many reasons. Standing between his knees, my hands holding his, I look up to his face. "David, I really like you. Like, *really* like. I believe this could work. I want us to work. I want it to be good for the both of us."

I can see in his face, realisation sliding into place. He is mentally bracing himself: There is *something* coming. I think there might be tears running down my face. "Before we do anything else, before *you* decide anything, there is something that you need to know about me."

I am having to fight to keep my voice steady. My fingers are numb. My lips are numb. David is absolutely still. Waiting. "I am trans* gender. I was born into a male body. Some years ago, I decided to live this life as the woman I am. It changes nothing about the Alice you know. But you need to *know* about my past".

Seconds pass, marked by my heart pounding in my ears.

His eyes never leave mine. I can still see emotions flitting to and fro. Surprise. Insecurity. Processing. Assessing. Deliberating. He breathes. Decides. Gentle as a butterfly, he kisses my lips, whispers, "It's not important". He kisses me again. Then, "Thank you for your trust".

A heartbeat later, my giraffe becomes a fluffy ball of fluster, as realisation hits him between the eyes, "I mean, yes, of course it is important. This means so much for you. But it is *not* important. I mean, what I mean is..."

I free him from his attempt to explain his colliding, contradicting, crashing thoughts. And yes, I know exactly what he means. It means, he understands. I stop him in mid-sentence with a kiss. My face is now really wet with tears, but now they are tears of joy and gratitude. And of sheer, utter relief.

I have just been set free.

I have no recollection of whether we played that board game or not. Probably not.

What I do remember is the quality of the light in his hair, his hoodie under my fingertips, his fragrance, and the taste of his lips. I remember that somehow, we ended up in the same bed, despite the fact he had a guest bed prepped for me.

I remember our first time with a clarity that is almost surreal.

The first time that I chose. That I wanted to experience this. To know what it feels like when I choose it. When I choose to open myself to him. I could taste David's surprise. And his fulfilment. His pleasure and his appreciation of my choice to trust. To give.

Turned out, my giraffe is quite the lion.

Growing together

To begin with, he was very shy to touch and caress me. David restrained himself in his passion. It was as if he were afraid, I would break. Or vanish. It required a lot of encouragement on my part, to put him at ease. It required a lot of trust and honesty on both our parts, to communicate openly about this. I suppose, I would like him to be more assertive. The Lion in him, is something he controls as tightly as I control my Dragon, and to me, sensuality is something very much about being permitted myself to relinquish control. At the same time, his gentleness, his patience remains core to my being able to trust. To my feeling safe. In his arms, I can permit myself to be utterly vulnerable.

Being together has been an experience of learning and adapting for us both, getting to know, trying out and experimenting. We laugh a lot. He will ice-cold remark how "a Wizard is never late" and have me squealing with giggles. Which makes me all the more aware of how much I adore him. And, yes, David was capable of taking any awkwardness *out* of the moments, when I have a relapse of insecurity and dysphoria.

In the meantime, David has discovered several spots, that when kissed, lead to loss of basic motoric control. His caresses and kisses make me feel singularly special. I *feel* his desire. I feel his desire for *me*. And he is entirely capable making my world slide into a knot, which proceeds to release itself in tingles that burn through my entire nervous system in successive radiating waves. Post coital glow is a renewable energy source. I am convinced of this. Not sure about the carbon footprint though.

But what is far more important, is that he makes me feel safe. As in, safe from ridicule and depreciation. Safe to let my guard down. Safe to be vulnerable. Safe to be myself, entirely. To speak my thoughts, my needs, my emotions. He takes everything I offer him, as a gift, and as a token of trust. And I am speechlessly grateful that he should love me. Which is tricky, because I do not want to fall into old patterns of dependency and self-denial just to please him.

He is relaxed and natural about things, where I am still very often caught in overcoming a moment of inner resistance. And he makes it so much easier to remember, how great life has become since I changed it. I realise this says a number of things about my own state of mind that are not altogether… …integrated. I have not reached the point where I take myself for granted and where I can act naturally or draw on all my resources and strengths without conscious effort. David actually empowers me in getting there.

He is capable of pointing out a newspaper article on the need to raise awareness about trans* in community-based outreach centres, because he knows I am active on many fronts to educate society. When I have a bad-hair-day with the persistent stubble on my upper lip, he is *so* capable of soothing my worries with a kiss that will make the world go away. He is not just at ease with my being trans*, he is openly, actively supportive. Which does not mean, he advertises. In the everyday life we share, my being trans* simply does not feature. There is no need. But he encourages me in my extracurricular activities, in mentoring and counselling peoples and families. He has my back in all the awareness projects I contribute to.

It is one of the things I so admire and love about David. That he is unafraid to look truth in the face. Even if it confronts him with hurt, challenges his comfort zone, he is willing to look at and talk through injuries and unmet needs.

Oh! And he is meticulous about coffee cups left lying around.

I learned that David had been through his rough spots too. As a matter of fact, he has had his own moments of truth, and I firmly believe that is what makes him so... ...empathic, mindful, feet-firmly-in-reality. I find he does his best to place emphasis on the truly important aspects of life. Those that make memories which make you smile or blush or cry years later.

Of course he isn't perfect. However, I like to think both of us have managed to *let go* of the requirement for perfection, and focus instead on what is real.

I told David about so many things that make me who I am. The transgressions. The baby I decided not to have. I told him not because I want pity, but because he needs to know if he is to know me. He looks at me. And I am not a freak or a monster. Not for what I am. And not for the decisions I made.

I am simply the woman who has his trust and his love.

Beyond that, David and I have grown to share so much more. The only way household chores became topic, was when he asked me where I kept my vacuum cleaner, or at what temperature he should wash my clothes. David loves to dance, even if he needs to be mindful of his injured knee. He will suggest films like "About Time" and "Walter Mitty", just as he enthuses about "Rocket the Racoon". And David can absolutely empathise with my idolising Susan Storm or Kate Kane. He also thinks Batman kicks serious butt. We both love binge-watching any trilogies we can get our hands on, and we both enjoy fantasy or sci-fi epics. I am delighted and charmed by how much of his boyish joy and curiosity he has kept, and how it is always present in one way or another in everything he does. I certainly have a very defined streak of the whimsical and frivolous, and with David, I can live this out to the fullest. He even seems to enjoy the darker side of my humour as well.

David is a loving Dad to Johannes, and doing his best to be a role-model of a cis-het* guy, who meets people at face-value. Every two weeks, David has Johannes for the weekend, and I do my best to spend as many of these weekends with "my two boys". I have grown very fond of Johannes, and he seems to have accepted me easily. Aside from his normal pubescent mood shifts, he treats me with affection and courtesy. He readily (mostly readily) accepts that I coach him in English or check his homework.

The three of us regularly sit over parlour games like Carcassonne, Quirkle, Flash-Point, Ticket-to-Ride or Forbidden-Island, something Johannes enjoys thoroughly. If we can pry him away from screens. Which is sometimes hard to justify, because after all, both David and I do enjoy computer games, and we play those too. Johannes seems to appreciate that I take his needs and interests seriously. And that usually gives me an opening, to bring his attention back to this world.

Closer to home

David is intelligent, with a broad education and a great curiosity to see the world. As a matter of fact, in many things, he is probably braver and more outgoing than me. Something he proved, when we were out-and-about in Namibia.

Some eighteen months after we met, David and I took a trip to Namibia and South Africa. Our first prolonged vacation together, our first experience of extended intimate proximity. We rented a vehicle and spent three weeks, driving on a round tour through the northern half of Namibia. Sightseeing, game viewing, marvelling at the immeasurable beauty of the landscape. Coming into contact with the locals, exploring towns and villages on foot. To be honest, I probably would not have done the latter on my own with as much ease.

On our return trip, we detoured via Johannesburg. My Dad was, at the time, still living in the house He and Amahle had shared. Some short few weeks later, my Father would move into a care home community, run by the Methodist church, where he had bough a tiny two room apartment for himself. Later still, he would get to know Khanyisile, with whom he would build a cautious and tender relationship.

For reasons beyond what I can truly name, introducing David to my Dad was very important to me. My Father welcomed David with heartfelt warmth. It relieved me to see them hitting it off so well, talking easily and amiably about jobs, work, house maintenance, and politics. And my Dad told David all kinds of anecdotes about my childhood. Must be a parent thing. There exist of my entire childhood maybe four or five photographs, no more. There are times when I am grateful for this.

My Dad took the time, to take us to all kinds of places, showing us around the most pretty spots of Johannesburg, and introducing us to his friends. We went to look at what would be his new apartment in the care home. I was glad to see that he would be safe and well catered for. And surrounded by people. But more than anything, I enjoyed our quiet conversations, being in the company of the two dearest men in my life.

We are sitting in the winter garden, my Dad's favourite spot in the house, sharing a break-fast of wholegrain bread and cheese, yoghurt and honey. Succulent, ripe Papaya with lemon juice, fragrant fresh coffee.

David has excused himself for a few minutes to go phone with Johannes.

I take the opportunity to have a little time alone with my Dad, "So. What do you think of David?"

My Dad smiles. "He is certainly seems to be a very charming guy. Very observant. But *my* opinion is hardly that important, right?" He looks at me earnestly.

"Yes," I look at my Dad, "he certainly looks out for me. It's taken a little getting used to. So far, we have been able to talk about pretty much anything. And this holiday has shown that we are very compatible, even in close quarters".

I blush slightly as I say, "With him, I can be completely myself. He makes me so happy".

"Yes." My Dad looks pleased. "Yes, you do look altogether happy". His face becomes pen-sive for a moment. Then he smiles warmly. "It has been a long time since I have seen a woman, who so wholeheartedly enjoys being a woman".

Wider circles

Some days after I had disclosed myself to David, I was in a meeting with my four colleagues. At some point Roddy broke the topic by stating, how there was something different about me. How I was positively glowing. I must have turned red as a beet, because he laughed from the bottom of his heart. He followed that up by inquiring whether I was happy, which turned up my afterglow another few notches. He simply smiled knowingly and said, "Well, okay then. Good for you." I understand that not many people would be comfortable with colleagues asking those kind of questions, but this is exemplary that my colleagues were (are) among my most trusted friends. Even if Stephan is strictly speaking my supervisor or boss.

Vanessa and Bart adopted David with their customary exuberant friendship. The two of them were grateful to see me radiantly happy (Vanessa's words). Bart does not thaw easily in the company of new people, but even he was put at ease by David's open and easy nature. And David's enthusiasm for comic superheroes. He filled in David on my obsessive-compulsive nature, something that still amuses Bart to no end. Vanessa was swept off her feet by David's manners. In a quiet moment to ourselves, she confided how she was extremely grateful I had found someone caring and gentlemanly.

True to her socialite heart, Athene had worked through her (extensive) roster of friends for someone with whom she could match me with. She practically *squeeed* when I let on, she could call off the search. I believe she started making plans for a dinner invitation the moment she got the news that I had a boyfriend. Eddie and David got on like a house on fire, sharing memories of Berlin, comparing notes on aged Scottish whiskies, exchanging ideas on music taste, and generally trying good-naturedly to one-up one another in dark humour. Athene and I just sat back and basked in the glow.

And of course Darren and Suzy are regulars on our list of friends to visit. We met for Sushi more than once in places we all like so well in Ulm. Or, the four of us, lounging in Darren and Suzy's garden, amiably chatting about latest developments and talking about our respective kids. It makes me aware just how much David has become part of my life, naturally accepted by my friends.

In the meantime, David and I have been to Berlin several times, sometimes with Johannes. I got to meet David's parents as well as his brothers and their annexes. I was grateful for the profusion of family members, particularly the grandchildren. This meant I was not so much in the centre of focus. But overall I felt at ease and at peace.

Each time in Berlin, we visited Josephine. In the meantime, Josephine had married Matteo, her long-term boyfriend from Zürich, and in the meantime, have two boys. I very fondly remember those visits, Josephine and David sharing their Berlin roots, David playing with the two boys, us four adults talking music, movies, science, and society. Josephine and Matteo took us to see their favourite haunts, restaurants, and eateries. Plus of course, they knew all the best playgrounds. Johannes may be in puberty, but give him a playground and put him among younger children, and he will completely forget his hormones.

I took David sightseeing in Switzerland. We visited Bern, introducing David to Evangeline, Seraphina and René. I showed him my favourite spots, where I had held Seraphina's hand, when she was a toddler. Discovering some new favourites together, strolling along the Aare River for hours, just breathing in the peace. Taking the time to explore the old city, tiptoeing down narrow medieval alleyways, marvelling at glamorous avenues. We toured Zürich, lingering along the most beautiful spots at the lake, where I used to go with my art classes. Ambling through the ancient nooks and crannies of the old quarters, built on the foundations laid by the romans. Seeking out adventures in restaurants. Introducing David to my Mum and Francesco.

Going out to dinner with Eirian and her partner Nicola, sharing plans and renewing bonds.

Clarity and reflections

There is something ironic, almost comical, about how my former self was so streamlined, so heteronorm and well-integrated in society.

Invisible.

And yet, here I am leading a life that is so close to heteronorm stealth. Going for walks with "my two boys", or dining in restaurants, permit me to bask in the glow of pretending to be just another mom with her family.

That being said, my internal dialogue is far from over. Despite all the insights and strengths I have discovered, lack of self-esteem, insecurity, anxiety remain challenges. Dysphoria is not something that can be removed surgically, and even if the body heals, I have come to find, the soul still bears the memories and scars of what went before. There are still days where I am emotionally so far out of sorts, where facing a working day is a challenge.

Another enlightenment in connection to this, is, how I lack a network of kinder-garten-playmates and school-friends, something most people grow up with and take for granted. This makes my social circles extremely small, and very far apart. It makes me shy, even sociophobic. Sometimes, even reaching out to people I love is difficult for me.

Echoes, luxury problems and responsibility

David and I are on our usual round near his home in Munich. Strolling past homes and gardens, over fields, through the forest, past the skater park, looping back through the town park, and back home. The sky is a deep, brilliant blue, streaked by wispy cirrus. The air still has a chill, but the sun is already showing its strength. Cherry is bursting into full bloom.

Spring!

We often take these walks as an opportunity to air out our minds, as well as our lungs. Discussing issues that are challenging, or exploring feelings, and sometimes the limits of our comfort zones. In my mind, it is almost exclusively me who pushes boundaries. My need for honesty and my requirement to live without masks still in conflict with my preconditioned reflex to blend in. To be invisible.

I ask David to imagine me disclosing my past to his family. Most particularly to his mother. And I ask, "When you think of that, how does that make you feel?"

I look up into David's face as he ambles next to me. True to his imperturbable nature, David declares that his feelings on the matter are unimportant, and that it is my decision alone. And regardless of how his mother reacts, it will not change how he sees me.

I disagree. "But *your* feelings *are* important. To me."

He muses, "There are two things you need to keep in mind. I only know Alice. My mother knows only Alice. *You* are all that is important. Who you were before doesn't matter." He pauses. "And. If I ever felt any kind of..." he searches for the words "...incongruency, then we would not be here today."

I flush in an overflow of emotion. The realization that I have been projecting my own insecurities. Again. The plain, matter-of-fact trust that David has in me. It leaves me feeling insufficient. Again. And guilty. That I expose him to all my drama.

I pause in my footsteps, making David turn to face me. "I am sorry I put you through so much. I just want... ...I want to be good for you."

"What makes you think you're not?" there is warmth in his face. "As I said. We wouldn't be here if it wasn't good. If You weren't good."

I am still trying to cope with my feeling of insufficiency, guilt over exposing him to all my turmoil. "I just feel, I am not an easy person to live with. You could have it so much easier with another woman. On a scale of complexity, I am probably high-maintenance."

David raises an eyebrow, his eyes take on a twinkling of mischief, his voice drips with theatrical scepticism and humorous implication. "You think?"

That does it. I am laughing so hard, I almost trip over my own feet.

I do have a significant need for warmth, for reaffirmation, for closeness, for proximity. I need to be aware of this, and I need to be aware of how deeply this contributes to my feeling fulfilled. And, as a consequence, what this drives me to seek.

And yet, even when I receive so much love and support, I mistrust it. And I need to be mindful how a much of this stems from insecurity. From the echoes of my dysphoria. And. From the repeated experience, that people I trusted turned away, or outright turned on me. This, more than anything else, makes it very hard for me to trust.

Sometimes, David appears so much at ease with who I am, what I am, that I wonder if he is denying reality. Sometimes, he appears so accommodating and caring, that it triggers my anxiety. I catch myself being hung-up over how he might be doing things and saying things simply to please me. Placing himself in a similar position *I was once in*, and how he might be subordinating his own true desires or needs to please me. And instead of permitting myself to just accept a gift for what it is, I end up distraught and obsessive.

I catch myself forcing issues or trying to impress decisions on David. Only to stop short, sometimes to break down in tears, because I realise that I am being manipulative and toxic. I do my best to explain the motivations and reasoning behind my behaviour. But I am worried that at some point, David will decide that I am simply too much of a "nut job" to be worth the effort. And he will abandon me.

Because somewhere in my mind is still the feeling, the conviction that I am unworthy of anyone's (David's) attention, never mind affection. That I am unworthy of anyone being good to me. That I am unlovable. Not good enough.

Daydreams

I sometimes wonder if my "awakening" had other of long-term repercussions. I am severely disconcerted and confused to find, that as well as being bisexual, I seem to be inclined to loving more than one person. I have caught myself developing feelings for someone other than David, that go quite beyond a crush. And please note, I say feelings.

The rational, analytical part of me wonders, how much of my insecurities is just my teenage Nancy being rebellious and adventurous. Which would be odd, because I am quite certain that Nancy is asexual. Or, what if my ambivalence is my dysphoria and anxiety, looking for ways to abandon him, before he abandons me? Or, simply feeling a natural attraction to characteristics and attributes, that are not David's immediate strong suits? I am aware. I have to be aware. There is a primal part of me, that has a longing, a yearning. For a superhuman lover, a perfect heroic gentleperson, a divine and omnipotent companion, bordering on a parent figure. To rise to my passion and feed my impulses when and where the urges take me, and to seduce me unto oblivion. To read my whims and conceits before they have even manifested themselves to me, to satisfy every hunger and aspiration. To embrace me into complete security, offer me a sanctuary of warm, gossamer bliss, safeguard me from the hardness of existence. To lift me above the weight and drudgery, from the ennui of the world. To take off me every responsibility. And I am aware of how someone like this *would be nothing but an empty reflection of my own desires and compulsions*. And. Were such a being to truly exist, they would reduce me to a vegetable.

And finally, how much has my history conditioned me to be drawn to people who are genuinely bad for me? Toxic and transgressive? That I mistake being humiliated and abused, for a meaningful connection? And since David offers me security and honesty instead, I find his behaviour unfamiliar, lacking the "adrenaline"? That his gentleness, his clarity and dedication, do not offer me the "thrills" I am accustomed to? That the absence of any emotional roller-coaster, I find our relationship "boring"?

In an ideal world, if a perfect world, I believe I would like to live in a polyamorous family. But then, in a truly perfect world, I would have been born biologically female. Nevertheless, I guess what I would really like, is to be part of a coparenting constellation of people, who resonate in love and commitment to each other. Maybe there is a flower child somewhere deep inside my soul after all?

At the same time, from what I remember of the hippy roots that my mother used to cultivate, then I am hardly so naïve to believe, that the breaking of traditions alone, guarantees the kind of commitment needed to make polyamory work. On the contrary. I expect such a constellation of people to demand so much more work and honesty, so much more reflection and self-reflection, than what the majority of humans are used to.

And yet, ultimately, none of these musings, none of these feelings or desires invalidate what I feel for David. Or how he is a most wonderful partner for me. How much I appreciate and love him for it, or that he makes me glow with happiness (his words). And since David has been deeply hurt in the past, polyamory is a no-go. So far, I have acknowledged my feelings, my insecurities, and what they imply. But I will not undertake anything that could threaten David's trust.

Intimacy. Does not mean spending a weekend in bed. But entrusting your significant other with what moves you and what enriches you. What lets your spirit grow. What brings your soul and your passion to bloom. Intimacy is knowing what permits your loved one lose all adult inhibition and shine like a child in an ice cream shop. Or blush like a teenager.

Commitment. Does not mean unchanging patterns 'til death do us part. Neither is it a predetermined number of chances, and then game-over. Commitment is getting up in the morning with purpose and intent, to take your significant other at face value. To entrust them with what is important to you, to entrust them with your needs and your desires. To share your hopes, your aspirations. And your sorrows and worries. To give them the trust, to give them the space, that permit them to share the same with you. Commitment is the conscious decision to make positive choices.

Mutual respect and appreciation, consent and commitment, all of these remain essentials I cannot and will not go without.

Regardless, all of this *does* contribute to my feeling insecure and *unworthy* of David. Guilty. Because I am unsure of how I can even permit these feelings, these ego-trips? Or these affections and desires for someone else? How can I be bored by this wonderful man? I keep thinking he deserves better. On the up-side, the though processes keep me reflective and aware. Prevent me from becoming complacent. Prevent me from taking things for granted.

Nightmares

David reacts always with consternation, sometimes with amusement, sometimes with alarm, at the lucidity of my dreams. I often tell him of my dreams in the morning.

I still dream. Of being asphyxiated. Of struggling against an assailant's crushing weight. Of being torn. Of my strength failing, and my entire world dissolving into a red haze. Or. Of being trapped in discussions, endlessly spiralling into an abyss of depreciation and ridicule. Of being stripped of my worth and my dignity. And I wake completely distraught, disorientated, and lost.

Despite that, despite the tears, I seem to dream silently.

I feel unsure of how much I should show David of this side of me. Which is plain silly. Because rationally, I know he would never judge me for having nightmares. He knows. He knows I was assaulted. He knows I decided to abort. He knows I am politically active. He knows I had my wild days before I met him. He knows I still go to see my beautician once every couple of weeks, to have my cats' whiskers removed. And more than anything else, he knows what it is like to be coerced and gaslighted, to be invalidated by the person you love.

Still. My nightmares leave me so utterly vulnerable, that I it takes me a while to reconstruct who I am and what I survived. And it takes me a while, to remind myself, that just because I have nightmares, does not make them true. It leaves me in a state of severe contradiction, of needing a warmth and solace, but not able to bear proximity. And when my pulse and my breathing has slowed, when my tears have dried, I feel silly to wake David. So. Instead, I reach out and just feel his ribs rise and fall. Feel his heartbeat. More often than not, he will briefly surface from sleep. He will pat my hand, or squeeze my fingers. He will snuggle a little closer, and then his breathing will grow slow and deep again.

And I am left alone with my thoughts. And yet not alone. And listening to his breathing permits me to drift off back to sleep so much more easily.

It is a curiosity, how close bliss and despair are.

I really want to bear him a child. Impossible and completely irrational as the wish may be, it remains a deep unfulfilled part of me. There are moments when where I feel so alive. So close to David, a heartbeat apart. It is sometimes a very bittersweet realisation. Because every once in a while, it underscores my loss, rather than my gain. For all the life I feel, for all the love I feel, it will never bud and blossom into something that breathes.

Which makes me feel utterly, utterly stupid, ungrateful.

And finally, I try to keep in mind, that *not everything is about me*.

Of course, David has bad days too. Frustration over his work, feeling the lack of appreciation, struggling with the lack of commitment of cooperation partners. Or anxiety about Johannes and his poor performance at school, being a pubescent teenager who is currently unable to focus on anything involving concentration and dedication. Or Johannes' mother exerting influence and being toxic, using Johannes as a tool of manipulation. The memory of her betrayal and the subsequent disillusionment colouring the mood of the present. David too, has ghost from the past that haunt him.

I need to be extremely wary not to project the causes of those moods on myself. I catch myself again and again, watching every reaction, weighing every word. Obsessing over what David might or might not have meant.

I do my best to be *aware* of all these emotions, needs and desires. Of the insecurities and moments of panic. Because if I do not address them, *the feelings still remain there*, in my mind, my heart. I do not want to sublimate my anxieties and dysphoria, my desires or attractions, into my being a passive-aggressive canine-female who antagonises her boyfriend because she feels a tension she does not have a name and a direction for. I do not want to be a hypocrite, who needs a sitting duck to blame, when the relationship crashes and burns.

The lengths to which our brains go to, to avoid having to look at painful truths is simply astounding. Hidden libraries and burning palaces of thought.

So, these remain topics that I still discuss with Dr Chamberlain regularly. How my dysphoria and my experiences of depreciation *have broken my innate ability to trust*. And how a part of me *expects* to be betrayed and wounded. How important it is to remain mindful with myself. Be patiently, gently, and kindly mindful, that I have these insecurities *and that they are there for good reasons*. But, as Dr Chamberlain also reminds me, that it is important to live in the present. And just because the insecurities are there, does not mean they are true.

I am strong. I am safe. I am capable of keeping myself safe.

And David keeps me safe.

But I still catch myself freezing up at the thought, should David ever ask me to marry him. Because I have no idea whatsoever what I would answer him. And I feel I am doing him wrong.

And more to the point, I don't even know what I would need, to permit myself that level of trust.

It starts today

Having said all that. I accept the responsibility.

To be the woman in love with this man. To be mindful of my patterns of dependency, of deference, of defence, and shutting the world out. To let him know of my thoughts and moods, my shortcomings and my insecurities. To let him know of my vulnerabilities and limits. To communicate appreciatively what I miss in our being together. And to sometimes take the initiative and just *do*. Not because this puts me in control. Control is an illusion. And if a relationship is about control, then it is not a partnership. But because I have sworn to myself, I will rather be sorry for having tried and failed, instead of putting my hands in my lap and waiting on miracles. And being sorry for having done nothing.

I do my best to be generous in my understanding and interpretation of his actions. To accept his limits. To be generous without being condescending or judgmental of him. To let him know I see his contribution, to let him feel how much I appreciate.

To always do my best to work on solutions, never on problems.

Above all, I do my utmost to always ensure he knows I will have his back and I will stand at his side. And that he is welcome in my arms and in my heart.

I was not able to cater to Wiebke's hurt child. Perhaps I can cater to David's instead? Up to a degree...

We say, we want a partner who understands us. We say "understand", but what do we truly mean? Do we, in actual fact, mean "control"? That we are in control? Of the situation? Of our partner? But control is an illusion. And the attempt to control is a transgression. A breach of trust.

We always say things like, "we don't understand our partner". But what we truly mean, is, that they have failed to fulfil our expectations. Our needs. But, did we communicate those needs? Were we honest? Open? Trusting? And. Were those expectations realistic? Were they justified? Were they within what we truly can expect from another human being, who has a right (and a duty) to their living their own life?

I have come to find, *I do not need to understand people I love.*

All I truly need, is to accept. Accept who my loved ones are, and see all the good things they are. See what they can be. And reflect to them the potential I see in them. Appreciate them. Share my joy, my insights, and my delight. Let those who share my life take part in what moves me, what is important to me and what I burn for. I need to be honest. With myself, with my loved ones. In my needs, my hopes, my emotions. Even in disappointment and hurt. That is something I was never good at, because implying someone else did not meet my needs, meant they were not good enough. Or maybe I was not good enough. And addressing that my needs were unmet, might have led to my being abandoned.

Which, incidentally, is the point at which I challenged a fair number of my potential partners, and where I continue to challenge David. Not many people are prepared for that kind of self-reflection. And even fewer prepared to share their insights.

We wish, that someone would love us unconditionally.

But there is no growth, no opportunity for evolution in that. And ultimately, the "unconditional" is a lie. Because we *do* have hopes. We *do* have expectations. Of course we do. It is part of what makes us human. And it is very human indeed, to hope for proof of their devotion, by how far they are willing to put their own needs aside for us. What do we truly want from the people we share our lives with? To what degree do we accept them as real people, with independent traits and needs? As opposed to them simply being reflections of our own egos?

I do my best to remain aware that *every choice counts.*

And be kind to myself as well. If I continue to measure myself against others, against the demands and needs of others? If I measure myself against the imbalances, and the perceived lack of import of my actions, my impotence? Those are things that make me dependant. Those are things that lead to giving myself up as a victim. I accept the responsibility to be self-determining and self-responsible. I do my best to stand by my mistakes. I do my best to permit myself satisfaction in proficiency and efficacy. To always be mindful of the truth of what I am. And as long as I do not pretend to be something I am not, I will always be free of the strain of upholding an illusion.

I want to evolve. I want to grow. And in that, I hope to continue to have the strength to face change, even welcome it. To not be content and complacent with what I am today. I do my best to keep in mind, that I would rather feel wretched for having tried and failed, rather than for having been passive and resigned.

I want more than to survive day to day. I want to live.

Gratitude

I find myself surrounded by people who accept and support me.

Friends, people whom I love. People who do not just tell me, I deserved to be happy, as a turn of phrase. People who truly make me feel like I do. I am not implying that this was different in the past. But in the past, I felt I needed to shut away so much of myself. And today I feel welcome. Appreciated.

All of me.

In both my private life, and in my professional environment, to experience their love, their respect, and their happiness at my successfully navigating the past few years, all these people make my days so much brighter.

In fact, considering my past, *I have been lucky beyond any description*. I still am.

Looking at my life, looking at my experiences, there are so many things where I was (am) privileged. Being born into Swiss middleclass and all that provided me with. Growing up in Africa and everything that taught me, all the wonders and the hardships I was able to witness there. Often without immediate impact on myself. Being able to go to schools that showed me how the world is populated by such a multitude of cultures. Schools that were able to convey a background which in turn empowered me, to not only make a self-sufficient living, but live comfortably.

I am trans* gender. And to put it bluntly, I think being trans* sucks *so* frikkin' badly. There were experiences I could have easily done without. But I survived. I was able to get myself out of a state in life where I would have died by degrees. I get to live in Europe. In a day and age where trans* is something that does not land me in jail. Or in a psychiatric ward. Or in a medical waste container. Or burnt at the stake.

I was so incredibly fortunate to meet the right people. Humans who by their empathy and by their expertise did what stood within their power to make my life better. Many of those people went out of their way in order to enabled me in my self-determination. People who believed me, and believed in me.

I am still a vocational trainer and a counsellor who generally kicks serious butt. Or at least I get taken seriously. Apparently, I contribute in ways that other people find genuinely helpful. I do my best to offer perspectives instead of micromanagement. Obviously, I still teach basic science laboratory stuff. But what makes my job so fulfilling, is that I get to contribute to empowering young adults in finding their own way, laying the foundations to their own paths. Building their own futures.

In the meantime, Roddy has moved on to other tasks, but we still meet every so often, and he still makes me blush when he grins at me and tells me how much I glow. Gerlind has gone into well-deserved retirement. And our team, our working family, has gained two new members, Lore (Hannelore) and Andy (Andromeda), with whom working has proven to be at least as much a joy and a privilege. Both wonderful young women with clarity of purpose and intent. Creative and inquisitive. Strict, but with an underlying kindness and fairness. It is good. It is right to have a new generation in our family of learning-coaches and minders.

And I am still one of those teachers who reads between the lines. And listens to things, other people seem to have little time or patience for. Be it dealing with the fallout as a survivor of a school killing spree (Not as often as in the US, but yes, in Germany too). Or coping with the repercussions after a suicide in a family, when that family responds by stonewalling.

And yes, sometimes I counsel students who approach me, because they feel lost and misrepresented by the gender roles provided and expected by society. And their own body simply does not seem to fit right.

I do my best to be there for others, trans* people like me, or their families and loved one. Or their employers and colleagues. And I offer them what support I can, in finding their own balanced and fitting path to follow. Some need a push, some need a hug. I do my best to remain mindful that different people have different thresholds, different limits to what they feel capable of tackling.

I get to be an aunt. On rare occasions, I get to attend, with humility and rapture, to Nimue's soprano. Or we share the anticipative companionship of cutting veggies in the kitchen, trying out new recipes and indulging our curiosity. I tell her of my students and of David, and she tells me of her studies, her university friends, and her Love. Our relationship has changed, grown. But then, that is hardly surprising. I am no longer thirty, and Nimue is a grown woman. The opinions, insights, and wisdoms we trade are those of close friends, both of whom have seen the rougher side of the globe and its societies. And the ups and downs of relationships.

Body image, self-esteem *will* continue to be challenges. I do my best, to not be ruled by my urges. Or insecurities. And sometimes, this is a *deliberate* decision. Sometimes it needs to be a deliberate decision: *I will not* spend the rest of my life in a state of obsession about blending in, and to what degree I am perceived as female. Nor will I spend the rest of my life in anxiety about being violated. Yes, I am trans*. But I do not permit other people to reduce me to this. *And I will not reduce myself either*. There comes a point where you just need to risk a leap, and *live*. And that means permitting yourself to let go of expectations, standards, and ideals, particularly those posed by the beauty industry or conservative societies.

So, yes. Being trans* sucks. But considering where I am in life today, considering the choices made and where those put me today; if I were given the proverbial three magical wishes, I would not risk losing what I have now, by changing my past.

…except perhaps to have that child…

I feel healed.

Which is not the same as whole. Not the same as unmarred. But I am no longer broken in a way that prevents me from feeling joy, or experiencing the beauty of this world, or the blessing of friendship and love.

More to the point. The past years have been something close to a rebirth in so many ways. *Everything* in my life has a new edge. Sharper, clearer, deeper, more colourful. More real. I have not done drugs, but occasionally I imagine this is what a "high" feels like. Everything has picked up again, all my interest, all the thing I loved to do are more fulfilling than ever. I take more joy and pride in my photography. I have renewed my dabbling in painting (I call it dabbling, because I hardly have time for it). I am still sociophobic, but I manage overcome that. Most of the time. I pursue concerts, performances, and theatre venues again, and I feel the pulse of lives touching. I breeze through galleries, I take in expositions, and it feels like swimming in new ideas. Even basic things, like walking through a farmers' market on a brisk Saturday morning, has taken on an invigorating rush, where I feel to be an engaging part of the throb and the hum of society.

I make myself. I continue to do so.

I make my own opportunities. I am wiser. I am tougher and more resilient than I used to be. I am strong. I am a survivor.

So, Yes. Life is good.

Let me rephrase. Life is not just good, **Life is Great!** I wake up on most mornings, and my first thoughts are of gratitude, of joy, and of anticipation.

To be *aware*, to be mindful of this, is a singular, inestimable gift.

This life is a gift.

To be loved is a gift.

More than enough reason to dance.

(12) Being Empowered

Evolution…

…means change.

One thing remains certain on this globe.

Things will continue to change.

We, as a species will continue to change.

If we welcome change…

If we seize the opportunity…

We will be better tomorrow,

than we were yesterday.

I follow a web comic called "Questionable Content".

Created by Jeph (Jeffrey) Jacques, 17.06.1980, US cartoonist, musician, illustrator, writer .

It is one of my favourites, mainly because it analyses closely how human interaction depends almost exclusively on how we treat one another. And how ready we are, to accept other norms as valid. Plus, one of the main protagonists, a cis-het* male, being liaised with an ftm trans* person, and his being completely matter-of-course level with this, is exactly the kind of behaviour I would wish for from people.

In one scene, Momo, who is an android AI, is talking to Marten, who is an "ordinary" human being. They are discussing the ramifications of there being sentient, self-aware (self-made) androids as members of society.

Momo tells Marten of her sadness at being hated by some people, for being a non-human. While at the same time she is supremely grateful for her circle of friends, for whom she is simply a person with special needs (for example, a charging port). And she expresses the hope, that one day, all of society will be as accepting of her kind of people, as her friends. Marten cautions her enthusiasm, reminding her that humanity is still trying to deal with racism, sexism, homophobia, etc.

To which she replies, with a mixture of wistfulness and exasperation, that she is aware that "one day" might indeed be one step up the evolutionary ladder.

Being trans* human

Science or fiction, this planet is changing. Humanity as a species is changing. Societies are changing. Our individual expectation and our desires, our needs are constantly evolving. And growing. What is also changing, is the available arable surface that we have on this globe, and it is not getting larger. The elements of which this lovely world is comprised are finite. There are only so many wind turbines that we can put up to generate power, before the whole planet is covered, and the air masses stagnate.

Spanish philosopher, writer and trans* woman Elizabeth Duval asks, "what comes after?" Evolution means letting go. Being able to relinquish control. And *trust* that we are equipped and prepared, as well as we possibly can be. *And take that step.* And *trust* that, even if we are confronted with the unknown and the unexpected, and we *WILL* be, then we have made it this far by our wits and our adaptability.

We need to trust, that there *will* be a place for us in the future as it unfolds.

In a world, where everyone wants to be powerful, too few focus on sharing. What if we gave that up? What if, instead of focusing on amassing wealth, or gaining influence, what if we followed our own paths? Instead of being constantly so driven and desperate to achieve a goal, what if we could actually slow down and enjoy the journey? Perhaps this transcendence, equanimity of being is becoming necessary to our species, simply to survive. Letting go of old patterns, outgrowing traditions and rituals.

Evolution

I believe. We are ready. We have the means.

The time is now. It is never too late. It is never too late to be good to yourself. on the contrary. It sets free so much energy and capacity for the creative. Live in the moment. Regardless of how many lives you believe you are going to live. If you are not experiencing the moment, you are wasting time. Also: being positive is a choice. Looking at the bright side, being proactively hopeful, being affirmative, is a decision we can actively make. Sometimes it takes patience. Sometimes it takes work, to overcome a darkness, or a difficulty. But on the whole, I stand by my statement.

To quote Margaret Atwood, Canadian Author and poet, "I hope that people will finally come to realise that there is only one 'race', the Human race, and that we are all members of it." The problem with our biological prerogatives, our finely honed instincts for survival, they are in fact *getting in the way* of approaching each other on equal terms. Being objectified and reduced to being different, is depreciative. Being hated for what you are, is painful. Pure and simple. Being tolerant, never mind inclusive, is such a challenge when all societies, all tribes and clans have been honed to pushing their gene to survival, regardless of costs or consequences. Let's face it, biology is a cold and heartless thing.

All the more reason, to be our best possible selves.

From experience of my own life, and from the lives that have touched mine, I am convinced the best way to achieve this, is to discover your full potential. You might say, "yeah, duh". No, not everyone is trans* gender, and not everyone needs to embrace their own inner dragon.

...perhaps...

But. I am convinced, all of us have areas in our life, where we limit ourselves. Not out of love, or out of compassion. But out of fear. Fear of retribution, fear of ostracism, fear of losing face, fear of losing our place in society. And in limiting yourself, you limit what you can bring into society.

For the record, if you find you have an innate tendency to harm other people, or to disrespect them, by all means, *please limit yourself. Let me rephrase:* **Limit yourself**. *Full stop. Despite my hope to engender tolerance, transgression and violence* deserve *no tolerance. They are inacceptable.*

NOT ACCEPTABLE.

I would like humans to evolve beyond biology. Grow better than primal urges, instincts rooted in fear. I hope for a global community that is emotionally mature. A community that takes on responsibility, instead of placing blame.

It is my profound hope, that our societies evolve to the point of where ethnic heritage, cultural background, sexual identity and preferences, are viewed with a natural respect and equanimity. I hope for a global society where people are measured and valued for the skills, the competency, and the intelligence they share. For the effort and the energy they bring to a project, for the compassion and the hospitality they offer others.

A society where it is natural that the variety and diversity is welcomed as an enrichment and a gift. A society that appreciates an abundancy of alternatives and ingenuities. Also, a society where an unsuccessful attempt is viewed as a natural learning opportunity, and not a dead end. A society where "not knowing" is not stamped as ignorance, but seen as an opportunity to grow.

A society, where requiring and asking for support, is acknowledged with respect and humility. As an insight, that the person asking requires resources or perspectives beyond what they have access to right now. Where support is guided by the honest desire to enable each other to be better together. A mature and stable society will no longer find its values challenged, when faced with gender dysphoric individuals. People who are secure in *their* own identity and self-expression, will no longer find themselves shaken, by people that look different.

Survival

There is always somebody stronger.

It does not matter how skilled, how powerful, how rich, how influential you are. We are mortal, we are vulnerable. And there will always be someone who can out-perform, out-wit, out-last you. No, we will not stop being vulnerable, not biologically, nor emotionally. And the likelihood of becoming biologically immortal is... ...not worth discussing.

Besides, it would change nothing.

We need to stop surviving, and start living.

Instead of fearing competition, we could be seeking inspiration for greatness. Seeking win-win outcomes. We need to accept that life is filled with ambivalence. And that there is no such thing as security. As individuals and as a species, we need to step out of the circle of competing against ourselves. We need to think longer long-term, and we need to wise up. It is an illusion that we can safeguard against all forms of harm. And it is a gross misjudgement to believe we can stop the world from changing.

And since we are on the topic: no! The world is not "going to go back to normal". Normal is an illusion. Yesterday is history. We need to look forward. And we need to find ways to live with the world as it evolves along with us. And that means dealing with multiple resistant Tuberculosis and all kinds of SARS variants. Dealing with microplastics and shortages of drinking water. Having enough energy to keep the internet online. But dealing with these challenges proactively, and in a way that builds in the strengths of humanity: the ability to care. To learn from one another. To support one another.

Life happens constantly along many borders and limits. It is a part of life, to constantly remind us of our vulnerability. Our finite existence. It is human, to avoid these challenges to the comfort zone, to avoid challenging our boundaries. We like to lull ourselves in routines of fulfilment and gratification. I find it necessary to observe very closely; when does a limit of inviolability become a zone of complacency? The best things, the most exhilarating and memorable things, happen outside the comfort zone. It is my conviction, that freedom to self-determination, to self-exploration and to self-expression are things that empower us to become better people.

Having said that. It is my own conclusion, that being good for myself, is not good enough. I want, I need to be good for others, as well as myself. Ego trips just do not cut it. Self-actualisation is important, but contribution to society just as important. A community only thrives, if we all contribute to it.

I do my best to prepare our students to living with ambivalence. In between lessons and experiments, my students ask me about my life. About Africa, about returning to Europe, about being married, about being different. About making changes. And one of the things I tell them, is, that there is no universal solution that I can teach them. I tell them, learning to live with double binds, setbacks, and hard choices, is a matter of your own inner conviction. That you have given it your best, and that if you fail today, then you try again tomorrow. From that, true resilience grows. And with it, the self-respect, and the assurance that you are growing. Evolving. Learning. Learning to be your best possible self. Empowered.

And from there share your best with the people you love, contribute to their growth and their security, such as it can be. And thereby contribute to our world as a whole. *Because everyone matters.*

So, yes. This planet will continue to change. Climate will continue to shift. Availability of resources will require adaptation. Language will evolve. And we, as a species, we, in our circle of loved ones, will continue to grow, change. Life will remain full of irritations and catastrophes, perturbance and heartbreak. Life will continue to be filled with insecurity and ambivalence.

We trans* gender are experts of the unknown.

We are connoisseurs of the ambivalent. We are virtuosos of imagination. We create whole worlds, to somehow permit ourselves to exist in two spheres at once.

We sit amongst the authorities of fear and loathing. We spend a significant part of our lives, being raised as someone we are not, being pressed into roles that abrade our self-esteem and our energy. We have finely tuned senses, enabling us to identify disharmonies and inequity. And we are experienced in addressing these, coming up with solutions. We come equipped with perseverance, and focus of purpose, tough enough to endure.

We are the avant-garde of questioning obsolete rituals, casting off old patterns, outgrowing traditions, breaking chains.

We are graduates of being powerless, lost and broken. We are phoenixes, risen from our own ashes. We are examples of surviving change. And coming out stronger, more adaptable, more resilient.

We are great at recognising patterns, at recognising traits and mechanisms. Recognising where people or processes share common ground. We intuitively perceive strengths and talents, and how best to employ them. We are resourceful and versatile, creative in overcoming obstacles.

We are pros of empowerment.

We are self-made.

And in that, there is utter horror and sheer blinding hope.

We offer you this fortune of expertise and insight. It is there for you to draw on. We offer you this treasure of imagination. Our ability to look beyond the obvious.

All we ask in return, is to be able to lead a life in dignity. To be a part of the world you walk and work in. We want to be a part of the community. We want to contribute.

Because we care. We are human.

From here on out

…it begins today.

We cannot prevent the future from unfolding. But we can decide to take part. In shaping the future into a place, where we want to see our children grow up in.

Humanity's history is rife with conflict over resources and rights.

We need to get out of the victim mind-set. We do not need a revolution. Revolutions are destructive and careless. Hate and anger comes easily to us humans. But to give in to this, is weak, and lazy. Violence engenders counter-violence. The attempt to control this, gives rise to an excess of rules, axioms, written and unwritten laws, all with the hidden purpose of preventing change. Of keeping the status quo, and thus maintaining the illusion of security. A mechanism founded in fear. The continuos right-wing drift of so many nations are the clearest sign of this: we segregate, and we divide, every nation scrabbling for its own advantage. Every tribe trying to secure the maximum resources. We do not need more rules, we certainly do not need more fear. We cannot afford to be weak and lazy anymore.

I would like to believe, that we are evolving beyond the point, where we are dependent on the biological prerogatives. And beyond the need to believe that we will be judged by an everlasting, but jaundiced, parent in the sky.

We all talk of wanting to do something for future generations.

How about we work on peaceful coexistence? What if being the fittest for survival is *not* about being the hardest, toughest, and most ruthless nation on the planet. Or the most bad-ass species. After all, some would argue, that place is already taken by the mantis shrimp. Or possibly the cockroach? What if our survival depends on how well we work and grow together?

We need to accept responsibility and self-responsibility. What we need is a gentle change that grows from the heart. We need the openness to see, and the fortitude and the readiness, to accept the humanity in the person opposite us.

And we need people who are prepared to lead by example.

There is an immediate correlation, between how closely our outward expression is congruent to our inner identity, and how confident we are about this. This, in turn, has everything to do, with how free we feel to express ourselves in our community. How free we are to evolve and *be* the person we truly are. And how the community shows its encouragement and appreciation for people being their best possible self. Such a society *will* engender people, citizens who themselves live and thrive on reciprocal respect and appreciation.

It remains my hope, that we as a species, can overcome our fear of that which is different. And instead, welcome it as an opportunity for growth.

Compassion

We humans are creatures of efficiency. A less kind way to describe it, would be to say: we are lazy. Efficiency is ruthless. Without loyalty, without love.

What does compassion mean? Possibly, that we are prepared to set aside the efficiency necessary to survive, along with our immediate need for gratification or triumphing. Over the recognition of the struggle of others, and the acknowledgement of the pain, the strife and sorrow in others. To feel a connection, a kinship, a sympathy. And to lend them our strength and our resources.

Possibly to our own immediate detriment. But to both our gain in the long term.

We *care*.

It is the basis of being human that we are able to empathise. This is what permits us to exist in a society. This is what permits us to thrive. And love.

What makes us human is the ability to look beyond what is immediately visible. And to engage our imagination. And to take part in the lives of our fellow humans. And in doing so, step out of our own limited borders of perception. Welcome and embrace someone, simply because we recognise a fellow human struggling with the same harsh environment.

Sometimes we are at an advantage over someone else. Instead of turning away, or lashing out, a part of being human, is to realise that we gain more in the long run from embracing and supporting this struggling individual. It does not matter if this is a brother, a sister, a... ...someone. And perhaps, they can actually help us learn something vitally important, that we might not have learnt by ourselves. This starts at an individual level, but it encompasses nations.

We need to stop asking ourselves, why are we so different. We need to start asking ourselves, and each other, how we are similar, familiar, alike. It is not about comparing or measuring. It is about finding common ground.

A common purpose.

Of where to go from here. And building a future for us all. I say, the future will look brighter, richer, and more colourful, the more different people are involved. Instead of counting people who are influenced. Making people count. Every single person is valued. Is heard, respected, and empowered. Every person should be given the opportunity to feel like they belong. That is what motivates people to contribute.

Motivated people care.

Hope

So, no. This book is not a call to arms. Not a demand to disown the rich. Not a petition to overthrow the establishment.

This book is an appeal. To be your best possible self. It is a proposal to look inside yourself, at what truly motivates you, to analyse your needs. To understand how your past has shaped you, your identity. And how it influences your view of the world, and how you interact with the world.

This is an invitation. To look beyond your own horizons. To realise and appreciate just how much there is, that is wonderful and worth experiencing. I have the hope, that you recognise the humanity in the people you meet. That you show compassion for their vulnerability, that you offer your heart and your hand in kinship and understanding.

This book is a prayer. To live your life with love and joy in your heart. It is a suggestion, that sometimes, it is a conscious choice to look for the silver lining, and to gift someone with a smile. Chances are, you will brighten *their* day, remind them of the brilliance of Life, and the exhilaration of sharing.

This book is a statement and a plea. That you owe it to yourself, to be kind to yourself. And to be kind others. Our interactions with other people follow intricate rhythms and melodies. And they sing most clearly, most powerfully, when they harmonise and resonate with each other. Life is a dance, and you owe it to yourself, to burn the floor, and weave trails of sparks.

I dare you. To leave no one a wallflower. Invite them, inspire them, set their soul alight.

It does not matter if we do not achieve this tomorrow. Or even next generation. But we are nothing if we do not strive. It is never too late.

There are not many rules to being human. One of them is, that we are all different. Unique. And yet, another rule is, that we are united in a common need for appreciation, solace, connectivity. Love. This is what sets us apart from simpler creatures. We strive to do more than survive. We create. We care. To be human is to be compassionate. To strive for a better world.

I have promised myself to be an example of how I would wish people to live together. I offer you my perspectives and my views, my experiences, and my conclusions. I ask you to look kindly and with patience upon me. And upon your fellow human beings.

Whatever our future will bring, I am convinced, there will be music. And I will dance. Burning my brightest possible. Until I dissolve into sparkles and become one with the music.

I invite you to join me.

We don't know what will come. But if you like, I will be there at your side.

And I will have your back.

Acknowledgements

Telling my parents about this book took an immense amount of strength. Quite frankly, there are things in my life, that I would have very much liked to spare them ever knowing.

At the same time, I am proud of my parents. *All of them*. And I am grateful, very much so. And they most certainly deserve to know that. I make sure they do; I tell them as often as I can. Whether they read this or not, is up to them.

The wonderful thing about writing an autobiography, is that you can elaborately thank people who have been good to you.

All names in this book are pseudonyms. I chose to do so for people's protection. The only exceptions are quotes of scientific literature or referencing quotes and titles of people whose works have had an influence.

So.

Thank you.

All you people who have contributed, enabled, and empowered.

You are loved.